Mindfulness with Breathing

Mindfulness
with Breathing
A Manual for Serious Beginners

Buddhadāsa Bhikkhu

*Translated from the Thai by
Santikaro Bhikkhu*

Foreword by Larry Rosenberg

Wisdom Publications • Boston

Wisdom Publications
361 Newbury Street
Boston, Massachusetts 02115
USA

First published in 1988

Revised edition published by Wisdom Publications in 1997

Library of Congress Cataloging-in-Publication Data

Phra Thēpwisutthimēthī (Ngūram), 1906–1993
    Mindfulness with breathing : a manual for serious beginners / Buddhadāsa Bhikkhu ; translated from the Thai by Santikaro Bhikkhu.
        p.   cm.
    ISBN 0-86171-111-4 (alk. paper)
        1. Meditation—Buddhism.   2. Ānāpānasmṛti.   3. Tipiṭaka. Suttapiṭaka. Majjhimanikāya. Ānāpānasatisutta—Criticism, interpretation, etc.   I. Santikaro, Bhikkhu, 1957–   .
    II. Tipiṭaka. Suttapiṭaka. Majjhimanikāya. Ānāpānasatisutta. English.   III. Title.
    BQ5612.P53 1996
    294.3'443—dc20   96–32332

0 86171 111 4

01 00 99 98 97
6 5 4 3 2

Designed by: L·J·SAWLIT

Wisdom Publications' books are printed on acid-free paper and meet the guidelines for permanence and durability of the Committee on Production Guidelines for Book Longevity of the Council on Library Resources.

Printed in the United States of America.

Contents

Anumodanā

To all Dhamma comrades, those helping to spread Dhamma:

Break out the funds to spread Dhamma to let faithful trust flow,
  Broadcast majestic Dhamma to radiate long living joy.
Release unexcelled Dhamma to tap the spring of virtue,
  Let safely peaceful delight flow like a cool mountain stream.
Dhamma leaves of many years sprouting anew, reaching out,
  To unfold and bloom in the Dhamma centers of all towns.
To spread lustrous Dhamma and in hearts glorified plant it,
  Before long, weeds of sorrow, pain, and affliction will flee.
As virtue revives and resounds throughout Thai society,
  All hearts feel certain love toward those born, aging, and dying.
Congratulations and blessings to all Dhamma comrades,
  You who share Dhamma to widen the people's prosperous joy.
Heartiest appreciation from Buddhadāsa Indapañño,
  Buddhist science ever shines beams of Bodhi long lasting.
In grateful service, fruits of merit and wholesome successes,
  Are all devoted in honor to Lord Father Buddha.
Thus may the Thai people be renowned for their virtue,
  May perfect success through Buddhist science awaken their hearts.
May the King and his family live long in triumphant strength,
  May joy long endure throughout this our world upon earth.

Buddhadāsa

Mokkhabalārāma
Chaiya, 2 November 2530 (1987)
Translated by Santikaro Bhikkhu
3 February 2531 (1988)

Publisher's Acknowledgment

THE PUBLISHER gratefully acknowledges the generous help of the Hershey Family Foundation in sponsoring the publication of this book.

Foreword

IN HAPPILY ACCEPTING the invitation to write about Ajahn Buddhadāsa's teaching of *ānāpānasati* I have come full circle from an encounter I had with him in Thailand a number of years ago. At that time, I had already corrected the misconception I had previously held, one which is shared by many practitioners, that *ānāpānasati* is simply a method to calm the mind, that it is solely *samatha*. According to this view, you calm the mind by paying continuous and exclusive attention to the breath until the mind is serene and fit to do some serious "looking." At this point, this view asserts, you can drop the breath and get on with the "real work" of *vipassanā*. However, I knew this was not so. The breath awareness teaching in the *Ānāpānasati Sutta* provides a clear and comprehensive way for us to develop *both samatha* and *vipassanā*. The Buddha himself is reported to have attained liberation using this very method. Before I met Ajahn Buddhadāsa, however, my understanding of this was largely conceptual.

This all changed during an intense two-hour meeting with Ajahn Buddhadāsa at his monastery, Suan Mokkh, in southern Thailand. The impact of this encounter changed my practice and teaching forever. Buddhadāsa was nearly eighty when I saw him, and though his health was not very good, he was still tireless in his teaching. He often taught informally, sitting in front of his hut in the forest with students—and wild chickens and a dog!—gathered around him. From time to time bus loads of people seeking his blessing would come to Suan Mokkh. He would patiently and lovingly care for these visitors and then resume our conversation at exactly the same point at which we had paused.

He was convinced that the *Ānāpānasati Sutta* provided a magnificent vehicle for practice and teaching. With detailed, painstaking, and quietly passionate instructions, he took me through the sixteen contemplations of the sutta step by step, contemplation by contemplation. It was a mixture of lecture and meditative reflection, and one of the most powerful pieces of teaching I have ever experienced.

His approach was rational and systematic, but also beautifully timed to open me up emotionally. Its effect was dramatic. As you will soon discover, the sutta is comprised of four tetrads, or four sets of four contemplations. Briefly, in the first tetrad we familiarize ourselves with the breath and the body; in the second, breathing with feelings; in the third, breathing with mental formations; and in the fourth set of contemplations we concern ourselves with the breath and discernment—pure *vipassanā*. This last set of contemplations, 13–16, is about impermanence, emptiness, and letting go into the freedom that emerges naturally from such clear seeing.

When Ajahn Buddhadāsa and I had completed the thirteenth contemplation he paused, seemingly to check if I had understood thus far. When he was convinced that I did, he quickly and decisively said, "Okay, now you can go back to contemplations 1–12, with which by now you are quite familiar. You will find that the object of each and every one of these contemplations is impermanent and empty: the body is empty; feelings are empty; mental formations are empty; and the in- and out-breaths, which have accompanied you throughout the contemplations, are also empty. Of course breathing is happening, but you will see that no matter how hard you look, there is no 'breather' to be found anywhere!" His warm, large smile and laughter ended the interview.

In this book, Ajahn Buddhadāsa will take you by the hand and lead you, as he did for me, all the way from the first attempt to observe the in- and out-breaths to the kinds of insight that have the power to liberate. Of course, you will begin with merely a set of instructions, but then you must take these clear words of teaching and put them into practice. If you do, you will not be disappointed. The beauty of this work is its seamless integration of theory and practice. You have in your hands a precious yogic manual, one that can decisively launch you into the practice of *vipassanā* meditation and set you firmly on the Buddha's path of liberation.

I bring both of my palms together in the heartfelt wish that these simple, clear teachings of Ajahn Buddhadāsa bring as much benefit into your life as they have already brought into mine. I bring both palms together with gratitude to this great servant of the Buddha.

Larry Rosenberg
Cambridge Insight Meditation Center

Preface to the Revised Edition

THE MAIN BODY of this manual comes from the series of lectures given during Suan Mokkh's September 1986 meditation course. For this course, Ajahn Poh (Venerable Bodhi Buddhadhammo, the initiator of these courses and currently Suan Mokkh's Abbot) asked Ajahn Buddhadāsa to give the meditation instruction to the retreatants directly: usually they are given by other monks, such as the translator. Each morning, after breakfast, the retreatants gathered at "the Curved Rock," Suan Mokkh's outdoor lecture area. Venerable Ajahn spoke in Thai, with this translator interpreting into English. The talks were recorded and many people, both foreign and Thai, requested copies of the series.

At the request of the Dhamma Study-Practice Group, the tapes were transcribed and edited for publication. The text follows the original Thai closely, although some of the translator's interpolations have been kept. Material from talks given during subsequent retreats was added as appendixes to make the manual more comprehensive. In this edition, however, the appendixes have been incorporated into the text. We also include a "Translator's Conclusion" based on a talk given by the interpreter as a summary of the Venerable Ajahn's seven lectures. The final word comes from our prime inspiration and original source: the Lord Buddha's "Mindfulness with Breathing Discourse" (*Ānāpānasati Sutta*). The complete text of this fundamental sutta is presented here in a new translation. We hope that the exquisite simplicity and directness of the Blessed One's words will gather all of the preceding explanations into one clear focus. That focus, of course, must aim at the only real purpose there is in life—*nibbāna*.

This revised edition has been prepared with the help of Wisdom Publications. The material is substantially the same as the previous editions; however, the following changes have been made. Material that was previously in appendixes (that which had been taken from talks given in the months after the main series on which this book is based) has been incorporated into the text, thus expanding chapters one and two into three chapters. The translator's introduction and conclusion have been revised, a few terms have been added to the glossary, and the usual attempts to make the book more accessible, readable, and accurate have been tried. We hope the reader approves of the results.

Santikaro Bhikkhu
Suan Atammayatārāma (Dawn Kiam)
2538 Rains Retreat (1995)

Translator's Introduction

MINDFULNESS WITH BREATHING is a meditation technique anchored in our breathing. It is an exquisite tool for exploring life through subtle awareness and an active investigation of breathing and of life. The breath is life; to stop breathing is to die. The breath is vital, natural, soothing, revealing. It is our constant companion. Wherever we go, at all times, the breath sustains life and provides the opportunity for spiritual development. In practicing mindfulness upon and through breathing, we develop and strengthen our mental abilities and spiritual qualities. We learn to relax the body and calm the mind. As the mind quiets and clears, we investigate how life unfolds as experienced through the mind and body. We discover the fundamental reality of human existence and learn to live our lives in harmony with that reality. And all the while, we are anchored in the breath, nourished and sustained by the breath, soothed and balanced by the breath, sensitive to breathing in and breathing out. This is our practice.

Mindfulness with breathing is the system of meditation, or mental cultivation (*citta-bhāvanā*), often practiced and most often taught by Buddha Gotama. For more than 2,500 years, this practice has been preserved and passed along. It continues to be a vital part of the lives of practicing Buddhists in Asia and around the world. Similar practices are found in other religious traditions as well. In fact, forms of mindfulness with breathing predate the Buddha's appearance. These were perfected by him to encompass his most profound teachings and discoveries. Thus, the comprehensive form of mindfulness with breathing taught by the Buddha leads to the realization of humanity's highest potential—spiritual awakening and liberation. It has other fruits as well, and so offers something of both immediate and long-term value, of both mundane and spiritual benefit to people at all stages of spiritual development.

In the Pali language of the Buddhist scriptures this practice is called *ānāpānasati*, which means "mindfulness with in-breaths and out-breaths." The complete system of practice is described in the Pali texts and further explained in their commentaries. Over the years, an extensive body of literature has developed. The Venerable Ajahn Buddhadāsa has drawn on these sources, especially the Buddha's words, for his own practice. Out of that experience, he has given a wide variety of explanations about how and why to practice mindfulness with breathing. This book contains some of his most cogent talks about this meditation practice.

The talks included here were chosen for two reasons. First, they were given to Westerners who were attending the monthly meditation courses at Suan Mokkh. In speaking to Western meditators, Ajahn Buddhadāsa uses a straightforward, no-frills approach. He does not go into the cultural interests of traditional Thai Buddhists; instead, he prefers a scientific, rational, analytical attitude. And rather than limit the instruction to Buddhists, he emphasizes the universal, natural humanness of *ānāpānasati*. Further, he endeavors to respond to the needs, difficulties, questions, and abilities of beginning Western meditators, especially our guests at Suan Mokkh.

Second, this manual is aimed at "serious beginners." By "beginner" we mean people who are fairly new to this practice and its theory. Some have just begun, while others have some practical experience but lack information about where and how to develop their practice further. Both types of beginners can benefit from an overall perspective and clear instructions concerning their current situation. By "serious" we mean those who have an interest that runs deeper than idle curiosity. A serious individual will read and reread this manual carefully, will think through this information adequately, and will apply the resulting understanding with sincerity and commitment. Although some people like to think that we do not have to read books about meditation, that we need only to do it, we must be careful to know what it is we are doing. In order to practice meaningfully, we must begin with some source of information that is sufficiently clear and complete. If we do not live near a competent teacher, a manual such as this is necessary. The beginner needs information simple enough to give a clear picture of the entire process, yet with enough detail to turn the picture into reality. This manual should strike the proper balance. There is enough to guide successful practice, but not so much as to complicate and overwhelm. Those who are serious will find what they need without difficulty.

If you have yet to sit down and "watch" your breath, this book will point out the benefits of doing so and will explain how to begin. Still, until you try it, and keep trying, it will be impossible to completely understand these words. So read this book through at least once, or as many times as it takes to get the gist of the practice. Then, as you practice, read and reread the sections most relevant to your particular stage. Only through applying them will these words become tangible. When properly put into practice, they will guide your development more securely. This manual should provide you with enough intellectual understanding to be clear about what you need to do and how to go about doing it. As you focus on the immediate requirements of today's learning, do not lose sight of the overall path, structure, method, and goal. Then you will practice with confidence and success.

In addition to its primary purpose—teaching how to practice *ānāpānasati* correctly—this manual serves another purpose that the casual reader might overlook. In the course of carefully studying in the way that has been recommended here, you will discover that every central teaching of Buddhism, true Buddhism in its pristine form, is mentioned here. Thus, this book provides an outline of the essential teachings of Buddhism. So in this way our intellectual study is neatly integrated with our mental cultivation practice. For how can we separate the two? To fully understand our practice we must do our Dhamma homework, and vice versa. Having both in one place will help those who are confused about what and how much to study. Just be sure that you understand all the things discussed here; that is enough.

We should always remember that meditation is the cultivation and practice of non-attachment. The Buddha taught only the middle way, and *ānāpānasati* is nothing but the middle way. It is neither an intense practice, nor can it be done without effort. It must be done with balance. Properly done, *ānāpānasati* is neither detached pushing away nor egoistic clinging; it is a practice of non-attachment. Be very careful about sitting down with ideas like, "I am sitting, I am watching, I am breathing, I am meditating. I am this, that is mine, my breathing, my body, my mind, my feelings, I, I, me, me, mine, mine…" Learn to let go of these attached feelings and ideas of "I" and "mine." Learn to stay balanced in the breathing with *sati*.

We do not cling to the technique we are using, nor do we cling to its theory. We do not use *ānāpānasati* to collect mundane trivia about the breath, ourselves, or anything else. We do not abuse it in the pursuit of attainments. Rather, we respectfully use *ānāpānasati* to develop the skills and learning we need, and all we need is to let go of attachments and thereby quench our *dukkha*.

The middle way is also a practice of correctness, of being skillful in the way we live. While practicing *ānāpānasati* correctly, we are also living correctly. We do no harm to any creature, neither to others nor to ourselves. This practice abuses no one. As we become established in this practice, we become familiar with a mode of being that is correct, balanced, and non-attached. We do not get caught up in extremes, in any of the dualistic traps. Although we may initially develop this wisdom in formal *bhāvanā* practice, we then perfect it within the informal meditation of daily life.

Attachment is a long-established habit for most of us. If we could drop it easily, we would become buddhas just like that! Instead, most of us must work at letting go of our attachments and the habit of clinging and grasping. *Ānāpānasati* is one way of letting go. We begin by letting go of our coarse attachments: attachments to the body, to aches and pains; attachments to agitation and impatience, to boredom and laziness; attachments to external disturbances and petty annoyances. Then, we find ourselves becoming attached to more subtle things, such as happy feelings. Once we let go of these, we discover attachments to higher, brighter, clearer, more refined states of awareness. Letting go of these, we begin to have some insight into reality and so we become attached to the insights. Finally, we learn to let go of everything. In this way, *ānāpānasati* is a systematic method of successively letting go of more and more subtle attachments until there is no attachment left at all.

The benefits of correct, sustained *ānāpānasati* practice are numerous. Some are specifically religious, whereas others are mundane. Although Ajahn Buddhadāsa covers them extensively in the seventh lecture, we should mention a few here at the beginning. First, *ānāpānasati* is good for both our physical and mental health. Long, deep, peaceful breathing is good for the body. Proper breathing calms us and helps us to let go of and eliminate the tension, high blood pressure, nervousness, and ulcers that ruin so many lives these days. We can learn the simple and beautiful act of sitting quietly, alive to our breathing, free of stress, worry, and anxiety. This gentle calm can be maintained in other daily activities and will allow us to do everything with more grace and skill. *Ānāpānasati* brings us into touch with reality and nature. We often live in our heads—in ideas, dreams, memories, plans, words, and the like. So we do not even have the opportunity to understand our own bodies, never taking the time to observe them (except when the excitement of illness or sex occurs). In *ānāpānasati*, through breathing, we become sensitive to our bodies and their nature. We ground ourselves in this basic reality of human existence, which provides the stability we need to cope wisely with feelings, emotions, thoughts, memories, and all the rest of our inner conditioning. No longer blown about by these experiences, we can accept them for what they are and learn the lessons they have to teach us. We begin to learn what is what, what is real and what is not, what is necessary and what is unnecessary, what is conflict and what is peace.

With *ānāpānasati* we learn to live in the present moment, the only place one can truly live. Dwelling in the past—which has died—or dreaming of the future—which brings death—is not really living as a human being ought to live. Each breath, however, is a living reality within the boundless here-now. To be aware of the breath is to live, ready to participate fully in whatever comes next. Lastly, *ānāpānasati* helps us to let go of the selfishness that is destroying our lives and our world. Our societies and planet are tortured by the lack of peace. The problem is so serious that even politicians and military-industrialists pay lip service to it. Still, very little is done to encourage the blossoming of genuine peace. Merely external—and superficial—solutions are tried, while the actual source of conflict is internal, within each of us. Conflict, strife, struggle, and competition, violence and crime, exploitation and dishonesty—these all arise out of our self-centered striving, which is born from selfish thinking. *Ānāpānasati* will guide us to the bottom of this nasty "I-ing" and "my-ing" that spawns self-ishness. It is not necessary to shout for peace when we need merely to breathe with wise awareness.

Many people who share our aspiration for peace—peace both for individual hearts and for the world we share—visit Suan Mokkh. We offer this manual to them and to all others who seek Lord Buddha's path of peace and who accept this as the duty and joy of all human beings. We hope that this book will enrich your practice of *ānāpānasati* and your life. May we all realize the purpose for which we were born.

Santikaro Bhikkhu

Acknowledgments

To the First Edition

DHAMMA PROJECTS GIVE us opportunities to join together in meritorious work and in service of our comrades in birth, aging, illness, and death. A number of friends have given freely of their energy, time, and skills. Although there is no better reward than the contentment and peace that comes with our doing our duty in Dhamma, nevertheless, we would like to acknowledge and bless our friends' contributions.

Those who helped are: Jiaranai Lansuchip, Supis Vajanarat, Pradittha Siripan, Dhammakamo Bhikkhu, Viriyanando Bhikkhu, John Busch, Kris Hoover, Sister Dhammadinnā, Wutichai Taveesaksirphol, Phra Dusadee Metankuro, Dr. Priya Tasanapradit, Amnuey Suwankiri, and the Dhamma Study-Practice Group. The support of certain special friends was invaluable: Ajahn Poh (Bodhi Buddhadhammo), Ajahn Runjuan Indrakamhaeng, and Mrs. Pratim Juanwiwat.

Lastly, Ajahn Buddhadasa, in line with the Blessed One's purpose, gives us the example and inspiration for a life of Dhamma service, which we humbly try to emulate in ways such as putting together this manual.

Phra Dusadee Metamkuro
Suan Mokkhabalārāma
Twelfth Lunar Month, 2530 (1987)

To the Revised Edition

The entire text was typed onto disk by Ms. Boonsom, while David Ollson and David Mendels helped check her work. Subsequent checking, proofreading, and correcting were undertaken by the Sangha of *Dawn Kiam*—Dhammavidu Bhikkhu, Samanera Sucitto,

Samanera Santipemo, Matthew Magnus, David Wayte, and the translator—during the Rains Retreat of 1995.

Finally, Wisdom and their capable editors, proofreaders, designers, and others have brought this project to fruition. On behalf of Suan Mokkhabalārāma and the Dhammadana Mulanidhi, we express appreciation, gratitude, and blessings for their efforts.

Santikaro Bhikkhu
Suan Atammayatārāma

Textual Notes

AJAHN BUDDHADĀSA FELT that committed students of Dhamma should become familiar with and deepen their understanding of important Pali terms. Translations into English often miss some, or much, of the original meaning. (Take as an example the Pali term *dukkha*.) By learning the Pali terms, we can explore the various meanings and connotations that arise in different contexts. In this volume, you will find Pali terms explained and sometimes translated (although not always in the same way) both in the text and in the glossary. The spelling we have used is according to Thai convention.

Pali has both singular and plural inflections, but Thai does not. The Pali-Thai terms herein are used like the English word *sheep*, sometimes with an article and sometimes not. Depending on the context and meaning, you can decide which cases are appropriate: singular, plural, both, or numberless.

Generally, Pali terms are italicized. The proper nouns Buddha, Dhamma, and Sangha are not italicized. Pali and Thai scripts do not use capital letters. In general, we have only capitalized Pali terms when they begin a sentence.

All notes have been added by the translator.

I

Why Practice Dhamma?

WHY DHAMMA? WHY PRACTICE DHAMMA?

Before we answer these questions, we need to understand the meaning of Dhamma. Then we can discuss the reasons why we must study and practice Dhamma.

DHAMMA AND THE SECRETS OF LIFE

A simple explanation of Dhamma is "the secret of nature that must be understood in order to develop life for the highest possible benefit."

To develop life to the highest level means to reach a stage of life that is free from all problems and all *dukkha* (unsatisfactoriness, suffering). Such a life is completely free from everything signified by the words *problem* and *dukkha*.

To understand our topic, it is also important to clarify the word *secret*. If we do not know the secret of something, then we are unable to be successful in obtaining the highest results and maximum benefits from it. For example, the exploration of outer space and developments in nuclear power have been possible through understanding the secrets of these things. The same is true of life. In order to develop our lives to the fullest, we must know life's secrets. Life, especially in the context of Dhamma, is a matter of nature (*dhamma-jāti*). This Pali word *dhamma-jāti* may not correspond exactly to the English word *nature*, but the two are close enough. Nature, in this context, means something that exists within itself, by itself, of itself, and as its own law. According to this understanding, nature is not opposed to humanity, as some Westerners believe, but encompasses humanity and all that human beings do and experience. Thus, in order to understand Dhamma, we must understand the secret of the nature of life.

DHAMMA: FOUR ASPECTS

The Dhamma of life has four aspects:

27

1. nature itself;
2. the law of nature;
3. the duties that must be performed according to that law of nature; and
4. the fruits or benefits that arise from the performance of that duty.

We should always keep these four interrelated meanings in mind.

Please investigate these truths within yourself, within this body and mind that you imagine to be yourself. Within each of us, various natures are compounded into a body, into a being. And there is the natural law that controls these natures. Further, according to the law of nature, there are the duties that must be performed correctly. Lastly, there are the results of the performance of these duties. If one's duties are performed correctly, the result will be well-being, tranquility, and ease. If they are performed incorrectly, however, the result will be *dukkha*: unsatisfactoriness, anguish, pain, frustration, suffering. Even at the beginning, we should observe carefully and see clearly that we can find all four aspects of Dhamma or nature within each of us. When we have thoroughly investigated the four meanings of nature, we will see that all life is made up of these four aspects. At present, however, we have yet to understand them correctly and completely. We have not truly penetrated the secret of what is called "life." As we have not yet realized the secret of Dhamma, we are unable to practice in a way that obtains the fullest benefit from life. Let us take the time to thoroughly study Dhamma and "the secret of life" so we might take full advantage of them.

DEVELOPING LIFE BEYOND *DUKKHA*

We must also consider the phrase "developing life." As we begin to practice, we do not know the secret of this either. We lack a clear understanding of the extent to which life can truly be developed. As we do not realize the highest benefits that are available to humanity, we take little interest in the secrets of life that are necessary to reach those highest levels. Our objective, then, is to understand how far life can be developed and to kindle interest in that development.

As beginners, we need only hold to the basic principle that "developing life" means "causing life to progress to the highest level," that is, beyond all problems and *dukkha*, beyond all the possible meanings and gradations of these two terms. For those unfamiliar with the word *dukkha*, we can tentatively translate it as "stress, unsatisfactoriness, conflict, agitation—all the things that disturb life." *Dukkha* is what we are running from all the time. *Dukkha* interferes with a life of calm and ease as well as with spiritual perfection. When life is developed beyond all *dukkha*, it reaches its highest possible level.

Now, some people do not know about their own problems. They do not understand *dukkha*, neither in general terms nor in their own lives. They look at themselves and say, "Oh! I don't have any problems; everything is okay." They accept all their difficulties and sorrow as normal and ordinary. Are we like this? We need to take a serious, detailed look into our own lives to see if there is anything that we can call "a problem." Is there any *dukkha*? Is there anything unsatisfactory or disturbing about life? Such questions are necessary when we choose to study Dhamma. If you have not looked inside, if you are unaware of your problems, if you feel no *dukkha*, then you cannot know why you are on retreat, why you have come to a meditation center, or why you are studying Dhamma. Please, take a good, clear look at your problems and *dukkha* before proceeding any further.

Developing Life Is Our Duty

There are four aspects of developing life. The first is to prevent from arising that which is dangerous to life. The second is to eliminate and destroy that which is dangerous that has already arisen in life. The third is to produce that which is useful and beneficial for life. The fourth is to maintain and preserve such beneficial elements so that they grow further. Again, these four aspects of developing life are: preventing new dangers, eliminating old dangers, creating beneficial elements, and maintaining and increasing the beneficial elements. These comprise what is called "developing life." Developing life is our duty. If such development is to happen, we must realize our true duty.

In order to fulfill our duty, we must have in our possession four very important *dhammas*,[1] four Dhamma tools. These four Dhamma tools are *sati* (mindfulness or reflective awareness), *sampajañña* (wisdom-in-action or ready comprehension), *paññā* (wisdom or spiritual knowledge) and *samādhi* (concentration, mental collectedness, and stability). These four tools will enable us to develop life.

In addition, the practice of *vipassanā*, or mental development, cultivates and trains the mind so that these four Dhamma tools are sufficiently enriched to develop our lives. We need to take an interest in studying the mental development of these four necessary *dhammas*.

THE KIND OF *ĀNĀPĀNASATI* WE NEED

There are many different systems and techniques of mental development, or *vipassanā*, for training the mind. Nevertheless, of all known techniques, the best is *ānāpānasati-bhāvanā*, the cultivation of mindfulness with breathing. This is the practice that we will discuss in detail throughout this book.

The correct and complete practice of *ānāpānasati-bhāvanā* is to take one truth or reality of nature and then observe, investigate, and scrutinize it in the mind with every inhalation and every exhalation. Thus, mindfulness with breathing allows us to contemplate any important natural truth while breathing in and breathing out.

Such study is of great importance and value. To know the truth of something, we must take that reality and contemplate, analyze, and study it wholeheartedly every time we breathe in and out. The object must be experienced continuously in the mind. Here, "continuously" means "with every in-breath and out-breath." Breathing in, know that object. Breathing out, know that object. Breathing in, understand that object. Breathing out, understand that object. This kind of contemplation is necessary, as well as beneficial, to our development of knowledge. Such study brings about a transformation in the mind-heart, that is to say, on the inside of life.

Actually, the meaning of *ānāpānasati* is quite broad: "to recall anything at all with *sati* while breathing in and breathing out." Imagine that while breathing in and breathing out you are thinking about your home or work; or about your family and friends. This too can be called *ānāpānasati*. However, this kind of thinking is not our purpose here. We need to recollect Dhamma, that is, the natural truths that free the mind from the suffering of *dukkha*. If we sufficiently investi-

gate these truths in the mind, we will be free of all our proble[m]
eliminate *dukkha*. In other words, we must acquire the four D[hamma]
tools mentioned earlier. This kind of *ānāpānasati* is the most us[eful]

FOUR OBJECTS TO CONTEMPLATE

What are the proper, correct, and necessary objects of contemplation
every time we breathe in and breathe out? There are four proper
objects of contemplation: the secrets of *kāya* (body), the secrets of
vedanā (feeling), the secrets of *citta* (mind), and the secrets of
dhamma. The secrets of these four objects are to be brought into the
mind and studied.

These objects are sufficiently important that you should memorize their Pali names. For your own clear understanding and future
reference, please remember: *kāya, vedanā, citta,* and *dhamma*. These
are the four most important topics. Because these four already exist
within us as the sources of all our problems, we must use them far
more than any other objects to train and develop the mind. Our
lack of understanding and inability to master[2] these four objects
ensures that they lead us to suffering. Therefore, it is absolutely necessary that we clearly distinguish and understand these four objects:
body, feeling, mind, and *dhamma*.

STAGE ONE: FLESH-BODY AND BREATH-BODY

Now, let us examine these four separately, beginning with *kāya*. The
Pali word *kāya* literally means "group" and can be applied to any
collection of things. In this case, *kāya* specifically means the groups
of elements that are compounded together into a physical flesh-and-
blood body. The English word *body* can also mean group; we must
simply be careful about which group we mean.

Let's observe for ourselves what makes up our bodies. What are the
organs? How many are there? What kinds of elements are present?
What parts and components come together to form a body? We
should note that there is one very important component which nourishes the rest of this body, namely, the breath. The breath too is called
kāya in that it is a collection of various elements. We will study the
establishment of the flesh-body and its relationship to the breath-body.

The breath-body is very important because it sustains life in the rest of the body. This relationship is crucial to our study. Although we lack the ability to control the general body, or flesh-body, directly, we can master it indirectly by using the breath. If we act in a certain way toward the breath-body, there will also be a specific effect upon the flesh-body. This is why we take the breath as the object of our training. Supervising the breath, to whatever degree, is equivalent to regulating the flesh-body to that same degree. This point will be more clearly understood when we have trained up to that particular stage of *ānāpānasati*.

Beginning our practice with the *kāya* (body), we study the breath in a special way. Every kind of breath is noted and analyzed. Long breaths, short breaths, calm breaths, violent breaths, fast breaths, slow breaths—we learn to know them all. We examine the nature, characteristics, and functions of each kind of breath that arises.

We should observe the influence of the different breaths upon the flesh-body. We need to see clearly the great effect that the breath has on the physical body. We observe both sides of this relationship until it becomes clear that the two, the flesh-body and the breath-body, are interconnected and inseparable. See that the breath-body conditions and affects the flesh-body. This is the first step. We make a special study of the breath and come to know the characteristics of all its different forms. In this way, we gain insight into the conditioning effect it has on the flesh-body. This, in turn, will allow us to master the flesh-body by means of regulating the breath.

The purpose of these beginning steps is to know the secrets of the *kāya*, the body. We know that the breath-body, our breathing, conditions the flesh-body. This important secret helps us to use the breath to gain mastery over the body. We discover that by making the breath calm we can relax the flesh-body. If our breathing is calm, the flesh-body will be likewise. Thus, we can regulate our body indirectly through our breathing. Furthermore, we learn that through calming the breath-body and the flesh-body we can experience happiness, joy, and other benefits.

STAGE TWO: OUR MASTERS, THE FEELINGS

Once we understand the secrets of the *kāya*, we turn to the secrets of the *vedanā* (feelings). The *vedanā* have the greatest power and influence over human beings; indeed, over all living things. This may come as a surprise to you. Nonetheless, the entire world—animals, humans, all living beings—depends on the *vedanā*. All are under the power of the feelings. At first, this may seem unbelievable, so let's examine it in more detail.

Our entire species is forced by the *vedanā* to do their bidding. When *sukha-vedanā* (pleasant feelings) are present, we try to increase these feelings. Pleasant feelings always pull the mind in a certain direction and condition certain activities. *Dukkha-vedanā* (unpleasant, disagreeable feelings) affect the mind and influence life in the opposite direction; again, the results are habitual responses. The mind struggles with these feelings, turning them into problems that cause *dukkha*.

Vedanā, or feelings, have great power over our actions. In fact, the whole world is under the command of these *vedanā*. For example, *taṭhā* (craving) can control the mind. Craving itself is first conditioned by feeling. Thus, the *vedanā* have the strongest and most powerful influence over our entire mind. Thus, it is especially important to understand the secrets of the *vedanā*.

People leave Europe and America to come to Suan Mokkh or go to other retreat centers in search of the conditions for *sukha-vedanā*. This is a fact. Even those people who remain at home work for the sake of nurturing *sukha-vedanā*. We are slaves to *vedanā*—*sukha-vedanā* in particular—all the time. Clearly, we must understand the *vedanā* in order to keep them under control.

In some Pali texts the *vedanā* are described as "conditioners of the mind" (*citta-sankhāra*). Mind, in this instance, arises from our thoughts, desires, and needs. We cannot endure the influence of the *vedanā*. We are not free within ourselves; we think and act under the power of *vedanā*. Feelings condition the mind and force us to act.

If we master the *vedanā*, we will master the world. This statement may seem peculiar at first. However, we shall be able to regulate the world when we are able to regulate the feelings as needed. Then we shall be able to govern the world as it needs to be governed. These days, nobody is interested in mastering the *vedanā*, and as a consequence, the world exists without any proper supervision. Wars, famines, corruption, pollution, all these crises and problems originate from our failure from the start to master the feelings. If we master the feelings, then we can master the world. It is important that we give this some serious thought.

According to Lord Buddha, the causes of everything in the world are rooted in the *vedanā*. All activities occur because the *vedanā* force us to desire and then to act out those desires. Even the rounds of rebirth within the cycle of *samsara*—the cycles of birth and death, of heaven and hell—are themselves conditioned by the *vedanā*. Everything originates in the feelings. To master the *vedanā* is to master the origin, the source, the birthplace of all things. Thus, it is absolutely necessary to understand these feelings correctly and comprehensively. Then we shall be able to master our feelings, and their secrets will never again deceive us into behaving foolishly.

Once we master the highest and most sublime *vedanā*, we can also master the lower, cruder, more petty *vedanā*. When we learn to control the most difficult feelings, we can control the easy, simple, childish feelings as well. For this reason we should strive to achieve the highest level of *vedanā*; namely, the feelings that are born from *samādhi*. If we can conquer the most pleasant *vedanā*, we can be victorious over all *vedanā*. Should you bother to give it a try? Should you endure any difficulties that might arise? Should you spend your precious time on this practice? Let us consider wisely.

It may seem curious that in striving to realize the highest *vedanā* our aim is to control and eliminate these feelings rather than to enjoy and indulge in them. Some people might think it strange to search for the highest *vedanā* only to master and control them. It is important to understand this point correctly. By eliminating these pleasant feelings we obtain something even better in return. We receive another kind of *vedanā*, a higher order of *vedanā*—one that perhaps should not even be called *vedanā*—something more like *nibbāna* or emancipation. So it is not so unusual or strange that we wish to achieve the best *vedanā* in order to eliminate the pleasant feelings.

There are three main points to learn regarding the *vedanā*. First, we must learn to know the *vedanā* themselves, those things that cause feeling in the mind. Second, we should understand how the *vedanā* condition the *citta*, the mind-heart. The *vedanā* stir up thoughts, memories, words, and actions. We need to know this conditioning of the mind. Third, we must discover that we can master the mind by mastering the *vedanā*, just as we can control the flesh-body by regulating the breath. We master the mind by correctly mastering the feelings that condition it, so that the *vedanā* condition the mind in only the proper way. We do this by regulating those elements that condition the feelings, which is equivalent to regulating the feelings themselves. These are the three important points to understand about the secrets of the *vedanā*.

Since the first and second stages of practice both follow the same principle, it is helpful to compare the two. In the stage regarding the body, we learn what conditions the flesh-body and we study it. We analyze that body-conditioner until we know it in great detail and how it conditions the body. Then, by regulating the body-conditioner, we master the body. In this way we make the body calmer and more peaceful. Likewise, that which conditions the mind is feeling. We calm the mind by controlling the *vedanā* so that they do not condition or stir up the mind; or if they do condition the mind, it is in a desirable way. Thus, the first stage regarding the *kāya* and the second stage regarding the *vedanā* follow the same basic principle and are similar in their method of practice.

STAGE THREE: THE SUBTLE MIND

First, we practice to know the secrets of the *kāya*. Second, we practice to know the secrets of the *vedanā*. Then, after fully mastering the first and second stages, we practice in order to know the secrets of the *citta*. The mind is the director and leader of life. The mind leads; the body is merely the tool that is led. If life is to follow the correct path, we must understand the *citta* correctly until we are able to master it. This requires a special study, because what we call "mind" is very subtle, complex, and profound. We cannot see it with our eyes; something special is needed to "see" it. Such study is fully within our ability with well-trained *sati*, but we must put forth special effort. Do not lose heart or give up! We are more than capable of studying the *citta* so that we may learn its secrets.

It is not possible to know the *citta* directly: that is, we cannot touch it or make direct contact with it. However, it is possible to know the *citta* through its thoughts. If we know the thoughts, we will know the mind. In the material world, for comparison, we cannot know the phenomenon "electricity" in itself. Instead, we know electricity through its properties: current, voltage, power, and so on. So it is with the *citta*. We cannot directly experience it, but we can experience its properties, the various thoughts. During each day, how many kinds of thoughts arise, how many levels of thoughts come up? We learn to observe these different thoughts; this is how we can know the *citta*.

We begin our study of the *citta* by observing the kinds of thoughts that arise. In what ways are these thoughts improper and in what ways are they correct? Does the mind think along defiled or undefiled lines, good or wicked lines? We observe all the possible types of thought until we can thoroughly understand the *citta*. In this way we gradually come to understand the true nature (*dhamma-jāti*) of the mind.

Because of having already trained the *kāya* and the *vedanā*, we are able at this stage to direct the mind as we require. The mind can be made to think in different ways, or it can be kept still. We can make the mind satisfied, or even dissatisfied, if we choose. The mind can experience different kinds of happiness and joy. It can be stilled, calmed, and concentrated in different ways and to different degrees. Finally, the mind can be liberated. We can direct our mind to let go of things that it loves or hates, or to which it is attached. The mind is liberated from all those objects. These secrets of the mind must be practiced in stage three of *ānāpānasati-bhāvanā*.

We must get to know all the different kinds of *citta*. We are able to make the mind glad and content; we can make it stop and be still. Lastly, we can make the mind let go of its attachments. As the mind lets go of things to which it is attached, things that are attached to the mind let go as well. We let go of it all. As we do this, we become expert and well versed in matters of the mind. This is the third lesson of *ānāpānasati*.

STAGE FOUR: REALIZING THE SUPREME DHAMMA

Having learned the secrets of the body, the feelings, and the mind, we come to the fourth stage, which concerns Dhamma. As mentioned, Dhamma is nature in all its meanings. In this stage, we take the ultimate truth of all natures as the object of our study. "Studying Dhamma" is to study the truth, the fact, that is, the supreme secret of nature. With this knowledge we can live life in the best way. We need to study the secret of the truth that controls life, the truth of *aniccaā, dukkhaā, anattā, suññatā,* and *tathatā.*

> *Aniccaā:* know that all conditioned things are imperma-
> nent and in endless flux.
> *Dukkhaā:* know that all concocted things are inherently
> unable to satisfy our desires.
> *Anattā:* know that all things are not-self.
> *Suññatā:* know that everything is void of selfhood, of "I"
> and "mine."
> *Tathatā:* know the thusness, the suchness, of all things.

Together, these are the one ultimate truth. We must observe these until they are fully realized so that the mind will never again lose its way. When the mind understands this truth of all reality, it will not make any errors but will keep itself on the path of correctness.

It may seem curious that all truth—*aniccaā, dukkhaā, anattā, suññatā*—ends up with *tathatā.* It may be surprising that the ultimate truth of everything in the universe comes down to nothing but thusness. In Thai, *tathatā* is translated "just like that." It is more difficult in English: "just such, only thus, thusness." It's hard to believe, isn't it? All truth boils down to the typical, ordinary words, "That's the way things are." When we see thusness, the highest Dhamma, nothing is regarded as good or bad, wrong or right, gain or loss, defeat or victory, merit or sin, happiness or suffering, having or lacking, positive or negative. The highest Dhamma is right here in "merely thus," for thusness is above and beyond all meanings of positive and negative, above all meanings of optimism and pessimism, beyond all dualities. This is the end. The truth to be known in stage four is the secret of nature that says all things are "only thus, just so."

To understand Dhamma sufficiently is the first step, but understanding it is not the end. We now see that as the mind begins to let go, to loosen up its attachments, these attachments dissolve away. We experience this until the point where attachment is extinguished. Once attachment is quenched, the final step is to experience that "the mind is free, everything is free." The Pali texts use the phrase "throwing back." The Buddha said that, at the end, we throw everything back. This means that we have been thieves all our lives by appropriating the things of nature as "I" and "mine." We have been stupid and have suffered for it. Now, we have become wise and are able to give things up. At this last step of practice we realize, "Oh! It isn't mine, it belongs to nature." We throw everything back to nature and never again steal anything.

The last step ends in this unusual way with our not being thieves anymore, with freedom from all influences of attachment. The final step of the development of *ānāpānasati* finishes here. To learn the secret of Dhamma is to know that we should be attached to nothing whatsoever, and then never again to become attached to anything. All is liberated. The case is closed. We are finished.

If we choose to give a name to this last step, we can call it "emancipation" or "salvation." All religions seem to have similar goals and to call these goals by similar names. *Our* understanding of emancipation is the meaning just described—ending attachment and throwing everything back to nature. In Buddhism, emancipation means to be free from every type and form of attachment, so that we may live our lives above the world. Although our bodies are in this world, our minds are beyond it. Thus, all of our problems disappear. This is how to develop life to its full potential, using this four-stage method of practice. There are many more details to consider, but we will leave them for later chapters.

In this chapter, we have given a general outline of this system of practice. With this background it should be easy to practice each step as we come to it. In the following chapters, we will describe the practice of *ānāpānasati* itself.

2

Getting Started

MANY DIFFERENT SYSTEMS, forms, styles, and methods of *samādhi-bhāvanā* (mental cultivation through concentration; meditation) or *vipassanā* (meditation for the sake of insight into impermanence, unsatisfactoriness, and not-self) are taught by various teachers under different names. We will discuss the *samadhi-bhāvanā* specifically introduced and recommended by Lord Buddha himself: *ānāpānasati*. This method appears in both brief references and detailed explanations in the Pali *Tipiṭika*. *Ānāpānasati* is the Buddha's system, "the Buddha's *samādhi-bhāvanā*." This system is not the Burmese or Chinese or Sri Lankan style that some people are clinging to these days. Likewise, it is not the system of "ajahn this," "master that," "guru this," or "teacher that" as others are so caught up in nowadays. Nor is it the style of Suan Mokkh or any other *wat*. Instead, this system is simply the correct way as recommended by the Buddha. He declared this form of *samādhi-bhavana* to be the one through which he himself realized the Dhamma of Perfect Awakening. Suan Mokkh practices as well as teaches this system. This book deals with this style in particular of *samādhi-bhāvanā*, or *vipassanā*. We recommend the practice of *ānāpānasati*, which is one system of *vipassanā*, the one used at Suan Mokkh and taught by the Buddha.

Ānāpānasati has many forms that are short, easy, and incomplete; we have chosen the form that is complete. Consequently, this sixteen-step form of *ānāpānasati* may seem long and detailed, as is fitting for anything complete. For some people it is too long, too detailed, or simply too much for what they need. This is true—it may be more than is necessary for certain people. But for those who want to study and train thoroughly, it is just right. If we want the technique to be complete, it must include all sixteen steps. This is required by nature. The Buddha never taught anything more than necessary or less than complete. Consequently, this sixteen-step *samādhi-bhāvanā* is neither too much nor too little. If you are patient enough to learn all sixteen steps, you will have the complete system. If you are unable to do all sixteen, there is a condensed version that is adequate for those so inclined. However, if you are interested in completeness, you must have the patience to train and practice *ānāpānasati* in its full form.

MODE OF LIVING

In order to practice *ānāpānasati* satisfactorily, some general preparations are needed. In other words, we must make some adjustments in our mode of living. Our lifestyle and our *ānāpānasati* practice are interrelated. Thus, we shall discuss the kind of lifestyle that supports Dhamma study and *citta-bhāvanā* practice before going into the details of the practice of *ānāpānasati* itself.

Here, we are discussing the *paccaya*. *Paccaya* is a Pali (and Thai) word whose meaning is similar to the English word *condition*, although it has other connotations as well. The *paccaya* are those things that are absolutely necessary for life; thus, they are sometimes translated as "the necessities, or requisites, of life." The *paccaya* are factors that support the existence of life. These necessities, the foundation of our lives, must be correct if we are to study Dhamma and practice meditation successfully. Thus, it is important to give your attention to this important matter.

Generally, most people only pay attention to the four material or bodily conditions: food, clothing, shelter, and medicine. However, it is equally important that we understand the fifth necessity, the *paccaya* for the mind-heart. The first four conditions are for the body alone. The *paccaya* for the mind is what amuses and coaxes the mind into contentment. We might describe this *paccaya* as "entertainment," since it entertains the mind properly and makes it content in the correct way. Without this condition there would be death— mental death. When the bodily necessities are lacking, the body dies; when the mental necessity is missing, the mind dies. We will get to know both the four physical and the one mental *paccaya*, although we are primarily concerned with the fifth necessity, the *paccaya* that nourishes and sustains the mind. Let's consider in detail these four physical and one mental *paccaya*.

THE MATERIAL NECESSITIES

Let us start with the first material necessity—food. We should eat food that is food. Do not eat food that is "bait." We should understand the crucial distinction between "food" and "bait." We eat food for the proper nourishment of life. We eat bait for the sake of deliciousness. Bait makes us unwise and causes us to eat foolishly, just like the bait on the hook that snags foolish fish. We must eat the kinds of food that are genuinely beneficial for the body, and we must eat in moderation. "Eating bait" means eating for the sake of deliciousness and fun. It is also usually expensive. We must stop swallowing bait and learn to eat only food that is proper and wholesome. This is especially important while staying in Dhamma centers.

If you are eating bait, you will be constantly hungry all day and night. You will always be sneaking off to eat yet more bait. Eating bait impairs our mental abilities. The mind surrenders to the bait and is not fit for the study and practice of Dhamma. On the other hand, when you eat food, it will be at appropriate times and in moderation. There will be little waste and no danger.

Our second condition is clothing. We should wear clothes that fulfill the real meaning and purpose of clothing: good health, protection against annoyances and discomfort, convenience and simplicity, and expression of culture.

Thus, we should wear clothing that is convenient, simple, and a sign of culture. Please do not wear clothing that destroys the culture of oneself or of others. This leads to inappropriateness in ourselves; it hampers mental tranquility. We should give some thought to the second *paccaya*, clothing.

INTIMATE WITH NATURE

The third condition is shelter; shelter should be adequate, modest, and not excessive. These days, worldly people live in housing that exceeds their needs, costs a great deal, causes difficulties, and leads to worries. Thus, housing becomes a source of ever-greater selfishness. The most appropriate housing for Dhamma practice is that closest to nature, close enough to be called "in camaraderie with nature." It seems that Europeans and Americans seldom live out in the open, on the ground, or close to nature. They tend to live in beautiful, fancy, expensive places. They seem to need to stay in hotels and do not seem to care for the simple monastery meeting hall.[3]

As a condition of our Dhamma practice, we should try to adapt ourselves to housing that is closer to nature. Living in such a way makes it easier to understand and to practice in harmony with nature. We can learn to be contented and even enjoy such plain and simple living together with nature. This will benefit and support our study and practice.

The Lord Buddha is an excellent example in these matters. The Buddha was born outdoors, was enlightened outdoors, taught sitting outside on the ground, lived outdoors, rested out in the open, and died (*parinibbāna*) outdoors. Clearly his life was intimate with nature. We take his example as our standard and are thus content with a simple, natural mode of living. We believe that the founders of all the great religions practiced plain living as well, although perhaps not as thoroughly as the Buddha, who was born, was enlightened, taught, lived, and died in the open air.

By developing a lifestyle that is intimate with nature, we are making it convenient for nature to speak to us. If we are intelligent listeners, we will hear nature's voice more clearly than if we were far away. Intimacy with nature can become the essence of our mode of living.

In English, the words *moderate* and *sufficient* can be vague, so it is important to understand them in their fuller, Thai meaning, as they have been explained above. We should also be careful about the words *good* and *well*, as in, "good living" and "eating well." We do not care for good living and good eating that have no limits. Instead, we prefer to live and eat correctly. All four material *paccaya* are based on the principles of sufficiency and appropriateness. Do not get carried away with good-good-good such that it becomes excessive and luxurious. That would be neither proper nor decent. Please acknowledge this understanding of the four material necessities.

THE MIND-HEART *PACCAYA*

The fifth necessity, which is so often neglected, is more important than the other four, so let's consider it in detail. The fifth *paccaya* is that which cajoles and entertains us, making us content, easing our anxiety and agitation, so that we are no longer hungry to the point of death.

Amusing the heart, making it satisfied and pleased, is crucial. This is the mental *paccaya* or necessity. We might call it different names, such as entertainment or amusement. The important point is that whatever we call it, it must be right for the mind. It must be nourishment, food for the mind, just as the other four are food for the body.

Much of the time, worldly people think of the fifth necessity as a matter of sex. But we are interested in something different. Sex can entertain the mind, but now we are ready for Dhamma-Dhamma-Dhamma to be our amusement. This means we use appropriate means to amuse and satisfy us. When we are aware of correctness and are satisfied with it, when we feel proper and are content, the heart is entertained and the mind is amused. This sense of correctness and contentedness need not have anything to do with sex.

There is a building at Suan Mokkh called the "Theater of Spiritual Entertainments."[4] It was built to provide entertainment for the heart. It is full of pictures that not only teach Dhamma but also amuse and please. This is one form the fifth *paccaya* can take. We should get to know this type of fifth necessity whose nature is not sexual but Dhammic. Let's not follow the majority who ignore the fact that sex is caught up in endless complexities and difficulties and who still cling to sex as their fifth necessity.

In summary, it is important that we adjust our mode of living to fit the study and practice of *citta-bhāvanā*. Then it will be easy and convenient for us to study and practice successfully. We will discover the "new life" that is above and beyond the influence of positivism and negativism.[5] We will be discussing the details later, for this matter is very subtle. We can say that "new life" is above all problems and beyond all aspects of *dukkha*. It is free, liberated, and emancipated because we practice Dhamma with the support and aid of all five *paccayas*. Let's endeavor to gather all five correct and proper conditions for our Dhamma practice.

PHYSICAL PREPARATIONS

Next, let's consider the immediate preparations for practicing *ānāpānasati*. First, we must choose a place that is suitable and appropriate for our practice. We select the best location available, knowing that we can never have a perfect situation. We try to find a place that is quiet and peaceful, where the conditions and weather are good and where there are no disturbances. But when good conditions are not available, we do the best we can with what we have. We must choose something, somewhere. We must be able to practice even while sitting on the train traveling from Bangkok. In this case, we can focus on the breath until we do not hear the noise of the wheels and do not feel the shaking as the train rattles over the rails. This shows that we can choose a location and use the conditions available to us in the best possible way.

We are not going to be defeated by circumstances, even on the train. Whether we have perfect conditions or not, we will make the best of them and do what we can. When we want to practice, we can use the sound of the train itself as a meditation object. Instead of the breath, the "clack-clack-clack" of the wheels on the rails can be our meditation object. In this way we cannot object to any location in the world, whether it is perfectly suitable or not. We will have no excuses regarding our choice of a proper location.

The next preliminary step is to prepare the body. Ideally, we need a body that is normal, free of disease, and without any respiratory or digestive abnormalities. More specifically, however, we can prepare the nose so that it functions smoothly and correctly. In ancient times, practitioners took clean lukewarm water in the palm of the hand, drew it up into the nose, and then blew the water out. If we do this two or three times, the nose will be clean and prepared, able to breathe well. The nose will then be much more sensitive to the breath. This is an example of getting our body ready.

TIME AND TEACHER

The time of practice is also important. When we are determined to practice earnestly, we need to choose the most suitable and appropriate time possible. However, if we cannot find a good time, we accept whatever we can get. We do not have to be enslaved to a certain time of day. Whenever possible, we should choose a time when there are no distractions or disturbances. But when there is no time that is completely free of distractions, we use the best time available. Then the mind learns to be undistracted regardless of how many disturbances are occurring. Actually, we are training the mind to be undisturbed no matter what is happening around us. The mind will learn to be peaceful. We should not limit ourselves to any certain time when things must be just right, or we will never find it. Some people do this until they cannot find any time to meditate at all! That is not right. We must always be flexible and able to practice at any time.

The next consideration involves what is called an *ācāriya* (teacher, master). In truth, even in the old training systems, they did not talk much about an *ācāriya*. Such a person was called a "good friend" (*kalyāna-mitta*). It is correct to refer to this person as "friend." A friend is an advisor who can help us with certain matters. We should not forget, however, the basic principle that no one can directly help someone else. Nowadays everyone wants a teacher to supervise them! But here, a good friend is someone who has extensive personal experience and knowledge about the meditation practice, or whatever else it is we are striving to do. Although he or she is able to answer questions and explain some difficulties, it is not necessary for a friend to sit over us and supervise every breath. A good friend who will answer questions and help us work through certain obstacles is more than enough. To have such a *kalyana-mitta* is one more thing to arrange.

SITTING POSTURE

With regard to the actual activity of meditation itself, the first thing to discuss is the sitting posture. It is important to sit in a way that is both stable and secure, so that when the mind becomes semiconscious, we will not fall over. We should be able to sit just like a pyramid. A pyramid cannot fall over because it has a very solid base and sides that rise up into a central pinnacle. There is no way that it can fall down. Consider how long the pyramids in Egypt have been sitting! So we learn to sit like a pyramid. The best way is to sit cross-legged. Put your legs out in front of you, then pull the right foot up onto the left thigh and the left foot up onto the right thigh. If you have yet to try sitting this way, or are not even used to sitting on the floor, you may need some time to train the body to sit in such a posture. It is worth the effort. You can patiently, gradually train yourself to sit this way. Then you will never fall over, as it will be impossible to fall forwards, backwards, or sideways. From ancient times this way of sitting has been called "the lotus posture" (*padmāsana*).

It is also important to sit upright, with the vertebrae and spine in proper alignment, without any bends or curves. The vertebrae should sit snugly one on top of the other so that they fit together properly. This is what is normal for the body. The spine is a vital part of the nervous system, so we should sit erect in order to keep it straight and correct. This is good posture.

If you have never sat like this, it may be difficult at first. Nevertheless, it is important that you try to do it. The first time, you may be able only to fold your legs in front without crossing them. That is enough to begin. Later, put one leg on top of the other, crossing one leg. Eventually, you will be able to cross both legs in a "full lotus" position. This way of sitting is as compact as a pyramid and will not tip over when the mind is concentrated or half-concentrated. A straight spine is necessary because it stimulates the correct kind of breathing. If the spine is bent, there will be another kind of breathing. Therefore, we must try to straighten the spine, even if it is a little difficult at first.[6]

Next, consider the hands. The most comfortable and easiest placement is to let the hands fall onto the knees. Another way is to lay one hand on top of the other in the lap. This second position may be uncomfortable because the hands can become hot. If we rest them on the knees, they will not get hot. Some groups advise people to fold their hands in the lap with the thumbs touching in order to aid concentration. That is how they do it in China, and this position can also be good. You should choose whichever position seems most suitable for you. The hands will not heat up if you leave them on the knees. Or you can lay them in the lap if that is comfortable. Or you can press your thumbs together to increase concentration a bit. You can choose the placement that is best for you from among these different positions of the hands.

COOL, CONCENTRATED EYES

Practitioners often ask, "Should we leave the eyes open or close them?" Many people believe that they must close their eyes, that they cannot meditate with open eyes. If you are serious about what you are doing and have a sufficiently strong mind, it is not difficult to practice with the eyes left open. Begin with the eyes open. Open them with the determination to gaze toward the tip of the nose. This is not impossible; it just takes a little effort. Gaze at the tip of the nose so that the eyes do not get involved with other things. When we close our eyes, we tend to grow sleepy, so be careful about closing the eyes. Also, when the eyes are closed, they tend to become warm and dry. Meditating with the eyes open will help us to stay awake and will keep the eyes cool and comfortable. Furthermore, this will help the mind to be concentrated; it will aid the development of *samādhi* (concentration or collectedness). As *samādhi* gradually develops, the eyes will naturally close by themselves. The eyelids will relax and drop shut on their own. This is nothing to worry about. The complete technique begins with the eyes open. Gaze at the tip of the nose until you develop *samādhi*, then the eyes will close on their own.

Practicing with the eyes open and gazing at the tip of the nose automatically produces a noticeable level of concentration. If we establish the entire mind in gazing at the tip of the nose, we will not see anything else. If we can do this, a certain level of *samādhi* is produced. We profit from having this much concentration right from the start. Merely look at the nose without seeing anything else. If all of the mind's attention is set on looking at the nose, then nothing else will be seen. This *samādhi* is not insignificant. Therefore, we should start with open eyes.

We are intent upon gazing at the nose, at feeling the nose, and at the same time we feel the body breathing. Both can be done concurrently. It may seem that both are being done at exactly the same moment, but they are not. There is nothing unnatural or supernatural about it. Because of the mind's great speed it is possible for the eyes to be gazing at the tip of the nose and to be aware of breathing in and breathing out at the same time. You can experience this for yourself.

FOLLOWING THE BREATH WITH MINDFULNESS

Finally, we come to noting, contemplating, our breathing. In order to begin, we must develop *sati* (mindfulness or reflective awareness) by being mindful of each in-breath and out-breath. We train in *sati* by noting that we are about to breathe in or breathe out. Let the

47

athing continue comfortably and normally. Let it be natural. Do
ot interfere with it in any way. Then contemplate each breath with
mindfulness. How are we breathing in? What is the out-breath like?
Use *sati* to note the ordinary breath.

We first develop and train *sati* by using a technique called "following," or "chasing." We imagine the in-breath starting from the
tip of the nose and ending at the navel. We imagine the out-breath
starting at the navel and ending at the tip of the nose. In between
these two points is the space through which the breath runs in and
out. We contemplate with *sati* the properties of this movement in
and out, from the tip of the nose to the navel and back again. Back
and forth. Do not allow any gaps or lapses. This is the first lesson:
contemplate the breath with *sati*.

Even though we are not medical students, we still know that the
breath only goes into the lungs, that it does not go all the way down
to the navel. Imagining that the breath ends at the navel is merely a
useful convention; we do not hold it to be true. It is just an assump-
tion based on our feeling and sensitivity of the movement of the
breathing. When we breathe, we feel movement all the way down to
the navel. We use that feeling as the basis of our practice and follow
the breath between the tip of the nose and the navel.

The distinction as to whether it is *sati* that follows the breath in
and out or whether *sati* forces the mind to follow the breath in and
out is not important at this point. All that matters is to contemplate
the breath as if chasing it, without ever losing it. The breath goes in
and stops a moment. Then it comes out and pauses a moment. In
and out, in and out, with short breaks in between. We must note
everything and not let anything slip by. We do not allow empty
spaces where the mind might wander but keep the mind constantly
focused on the breathing in and out.

This is the first lesson to learn, the foundation for all the rest. It
may not be so easy. Maybe it will take three days, three weeks, or
three months until we are able to do it. This is the first step, the first
task that we must accomplish. Here we are merely explaining the
method of training; it is the practice that counts. You may not get
very far in a ten-day course at Suan Mokkh or some other meditation center, but it is important to know what needs to be done and

to get started doing it. Once you correctly understand the method, you can practice on your own until you are successful. So begin with this simple step: contemplate the breath as it moves between the nose and the navel without leaving any chances for the mind to wander elsewhere.

MANY KINDS OF BREATH

As we practice "following," we have the opportunity to observe the various characteristics of the breath. For example, we can feel the long and the short duration of the breath. Thus, we learn naturally about the long breath and short breath. We can observe the coarse and fine nature of the breath. Further, we can observe its smoothness and bumpiness. Later, we will observe the reactions to these qualities. In this first step, however, we contemplate the different kinds of breath: long and short, coarse and fine, easy and uneasy. Begin to observe the various kinds by experiencing them with *sati*.

We must learn to observe in greater detail, that is, to observe the reaction or influence of each different kind of breathing. What reactions do they cause? How do they influence our awareness? For example, when each breath is long, how does this affect our awareness? What reactions do short breaths cause? What are the influences of coarse and fine breathing, of comfortable and uncomfortable breathing? We should observe the different types of breath and their various influences until we can distinguish clearly how the long and short breaths, coarse and fine breaths, and comfortable and uncomfortable breaths differ. We must learn to know the reactions to these various properties of the breath. Likewise, we must learn to know when these qualities influence our awareness, our sensitivity, our mind.

It is also important for us to note the effect or flavor of each kind of breath. The flavors that arise as different kinds of feeling are: happiness, unhappiness, *dukkha*, annoyance, and contentment. We observe and experience the flavors or effects caused by the long breath and the short breath, by the coarse breath and the fine breath, and by the easy breath and the uneasy breath. Find out why they have different flavors. For instance, we can see that the long breath gives a greater sense of peace and well-being; it has a happier taste than the short breath. Different kinds of breath bring different kinds of happiness. We learn to analyze and distinguish the various flavors that characterize the different kinds of breathing we have scrutinized.

Finally, we can discover the various causes that render our breathing either long or short. We gradually learn this by ourselves. What causes the breathing to be long? What kind of mood makes the breath long? What kind of mood makes it short? Thus, we also come to know the causes and conditions that make the breath long or short.

There is a method that we can use to regulate the breath in these beginning steps to make it longer or shorter. This technique is called "counting," and it trains us to change the length of our breathing. For example, as we inhale, we count from one to five. If during one breath we count at the same pace but from one to ten, that breath will lengthen accordingly. During an ordinary breath we only count to five. For a short breath we might count to three and that shortens the breath as we wish. We should always count at the same speed, for if we change the pace of counting, it will negate the effect of counting higher or lower. By counting, we can regulate the duration of each breath. By using this special training technique we can lengthen or shorten the breath. We do not have to use it all the time, but we can employ it occasionally to help us regulate the breath or to get to know it better. We can give it a try whenever we choose.

In this chapter, we have described various preparations for our practice and the actual establishment of mindfulness on breathing. This practice is the foundation for a more detailed examination of the four stages that were described in the first chapter. Some meditators may be satisfied with just this level of practice; it can be quite difficult in and of itself at the start. Nonetheless, let's continue our study of the first stage: contemplation of the body.

3

Bodies of Breath

As WE HAVE MENTIONED before, altogether there are four groups that we must contemplate, each group corresponding to one of our four fundamental objects of study. Each group includes four steps, or *dhammas*; hence they may be called "tetrads." In all, therefore, there are four tetrads, or groups, each of which contains four steps. This makes a total of sixteen *dhammas*. Of these sixteen, the breath is directly contemplated in only two steps. The remaining fourteen steps focus on other objects.

The first of our four objects of study is *ānāpānasati* focused on the *kāya*. In this chapter we will examine the practice of the first two of the four steps of *ānāpānasati* focused on the *kāya*.

KĀYĀNUPASSANĀ

In the *kāya* tetrad, or *kāyānupassanā* (contemplation of the body), we study and understand the breath. We learn to understand the different kinds of breath, their various qualities and characteristics, and the influences they produce. We get to know the breath in all aspects and from all angles in order for it to be correct.

To put it briefly, we must have correct *prana*. *Prāna* is a Sanskrit word, the Pali equivalent is *pāna*. Ordinarily, this word means "life" or "life force" or "that which preserves and nurtures life." We must understand it correctly; our *prāna* should be healthy and correct. Then our lives will be correct. Thus, it is necessary to study the subject of the breath.

In India every style of yoga—and there are dozens of styles—has trainings involving the *prāna*. These trainings are called *prāṇāyāma*, which means "control of the *prāna*" or "breath control." To control the breath is to control life. When the *prāna* enters the body, it is called *āna* and when it leaves it is called *apāna*. The two words combined become *ānāpāna*, that is, the *prāna* enters and the *prāna* exits. To control the *prāna* is to control that which enters to preserve life.

Then we live a life that is fresh and cheerful, ready and fit for training and practice. Such *prāṇa* training can be found even in Buddhism.

Prāṇāyāma is the first subject of *ānāpānasati*. Although this may seem surprising, it does not contradict our principles at all. In fact, *ānāpānasati* is the equivalent of any system of yoga; indeed, it actually improves on all of them. This system of *kāyānupassanā* (contemplation on the body) takes up the *prāṇāyāma* of the Indian yogas and improves upon them in appropriateness and practicability.[7] Thus, our first item of study is this system of training known as *kāyānupassanā*.

If we adjust the *prāṇa*-body, so that it is good, healthy, and calm, it makes the flesh-body good, healthy, and calm as well. Calm and healthy *prāṇa* brings the greatest peace and well-being in this life. This is why we must understand both *kāya* (bodies): the flesh-body and the breath-body. Then we shall be able to cultivate the "good" until there is good peace and good calm. The word *good* here means "fit and proper to be used in performing duties and work."

The last item of this tetrad is calming the body-conditioner, that is, making the preservers of the body peaceful and calm. By calming the breath, which conditions the body, then the body too becomes tranquil. The *citta* will feel this tranquility and will also be calmed. When the *citta* is calm, it is ready to perform its further duties.

This is the subject matter of the *kāya*. It is important to note that the more you understand these facts, the more benefits this training will bring; you will become able to make this the best life possible. So we begin with learning about the *kāya* as the first tetrad.

THE BUDDHA'S *PRĀṆĀYĀMA*

It is essential that we understand this profound truth: the *prāṇa*-body is the conditioner of the flesh-body. We ought to know that there are these two *kāya* or levels of *kāya*. We know about the first level, the flesh-body, but we hardly know the *prāṇa*-body at all. Therefore, it is very important to understand the *prāṇa*-body, as it can condition the flesh-body in beneficial ways. In India, the *prāṇāyāma* is considered to be the highest and most important subject for study. While different schools vary in their explanations and meanings for the *prāṇa*-body, all schools seek to regulate the *prāṇa*-body so that it conditions the flesh-body appropriately. We need to study and train the breath in order to use it to condition the flesh-body. Since we cannot regulate the flesh-body directly, we regulate it indirectly. We study the *prāṇa*-body and practice regulating it. By learning to regulate the *prāṇa*-body, we regulate the flesh-body, making it calm and peaceful.

We develop this knowledge through practice and training until we are able to regulate the *prāṇa*. In this way we gradually develop a good, healthy body that is ready for concentrating the *citta*. Both the body and mind are prepared to do their respective duties. The first tetrad, the *kāya*, has these characteristics, this objective and method of practice. We should examine this tetrad carefully. Is it necessary or not? Is it worth our time and effort to study and practice? If so, then we should wholeheartedly commit ourselves to this study and train in it until we are successful. This is the way to cultivate the best *prāṇāyāma*—Buddhist *prāṇāyāma*—through the practice of *vipassanā-bhāvanā* (the cultivation of insight or direct realization).

There are four steps in the practice of the *kāya* tetrad: knowing the long breath, knowing the short breath, knowing how the breath regulates the body, and contemplating the breath in order to calm the body. These four steps are not difficult if we sincerely observe and genuinely study in a scientific way.

Before the Buddha's time people practiced many types of *prāṇāyāma*. When Lord Buddha appeared, he too practiced *prāṇāyāma*; he then incorporated it into this system of contemplating the breath. And through this system of contemplating the breath, we regulate life and the body.

There are many advantages and benefits to *prāṇāyāma* that are not directly concerned with religion or Dhamma. These extra incentives may serve to interest you in *prāṇāyāma* or breath control and encourage you to manage it correctly. First, you can live longer through practicing *prāṇāyāma*. Or you can make yourself die immediately, even today, if you so wish. In fact, with the practice of *prāṇāyāma* you can die during any breath you choose. On the other hand, you can have a healthy breath and a good, healthy body with *prāṇāyāma*. You can play sports, drive a car, work in an office, or do whatever you choose if you regulate the breath or *prāṇa* in a way that is in accordance with your aims. You should know that these are some of the side-benefits of *ānāpānasati* outside the scope of religion or Dhamma proper.

STEP ONE: THE LONG BREATH

Let's consider in more detail the first two steps of the first tetrad, the practice concerning the *kāya* (body). Having followed the instructions in the last chapter, we have developed a preliminary understanding of the breath. We know about the various properties of the breath: long duration, shortness, coarseness, fineness, easiness, and uneasiness. Our knowledge extends to the properties connected with the breath and how our mind reacts toward and is influenced by these properties. We even know how to control the length of each breath. The next step is to enter a course of training with the breathing. We begin with the long breath.

The first lesson is the contemplation of the long breath. Having learned how to make the breath long and to keep it long, we are able to breathe long whenever we need to. In this first lesson, we will study exclusively the nature of the long breath. When a breath is long, how pleasant is it? Is it natural and ordinary? What kinds of calmness and happiness arise? In what ways is it different from a short breath? We begin by studying just the long breath to find out its properties, qualities, influence, and flavor. We should sit and investigate only the long breath. This is lesson one: understanding all matters connected to long breathing.

Finally, we observe how the body works in relation to the long breath. How does the body move when there is a long inhalation? In what places does the body expand? Where does it contract? When there is the deepest possible long breath, does the chest expand or contract? Does the abdomen expand or contract? These are things to examine. As you observe, you may learn that the process happens differently than you might have thought. Most people have the simple idea that when we breathe in, the chest expands, and when we breathe out, the chest contracts. In studying the breath carefully, however, we find that in taking a very long inhalation, the abdomen will contract and the chest will expand. We find the reverse of what common sense teaches. Thus, we investigate the very long breath, the longest possible breath, to see what changes occur. We do not take anything for granted but instead learn these basic facts for ourselves.

In order to know the nature of the long breath, we study all the secrets and attributes of the long breath. We are able to contemplate its long duration, learning to protect and maintain it. In fact, we become expert in all matters concerned with the long breath. Practicing with the long breath is lesson one.

It is extremely important that we learn the interrelationship between each type of breath and the body. We shall find there is a very close interconnection between them. As we learn the effects that the long breath has on the body, we discover the happiness and comfort the long breath brings. Further, we come to understand more deeply the secret of the two *kāya*: the breath-body and the flesh-body. We can observe this even at this early stage, although we will not discuss it specifically until step three. Still, in this lesson, we should begin to realize how the breath and the body are interconnected. Therefore, when breathing long, or in any way, we observe how the rest of the body is affected. We learn in a deeper way, through personal experience rather than through thinking, that the breath is intimately associated with the body.

STEP TWO: THE SHORT BREATH

Our second lesson concerns the short breath. We practice this step in exactly the same way as we practiced the long breath, only now we focus on the short breath. Whatever we learned about the long breath, we shall learn the equivalent facts about the short breath.

For instance, we observe and feel immediately that the long breath brings ease and comfort while the short breath leads to abnormality, that is, uneasiness, agitation, and discomfort. Thus, through our ability to regulate the breath, we know how to make the body either comfortable or uncomfortable. We need to know the complementary differences between the two kinds of breath as clearly as possible. So here we are particularly interested in the short breath. We study everything, every aspect, every property of the short breath until we know it as extensively as we know the long breath. Although the two kinds of breath have opposite natures, our way of studying them is identical.

Of special interest is the observation that when we breathe long, the breath is fine, and when we breathe short, the breath is rough. Once we learn to make the breath fine or coarse as we wish, we can use this ability to our advantage. The benefit is that the fine breath will calm our body. It becomes cool. When we wish to cool down our body, we bring out the fine breath. When we require the fine breath, we simply make the breath longer. This is one of the fine points we need to study.

Another example is that when we are angry, the breath becomes short. When the breath is short, the body is disturbed. If we make the breath long, our anger will not continue. When we are angry, the breath is short and rough, and the body is rough. We can drive away such anger by breathing long. The body will be relaxed, and the anger will disappear. This is an example of the many different interactions and relationships between the breath, the body, and the mind. It is important that we understand the relationship and differences between long and short breathing. We must experience this relationship and feel it for ourselves so that we become experts.

BREATHING AWAY EMOTIONS

Let's summarize these first steps: it is possible to regulate, control, limit, and manage the emotions by using the breath. We can make the emotions correct, useful, and beneficial through the breath. We develop the ability to control the breath itself through knowledge we have gained about the breath. If we train our breathing, we can control our emotions, that is, we can cope with the happiness and pain in our lives. We should practice until we feel this; our practice is not complete until we can see this clearly.

When you are sitting in meditation and a mosquito bites you, you may develop an evil emotion. How can you get rid of it? To drive it away, improve the breath. Make the breath long, make it fine, make it chase away that wicked emotion. This is the best method to solve such problems and is another example of the beneficial knowledge and useful abilities that we are learning.

The topics and facts to be studied in the first lesson about the long breath and in the second lesson about the short breath are the same. The only difference is that everything is complementary. The number and type of things to study are equal, but the differences between long and short breathing lead to complementary sets of facts.

This completes our discussion of the first two lessons of the first tetrad. Two more lessons of this tetrad remain to be considered. Please practice what you have read as you prepare for what comes next.

4

Calming the *Kāya*

NEXT, WE WILL CONSIDER steps three and four of the first tetrad, that is, the remaining steps concerned with the *kaya* (body).

STEP THREE: EXPERIENCING ALL BODIES

In step three, the aim is to experience all *kāya*, all bodies. The essence of this step is to feel all bodies while breathing in and breathing out. While practicing the earlier steps of *ānāpānasati*, we began to observe that the breath conditions our flesh-and-blood body. This next step, therefore, does not involve anything new; we merely investigate this fact more profoundly, clearly, and carefully than before. We contemplate in a deeper way that there are two *kāya* (bodies). We should continuously observe this while breathing in and breathing out.

The practitioner will recall that the breath is the conditioner of the flesh-body. Here, we are distinguishing between two entities, both of which are called *kaya* (body). The breath is a body in that it is a group, a collection. The flesh-body is also a *kāya* because it too is a group or collection. Thus, there are two groups, two bodies. One group is the breath that conditions the flesh-body group. We should analyze this experience to see clearly that there are two groups and that they condition each other. Contemplate this thoroughly until it becomes obvious.

The meaning of the word *body* includes the idea of a *group*. In the original Pali language, Lord Buddha used this word *kāya* in expressing, for example, "*sabbakāyampaṭisaṁveti*" (experiencing all bodies). In Thai, *kāya* comes from the Pali *kāya* and can also mean "group, pile, heap, division." This term can be applied not only to our human forms; it can refer to other things as well. For instance, in Pali a squad of soldiers is a *kāya* of soldiers. *Kāya* means "group, heap, collection"; we should not understand it only in terms of flesh-bodies. The breath is also called *kāya* or group. We must correctly understand the meaning of *kāya* in order to know what is meant by "experiencing all bodies." Then we can understand both the breath-body group and the flesh-body group.

The specific aim of this third step is to come to understand (1) that there are two groups and (2) that one group conditions, nourishes, and supports the other group. The breath-body group nourishes the flesh-body group. Actually, we have experienced this since the beginning of our *ānāpānasati* practice. Earlier, we learned that when the breath is coarse, the flesh-body becomes aggravated, and when the breath is fine, the body calms down. We have observed these facts while practicing steps one and two. In this step, we scrutinize this fact until these two groups become utterly clear. One group conditions and nourishes the other. We should know clearly the difference between them.

THE THREE MEANINGS OF *SANKHĀRA*

We are gradually acquiring the inner, mental experience that these two bodies condition each other. The body that is the causal conditioner is given the name *kāya-sankhāra* (body-conditioner) to distinguish it from the one affected by the conditioning, the "conditioned body." We should work on this fact in the mind to see if it is physically tangible. Observe the one group as it conditions and nurtures the other. See them arise together, fall together, coarsen together, become fine together, grow comfortable together, and become uncomfortable together. Realize how intimately they are connected. This is what is meant by "seeing all bodies." Watch both bodies together and see them condition each other. This is valuable for seeing truth more extensively, even for realizing *anattā*. In observing this interrelationship, we learn that what is occurring is merely a natural process of conditioning. There is no *attā*, no self, no soul involved. Although it is beyond the specific objective of this step, such an understanding can have the highest benefit. For now, however, our purpose in understanding this conditioning is to be able to calm the flesh-body by regulating the breath-body.

Let us discuss all the meanings of the term *sankhāra*, a very common and important word in the Pali scriptures. We may encounter problems because of the different uses and meanings of the word *sankhāra*. Language, at times, can be uncertain and unreliable. The single word *sankhāra* can mean "conditioner," the cause that conditions; it can mean "condition," the result of the action of conditioning; and it can mean "conditioning," the activity or process of conditioning. We use the same word for the subject of the conditioning, "the concocter," as well as the object, "the concoction." We even use it for the activity, "the concocting," itself. This may be a bit confusing, so we should remember that *sankhāra* has three meanings. The correct meaning depends on the context. This knowledge will be valuable in our further studies.

You should study the three meanings of *sankhāra* in your body. There is no need to study it in books or in a theoretical way. The body itself is a *sankhāra*. It has been conditioned by a variety of causes and by the many elements of which it is formed. Thus, it is a *sankhāra* in the meaning of "condition." Once this body exists, it causes the arising of other things, such as thoughts, feelings, and actions. These thoughts and actions could never happen without the body. Thus, it is a "conditioner" because it causes other actions. Lastly, in this flesh-body *sankhāra* of ours, the process of conditioning goes on constantly. We can discover all three aspects of the word *sankhāra* within this very body. If you study the meaning of *sankhāra* in this comprehensive way, you will find it possible to realize more and more profound Dhamma.

EXPERIENCING *SANKHĀRA*

In step three, "experiencing all bodies"—experiencing both the breath and this flesh-body—each of these three meanings is practiced. First, we contemplate the flesh-body as that which is conditioned by the breath. Then we observe the breath as the conditioner of the flesh-body. Lastly, we observe the activity of conditioning that always exists simultaneously between the breath and the flesh-body. Thus, in the practice of step three we see the conditioner, the condition, and the process of conditioning. This conditioning of the body is the physical level of *sankhāra*; we have yet to see the process at work on the mental level. Step three is the work of seeing these three elements together, simultaneously and continuously, within the mind. In this way we see everything concerning the term, especially as it relates to the *kāya* and its activity.

When we have plainly and clearly understood *sankhāra* as explained above, we will be able to experience all three of these meanings of *sankhāra* together in one moment. Even during the span of only one inhalation or one exhalation, in just a single stroke of the breath, we can experience all three elements. If we are successful, then we will have "fully experienced the *kāya-sankhāra*" (body-conditioner) and will have completed step three.

The essence of practicing step three is to know that there are two *kāya* and to regulate one *kāya* through the other. That is, we regulate the flesh-body through the breath-body. Once we have understood this clearly and are convinced by our experience of this process with each in-breath and out-breath, then we have realized success in our practice of step three.

STEP FOUR: CALMING THE BREATH

Once we know that we can regulate the flesh-body with the breath-body, we begin to practice step four. Lord Buddha described step four as "calming the body-conditioner" (*passambhayaṁ kāyasankhāraṁ*). Step four is calming the body-conditioner (*kāya-sankhāra*) while breathing in and calming the body-conditioner while breathing out. This means that as we inhale and exhale we make the body-conditioner (breath) calmer and calmer. Let's explore this in more detail.

"Calming the body-conditioner" refers to calming the breath-body. In step four, the aim of our practice is to calm the breath; using various techniques which are available to us, we make it fine and peaceful. If we can calm the breath, the results will be very interesting and powerful. First of all, the flesh-body will simultaneously become very gentle, relaxed, and tranquil. Then there will also arise a calming of the mind. There will be other results as well, which we will discuss at a later point. The immediate lesson is to calm the breath; managing the breath is the first point to be considered in the practice of step four.

FIVE SKILLFUL TRICKS

In practicing step four, there are various methods, or techniques—we could even call them tricks—to use in calming the breath. It is important to note that these are a higher order of methods that we use over more crude and foolish techniques. Thus, we call them "skillful means." The tricks, or skillful means, to use on the breath come in five stages:

1. following the breath;
2. guarding the breath at a certain point;
3. giving rise to an imaginary image at that guarding point;
4. manipulating these images in such a way as to gain power over them; and
5. selecting one image and contemplating it in a most concentrated way until the breath becomes truly calm and peaceful.

These are our five techniques, or skillful means: following, guarding, raising a mental image, playing with the different mental images, and choosing one image to be the specific object of *samādhi* (concentration, collectedness) until there is complete calmness.

The first stage—following or chasing—we have actually been doing from the beginning. We use hunting or following with the long and short breaths. Now, we merely repeat or review it until we become skilled at following the breath. This does not require further explanation since we have already done it many times in steps one, two, and three.

The second technique is guarding: choosing one point along the breath's path and watching or guarding the breath there. We no longer follow the breath, but the results are the same as if we continued to do so. This *citta*, this *sati*, is not allowed to go anywhere; it must stay at the chosen point. It guards the breath passing in and passing out; hence, the results are equivalent to following, except that guarding is more subtle.

Generally, we use the furthest point on the nose where the breath makes contact, usually at the tip. This point is the easiest and simplest to guard, unless you have a hooked nose that comes down low and a high upper lip. Then you might feel the breath's touch just above the upper lip. For each of us the point will be in a different place, depending on the shape and structure of our nose and lip.

Find the place where you can observe the breath most easily. If you have difficulty finding it while breathing normally, take a few deep, strong breaths, and the spot will become obvious. The exact location is not important; just find that point on your nose, or even on the upper lip, where you feel the breath most clearly. Once you find it, guard that point as the breath passes in and out. The mind, the *sati*, stays right at that point and contemplates the breath as it goes in and out. Just breathe in and breathe out with the mind guarding that point; this is stage two in our series of skillful means.

We can observe that when we do not note the breath and just let it go as it pleases, it has a certain feel. The breath becomes finer and gentler as soon as we begin to note it, even when merely following it. It adjusts itself and becomes subtler in order to deceive us. It plays tricks like this. Then, when we stop chasing and start to guard the breath at a specific point on the nose, the breath calms down even more. You can verify this through your own experience.

A MENTAL IMAGE APPEARS

If we create a mental image (*nimitta*) at the guarding point, the breath will be further refined and calmed. This mental image is not real, but imaginary. It is created by the *citta*, it is mind-made. You can close your eyes and "see" it, you can open your eyes and still "see" it. The image is like a hallucination the mind creates by itself to calm the breath. To do this the mind must be subtle. The breath, indeed all the faculties, must be refined in order for a mental image to arise. The breath must become finer and calmer until the image is created.

The mental image can be any shape or form, depending on what is appropriate for the body of each person. Some people might create a sphere—red, white, green, or any color. The mental image can be a candle flame, or a puff of cotton, or a wisp of smoke. It can look like the sun, or the moon, or a star. Even the image of a spider's web glimmering in the sunlight is within the abilities of the mind's creative powers. The kind of image depends on the one who creates it. The mind merely inclines in a certain way and the image arises by itself. It is a purely mental phenomenon that has no physical reality. The third technique is complete when we are able to create a mental image at the guarding point.

Skillful means number four is to change the image or alternate between images according to our requirements. We can change from one image to another, changing them in all the ways that we wish. How is this possible? Because the mind creates the images in the first place, it has the ability to change them, to manipulate them, to play with them. This can all be done easily; it is well within the mind's capabilities. At the same time, as we do this, we are developing our ability to master the mind in increasingly subtle and powerful ways.

Because we can now control the mind more than before, the *citta* automatically grows more subtle and refined by itself. The *citta* becomes more and more calm until eventually we are able to calm the mind completely. We merely control the images, changing them according to the mind's tendencies. Depending on the mind's inclination, we can experiment with changing the images in ways that calm the breath more and more. Although this is nothing more than a trick, it is a more advanced trick that enables us to have greater influence over the mind. Then the breath calms down automatically. The breath must become calmer for us to manipulate the images. Although the mind also calms down, the emphasis at the present is on calming the breath. The fourth technique is controlling the mental images as we wish.

THE FINAL IMAGE

If we observe the process of calming, we watch and see that when we train in the prescribed way, the breath automatically becomes more refined and calms down by itself. When the breath is calmed, the flesh-body automatically calms down accordingly. Now when the body calms down, this has an effect on the mind. The *citta* becomes calm in proportion to the calming of the body, but this calming of the mind is the aim of a later step. Here, by calming the breath in this most refined way, the body will calm down accordingly. So we observe the calming process while practicing this step.

The fifth skillful means is choosing the single most appropriate *nimitta* (image) and not changing it again. We choose the one image that is most fitting and proper, and then contemplate it with our full attention in order to develop a complete measure of *samadhi* (mental stability and integration). We should choose an image that is soothing, relaxing, and easy to focus on. The image should not stir up thoughts and emotions or contain any special significance or meaning. A mere white point or dot will suffice.

Indeed, the best kind of image is neutral. A colored image will brew thoughts and feelings, as will attractive, interesting, fancy, or complicated images. Some people like to use a picture of the Buddha as their *nimitta*, but this can cause thinking and distraction; the thoughts will merely follow the image that is seen, rather than easing into stillness. Therefore, we should take an image that has no meaning or mental associations and is natural. A white spot is perfectly suitable; so is a tiny spot of light. Some people prefer a Buddha image or whatever suits their fancy, but we do not. We take a spot that is easy to contemplate and does not stir up any thoughts. We choose such an image and focus all of the mind on it, for the purpose of developing concentration. We focus on just this simple point so that the *citta* does not wander anywhere else. The *citta* gathers together on this single spot. Concentrating everything on this one point is the fifth of our skillful means.

PERFECT CONCENTRATION

We should select an object (*nimitta*) to contemplate that is the most appropriate for the mind. Ordinarily, the mind is scattered, spreading and radiating outward in all directions. Now, we must turn inward onto one focal point to end that outward flowing. In Pali this state is called *ekaggatā*, which means "to have a single peak, focus, or apex." Everything gathers at this single focus. We have found an image that is the most appropriate—a tiny central point—and now the mind focuses in on it. The mental flow is collected at this point in the same way that a magnifying glass collects the sun's rays and focuses them into a single point powerful enough to ignite a flame. This example illustrates the power that is harnessed when all of the mind's energy is gathered into one point. Once the mind focuses on the object we have chosen, its radiance gathers there and becomes *ekaggatā*: one-pointed, one-peaked, one-pinnacled.

When the mind is one-pointed, there are no other feelings, thoughts, or objects of that mind. There remain only the *jhānaṅga* (factors of *jhāna*). At the first level of one-pointedness there are five factors. At this first level the mind is still coarse enough to perform the function of contemplating the object. The mind noting its object is called *vitakka*. The mind experiencing that object is called *vicāra*. The mind is satisfied or contented (*pīti*) because of the *vitakka* and *vicāra*. And once there is *pīti*, the feeling of joy (*sukha*) arises at the same instant. Lastly, one-pointedness of mind (*ekaggatā*) continues as before. Thus, the mind on this level of *samādhi* (concentration) has five factors: noting (*vitakka*), experiencing (*vicāra*), contentment (*pīti*), joy (*sukha*), and one-pointedness (*ekaggatā*). These five factors indicate that the mind has entered the first level of perfect *samādhi*. This kind of concentrated awareness does not include any thinking, yet these five activities of the mind occur. We call them factors of *jhāna*. If all five are present, then we are successful in having perfect *samādhi*, although only the first stage. That sounds strange— perfect, but only the first stage of perfection.

AT THE PEAK

Let's take a closer look at *ekaggatā*. This Pali word is commonly translated as "one-pointedness," although literally, the Pali term means "to have one single (*eka*) peak (*agga*; Thai, *yod*)." The Thai word *yod* (rhymes with *laud*) can mean either the very top, peak, apex, or pinnacle of something, such as a mountain or a pyramid, or the new tip or growing point of a plant. The word *point* in English does not have quite the same meaning, as a point can be anywhere, off to the side or even down very low. This is why Pali uses the word *agga* (peak, summit, or zenith). *Ekaggatā* is like being the peak of a pyramid. It would not be proper for such a mind to be at some low point; it must be on a high level. The one-pointed mind is gathered together from low levels up to one high point or peak. This is the proper meaning of *ekaggatā*.

We should not worry, however, if at first the mind collects itself at a focal point that may not be the highest. It is a start. Whenever there is *ekaggatā*, it is the beginning of something most useful; whenever there is some *ekaggatā*, there is *samādhi*. In our practice of step four of *ānāpānasati*, it is not necessary to enter *jhāna* completely. In the practice of *ānāpānasati* these very refined levels of concentration are not necessary. We need only to have a sufficient and appropriate level of concentration to continue with our practice: that is, enough *samādhi* that feelings of *pīti* and *sukha* (contentment and happiness) are also present. We shall need the feelings of *pīti* and *sukha* in the next steps of our study. If we can progress further into *jhāna*, into the material absorptions (*rupa-jhāna*), that will be useful; it will make the next steps easier. But even if we do not reach *jhāna*, as long as some feelings of *pīti* and *sukha* are present, we are doing fine. With any luck, that will not prove to be too difficult.

When the feelings *pīti* and *sukha* are strong enough for the mind to feel them clearly, there is sufficient concentration to go on to step five. If you enter the first, second, third, or fourth *rupa-jhāna*, it is better still. But sufficient *samādhi* to experience *pīti* and *sukha* distinctly is enough for step four.

IT'S EASY WHEN…

If you apply the method correctly, this practice is not difficult. If you have been reading carefully, then you understand the proper way to do this practice. If you follow the technique correctly, it will not be too difficult. You might even finish in a short time. If you do not practice according to the method, then it may be very difficult. You may never finish. It could take three days or three weeks for some, three months or even three years for others. Who can say?

If you are still at the beginning, working on step one, this does not mean you should not pay attention to the instructions about step four. If you do not know what to do, then it will be very difficult to practice when the time comes. Instructions are given as clearly as possible, so that you will understand the proper way to do this practice. Many people, however, do not like to follow instructions. They prefer to mix everything up with their own ideas and opinions. They like to make a hodgepodge out of things they read and hear from different places. If you want to make this practice successful and easy for yourself, you should follow these instructions, which explain the most proper and efficient way of using this technique.

Practicing according to the method is not difficult; not following the technique brings many difficulties. Therefore, if you learn the correct method and apply it, you will achieve the expected results. Beyond that, there is nothing else to do except repeat these steps many times until you can very quickly calm the breath and the body. You should practice until these steps require no effort and you have become well-versed in these activities.

We should not forget: in every step, in every stage and interval of the practice, we must note the breathing in and breathing out. This is the background and foundation of our *sati*. This is how to be supremely mindful. If we note the inhalations and exhalations at each stage of practice, we will meet with success in the first tetrad of *ānāpānasati*. This is the theoretical background of *ānāpānasati* and the principles on which we practice it.

This completes our discussion of the first tetrad of *ānāpānasati*, that is, the four steps concerning the *kāya* (body). The next chapter deals with the *vedanā* (feelings) and the tetrad, or four steps, concerning them.

5

Mastering the *Vedanā*

IN THIS CHAPTER, we will discuss the second tetrad of *ānāpānasati*, which deals with the feelings. It is called *"vedananupassanā"* (contemplation of feeling). The first two steps of this tetrad take *pīti* (contentment) and *sukha* (joy) as the subjects of our detailed examination and study. This practice develops out of the practice of the previous step. Once the body-conditioner, the breath, is calmed, feelings of *pīti* and *sukha* appear. We then take *pīti* and *sukha* as the next objects of our practice.

If we calm the *kāya-sankhāra* (body-conditioner) to the extent of entering *jhāna* (the first *jhāna* and so forth), then *pīti* and *sukha* will be full and complete as factors of *jhāna*. However, if we are unable to reach *jhāna* and are only able to calm the body-conditioner partially, there will likely be a degree of *pīti* and *sukha* present proportionate to the extent of that calming. Thus, even those practitioners who are unable to bring about *jhāna* can still manage enough *pīti* and *sukha* to practice these steps.

Pīti (contentment) arises from our successfully inducing *samādhi* in the previous steps, when we calmed the body-conditioner, or breath. Contentment or satisfaction arises with this success. Once there is contentment, happiness (*sukha*) will surely follow. Joy arises out of satisfaction. Thus, it is possible for us to experience sufficient *pīti* and *sukha* to be able to practice steps five and six.

PĪTI IS NOT PEACEFUL

Next, we observe that there are different levels to *pīti*, such as contentment, satisfaction, and rapture. We must know these energetic gradations of *pīti*. Most importantly, we should be aware that *pīti* is not peaceful. There is a kind of excitement or disturbance in *pīti*; only when it becomes *sukha* is it tranquil. *Pīti* has varying levels, but all are characterized as stimulating, as causing the *citta* to tremble

:e. *Sukha* is the opposite; it calms and soothes the mind.
ɔw *pīti* and *sukha* differ.

ne of the second tetrad, "experiencing *pīti*" (*pīti-paṭsaāvedi*),
consists of contemplating *pīti* every time we breathe in and breathe
out. We must keep watching until we find the *pīti* that has arisen
from calming the body-conditioner. Find out what this feeling is like.
Fully experience it. Take it as the new object for the mind to contemplate. The *citta* is absorbed in contemplating it the same as if there
was *ekaggatā*. The mind is absorbed with the single object, *pīti*.

Throughout our practice we have contemplated a number of
objects: the long breath, the short breath, all bodies, and calming
the bodies. Now we switch to *pīti*. This *pīti* has stimulating power.
It makes the mind quiver, shake, and tremble. It should be easy to
understand the various degrees of *pīti* through the different English
words we can use. How stimulating is contentment? To what degree
is satisfaction stimulating? And how stimulating is rapture? We must
observe and find out for ourselves. The mind focuses upon *pīti* and
fully experiences it with every inhalation and exhalation. This is the
essence of the practice of step five.

Briefly, we breathe, and we experience *pīti* with every breath.
Breathing in and out, we fully experience this feeling of contentment and, simultaneously, are aware of each in-breath and each
out-breath. There is a very pleasant feeling of well-being when this
step is being practiced. This work is fun to do; it is a most enjoy-
able lesson.

STUDY THE FLAVOR OF *PĪTI*

In each moment that we breathe with the experience of *pīti*, we are
simultaneously studying and training. Earlier, we trained and studied while breathing long, breathing short, and so forth. Now, we
study and train as we experience *pīti* in the mind. What is *pīti* like?
Is it heavy? Is it light? How coarse is it? How subtle? This can be
called "knowing its flavor." In particular, investigate the influence its
flavor has on the mind and on the thoughts. Study in order to
understand the nature of *pīti*, just as we studied to understand the
nature of the breath during the practice of the previous tetrad. This
is how to practice this step.

Most important, study and observe the power *pīti* has over the mind. What influence does *pīti* have on the mind and thoughts? Carefully observe the mind when *pīti* is not present. Once *pīti* arises, what is the *citta* like? What is the effect of an abundance of *pīti*? How is the mind when there is only minimal *pīti*? When *pīti* is intense, as in rapture, how much greater is the stimulation to the mind? See how the coarsest kinds of *pīti* differ from the medium levels and the finest types. Then, see how their influence upon the mind differs. This is the crucial point of this step of practice.

Finally, we realize that *pīti* stimulates the mind in a coarse way; it lacks a refined and subtle effect like *sukha*. In this step, understand the nature, facts, and secrets of this phenomenon known as *pīti*. Observe its relationship to the mind until the entire experience is completely familiar.

SUKHA SOOTHES THE MIND

In the second step of this second tetrad—or step six overall—"experiencing *sukha*" (*sukha-paṭisaāvedi*), we contemplate *sukha* (happiness) with every inhalation and exhalation. We focus on *sukha* as arising out of *pīti*. When *pīti* has finished stimulating the *citta* in its coarse way, *pīti* loses energy. That is, it calms down and transforms into *sukha*. These two feelings are very different; *sukha* does not stimulate or excite; it calms down and soothes. Here we contemplate *sukha* as the agent that makes the *citta* tranquil. Usually *pīti* obscures *sukha*, but when *pīti* fades away, *sukha* remains. The coarse feeling gives way to calm. Taste the tranquil flavor of *sukha* with every inhalation and exhalation. This is the gist of step six.

As we contemplate *sukha* within the mind, our method of studying and training is identical to our practice with the breath and *pīti*. How light is *sukha*? How heavy? How coarse is it? How subtle? How does *sukha* flavor awareness and experience? In Thai and Pali we use the word *drink* to describe this experiencing. We drink the flavor of *sukha* while breathing in and breathing out, at the same time studying its nature and truth.

When the power of *pīti* is present, the breath is rough. When the influence of *sukha* is present, the breath is fine. Moreover, when *pīti* manifests its power, the flesh-body is coarse. When *sukha* manifests its influence, the body calms down and becomes subtle. There are similar effects on the *citta* as well. When *pīti* shows its power, it disturbs the mind proportionately, whereas the influence of *sukha* calms and relaxes the mind. That the two feelings are opposites is what we must observe with every in-breath and out-breath.

To summarize, once *pīti* and *sukha* arise, they have different effects upon the breath. *Pīti* will make the breath coarse, while *sukha* will make it calm. They also have different effects upon the body: *pīti* makes it coarse or agitated, while *sukha* soothes it. Finally, they have different effects upon the mind. The presence of *pīti* excites the mind, while the presence of *sukha* calms it. When you can experience this distinction directly, rather than through thought, you will have met with success in the practice of this step.

It is possible to experience some difficulties on this step. While we are contemplating *sukha*, *pīti* might interfere. It may predominate such that the feeling of *sukha* disappears. Therefore, we maintain that feeling of *sukha* for as long as needed to prevent *pīti* from arising. *Pīti* is much stronger and coarser than *sukha*. If *pīti* interferes, the contemplation of *sukha* is ruined and real tranquility will not arise. Superb effort in our contemplation of *sukha* is needed to ensure that it does not fade away. We should not let any other feelings interfere. In this step we should feel saturated with happiness, certainly a wonderful way to meet with success in the practice of step six.

EXPERIENCING THE MIND-CONDITIONER

Now we come to step seven: "experiencing the mind-conditioner" (*citta-sankhāra-paṭsaāvedi*). If we have successfully completed step six, then we are familiar with the feelings of *pīti* and *sukha*. What does the arising of *pīti* do to the *citta*? How does the arising of *sukha* influence the *citta*? What kind of thoughts does *pīti* condition? And what thoughts does *sukha* condition? We have noted and scrutinized these effects since steps five and six. Once we come to step seven, it is easy to realize, "Oh, *pīti* and *sukha* are mind-conditioners." These *vedanā* are mind-conditioners in the same way that the breath is the body-conditioner. The method of study and observation is the same in this step as in step three.

We have observed that *pīti* is coarse and excited, whereas *sukha* is fine and peaceful. Thus, when *pīti* conditions a thought, that thought is coarse. On the other hand, when a thought arises through *sukha*, that thought is calm and tranquil. Thus, we realize the way that the *vedanā* condition thoughts. We learn that feelings condition both coarse thoughts and subtle thoughts. This activity is called "conditioning the mind."

When *pīti* is strong, it causes trembling in the body. If it is very strong, the body might even dance or bounce with joy. This feeling is coarse and powerful. On the other hand, *sukha* is calming, soothing, and relaxing. We learn that the characteristics of *pīti* and *sukha* are very different. When *pīti* dominates the mind, it is impossible to think subtle thoughts. We feel a tingling all over; it makes the hair stand up all over the body. So we need to be able to control *pīti*. However, *sukha* has advantages in that it leads to tranquil, refined states; it can cause subtle and profound thoughts. These two feelings might be called opponents or foes, but this does not really matter, for we have learned how to regulate them. We can control them by training according to the method of step seven. This is called "understanding the *citta-sankhāra* sufficiently."

FRIENDS AND FOES

It is important that we now observe and understand a different secret: these two feelings must arise together. That is, if we are not contented or satisfied, happiness cannot occur. Contentment gives rise to happiness; joy arises from satisfaction. Contentment and satisfaction are the group of stimulating, pleasant feelings called *pīti*. Although happiness and joy belong in the group of soothing feelings, they cannot exist without satisfaction. We observe that where there is happiness, satisfaction must always arise first. *Pīti* leads the way. We are satisfied when we experience success; we get excited and disturbed by that success. Once *pīti* loses strength, when the mind gets tired of agitation and excitement, then *sukha* remains. The feeling calms down. So the two are comrades while at the same time opposing each other; they are comrades in that they must arise together. There must first be contentment for there to be joy. We need to be careful about this, acting toward these two in an extremely subtle and refined way. It is an art, a spiritual art of controlling *pīti* and *sukha* so that they benefit our lives. This is the secret that we ought to know concerning *pīti* and *sukha*.

We have discovered that *pīti* is a foe of *vipassanā*, whereas *sukha*, happiness-joy, is a friend, a supporter. *Vipassanā* means "seeing clearly," having direct insight into the truth of *aniccaā* (impermanence), *dukkhaā* (unsatisfactoriness), and *anattā* (not-self). We require a very refined mind to realize *aniccaā*, *dukkhaā*, and *anattā* through *vipassanā*. Should *pīti* arise, *vipassanā* is impossible. The mind becomes clouded and restless. *Pīti* must be driven away, for it is the enemy of *vipassanā*, that is, of clear, subtle mental vision. However, *sukha* is quite the opposite. *Sukha* soothes and calms, making the mind active and ready for *vipassanā*. For this reason, we must acquire the ability to regulate *pīti* and *sukha*.

We have realized that feelings (*pīti* and *sukha*) are mind-conditioners. When *pīti* conditions the *citta*, it is coarse and its thoughts are coarse; both the mind and thoughts are coarse. When *sukha* conditions or supports the *citta*, it is subtle and tranquil, and its thoughts are subtle and tranquil. Both feelings condition the mind, but from different angles. The *vedanā* are conditioners of the *citta*; thus they get the name "mind-conditioner" (*citta-sankhāra*).

We contemplate this fact in the mind every time we breathe in and breathe out. This is the practice of step seven.

CALMING THE FEELINGS

Step eight is "calming the mind-conditioner" (*passambhayaā citta-sankhārā*) while breathing in and breathing out. We make the *citta-sankhāra*, the *vedanā*, calm and peaceful by lessening their energy while breathing in and breathing out. There are two approaches for us to use: the *samādhi* (concentration) method and the *paññā* (wisdom) method.

THE CONCENTRATION METHOD

We can calm *pīti's* impulse with the *samādhi* method, in which we develop a higher level of concentration that removes *pīti* and *sukha* from what is felt. As we have only just begun our training, we are probably not yet able to do this. Still, we should know that these feelings can be driven away by developing a higher level of *samādhi*, such as the third or fourth *jhāna*. Or alternatively, we can lessen the energy of *pīti* by bringing another kind of thought into the mind to intervene and suppress that satisfied feeling. Either technique uses the power of *samādhi*. Generally, it is not necessary to drive away *sukha*. In fact, we ought to preserve it as a support for further practice. Here, our objective is to control *pīti* with *samādhi* techniques, either by changing the mind's object or by having a higher degree of concentration or *jhāna*. Either method will calm down *pīti*.

Another possibility is to bring in the true meaning of the word *samādhi* to drive away *pīti*. The real meaning of *samādhi* is "having *ekaggatā-citta* with *nibbāna* as its object." We have already learned that *ekaggatā-citta* is the mind gathered together into one pinnacle, or peak; true *samādhi* has *nibbāna* or *santi* (spiritual tranquility) as its object. So when *pīti* causes complications, disturbances, and difficulties, we chase it away because we do not want or need it. We aim at the one-pinnacled mind that has *santi* or *nibbāna* as its object. The feeling of *pīti* dissolves because we do not want it anymore. This is a skillful means that uses *samādhi* to drive away *pīti*.

THE WISDOM METHOD

Next is the method that uses *paññā* (wisdom) to diminish the strength of *pīti*, to eradicate the influence of *pīti*, or even of *sukha* if we wish. We use the *paññā* that realizes the true nature (characteristics, qualities, conditions) of all things to understand how *pīti* arises and what will cause it to cease. *Pīti* bubbles up when a satisfying condition is achieved. *Pīti* ceases because of the lack of that satisfying condition, and thus we realize that it is illusory and not real. Once we see wisely in this way, the feeling of being agitated by *pīti* will abate.

Another wisdom method is to contemplate the *assāda* and *ādīnava* of *pīti*. *Assāda* is an element's attractive quality, its charm that deliciously tempts the heart. *Pīti* has an enchanting flavor. *Ādīnava* is an element's unhealthy consequences. The *ādīnava* of *pīti* is the fact that it excites and disturbs, that it drives away tranquility and is the foe of *vipassanā*. Once we realize this, *pīti* dissolves. If we see its arising and ceasing, its charm and unwholesomeness, then it dissolves and disappears. This is how to drive off *pīti* with the *paññā* technique.

We should understand completely the meanings of *āssāda* and *ādīnava*. The Pali words are even better than the English translations. *Āssāda* is the attractive, satisfying, lovely, infatuating quality or charm of something. *Ādīnava* is the unsound or noxious quality of a thing. There is no excuse for us to be deceived by these two. Once we see them, we will know that being pleased by and falling in love with anything is positive foolishness, and to hate something is negative foolishness. If we know that these two constantly deceive and lure us into loving and hating, then we will learn from them not to indulge in liking and disliking, and we will be freed from the power of objects. For example, money has both *āssāda* and *ādīnava*. Once we know these two, money will not mislead us or make us crazy.

The safest thing we can do is to understand this pair fully. Know the *āssāda* and *ādīnava* of *pīti* and you will tire of *pīti*. It will flee by itself. This is how to use the wisdom method to chase away *pīti*. Even *sukha* should not be indulged. Although we may save some *sukha* for a beneficial purpose, we do not get lost in it. We should remember *āssāda* and *ādīnava* for the rest of our lives. Then they will become the kind of charm or talisman that truly protects rather than endangers.

At this point, the mind is able to regulate the feelings. It has developed the kind of mastery and self-control where the feelings no longer have the power to drag us this way or that. We have discussed the *sukha-vedanā*, the group of pleasant feelings, that pull the mind in an agreeable direction, in a positive way. There is another set of *vedanā* that pull us in a negative way, in an undesirable, unsatisfactory direction. We also need to be aware of these unpleasant feelings, the *dukkha-vedanā*, and how to keep these feelings of displeasure and unhappiness from dragging us into a state of *dukkha*. They can be overcome with the same method as we used on *pīti*. We can control all happy or unhappy feelings. In fact, we become controllers of all feelings without exception. We practice by bringing any *vedanā* into the mind and experiencing it fully. Then we scrutinize it with *paññā* to drive that feeling away. Experience this ability to drive away any kind of *vedanā*. Know that the feelings cannot condition the *citta* anymore. Rehearse this technique with every inhalation and exhalation until you become deft and expert at it. Thus, you will meet with success in the practice of step eight.

WHY BOTHER?

One last point to consider is why we bother talking so much about the feelings. Why is it necessary to include them in this line of practice? Why not hurry on to *vipassanā* and get to *nibbāna* as fast as possible? The reason is that we must understand the *vedanā* and regulate them to help us control the mind as our practice continues on to the realization of the path, fruitions, and *nibbānas* (*magga-phala-nibbāna*), which is our primary purpose.

We also have a special secondary purpose. That is, once we can regulate the feelings, we will be able to keep our life on the correct path. When we are foolish about the *vedanā*, we become slaves to materialism. This happens when we indulge in material pleasures, that is, the flavors of feelings. All the crises in this world have their origin in people not understanding the *vedanā*, giving in to the *vedanā*, being enamored with the *vedanā*. The feelings entice us to act in ways that lead to disagreements, quarrels, conflicts, and eventually, war. Sometimes they even lead to world wars, all because people act unwisely through the deceptions of *vedanā*.

By now we surely realize that the feelings must be understood. We must know their secrets and learn to regulate them if there is to be peace in this world. There is no need to talk of realizing *nibbāna*, when merely living on this planet in peace with others—or even with ourselves—is more than we can manage right now. It is clearly important that we take advantage of this ability to control the feelings for the rest of our lives. This tetrad has been included in the practice of *ānāpānasati* because of the great power and importance of the *vedanā*.

This is the second tetrad of *ānāpānasati*. It is the foundation for the third tetrad, contemplation of mind, which we will consider next.

6

Contemplating the *Citta*

OUR STUDY OF THE THIRD TETRAD of *ānāpānasati* is concerned with the *citta,* the mind-heart, and is known as *cittānupassana* (contemplation of *citta*).

Before specifically discussing the third tetrad, there is a very important point that we sometimes forget to stress. Every time you sit down to practice *ānāpānasati*—every sitting and every session—you must begin with step one, experiencing the long breath. It does not matter which step you were doing yesterday, today you must start again at the very beginning. Each session is brand new. From the long breath, move on to the short breath, and so on. Progress from one step to the next, completely fulfilling each step before moving on, until you come to the step where you left off the last time. Each step depends upon the previous one. If you are unable to do the first step, then there is no possibility of going on to further steps. Even now, when we intend to do *cittānupassanā*, we must start at step one. This holds true for all sixteen steps. With every inhalation and exhalation, we practice in this way. Do not forget. We always begin practicing with step one—every time, every session, every step that we practice.

After successfully completing the first two tetrads, we begin to work on the third, *cittānupassanā* (contemplation of mind). The first step of this tetrad is contemplating or experiencing the mind in all its aspects. This is called *citta-paṭisaāvedī* (experiencing the condition or state of the mind during any given moment). Many different states of mind have arisen since the beginning of the practice. We must observe the state of the mind at each step. What is its condition now? How is it changing? What arises in the *citta*? What are the mind's characteristics at this moment? In previous steps, we have emphasized certain things that the mind knows or experiences. Now, we are ready to observe *citta* itself. We must observe until we know directly what the mind is like in this moment. What kind of experience is it? Step nine begins with experiencing the *citta* through each moment of practice.

DEFILED OR NOT?

There are many different characteristics of the mind to contemplate, but they all must happen naturally by themselves. We observe these characteristics as they really exist, in the very moment of their existence. As it is said in the traditional way of speaking, the characteristics to note begin with "whether the mind has lust (*rāga*) or is free of lust." The meaning of *rāga* is broad. Sexual lust is called *rāga*; lust toward objects such as money, jewelry, gold, food, housing, and possessions is also called *rāga*. There can also be lust toward individuals: for instance, love (nonsexual) of one's employees or servants. The Pali term *rāga* has this wide array of meanings, both sexual and nonsexual. Does the *citta* have any of these types of *rāga* at this moment, or is it free of lust? If there is lust, then thoroughly contemplate its presence to distinguish what kind of lust it is. Know what it is to have *rāga* in the mind. If there is no lust, then contemplate its absence. Breathe in and breathe out while experiencing the actual state of mind in this moment.

The next characteristic of mind to contemplate is *dosa* (anger, hatred, aversion). The meaning of *dosa* is also broad. Sometimes an external object—a person or situation—causes us to be angry. Any dislike in the mind is *dosa*; it can even arise from within, without any external object. When the mind is oppressed, irritated, offended, or resentful, it is called *dosa*. We contemplate whether this mind has *dosa*. If the *citta* is free of anger and hatred, then know that state. This is the second characteristic to observe.

The third characteristic to observe is *moha* (delusion and confusion). *Moha* is feeling infatuated with something because of not knowing that object as it really is. For example, when we are doubtful about something, we cannot help but think about it. Or when there is hope or expectation, we cannot avoid dwelling on it. *Moha* can mean "astray or lost," and it can mean "dark or dim," that is, full of doubt and ignorance. When one kind of thought or another ferments in the mind, it is called *moha*. We should know whether or not there is delusion in the mind. If there is *moha*, then realize it and contemplate it. If the *citta* is empty of delusion, then contemplate its absence. Always contemplate this state of mind while breathing in and breathing out. This is the third characteristic.

There is a simple way of distinguishing among these three states: *rāga*, *dosa*, and *moha*. If there is any feeling of wanting, that is, wanting to gather toward, to pull in, to hug and to hold, such a feeling is *rāga*. It has a most positive character. The second, *dosa*, does not like, does not want. It has a negative character. *Dosa* pushes away, knocks away, even to the extent of wanting to kill. *Rāga* pulls in and *dosa* pushes away. The third, *moha*, is ignorant. It does not know what is wrong and right, good and evil, according to reality. It is running around in circles. This is how the three differ. One gathers in, one pushes away, and one runs in circles. We should be able to observe the differences and to call them by their correct names. We know *rāga*, *dosa*, and *moha* by observing their activities of pulling in, pushing away, and running in circles.

Next, we need to know whether the mind is distracted or undistracted. The distracted mind lacks one-pointedness; it is unable to rest and relax and has no stillness or calm. Further, distraction annoys us. Is the *citta* distracted? Or is it free of distraction, in a state of normality? We contemplate the mind's character while breathing in and breathing out. We practice in order to know all types of *citta*.

COMMON OR EXALTED?

Next, we observe whether there is a superior state of mind, one better than usual, or merely a common state. In Pali, the superior state is called *mahaggatā*. In ordinary language we would say there is an awareness that is sharper than usual, more satisfying than usual, higher than usual. Does our *citta* have such an awareness now? If so, contemplate it. If not, know that a common state of mind exists at this moment. Contemplate this pair while breathing in and breathing out.

Another pair of states to consider is whether or not this mind is supreme and unsurpassed. That is, has our *citta* achieved that most advanced state where there is nothing better? Or has our mind not yet reached the most advanced state so that there are finer things yet to come? This one is difficult to know because the supreme, most developed state of mind is the *citta* of an *arahant* ("worthy one," fully awakened, perfected human being). If we are not yet *arahants*, common sense tells us whether we have the type of *citta* that is most satisfying or whether there is still something more to be developed. Do we feel that we have achieved final satisfaction? Or do we feel that there should be something even more satisfying than this? This pair is about the *citta* having or not having something superior to it. If there is this highest mind, contemplate it clearly in order to understand it. Breathe in and breathe out with this kind of awareness.

The next pair is whether or not the mind is concentrated. Is it or is it not in *samādhi*? Concentrate the *citta*. Even if the mind is not in full *samādhi* right now, the influence of *samādhi* will probably keep it concentrated. This too can be called a concentrated mind. Know whether the mind is concentrated or not while breathing in and breathing out.

The last pair is to see if the mind has been liberated, if it is empty of attachment (*upādāna*), not grasping or clinging to anything, or if it is not yet liberated and still clinging to something. Does the mind have attachment or not? This is what we mean by asking whether or not the *citta* is liberated. Right now, is there anything arresting the mind or is it free? Whatever the case, know it clearly. Breathe in and out with this awareness. Make it as distinct as possible.

KNOWING OURSELVES

By practicing like this, we learn to know ourselves and the kinds of thoughts that are typical for us. Then we understand ourselves well. What kinds of *citta* are habitual in us? Generally, the mind's thoughts tend to follow some object. By observing these tendencies, we know ourselves better. This is a special benefit of this step. Our primary aim, however, is to know our mind as completely as possible. Thoroughly understanding our own *citta* is the specific objective of this step. This is how to practice step one of the third tetrad, that is, step nine overall.

DELIGHTING THE MIND

Step two of this tetrad is delighting the mind (*abhippamodayaā cittaā*). From the beginning, we have been training in various ways of controlling the mind. In the second tetrad, we developed the mind's ability to be independent of feeling and to have control over the *vedanā*. This means the mind is under control.[8] Once we fully know the various mental states and conditions, both positive and negative, then we can put the *citta* into any state that is appropriate or desirable. Step ten is to make the mind joyful, delighted, and content. It is important to be able to control the mind so that it feels satisfied and glad while breathing in and out.

When the mind is sad, sorrowful, or without joy, we can let go of the sorrow and bring the mind into a joyful state. Or even when the mind is in a normal state, we can always gladden or delight it by using this technique. This is very useful. We do not have to endure a sorrowful mind because we can control it. Whenever needed, we can have the energy to do whatever work is required. We can be joyful at any time. But be careful—the words *joyfulness* and *delight* have two types of meaning. There is the ordinary, worldly kind of delight that is rooted in materialism and sensuality. Although this is one kind of joy, it is not the specific kind of joy we are interested in. We require the delight that comes with knowing and using Dhamma. We need not depend on material or sensual stimulants, for we have Dhamma to help delight the *citta*. Thus, there are two kinds of joyfulness: defiled joyfulness and joyfulness free of defilement (*kilesa*). Both kinds of joy are available to us. If you want defiled joyfulness, it is very easy to obtain. The delight derived from Dhamma, however, must be achieved correctly. For this reason, we ought to examine it more closely.

DELIGHTED BY DHAMMA

It is easy to delight the mind when we understand the cause of joyfulness. Joyfulness comes from the feeling of being successful, of having correctly and successfully completed an activity. An easy way to delight the mind is to return to practicing steps one, two, and three again. Go back to the beginning and practice each step successfully. Then there will be contentment and joyfulness with each completed step. This kind of gladness is associated with Dhamma. We return to practicing step one again, but now we focus specifically upon the feeling of success, contentment, and joyful delight. Proceed through each of the steps in the same way until you arrive at the feeling of joyfulness that satisfies us the most. Joyfulness comes from contentment, and contentment comes from achieving success in some activity. By being certain that we are safe and liberated from bondage, we will experience contentment and joyfulness.

An easy method is to reflect upon achieving what is good. We have obtained the good life, a life that has discovered the Dhamma and is certain to eradicate *dukkha*. We are the most fortunate of human beings, one who has found Dhamma and is able to eliminate *dukkha*. By reflecting in this way, we are joyful and happy. This is the way to be exceedingly glad and delighted. Obtaining what is good, achieving the good life, being a good human being, discovering enough Dhamma to ensure that we will not suffer—this kind of reflection is a simple way for the *citta* to experience joy.

When we are certain that we can extinguish *dukkha*, or when we have gained the best that humans can possibly achieve, then it is normal for us to be joyful and content. We study the Dhamma to understand what will eradicate suffering, to realize our maximum human potential. Then we are content. We are able to delight and gladden the *citta* using this skillful technique.

CONCENTRATING THE MIND

Once we are able to delight the mind as we wish, we train in the next step. The objective of step eleven is to concentrate the mind (*samādahaā citta*). This step is not difficult because we have been practicing with concentration from the beginning, especially in step four (calming the body-conditioner) and step eight (calming the mind-conditioner). If we could do it before, then we can do it now. So we concentrate the mind in *samādhi* and immediately drive away any unwanted feelings. Then the *citta* is concentrated and happy and is skillfully able to perform various duties. This ability is most advantageous.

This brings us to a common problem. Most people misunderstand, thinking that if the mind is in *samādhi*, we must sit absolutely still—stiff and unable to move. Or they think that in *samādhi* we should experience no sensation whatsoever. This is wrong understanding. To sit still and stiff like a log is only a training exercise in higher levels of *samādhi*. Developing the deeper concentrations of the second, third, and fourth *jhāna*, up to the point where the body does not breathe, are just training exercises. Nevertheless, if the mind is able to develop these very high levels of concentration, it should have no problems with the lower levels. Here in step eleven, concentrating the mind means to train the mind so that it has good qualities and is ready for work. It is prepared to perform its duties as needed. From the previous step the *citta* knows how to be happy. When it is happy, the *citta* is highly capable of performing its functions. We should not misunderstand and think that when the mind is in *samādhi*, we must be rigid like a rock or a log.

STABILITY, PURITY, ACTIVENESS

If the mind has correct *samādhi*, we will observe in the mind three distinct qualities. The quality of mind that is firm, steady, undistracted, and focused on a single object is called *samāhito* (stability, collectedness). That mind is clear and pure, not disturbed by anything, unobscured by defilement. A mind empty of defilement is called *parisuddho* (purity). Such a *citta* is fit and supremely prepared to perform the duties of the mind. This is called *kammanīyo* (activeness, readiness). It might be wise to memorize these three words: *samāhito* (stability), *parisuddho* (purity), and *kammanīyo* (activeness). For correct concentration all three of these qualities must be present. This kind of concentration can be used not only in formal meditation practice but in any of the necessary activities of life.

These three qualities can be present while walking, standing, sitting, or lying down. There is an interesting passage in a Pali text; it states that if these three qualities are present while standing, that is called "divine standing." If these three qualities are present while walking, then that is "divine walking." If all three are present while sitting, that is "divine sitting." If these qualities are present while lying down, then it is "divine lying down." Obviously, concentration is more than sitting like a lump of rock or a block of wood—stiff, rigid, and dead to the world. Instead, with concentration the *citta* is perfectly ready to perform its duty, namely, to grow in knowledge and understanding from moment to moment. At the very least, the *citta* will be happy when these three qualities are present, and being happy is also a duty of the *citta*.

The practitioner whose mind is concentrated with these three qualities is known as "one who has a concentrated mind." The Pali word is *samāhito* (one who is concentrated). In Pali, Lord Buddha is quoted as saying, "When the mind is concentrated, it knows all *dhammas* as they truly are" (*samāhito yathābhutaā pajānāti*). This is the supreme benefit of *samāhito*: the *citta* is concentrated on knowing all things as they really are. If there are any problems in life that we cannot answer, then concentrate the mind and the answers will automatically come. Wherever it goes, the concentrated mind sees things according to reality. If we look within ourselves, we see all things according to truth. This means that if the *citta* is accompanied by the three qualities of *samāhito*, we will easily see *aniccaā*, *dukkhaā*, and *anattā*.

We can observe that these three qualities are interdependent; they are interconnected in a single unity. There cannot be purity of mind without stability of mind. If there is no purity, there is also no stability. And there must be stability and purity for there to be activeness. The three work together as the three factors of the concentrated mind. Moreover, the three must be equal and unified to be called *samāhito*. Then they become extremely beneficial, valuable, and powerful. This kind of concentration is able to solve the questions of life, including both the natural problems of this material world and the questions of a "supernatural" order above the world.

Finally, we must understand this essential point: when the mind is in *samādhi*, we can walk or stand or sit or lie down or work or taste the fruit of our labor or help others or help ourselves. The *samādhi-citta* can be used on any problem, in any situation. It can be used to solve all problems. Be interested in this word *samāhito*— one who has *samādhi* and is able to perform every kind of duty.

LIBERATING THE MIND

While breathing in and breathing out, we practice until we are capable of having the mind of *samāhito* with three qualities. We have then completed step eleven. We now come to step twelve, which is liberating the mind (*vimocayaā-citta*). Liberating the mind means not letting the mind become attached to anything. We make the mind let go of anything it is grasping. Such a mind is spotlessly clean; it is free. Liberating the mind from all attachments has two aspects: the mind can let go of all these things, or we can take these things away from the mind. The results are the same. We take away all the things that the *citta* should not hold on to. Then we observe if there is anything to which the *citta* continues to cling. If so, we try to release those things from the mind. This is step twelve.

It is essential that we thoroughly understand what is called "attachment." Although it is a mental phenomenon, we use words from the physical-mental realm to discuss it. We use words like *cling*, *grasp*, and *be attached*. Yet, it is a mental activity. The mind is ignorant and acts out of ignorance. Thus, it causes the activity we call clinging or grasping or being attached. We ought to study this carefully, for it is something that exists in all people, in everyone's daily life. Briefly, attachment is to regard something as "I" or "mine." If we understand attachment, then the practice of this step will go smoothly.

The most direct way to practice step twelve is to examine the danger, the pain, and the suffering present in any moment that we cling to something as "I" or "mine." Scrutinize the dangerous and painful consequences that all attachment inevitably brings. Then examine and realize the benefits and advantages of non-attachment. When we are not attached, what benefits do we receive? What kind of happiness is present? Observe carefully. When we grasp onto something, what type and degree of pain and suffering results? Examine both sides of the coin. Contemplate the suffering of attachment and the value of non-attachment as they continuously alternate in the mind. Through this kind of contemplation the mind is automatically liberated. The mind will naturally let go of things, and things will naturally let go of the mind through observing these two facts. Observe until you see the penalty and lowliness of attachment. Observe until you see the advantages of non-attachment. Observe this every time you breathe in and out. This is how to practice this step.

FOUR KINDS OF ATTACHMENT

The objects of attachment are numerous. Furthermore, they are subtle and profound. By this we mean that they are difficult to see, hear, and understand. Nevertheless, we can identify four types, or modes, of attachment. The first category is all the material objects valued by sensuality (*kāma*), such as possessions, necessities, gems, jewelry, gold, and money; or in other words, the things we see, hear, smell, taste, feel, and think about. All these are the foundations of sensuality and sexuality. These are objects of attachment to sexuality.

The other three categories are immaterial objects of attachment. The second category consists of our incorrect opinions, beliefs, views, and theories. These are the things that we cannot understand, that we cannot possibly know, but because of *avijjā* (ignorance) we accept and are attached to them. We have many such incorrect opinions and views.

The third category includes the traditional activities and practices that we follow. All of them, both the religious and the secular, are superstitious. There are many of these customs with which we identify.

Last and most important of all is the category of all the things that we are attached to as "I" or "mine." These four main categories of attachment include all the things that we grasp. Observe them and see the pain and suffering of clinging to them. See the value of not clinging to them. Continually examine every kind of attachment with every inhalation and exhalation. In this way they are released in an automatic letting go. Release the objects of attachment. Let go, let go, let go.

When we look at Christianity, we see that it shares this concern about attachment. In fact, the primary symbol of Christianity—the cross—teaches the "I" (the upright) and the cutting of the "I" (the cross-member). This symbolizes getting rid of attachment. All religions agree on their major goal: the eradication of attachment to "I" and "mine." This is the highest, most sublime practice. It removes those fundamental difficulties—selfishness in particular—that are the source of all other problems. Cut out selfishness and problems end. We should become interested in letting go of all things. Letting go of the four types of attachment is the best thing we can do.

The mind must also let go of the things that are disturbing the *citta* right at this moment, such as the *nivarata* (hindrances). These are moods that arise in the mind out of habit and tendencies of thought. The five *nivarata* are feelings of sensuality, aversion, depression and drowsiness, agitation and distraction, and doubt and uncertainty. We must drive away these five *nivarata*. Furthermore, the *kilesa* (defilements)—the emotions of *lobha* (greed), *dosa* (anger), and *moha* (delusion)—must go. Any feelings of liking and disliking, any moods of satisfaction and dissatisfaction, any attachments to dualistic things must be removed. Eventually, we will realize that no problems remain that will put the *citta* into *dukkha*. If there is attachment, there is *dukkha*. When the mind is empty of attachment, it experiences no *dukkha* because there is no foundation for *dukkha*.

Whenever the mind sees something clinging to it, it releases that object. Practicing like this every time we breathe in and breathe out is step twelve, the last step of the third tetrad. Altogether there are four steps that deal exclusively with the *citta*: experiencing the different states of mind, gladdening the mind, concentrating the mind, and liberating the mind. Through them we successfully complete our study of the mind.

So far, we have discussed three of the four tetrads. The next chapter concerns the remaining tetrad, the most important of all.

7

The Supreme

IN THIS CHAPTER, we will discuss the fourth tetrad, the final four steps of *ānāpānasati*. In this tetrad we specifically study and examine Dhamma, or truth. You will recall that the first tetrad concerned the breath and the body. The second tetrad dealt with those feelings that result from the calming of the body-conditioner, the breathing. We studied the mind's feelings although not yet the mind (*citta*) itself. We studied the mind-conditioners and learned about the conditioning of the *citta*. Then we learned to control the *citta-sankhāra*, the mind-conditioners. In the third tetrad we studied the *citta* and practiced various ways of controlling the mind. Now that this well-trained mind has been brought under control, in the fourth tetrad we use it to study Dhamma, the truth of nature. Please observe how the four tetrads are interconnected: first, the *kāya-sankhāra*; second, the *citta-sankhāra*; third the *citta* itself; and finally Dhamma, the facts (*saccadhamma*) of nature (*dhamma-jāti*).

The reasoning here is simple. Once the mind is under our power and within our control, we put this mind to work. The mind has a great deal of *kammaniyo*, readiness or activeness, from the practice of concentrating the mind in the third tetrad. The mind is fit and ready to do its duties. In Pali another word is used in this context—*mudu* (gentle). Whereas before the *citta* was hard and stiff, now it is gentle and supple. The mind is very sensitive and quick, in a condition that is ready to be used. Consequently, we use the mind to do the work of the fourth tetrad, where the first duty is to contemplate impermanence.

THE IMPERMANENCE OF *ĀNĀPĀNASATI*

From the beginning, a fundamental principle of this entire practice has been to use elements already existing within us as the objects of our study and practice. We prefer not to use external objects. Once we completely understand the internals, we can extrapolate to the externals. We should not forget this important principle: we must examine things that exist internally. Therefore, for this step of *aniccānupassī* (contemplating impermanence), we return to the beginning step. First, we contemplate just the breath until we see that it is impermanent. We observe that the breath changes and becomes long. Its long duration is impermanent, always changing, getting longer or shorter. Its shortness is impermanent as well. The various conditions and characteristics of the breath are impermanent. The breath's effect on the body is also impermanent.

Next, observe that both bodies—the breath-body and the flesh-body—are impermanent. Then, watch the calming of the breath; here, impermanence becomes even more obvious. The breath changes from coarse to calm, but even that calmness is impermanent. The state of the breath keeps changing. Contemplate each step, one at a time, until each phase is seen to be impermanent.

Eventually, the feelings of *pīti* and *sukha* arise. Watch them one by one. See impermanence in each and every aspect of these *vedanā*. Contemplate the impermanence of the conditioning of the mind by the feelings. The calming of these feelings is impermanent as well.

Next, we watch the *citta* itself; it, too, is impermanent. The gladdening and refreshing of the mind as it changes to delight and joyfulness is impermanent. Contemplate the impermanence of this freshness and delight along with its various conditions and flavors. Concentration itself is impermanent for it changes to non-concentration. The activeness of *samādhi* is impermanent. Impermanence manifests right there in that activeness. Even the liberating of the mind is only a temporary liberation here and thus is also impermanent.

Realize impermanence in each and every step, in each and every one of the interconnected points, phases, and aspects of this practice. Directly experience impermanence in everything. Redo each of the steps. Make the impermanence of each step absolutely clear, undoubtedly obvious, completely certain. This is how we contemplate the impermanence of all these passing phenomena, which are collectively known as *sankhāra*. In step thirteen, we contemplate the impermanence of the *sankhāra* (conditioned things, concoctions).

MORE TO IT THAN JUST IMPERMANENCE

Now, observe that in the realization of impermanence there is the simultaneous realization of many other aspects. When impermanence is truly seen, it also has the characteristic of *dukkhaṁ*, namely, it is painful and unbearable. We can also find the characteristic of not-self (*anattā*) in it. As these things are always changing, impermanent, unsatisfactory, and beyond our control, we realize *anattā* as well. Then we see that they are void of selfhood, which is *suññata*. We see that they are just thus, just like that. Impermanence is just thus, just like that, thusness. And so, *tathatā* is seen as well.

Please understand that the realizations of these truths are interrelated. From seeing impermanence, we see unsatisfactoriness, see *anattā*, see *suññatā*, see *tathatā*, and see *idappaccayatā* (conditionality, the law of cause and effect) as well. Each continues into the next. A complete realization of impermanence must include unsatisfactoriness, not-self, voidness, thusness, and the law of causality. When we see all of these, then we have seen impermanence completely and in the most profound way. This is how we fully realize the impermanence of the *sankhāra*.

We have already explained *sankhāra* and practiced it in lessons three and seven.[9] Remember that there are three meanings to this word: the conditions that are concocted, the concocters that condition other things, and the activity of conditioning or concocting. Various causes, conditions, and ingredients must be concocted and compounded in order to use the term *sankhāra*. The characteristic of conditioners is impermanence. The characteristic of things conditioned is impermanence. The characteristic of the activity or process of conditioning is impermanence. To see all three aspects like this is to realize impermanence in the most profound and complete way.

Merely seeing *aniccaṁ* by itself, rather than seeing it completely in all of its characteristics, is nothing extraordinary. To be complete, the realization must encompass *dukkhaṁ*, *anattā*, *suññatā*, *tathatā*, and *idappaccayatā*. To see *aniccaṁ* alone, in an incomplete way that does not include *dukkhaṁ* and *anattā*, is neither profound nor sufficient to solve our problems. Thus, "realizing *aniccaṁ*" in this context must encompass a realization as deep as *dukkhaṁ*, *anattā*, *suññatā*, *tathatā*, and *idappaccayatā*.

This is illustrated in the following story. In *The Basket of Discourses* (*suttanta-piṭaka*) of the Pali Canon, the Buddha mentioned that there was a religious teacher at that time named Araka who taught about impermanence as often as the Buddha did, but went no further and said nothing about *dukkhaṁ* and *anattā*. This is interesting because at the time of the Buddha there lived the Greek philosopher Heraclitus. The Buddha said that Araka lived in a distant land where he taught about impermanence or flux. The Blessed One was probably referring to Heraclitus, whose central teaching was *panta rhei* (Greek, "everything flows" or "all is flux"). Heraclitus taught only impermanence, however, and was unable to extend this insight to include *dukkhaṁ, anattā, suññatā, tathatā,* and *idappaccayatā.* Thus, it was not a successful teaching. Otherwise, another buddha would have arisen right then and there. Knowledge about impermanence was well spread both within India and abroad. "Distant land" probably meant a foreign country; thus we might suppose that Araka and Heraclitus were the same person.

The essential point is that seeing *aniccaṁ* alone is not enough. We must see *aniccaṁ* such that it shines onto *dukkhaṁ, anattā, suññatā, tathatā,* and *idappaccayatā*—the entire string of realization. The short phrase *aniccānupassī* (contemplating impermanence) includes the realization of unsatisfactoriness, not-self, voidness, thusness, and conditionality as well.

DISSOLVING ATTACHMENT

Now, observe—study closely until you see it—that the realization of *aniccaṁ* dissolves *upādāna,* dissolves attachment. This is crucial. Realizing *aniccaṁ* dissolves attachment because we realize the pain and suffering of that attachment. *Upādāna* dissolves until less and less remains. Such is the result of realizing impermanence. It makes us weary, bored, and disenchanted with all the things to which we continue to be attached and were ever attached. Then *upādāna* begins to dissolve. This is the result of truly seeing impermanence.

The second step of this tetrad, or step fourteen overall, is contemplating fading away (*virāgānupassī*). We already began to observe this in step thirteen when the contemplation of impermanence led to the dissolving of attachment. Now we focus upon and study dissolving, or *virāga*. *Vi*, in this case, means "not" or "not having." *Rāga* is another name for attachment. Thus, *virāga* means "without attachment." Watching attachment dissolve is like watching the stains in a cloth slowly fade away, bleached out by sunlight, until the cloth is white. This is a material analogy of *virāga* that helps to explain the mental fading away of attachment. *Upādāna* dissolves under the light of seeing things as they truly are—*aniccaṁ, dukkhaṁ, anattā, suññatā, tathatā,* and *idappaccayatā.* We know that attachment is lessening when we are even-minded toward *sankhāra*, namely, toward all things to which we were once attached. When we are unprejudiced toward them all, we realize *virāga*, the fading away of attachment. Contemplate this with every inhalation and exhalation. This is how to practice step fourteen.

The result of this fading away of attachment is the even-minded stillness of non-attachment. We can observe this quite easily, for example, as our erotic love for things to which we were once attached begins to fade. Anger toward past, or even present, objects of our displeasure dissolves away. We are no longer afraid of the things we once feared. We are gradually less and less afraid until fear disappears. The same is true for hatred, envy, jealousy, worry, anxiety, longing after the past, and so on. Each of these indicators lessens and shrinks until the mind is able to keep still and silent. The phrase "keep still and silent" means simply not to grasp, cling, or regard anything as "I" or "mine." Contemplate impermanence until the attachment dissolves, until we can remain still, silent, and even-minded. This is how to practice this step.

QUENCHING *DUKKHA*

Step fifteen, *nirodhānupassī*, is the study and contemplation of the quenching of attachment. We observe the cessation of attachment, the nonexistence of attachment, while breathing in and breathing out. We can observe quenching or cessation from a variety of perspectives: the quenching of attachment to "self"; the quenching of selfishness; the quenching of greed, anger, and delusion; and the quenching of all experiences of *dukkha*. All occur with the quenching of attachment. There are many forms of *nirodha*.

When we speak of quenching, remember that the ending of

dukkha is what the practice of Dhamma is all about. Here, we observe different aspects of *dukkha* to see how they are quenched. The first aspect is the ending of fearfulness, the horror of birth, aging, illness, and death. Aging, illness, and death will never again terrify our mind. This is one type of quenching. The next aspect is the cessation of the various symptoms or conditions of *dukkha*, such as sorrow, grief, lamentation, despair, sadness, pain, frustration, and depression. All of these symptoms of *dukkha* are quenched. The third aspect is related to our hopes and wants, to attractive and unattractive things. Experiencing things we do not like is *dukkha*. Being separated from the things we like is *dukkha*. Not getting what we want is *dukkha*. These aspects of *dukkha* are quenched as well.

Lastly, clinging to one of the five *khandha* (groups, aggregates, clusters), grasping the five groups (*pañca-khandha*), as "self" or "belonging to self," as "I" or "mine" is *dukkha*. These five groups of things to which the mind habitually is attached are body, feeling, perception, thought, and sense-consciousness. These are the summation of all *dukkha*, the burdens of life. A full realization of this step must include all four aspects of *dukkha's* quenching. Quench the fear of birth, aging, illness, and death. Quench the symptoms of *dukkha*, such as pain, sorrow, sadness, and despair. Quench the wants and desires of agreeable and disagreeable things. Finally, quench the view of any of the five *khandha* as "self." When these four aspects are quenched, then *dukkha* is quenched. We should not underestimate this important realization.

Thus, we realize the voidness or nonexistence of attachment through the quenching, disappearing, and ending of attachment. We experience the absence of attachment, in any of the aspects mentioned above, while we breathe in and breathe out. Or more simply, we drink, taste, and savor the flavor of *nibbāna*. *Nirodha* and *nibbāna* are synonyms; we can use them interchangeably. Thus, to contemplate the quenching of attachment is to contemplate *nibbāna*.

THROWING IT ALL BACK

The last step, the fourth step of the fourth tetrad, the sixteenth step of *ānāpānasati* is called *patinissaggānupassī* (contemplating throwing back). *Patinissaggā* is a curious word; it means to throw back or give back. When we arrive at this step, we contemplate our throwing back, our returning, everything to which we were once attached. This is step sixteen.

There is a simple metaphor for explaining this step. Throughout our lives we have been thieves. All along, we have been stealing things that exist naturally, that belong to nature, namely, the *sankhāra*. We have plundered them and taken them to be our selves and our possessions. We are nothing but thieves. For this we are being punished by *dukkha*. We suffer *dukkha* because of all our attachment and thieving. As soon as we observe the way things really are through the succession of steps in this tetrad, we let go. We cease being thieves. We return everything to its original owner—nature. It all belongs to nature. Don't claim anything to be "I" or "mine" ever again! Our goal is made clear by this metaphor.

DROPPING THE BURDENS OF LIFE

The following example illustrates a similar point. In the past we went around foolishly picking up heavy objects, such as boulders.[10] We lugged them along wherever we went. For this we constantly suffered *dukkha*. How many years has this gone on? Now, however, we realize how unwise we were in creating such problems for ourselves. We realize how burdensome these boulders are, and we just toss them away. Without these burdens we are light; all our problems disappear. Before, life itself seemed to be a burden because of our stupidity. We clung to those natural *sankhāra*, carried them everywhere, and thus weighed ourselves down terribly. Now we throw them off. This is another metaphor that describes the final step of *ānāpānasati*.

The practice of this last step is to train in throwing away the burdens of life. Throw them away until no burdens remain. Before, we lived under their weight; their heaviness oppressed us. This is called "living beneath the world" or "drowning in the world." Once we can toss away the burdens that hold us down, that trap us beneath the world, we ascend. We are above the world. We are "lords of the world." This is the true meaning of freedom and well-being.

You should remember the meanings of these two conditions. "Living beneath the world" is *lokiya*. "Living above the world" is *lokuttara.* During the practice of step sixteen every problem related to these two meanings will be solved. Let us understand clearly and perfectly that whenever we are foolish, we pick up weights and pile them up as burdens of life. Once we know what they are doing to us, we throw them off. Now we no longer have any burdens. Living under the world and living above the world are totally different. Whoever wants to be free, to be at ease, to be above the world, ought to try their best to practice according to this truth as much as possible—starting right now.

THE SUPREME EMANCIPATION

Be well aware that this is the way to emancipation. *Ānāpānasati* successfully practiced through this final step brings emancipation, or liberation. When we are liberated from all bonds, we either let go of all burdens or release ourselves out from under those burdens. Whether we say "letting go of ourselves" or "letting go of the burdens," the meaning of the realization is the same. There is "letting go," and the result is emancipation. Or it might be called "salvation," "deliverance," "release," or "liberation." They all signify that we have obtained the best thing possible for human beings. We have not wasted our lives and the opportunity of having found the Dhamma, which is the best thing that human beings can obtain. This is the end of the story.

We have completed a thorough discussion of all the lessons and tetrads of *ānāpānasati* as taught by the Lord Buddha. You should now have a good understanding of the entire process as well as of the individual steps. Before finishing our discussion, let's consider the wonderful fruits and benefits of practicing *ānāpānasati*.

8

The Highest Benefits

IN THIS CHAPTER, we will summarize all of the inquiries into *anāpānasati* covered by the previous chapters. We will summarize the sixteen steps in terms of their essential characteristics, their value and benefits, and the means of realizing those benefits. We shall examine these benefits carefully, so that we will be able to make full use of them according to their meaning.

Let us not forget that we are talking about nature, about four aspects of nature, and the law of nature manifest in these four aspects: *kāya*, *vedanā*, *citta*, and Dhamma. These are nature, pure and simple. So we should understand *dhamma-jāti* (see chapter 1). *Dhamma-jāti* both *is* the law of nature and *follows* the law of nature; nature and its law can never be separated. As living creatures, our duty is to understand and use nature for our highest benefit. Although we cannot control it, we can use it to our advantage when we act correctly according to its law. We know these four natures for the benefit of our life, however long it may last.

KĀYA: COOLING EMOTIONS

The first subject in the practice of mindfulness with breathing is the *kāya* (the body, bodies). We can understand without explanation the body's importance in life. It is the foundation for the mind. We require a *kāya* that is ready and able to maintain and support itself, as well as the mind, in ways beneficial for life. Further, we need to understand how to control this *kāya* according to our needs through the technique of regulating the breath. There are many advantages in knowing how to regulate the breath. First, we can change our moods and emotions. For example, when we are angry, we can quickly let go of that anger by breathing long. By breathing deep and long, the anger will disappear. When we are worried and unable to think straight, we breathe longer and longer to force away that worry. Or we can also change from one train of thought to another

99

by breathing long, which will wipe out the unwanted thoughts or emotions and replace them with something more orderly and normal. Through this practice, we are able to think what needs to be thought. We can see that there is more to *kāya* than just the flesh-body; it carries over to the *citta* as well.

The breath alone is well worth knowing, even if only in terms of health. If we know how to breathe properly, we will have good health. Thus, the body and everything associated with the body—the breath, the emotions, our health—is considered to be a very important subject. It is hoped that you will be able to get the fullest benefits from this stage of *ānāpānasati*.

VEDANĀ: STOPPING THE SPINNING

The feelings are the second item. If you are unaware of the feelings, you might think they are unimportant. In reality, they are of the greatest importance to human beings in that they spin us around at their will. Furthermore, they also spin the whole world around. Whatever feelings we desire—and everyone craves them—incite us to all kinds of behavior. Everyone chases after pleasant feelings and runs away from unpleasant feelings. This is how the *vedanā* keep the whole world spinning. The feelings in people are the causes of all the new, strange inventions and creations that humanity constantly produces. Art, culture, and technology were discovered and produced for the sake of the feelings, which have such great power to force us to follow them. *Vedanā* causes desire. Want is born out of feeling and follows feeling. Consequently, we act according to our desires, causing all manner of occurrences to happen. Even our search for money is a response to *vedanā*, whether because of sensuality and sex or merely because of the ordinary feeling of wishing to be at ease.

We should get to know the things that dominate humanity. The *vedanā* have tremendous power and influence over us. If we cannot control the feelings, we will rise and fall at their whim. This is *dukkha*. We will act out of *vedanā*, which are trapped in ignorance (*avijjā*) and, thus, are incorrect. Animals, too, are directed and compelled by feelings. All their activities are merely searching, hunting, and chasing after the desired *vedanā*. Likewise, people search and hunt for the feelings they want.

Even when you do a meditation retreat, you are hoping to find something that will produce the *vedanā* that please you. Is it not true that in so doing you hope to experience pleasant feelings, such as those that arise from the peace and quiet of a monastery or the joy of meditation? Or that you are trying to get away from some of the agitation, conflict, sorrow, and suffering in the world? These *vedanā* cause all kinds of activity and searching; they compel every kind of effort and endeavor. In effect, they are the masters or dictators of our lives in the most profound way. When we can control them, they do us no harm. When we are unable to control them, we become their slaves. What a pitiful state it is to be a slave to *vedanā*!

There are two kinds of *vedanā*: foolish feelings conditioned by *avijjā* (ignorance) and wise feelings conditioned by *vijjā* (correct knowledge). If we are foolish at the moment of *phassa* (sensory contact), foolish feelings arise. If we are clever and knowledgeable at the moment of *phassa*, wise feelings arise. Foolish feelings lead to ignorant desire, or *taṇhā* (craving). Wise feelings lead to correct desire, to wanting what we ought to want in the right way, that is, to wise wanting. We should make sure that the *vedanā* are always wise feelings. Foolish feelings cause *taṇhā*, or craving, which in turn drags us along behind foolish desires; it also makes us chase after unintelligent needs. Craving can turn wise wants and needs into stupid desires. Foolish *taṇhā* leads us around and around the world, yet we still put up with it. Sometimes we even want to go to the moon! As long as craving remains, there will be no end to it all: endless comings and goings, endless inventions and concoctions, endless desires for the luxurious life. Hence, the benefits of controlling the *vedanā* are enormous. Do not allow them to stir up foolish desires and wants. Let us be interested in the *vedanā* from this perspective.

CITTA: WORKING CORRECTLY

Now we come to the *citta*. Our studies have clearly shown the significance of the *citta* (mind-heart). On the other hand, like the *kāya* and *vedanā*, if the *citta* is established or exists in the wrong way, problems will arise and *dukkha* will occur.

We must understand that we apply three different names to the mind depending on the function that it performs. When it thinks, we call the mind *citta*. When it is aware, feeling, experiencing, and knowing, we call the mind *mano*. And we call the basic function of being conscious at the sense doors in order to see, hear, smell, taste, touch, and think *viññāna*. We focus on the function that the mind performs and name it accordingly; in the case of thinking we name it *citta*, in the case of knowing we name it *mano*, and in the case of basic sensory consciousness we name it *viññāna*.

When the *citta* performs correctly, there are good results, but in order to work correctly the *citta* must be under control. If we do not control it, it will not be correct. When it is not correct, it is said that "nothing will be left in the world." By this we mean that the world exists because we have *citta*; if we did not have *citta*, it would be as if there was no world. If we keep the mind under control and dwelling in correctness, we will receive the fruits of calmness, quiet, and peace. Thoroughly understanding the *citta* to keep it under control is the highest knowledge for human beings to have. We must be especially interested in this.

DHAMMA: TWO BASIC FACTS

Lastly, we come to Dhamma, or truth. In all things—both those that make up "me" and those that are connected with "me"—there is truth that must be known. If we do not know such truth, or understand it incorrectly, our involvement with life is incorrect. This causes problems and leads to *dukkha*. Such knowledge can be summarized in two areas: that which is compounded (*sankhāra*, concoctions), that is, those things that have causes and conditions, and their opposite, that which is non-compounded. These subjects can be studied through the metaphysical terms "phenomenal" and "noumenal." Noumenal is the opposite of phenomenal; in principle, they are a pair. If something is phenomenal, it is compounded and must exhibit the truth of impermanence (*aniccaṁ*). If something is noumenal, it is non-compounded and is not *aniccaṁ* but *niccaṁ* (permanent). Therefore, we study the *aniccaṁ* of all things until we know well the truth of impermanence. Then we do not become attached to anything. The mind that is not attached to anything will proceed to realize that which is permanent (*niccaṁ*), which is beyond impermanence, namely, the noumenon: *nibbāna*. Understanding these two realities—the conditioned and the unconditioned—is of the utmost importance. It is the most important principle of all. The practice of the Dhamma tetrad of *ānāpānasati* leads to knowing these two realities.

This is the essence of our study within these four areas, and the knowledge and benefits such study brings. That is the essence of *ānāpānasati*.

THE FOUR COMRADE DHAMMAS

There are further benefits from practicing *ānāpānasati*. Through the practice of *ānāpānasati* we also obtain what are called the "four comrade *dhammas*." The four comrade *dhammas* are *sati*, *paññā*, *sampajaññā*, and *samādhi*. While we are living in this world, the four comrade *dhammas* enable us to subdue all threats; with them we can rid ourselves of *dukkha*. We must use these four comrades to live, whether inside or outside the monastery, in family life, or wherever we find ourselves.

First, we have *sati* (mindfulness, reflective awareness). When a sense object makes contact, *sati* is there and brings *paññā* (wisdom) to the experience. Once it arrives, *paññā* transforms into *sampajaññā* (wisdom-in-action), the specific application of wisdom required by the situation. Then, *samādhi's* power and strength are added to *sampajaññā*. With all four comrades we are able to conquer every kind of object that comes in through the eyes, ears, nose, tongue, body, and mind. The four comrade *dhammas* are unsurpassed guardians. They watch over and protect us as God is said to do. If we correctly practice *ānāpānasati*, we will acquire the four comrade *dhammas*.

PRACTICING FUNDAMENTAL TRUTHS

Another benefit of practicing *ānāpānasati* is that we are able to practice in accordance with the principle of *paticca-samuppāda* (dependent co-origination, conditioned co-arising). The theory of *paticca-samuppāda* is complex and lengthy. For those unfamiliar with it, conditioned co-arising explains the causal origination of *dukkha*. A series of causes, each dependent on a previous cause, leads to suffering. Lord Buddha taught many variations on this theme, but because of its great subtlety and profundity it is difficult to understand.

Nonetheless, it is worth making an effort to study it.[11] Once we come to its practical application, however, dependent co-origination is exquisitely simple. In practice, it means having *sati* in the moment of *phassa* (sense contact). That is all. *Phassa* is the meeting of an internal sense organ, a corresponding external sense object, and the appropriate type of sense consciousness (*viññāna*). Simply having *sati* in the moment of *phassa* completely solves all the possible problems of *paticca-samuppāda*. In other words, before conditioned co-arising can develop, *sati* should be right there at the moment of contact. Do not let it be ignorant *phassa*. If *sati* is present, then that contact will not lead to ignorant feeling and ignorant feeling will not lead to foolish craving (*tathā*). It will all stop right there at contact. This is another advantage of training in *ānāpānasati*: it makes *sati* sufficiently abundant, fast, and capable of performing its duty in the moment of *phassa* to stop the stream of *paticca-samuppāda* right then and there. This is an enormous benefit of practicing *ānāpānasati*.

Yet another benefit is that we are able to practice according to the principles of the four *ariya-sacca* with ease and completeness. We know about the Four Noble Truths. The essence of this set of laws is that *dukkha* is born out of ignorant desire (*tathā*). If there is *tathā*, there must be *dukkha*. When we use *sati* to stop *tathā* and to cut it off, there is no *dukkha*. Through preventing ignorant sense experience (*phassa*), there is no ignorant feeling (*vedanā*) and *tathā* is not stirred up. This is the most beneficial way to practice the Four Noble Truths. You can stop *tathā* through the speed and power of the *sati* that you have developed by practicing *ānāpānasati* in all four tetrads.

THE HEART OF THE TRIPLE GEM

A further benefit is that *ānāpānasati* easily, completely, and perfectly brings us the Triple Gem (*tiratana*), the Three Refuges of Buddhism. This is because the essence or nucleus of Buddha, Dhamma, and Sangha is in cleanliness, clarity, and calm. The state of *citta* that is clean, clear, and calm is the essence of Buddha, Dhamma, and Sangha. Please be careful about these three words. Lord Buddha is not some physical body or image. Rather, the state of mind that is clean, clear, and calm is the true Lord Buddha. In seeing the Dhamma, the Buddha is seen. The heart of the Dhamma is this cleanliness, clarity, and calmness itself. Then, the Sangha are those who through successful practice have clean, clear, and calm minds. All three words are very important. The first person to realize perfect cleanliness, clarity, and calm is called "Buddha," the truth that is realized is called "Dhamma," and those people who follow and practice accordingly are called "Sangha." When we practice *anāpānasati*, we make our *citta* clean, clear, and calm, as we have explained in detail throughout this book. These qualities are the fruit of *viraga*, *nirodha*, and *patinissagga* (steps fourteen through sixteen). Through them there is cleanliness, clarity, and calmness; thus, we can say the genuine Buddha, Dhamma, and Sangha are in our hearts. This is another of the unsurpassed benefits of *anāpānasati*.

BUDDHISM IN ITS ENTIRETY

The next benefit in practicing *anāpānasati* is that we practice the most fundamental principles of Buddhism, namely, *sīla*, *samādhi*, and *paññā*. These three factors are wholly present in the practitioner of *anāpānasati*.

The unshakable determination to practice is *sīla* (virtue). Moreover, when the mind is set on correct action, that too is *sīla*. In the intention necessary to practice every step of *anāpānasati* there is a natural *sīla*, automatically, without our having to specifically practice it. Then there is *samādhi* (concentration) as well. Because of this intention, we practice until *samādhi* arises. Then *paññā* (wisdom) develops, especially in the fourth tetrad, in which we contemplate the most perfect wisdom. In practicing *anāpānasati* correctly the most fundamental principle of Buddhism is fulfilled; it leads to *sīla*, *samādhi*, and *paññā* in full measure. This is an enormous benefit: practicing Buddhism in its entirety.

When we study Buddhism in more detail, we learn about the seven *bojjhaṅga* (factors of awakening). In the *Ānāpānasati Sutta*, the Buddha asserts that fully practicing the sixteen steps of *anāpānasati* perfects the four *satipaṭṭhāna* (applications of mindfulness). Through the perfection of the four *satipaṭṭhāna* (the subjects of the four tetrads—body, feeling, mind, and Dhamma), the seven *bojjhaṅga* are perfected. Then full awakening is assured. The seven *bojjhaṅga* are the very factors that lead to the enlightenment of the *arahant* (a human being who is liberated from all *dukkha*). It would take another book to go into all the details. For now we will simply list the names of these factors: *sati*, *dhammavicaya* (investigation of Dhamma), *viriya* (effort), *pīti* (contentment, satisfaction), *passaddhi* (tranquility), *samādhi* (concentration, collectedness), and *upekkhā* (equanimity, even-mindedness). When *ānāpānasati* is complete, these seven factors are complete. When these seven factors are complete, perfect awakening is assured. Although there is not enough space to explain further, we should understand that the seven *bojjhaṅga* are a certainty when we practice *ānāpānasati* completely. The recorded words of the Buddha clearly state this.[12] You can verify its truth by yourself.

NIBBĀNA HERE AND NOW

The greatest possible benefit of the practice of mindfulness with breathing is that without having to die we will have *nibbāna* in this very life. By this is meant *nibbāna* here and now, having nothing to do with death. *Nibbāna* means "coolness." The word *nibbuto* also means "coolness," referring to a temporary coolness, not yet continual, not yet perfect. Nevertheless, the flavor is the same as perfect *nibbāna*. *Nibbuto* is like the sample a salesman shows of a product that we might actually buy. They must be alike. So we have a sample of *nibbāna* to taste for a little while. It is called temporary *nibbāna* or *sāmāyika-nibbāna*.

Coolness can also be the *nibbāna* that happens due to "that factor." In Pali it is called "that factor," which means something like "coincidental." For example, when there is *sati* focusing on the breath, the *citta* is cool. *Ānāpānasati* is "that factor," the agent, the cause, that brings about the coolness here and now. This is *tadaḍga-nibbāna*, coincidental *nibbāna*. This coolness occurs because there is no defilement; when there is no defilement, the *citta* is cool. When there is no fire, there is coolness. Here *ānāpānasati* eliminates the fires, that is, the defilements. Although it is only temporary, the fires disperse and there is coolness for a while. There is *nibbāna* for a period due to "that factor," that tool, namely *ānāpānasati*. Although momentary, not yet perfect and perpetual, the flavor of *nibbāna* is savored as a sample, a taste. *Ānāpānasati* helps us to sample *nibbāna* little by little, moment by moment, during this very life. And nothing has to die! Then, the duration of that coolness is lengthened, its extent broadened, and its frequency increased until there is perfect *nibbāna*. If attained, this benefit is the most satisfying, the most worthwhile.

It is important that we correctly understand this word *nibbāna*. It means "cool" and has nothing to do with dying. We use the term *parinibbāna* if we are referring to the kind of *nibbāna* associated with death, such as the death of an *arahant*. Just *nibbāna* without the prefix "*pari*" simply means "cool," the absence of heat. Imagine that everything is going right for you: you have good health, economic security, a good family, good friends, and good surroundings. Then, according to the meaning of *nibbāna*, this life of yours is cool. It may not be perfect *nibbāna*, because to be perfect it must include a cool mind, but it is cool just the same.

Nibbāna means "cool." We can even use this word with regard to material things. A burning charcoal that gradually cools down until it is no longer hot is said to *nibbāna*. When soup is too hot to eat, we wait for it to cool off; we then say that the soup is *nibbāna* enough to consume. We might even apply it to fierce and dangerous animals captured from the forest, then tamed and trained until fully domesticated. They too can be said to *nibbāna*. In the Pali texts, *nibbāna* is used regarding material things, animals, and people. If something is cool rather than hot, it is *nibbāna* in one sense or another. And it need not die. Through practicing *ānāpānasati* we will receive the most satisfying sort of *nibbāna*—cool in body, cool in mind, cool in all aspects.

In short, we have a cool life here and now; our life is *nibbāna* in the sense just discussed. In Pali, this is called *nibbuto*, meaning "one who is cooled" or "one who has *nibbāna*." This reality is called *nibbāna*. This kind of person is called *nibbuto*.

THE LAST BREATH

There are many other benefits of practicing *ānāpānasati* that we could cite, but space does not permit it. One last item, however, should be mentioned: we will know the last breath of our life. That is, we will know the breath in which we will die. This does not mean that we will choose the moment of our death; it just means that by becoming well versed in our practice of *ānāpānasati* we will become experts regarding the breath. We will know instantly whether we are going to die during this present breath or not. Thus, we will be able to predict the final breath of our life.

Lord Buddha himself declared that he realized Perfect Self-Awakening (*anuttara sammāsambodhi*) through the practice of *ānāpānasati*. So he offered it to us as the best system to practice. He advised us to use this practice for our own welfare, for the welfare of others, for the welfare of everyone. There is no better way to practice Dhamma than mindfulness with breathing. May you give careful attention to it.

Our discussion of *ānāpānasati-bhāvana* is now sufficiently complete. We conclude this final chapter here, and with it the teaching on mindfulness with breathing for serious beginners.

Translator's Conclusion:
Summary and Suggestions for Practice

Following Ajahn Buddhadāsa's lectures, the translator was asked to give a summary. Based on the experience of the ongoing retreat, emphasis was placed on attitudes and techniques that would help beginners get off to a correct start. The following section is based on that talk.

I WILL ATTEMPT TO REVIEW and add to some of the main points from the preceding chapters, mainly those with which our Western readers might have the most trouble and confusion. Some of these are practical hints and tips to use in establishing the practice of *ānāpānasati*. The rest involve right view (*sammā-diṭṭhi*). The more our attitude is correct, the more our practice of *ānāpānasati* will be correct and will lead to the quenching of all *dukkha* through the end of attachment. Although I do not claim to be a meditation master, I hope that this information will be of some practical benefit to you. It is based on the experience of leading *ānāpānasati* monthly for many years, frequent discussions with Ajahn Buddhadāsa, and personal practice.

NATURAL EVOLUTION/INTENTIONAL PRACTICE

Let's begin with a distinction that is generally overlooked. When we talk about *ānāpānasati*, we also talk about a natural evolution of the mind, of human life. This natural evolution is not the same as our meditation practice, although the two happen together and mutually support each other. The sixteen steps of *ānāpānasati* are based on the contemplation of sixteen distinct objects (including, but not limited to, the breath) while we maintain awareness of breathing in and breathing out. In our study of life, we focus on these sixteen living objects. At the same time, these sixteen objects arise naturally out of our cultivation of the mind (*citta-bhāvanā*). The mind must follow a certain path of evolution from wherever it "is" to what is called "awakening" or "liberation." This path is fundamentally the same for all beings, a natural evolution that is both the duty and the privilege of us all. *Ānāpānasati* meditation is not that evolution itself; rather, *ānāpānasati* is the studying and nurturing of that evolution. As that evolution takes place—and it has already begun—we use *ānāpānasati* to study and understand it. Through that understanding we can use *ānāpānasati* to further support, nurture, and nudge that evolution along. Thus, the practice and the progress are interconnected and inseparable but not identical.

People often confuse the two. We often hear, "Oh! I had rapture, I got *pīti*, I had contentment. I must be on step five." The same confusion occurs regarding most of the steps, and some of us think that we are doing them all in one short sitting. The feeling of contentment, as well as the other objects, will be arising all the time, coming and going all the time, part of the natural process that is taking place. In step five, however, we only start to work with *pīti* at the proper time, which is after the first four steps have been completed and *pīti* manifests clearly and steadily. Even while we are practicing step one, feelings of contentment and joy arise to some degree. This is nothing to get excited about. We might even become aware of impermanence during step one, but that is not step thirteen unless we intentionally contemplate that impermanence. (In the case of impermanence, if it is a genuine insight and not just talking to oneself, it is worth following up immediately. With the first twelve steps, however, it is best to take them patiently, one at a time.) At any one time, we have the intention to practice one specific step or object. All other objects are to be left alone. If the mind should wander, merely note it, let go, and return to the current object or lesson while breathing in and out.

There is this difference between what is happening naturally and what we are practicing specifically. To summarize, on the natural side there are the sixteen objects that occur naturally whenever the conditions are present. On the practical side, we systematically contemplate and train upon these sixteen things one by one. Please be clear about this. It will help you to know what you need to do and when, and to practice efficiently.

Another aspect of this natural evolution is that the mind evolves from cruder states of happiness to more subtle states of happiness. When we begin meditating, we are still interested in rather crude kinds of happiness, usually sensual and sexual happiness. Through meditation we come across refined levels of joy. As *citta-bhāvanā* continues, we discover even more sublime levels of bliss. Once we learn of a higher or more refined level of happiness, then it is quite easy to let go of the coarser kinds. Thus, in this practice there is a natural progression of the mind letting go of a crude happiness through the discovery of a better happiness. Then the mind becomes attached to that better happiness until it finds an even higher level of joy. It can then let go of what is now a lower level of happiness to enjoy the higher level. This proceeds by fits and starts until we learn that supreme happiness is not to become attached to or indulge in any form of happiness.

ONE STEP AT A TIME, PLEASE

Ānāpānasati must be practiced one step at a time. We only get confused and distracted by trying to do two or more things at once. We should be satisfied with the step we are on and be willing to practice correctly, for as long as it takes. We should not jump around from this step to that, merely because we are restless, bored, or full of desires. Do not listen when you find yourself thinking, "Today I'll try all sixteen steps," or "Let's do the first tetrad this week, and the second next week, and then the third," or "What if I start with sixteen and work backwards?" Don't just leaf through this book and choose something that interests you. We must take the lessons one by one, because *anāpānasati* is based on the natural evolution already described. To make the most of this natural fact, it is best to follow *ānāpānasati* as it has been taught by the Buddha.

We should always start at the beginning. Each session starts with firmly establishing *sati* in the breathing and then practicing step one. After you are skilled in step one, after you know it well and can do it with ease, then go on to step two. Practice step two until you are expert in it and have learned what you need to know about it. Then, you can go to step three. Do not fall into the confusion of a little of step one, then a bit of step two, then some of this and some of that. We are often impatient with where we are and want to get somewhere else. We would be wise to restrain that urge. Practice the steps one at a time, remaining with each step until you are an expert in it.

Each session is brand new. Each sitting or walking period is brand new. In fact, each breath is new. So each session must start with step one. Even if you were working with step three or four yesterday, or before lunch, unless you have kept it going throughout the interim, you must start at the beginning, as is only natural. If you have already succeeded with step one, now you must review it at the start of each session until the knowledge of it is directly here and now, rather than mere memory. Each step must be reviewed in the same way to make sure that we are expert in it right now. Depending on conditions—primarily internal—some sessions will not get past step one and others will get as far as our overall progress. We never know until we do it. Without expectation we practice step by step, seeing what happens and learning what we can.

This is merely the way things are. Each step depends on the previous steps. The conditions for step five are the completion of steps one through four. We are ready for step ten only when we have gone through the first nine successfully. Once we can accept things as they are, we can stop desiring that they be otherwise. By accepting the nature of these steps—that is, the nature of our own bodies, breathing, and minds—we can practice wisely, without impatience, boredom, and frustration.

PATIENCE AND PROGRESS

Finally, let's remember that *khanti* (patience, endurance) is a necessary spiritual tool. The Buddha said:

> Patient endurance is the supreme incinerator of defilement.
> (*Khantī paramaṁ tapo titikkhā*)[13]

We are often in the habit of judging and measuring ourselves against various standards. Some of us are competitive and judge ourselves according to others. Sometimes we judge ourselves according to the various ideals we have. Many people, when they learn about the sixteen steps of *ānāpānasati*, judge themselves according to these steps. We foolishly think, "I am a better person when practicing step four than when practicing only step one." We all want to be good and practice step four and then five and then six. Such thinking will not do us any good.

Do not measure progress according to these sixteen steps. Measure progress according to the development of spiritual qualities, such as *sati*, perseverance, understanding, confidence, calmness, friendliness, compassion, balance, and so forth. Measure it against the diminishing of attachment and the disappearance of greed, anger, and delusion. These results of correct practice will increase noticeably even during step one. Even if we stick with little old step one for the rest of our lives, if we do it properly, these qualities will grow and attachment will diminish. There will be less and less *dukkha*, and that is all that matters.

Getting to step sixteen is not so important. In fact, step one can be enough. The reality of *nibbāna* is unconditioned and not caught within time. So you never know when *nibbāna* will be realized; maybe even during step one. You need not hurry to get on to steps two or three or ten. Step one might be enough if you just do it right. Do it with patience, with balance, with clarity, with wisdom. Do it without clinging and grasping. Just do it.

We find that when we have more patience and endurance in our *ānāpānasati* practice, then patience and endurance are more a part of our daily lives. They help us to live a clean, clear, calm life. So let us be very, very patient. Learn to sit still. Learn to forget about all those "things that I have to do." Learn to keep plugging away at step one until it is complete. And then proceed to step two. Do each step properly and do not hurry. With patience the mind will develop, it will "get somewhere." As long as there is impatience and desire to move on, you are learning little of consequence and experiencing much *dukkha*.

Regarding attitude or right view: discover the natural evolution; study it systematically; always start anew; take things one step at a time; be patient; put aside expectations, desires, and demands; stay balanced; learn to identify and let go of the attachments that creep into your practice. In short, practice to understand *dukkha* and to realize the end of *dukkha*. Accept that *nibbāna* is the reason for practicing *ānāpānasati* and be delighted with this great opportunity.

GETTING STARTED: ESTABLISHING *SATI*

Any practice of *citta-bhāvanā* begins with taking up *sati* and establishing it upon the initial meditation object; thus, we begin by establishing *sati* on our first object, the breath. This can be called the "preliminary step," or "lesson zero," if we wish to number it. There are various ways of being mindful of the breath. We can arrange them progressively from coarse to subtle in a way that corresponds to the first four steps. The following is a simple approach that should work well for most people, but you need not follow it blindly. As always, you must find what works best for you. Remember, never go by mere opinions or biases, learn from experience.

(1) Once you are seated comfortably and are relaxed and still, feel the breathing, which is now easily noted within the quiet and still body. Direct attention to the breathing in a firm and gentle way. Maintain this watchfulness of the breathing and become familiar with both the breathing and the mindfulness of it. This attention to the breathing can be general, that is, not focused on any one specific place.

(2) Note the three primary segments of each breath: beginning, middle, and end. During the inhalation these correspond to the nose, the middle of the chest, and the abdomen. During the exhalation the reverse is true, beginning at the belly and ending at the nose. Watch and wait at the nose until the incoming breath is felt there. Then, skip to the middle of the chest and watch there until the breath is felt. Next, skip to the abdomen and watch there until the breath is felt. Continue watching as the inhalation ends and wait for the exhalation to begin. Once the exhalation is felt at the abdomen, go to the middle of the chest and then to the nose. Observe at the nose as the exhalation ends and wait for the new inhalation to be felt, then skip to the chest, and so on. With *sati*, note the breath at each of these points as it passes in and out, in and out. Be careful to patiently observe at each point until the breathing (the movement of the breath itself or of the organs used for breathing) is felt. Only then does the mind jump to the next point. This hopping from point to point is a relatively easy way to establish *sati* on the breath. It is a good way to get started. It becomes, however, somewhat crude and agitating after a while. Once we are skilled at it, we will want a more refined and peaceful way to be mindful of the breath.

(3) Next, we connect the three points into a continuous sweep or flow. This more closely approximates the breath itself. We call this

"following, chasing, hunting, stalking." While breathing naturally, without any forcing or manipulating of the breath, *sati* follows the breath in and out, between the tip of the nose and the navel. Follow the breath, do not lead it. Track the succession of physical sensations—which must be felt, experienced—in and out.

(4) Once following becomes easy and constant, it will begin to feel unnecessarily busy and disruptive. Now we are ready for guarding, a more peaceful way to practice *sati* with the breathing. By this time, a certain point in the nose will stand out. This is right where the breath is felt most clearly and distinctly. Although some people may feel that there are two points, one in each nostril, do not make things unnecessarily complicated. Simply note one point that covers both nostrils. This is called the "guarding point." We choose a point in the nose because it is more subtle, exact, and distinct than other places such as the abdomen or chest where the movements are large and coarse. To calm the breath, we must use a point that is small, focused, and suitably refined. With *sati*, fix the *citta* on this point. Allow the *citta* to gather itself at this point. Do so by simultaneously calming the breath and becoming more sensitive (through *sati*) to the increasingly subtle sensations at the guarding point. Continue to calm the body-conditioner until proper and sufficient *samādhi* develops.

We can always begin with the first technique. The second and third techniques are suitable for steps one and two. Step three is best done by following, although guarding can also be used. Step four should begin with following and then take up guarding.

If at first our breaths are short and shallow, with movement in the chest only and not in the abdomen, then simply follow the breath down as far as it goes. After *sati* is established, we will relax and the breathing will become deeper. Just sitting still for ten or fifteen minutes also helps. Before long we will feel movement in the abdomen. If we see that the breath is passing by many places at the same time, do not use this as an opportunity to complicate matters. Keep it simple. A simple flow from the tip of the nose to the navel and from the navel to the tip of the nose is sufficient for our purposes. Do not look for or create complex breathing patterns. Do not try to watch every separate movement at once. If we merely observe the breath, the process will remain simple. If we spend our time thinking about the breath, it is easy to get confused.

This is a good opportunity to emphasize that *sati* is not "thinking about" something. *Sati* is reflective attention, awareness, watchfulness, observance, scrutiny. There is no need for concepts, labels, words, and pictures. Such things only get in the way of directly experiencing the breathing in and out. We can compare "following" the breath to walking along a river. The water flows; we walk along and watch it flow. We need not talk to ourselves, "river, river—flowing, flowing—this, that—blah, blah, blah," to see the river. In such a case, if we are not careful, we will stop watching the river and get lost in our words and thoughts. We do enough of that already. Why bring it into our *ānāpānasati* practice, too?

TRICKS TO AID *SATI*

If it is too much of a struggle to keep the mind on the breath while following, there are some tricks or aids we can use. The first is to aim the eyes at the tip of the nose, as Ajahn Buddhadāsa suggests. Do this in a relaxed and gentle way. Do not cross the eyes or create tensions; this will only lead to headaches, not to *sati*. At first you may be able only to gaze a little beyond or in front of the nose, but as the body and face relax, you will be able to gaze at the tip itself. Even when the eyelids are closed, we can aim the eyes at the tip of the nose.

A second trick is to breathe loudly. Breathe loud and strong enough to hear the breath. The ears as well as the eyes can support *sati*. This can be particularly useful at the beginning of a session or after a disturbance. After following is established, we naturally drop the loud breathing as it will become annoying. You should try some loud breathing, however, at the beginning of a session or whenever you find it difficult to establish *sati*.

The third trick is counting. We can gang up on the breath with the eyes, the ears, and now the intellect. Count each inhalation as it begins, one number for each breath. If the mind wanders, start over with "one." If we can count to "ten" without the mind wandering, go back to "one" anyway. For our purposes here, a simple count of each breath is enough. The method of counting explained by Ajahn

Buddhadāsa serves another purpose and comes later. Again, once *sati* is well established, counting is unnecessary and should be dropped. With training, *sati* becomes more subtle, alert, and natural.

These tricks are to help us get started and should not be confused with lessons one, two, and so on. After becoming familiar with them, you will always have them at your service, whether in meditation or ordinary life.

LONG AND SHORT BREATHS

As *sati* is established (techniques two or three), we begin to notice the long and short breathing. The mind may occasionally still wander, but it stays with the breath enough to learn what the breath is like. The first and easiest quality to note is length, in terms of both time and extent of physical movement. For our purposes, an exact dividing line between short and long is not important. Become familiar with your own breathing and learn what your longest breaths and shortest breaths are like relative to each other. There is no need to compare your breath to anyone else's.

Generally, you will find that abdominal breathing is longer than chest breathing, that is, if abdominal breathing comes naturally. This is something we observe, however; it is not something we desire or force. We are not "supposed" to breathe in a certain way, and we do not use *ānāpānasati* to develop any special way of breathing. So do not try to force abdominal breathing since the results would not be very relaxing. When abdominal breathing occurs naturally, however, you will see that it is longer, more relaxed, and healthier.

In fact, long breathing is more "not doing" than "doing." In other words, don't hurry the inhalation or squeeze out the exhalation. Let the inhalation naturally flow in by itself; the body knows exactly how to do it. Release the exhalation naturally, without pushing it out or cutting it off abruptly. Both require a relaxed diaphragm and abdomen, so let go of all those tensions down there. It is important to be patient during the transitions from inhalation to exhalation and from exhalation to inhalation. Watch carefully but gently as one ends, and wait calmly for the next to begin by itself.

Should your breaths become very long, you will discover an interesting point. You may have thought it strange when Ajahn

Buddhadāsa said that the chest expands and the abdomen contracts with the long in-breath. Common sense says that the abdomen expands on the in-breath and contracts on the out-breath; common sense seems to contradict Ajahn Buddhadāsa. Which is right? First, we observe normal breathing: as we inhale, the diaphragm drops and pushes the tummy outward; when we exhale, the tummy falls in again. This is ordinary abdominal breathing before it becomes very long. It is a simple movement of the abdomen expanding (or rising) with the in-breath and contracting (or falling) with the out-breath. Some people will consider this short whereas others will feel it is relatively long.

Now, there is a limit to how far the abdomen can expand. As we relax and breath more deeply, this limit will be reached. At that point there is, however, room left in the lungs for more air. If we continue to breathe in, the chest will then expand. This, in turn, pulls up and flattens the tummy. This is what Ajahn Buddhadāsa referred to. A very long inhalation begins just like a normal breath; the abdomen expands but the chest barely moves at all. After the abdomen's limit is reached the chest expands and the abdomen contracts. When the breath is really long, you will discover this for yourself. The opposite movements occur (roughly) with the very long exhalations. So, the very long breath is an ordinary breath plus more. Until the body becomes very relaxed through *ānāpānasati*, many of us will seldom experience this very long breathing. Eventually, it will happen more and more regularly—even outside formal sittings.

Any breathing that is less than long can be considered short. There are a few ways, however, to describe short breathing in more detail. The first is that if it feels short to you, then it *is* short. Such a definition may be helpful for neophytes. The second definition is more precise; chest breathing, breathing in which all the movement is in the chest with little or none in the abdomen, is clearly short and shallow (and usually rather fast). The third description is most appropriate for those who are committed to a long-term practice of *ānāpānasati*. The "normal breath" discussed above is considered short; that is, anything less than a full long breath that expands the belly and then the chest is short. When starting out, be flexible about the distinction between long and short. As you gain experience, you'll find the third definition to be the most useful.

Even when *sati* is less than firmly established, we will be learning about long and short breathing. Steps one and two really begin, however, when *sati* can follow the breath without faltering. Sounds, thoughts, and other phenomena may occasionally wander through, but the mind does not get caught up in them. We are able to stay with the breath, observe it, and learn. If the mind still wanders a great deal, consider yourself to be on the "preliminary step," that is, still getting started. Focus attention solely on establishing *sati* on the in-breaths and out-breaths. Until you are successful, that should be your only concern.

If we are impatient to get through step one and want to move on to "more interesting things," we can check such thoughts by asking ourselves: "Is the body relaxed enough to sit like this for an hour or more, comfortably, without any desire to move?" When the breathing is truly long, it is possible to sit comfortably for long periods of time. If we are restlessly changing positions every ten or fifteen minutes, it is best to be content with step one. Learn how to sit still, relax, and allow the breath to become long, slow, gentle, and smooth. Then, we will be able to sit for long periods of time with ease. This requires self-discipline—not self-torture. Train yourself wisely, with balance.

STEP THREE: A NEW OBJECT

In steps one and two the breathing is the only object of our attention. Beginning with step three, we take up other objects, in this case "all bodies." Here, we focus on the influence of the breathing upon the rest of the body. Note that the focus is no longer the breathing itself, although the breathing and its influence are closely associated. At this time, the awareness of breathing in and out moves into the background where it remains clear and constant. While the mind focuses on the new object, we always know whether we are breathing in or out. This holds true for the rest of the sixteen steps.

Studying the influence of the breathing upon the body involves more than just long and short breaths. Length was a convenient way to begin. Now, we should also notice speed (fast-slow) and texture (coarse-subtle). Texture, or quality, is the most important because it has the greatest influence on the calmness of the body. In this step, we will discover the kind of breathing that most effectively calms the body. Then we are ready for step four.

LIFE IS MEDITATION

These suggestions and tips should be enough to help you get started and to develop a wise meditation practice. Please note the following observations as well.

There is more to meditation (*citta-bhāvanā*, mental cultivation) than sitting. Our formal sitting and walking practice is very important, and there are few people who do not need it, but we are interested, most of all, in living life—life free of *dukkha*. Our lives involve more than sitting, and *ānāpānasati* can help us in other areas of life as well.

First, the skills and knowledge developed through formal practice can be used and expanded upon throughout our daily activities. Second, we can be aware of, if not concentrated on, the breath while performing most duties. If this is developed properly, the breath regulates the body in a state of correctness and anchors the mind in purity, stability, tranquility, clarity, strength, and alertness. Third, the mind can go to the breath and focus upon it when harmful mental states arise. In doing so, the breath should not be treated as an escape. Nevertheless, it is often the most skillful means out of an unwholesome thought, emotion, or mood.

As you grow to love this practice and its benefits, you will seek out opportunities to practice whenever you can. This can be frustrating, however, in our busy, time-poor world. Fortunately, a wonderful quality of *ānāpānasati* is that we can practice it anywhere without doing anything special. For example, when finding yourself waiting in a line or office, or at a traffic light, don't waste your precious time being bored or nervous! Practice *ānāpānasati*, at least until the light turns green. There is no need to close your eyes or to sit in a way that draws attention to yourself. You can practice while standing or in whatever position you may find yourself. When making a telephone call to somebody, there is time for a few mindful breaths even while waiting for that person to pick up the phone.

Computers often make us wait: a chance to come back to the reality of breathing in and out, of being alive and awake. You can probably find a couple hours for such practice even in your busiest day. These are just a few ways to integrate *ānāpānasati* into your life as a whole.

SATIPATTHĀNA IS ĀNĀPĀNASATI

Even the theory of *ānāpānasati* can be used throughout the meditation of daily life. Once we have taken the time to study and understand the sixteen steps (which may involve some supplementary reading), we need not limit their application to breathing alone. Ajahn Buddhadāsa points out that both versions of the *Satipatthāna Sutta*[14] lack a clearly defined method of practice, whereas the *Ānāpānasati Sutta* outlines a complete progressive system of practice:

> Another common problem is that some people cling to and are stuck on the word *satipatthāna* (foundations of mindfulness) far too much. Some go so far as to think that *ānāpānasati* has nothing to do with the four foundations of mindfulness. Some even reject *ānāpānasati* out of hand. In some places they really hang onto the word *satipatthāna*. They cling to the *satipatthāna* of the *Digha-nikāya* (*Long Discourses*), which is nothing more than a long list of names, a lengthy catalog of sets of dhammas. Although there are whole groups of dhammas, no method of practice is given or explained. This is what is generally taken to be *satipatthāna*. Then it is adjusted and rearranged into different practices, which become new systems that are called *satipatthāna* practices or meditation.[15]
>
> Then, the followers of such techniques deny, or even despise, the *ānāpānasati* approach, asserting that it is not *satipatthāna*. In truth, *ānāpānasati* is the heart of *satipatthāna*, the heart of all four foundations of mindfulness. The sixteen steps are a straightforward and clear practice, not just a list of names or dhammas, like in the *Mahāsatipatthāna Sutta* (*Digha-nikāya* 22). Therefore, let us not fall into the misunderstanding that *ānāpānasati* is not *satipatthāna*; otherwise, we might lose interest in it, thinking

that it is wrong. Unfortunately, this misunderstanding is common. Let us reiterate that *ānāpānasati* is the heart of all four *satipaṭṭhāna* in a form that can be readily practiced.

We have taken time to consider the words *satipaṭṭhāna* and *ānāpānasati* for the sake of ending any misunderstandings that might lead to a narrow-minded lack of consideration for what others are practicing. So please understand correctly that whether we call it *satipaṭṭhāna* or *ānāpānasati* there are only four matters of importance: *kāya*, *vedanā*, *citta*, and Dhamma. However, in the *Mahāsatipaṭṭhāna Sutta* there's no explanation of how to practice these four things. It only gives and expands upon the names of *dhammas*. For example, the matter of *kāya* (body) is spread out over corpse meditations, *sati-sampajaññā* in daily activities, the postures, and other things, more than can be remembered. This sutta merely catalogs groups of *dhammas* under the four areas of study.

The *Ānāpānasati Sutta,* on the other hand, shows how to practice the four foundations in a systematic progression that ends with emancipation from all *dukkha.* The sixteen steps work through the four foundations, each one developing upon the previous one and supporting the next. If you practice all sixteen steps fully, the heart of the *satipaṭṭhāna* arises perfectly. In short, the *satipaṭṭhāna* suttas are simply lists of names. The *Ānāpānasati Sutta* clearly shows how to practice the four foundations without anything extra or surplus, without mentioning unrelated matters.[16]

The four foundations and mindfulness of them are the basis for all meditation practice; we should at every opportunity work to develop the four foundations of mindfulness. You will see that the sixteen steps provide a general structure for all *satipaṭṭhāna* practice. These are the sixteen things that we should contemplate every chance we can, whenever these *dhammas* occur. Although most bodily processes are not open to the systematic and complete treatment we use with the breathing, we can use the sixteen steps to identify the things most worthy of our attention.

CONDENSED VERSION

Some people may feel intimidated or put off by all the steps. In this regard, Ajahn Buddhadāsa has given the following advice:

> If some people feel that sixteen steps are too much, that is all right. It is possible to condense the sixteen down to two steps. One—train the *citta* (mind) to be adequately and properly concentrated. Two—with that *samādhi*, skip over to contemplate *aniccaṁ*, *dukkhaṁ*, and *anattā* right away. Just these two steps, if they are performed with every inhalation and exhalation, can also be considered *ānāpānasati*. If you do not like the complete sixteen-steps practice, or if you think that it is too theoretical, too much to study, or too detailed, then just take these two steps. Concentrate the *citta* by contemplating the breath. When you feel that there is sufficient *samādhi*, examine everything that you know and experience so that you realize how they are impermanent, how they are unsatisfactory, and how they are not-self. Just this much is enough to get the desired results, namely—letting go! release! no attachment! Finally, note the ending of *kilesa* (defilement) and the ceasing of attachment when you fully see *aniccaṁ-dukkhaṁ*. Thus, you can take this short approach if you wish.
>
> Here, however, we want you to understand the complete system; thus, we must speak about the sixteen-step practice. Once you fully understand the entire sixteen steps, you can abridge them for yourself. Decrease them until you are satisfied enough to practice with confidence. You might end up with two steps, or five steps, or whatever suits you. This is our purpose in the way we explain *ānāpānasati*. We explain the system of practice in full, then you can shorten it for yourself depending on what pleases you.
>
> This is why we have studied and explained the sixteen-step method in full, because it will reveal the secrets of nature through its scientific approach. This is a science that leads to a natural understanding of *kāya*, *vedanā*, *citta*,

and Dhamma, in the best and most complete way possible, through the perspective and approach of natural science. This method is a scientific approach that can regulate these four things. First, study the complete sixteen steps, then you may trim them down by yourself. Choose for yourself what you need. Practice only two or three steps if you want. Keep just two or three or five steps as you like.[17]

THE SHORTCUT METHOD FOR ORDINARY PEOPLE

We will begin by speaking for those who do not like "a lot." By "a lot" they seem to mean too much, or a surplus. Well, the surplus is not necessary. We will take just what is sufficient for ordinary people, which is called "the shortcut method." The essence of this method is to adequately concentrate the mind, which any ordinary person can do, and then take that concentrated *citta* to observe *aniccaṁ-dukkhaṁ-anattā*—the three characteristics of being—until realizing *suññatā* and *tathatā*. With this practice it is possible to realize the benefits of *samādhi* as well as the full-scale result of extinguishing *dukkha*, but there will not be any additional special qualities. Such special abilities are not necessary anyway. Therefore, make the mind sufficiently concentrated, then examine *aniccaṁ* and *dukkhaṁ*. Just practice sufficiently the first tetrad of *ānāpānasati*, then practice sufficiently the fourth tetrad. That is all! Sufficient is not a lot, nor is it good enough. This is the shortcut for ordinary people.

Now let's look at the method of practicing the first tetrad. If you make the breath fine, the entire body will be subtle, that is, tranquil and cool. Just this much is sufficient for having a mind good enough to do *vipassanā*. Then the *citta* is on a level that it can use to contemplate *aniccaṁ-dukkhaṁ-anattā*, which manifests in every part and particle of our bodies. We contemplate the impermanence, unsatisfactoriness, and selflessness of every organ and component in our bodies—both concrete and mental—until we realize suchness. When we see suchness, we do not fall under the power of dualism. It is enough. This much is enough to penetrate higher and higher into the Dhamma until realizing the highest. This is the shortcut for ordinary people. Those living in the common, ordinary world—even those living the household life—are able to do at least this much.[18]

SIXTEEN STEPS TO EVERYTHING

We can use any bodily activity as a basis for *sati*. The more necessary and central to life (like breathing) that activity is, the better. First, get to know that activity from all angles (long-short may or may not be relevant). Second, see what influence that activity has on the flesh-body. Third, find the right way to perform that activity so that it has the optimal effect on the body and allows the mind to find an appropriate degree and type of concentration. This corresponds to the first tetrad (*kāya*). Next, examine the feelings associated with that activity, especially the pleasant feelings that arise when the activity is done well and successfully. Study the influence these feelings have on the mind, then calm that influence. This covers the second tetrad (*vedanā*). The third tetrad (*citta*) begins with experiencing the different types of mind that arise during that activity. Then we train to gladden, concentrate, and liberate the mind while that activity is taking place. Finally, the fourth and most important tetrad (Dhamma) is to contemplate all aspects of that activity—body, feeling, and mind—as *aniccaṁ*, *dukkhaṁ*, and *anattā*. Contemplate the fading away and extinction of attachment. Contemplate the tossing back to nature of everything associated with that basic activity.

Ānāpānasati explains how to use everything we do as *satipaṭṭhāna* practice. When possible, practice *ānāpānasati* directly. Otherwise, practice it indirectly through a parallel practice. The knowledge we gain through parallel *citta-bhāvanā* will supplement and support our regular *ānāpānasati* practice, and vice versa. Once we appreciate the possibilities inherent in the sixteen steps, there will be constant opportunities to develop the *citta* even in the "most difficult conditions." The sixteen steps—especially the first and last tetrads—are enough meditation theory to eliminate *dukkha* from life. May you use them well.

NOTHING SURPLUS

While simplified versions of *ānāpānasati* are common, Ajahn Buddhadāsa maintains that the sixteen-step approach of the Buddha is the most effective.

> You can see for yourself whether it is a lot or not, surplus or not. We begin our study with *dukkha* itself and the cause of *dukkha's* arising. Then we study the foundations on which *dukkha* grows: the body and the *vedanā*. We go on to study that thing that experiences either *dukkha* or the absence of *dukkha*, namely, the *citta*. Lastly, we study Dhamma—the truth of all things—so that the *citta* knows, knows, knows, until it does not become attached to anything. Know letting go. There is a great deal to be done. To do it, our practice must be complete. Thus, we have the sixteen steps. As I explain it to you, it does not seem the least bit excessive. Really, there are so many matters to study and know in life that to have only sixteen steps is not very much at all. Some may say that it is too much, that they do not want to study and practice. If they do not think that it can help them, well, whatever suits them. Anyone who does not want to study and train in the complete sixteen steps can follow a condensed practice as previously explained. That is still enough to get something beneficial out of Buddhism through the technique of *samādhi-bhāvanā*.[19]

LORD BUDDHA'S *VIPASSANĀ*

What is real *vipassanā*? Propaganda put out by certain meditation teachers might lead one to believe that only the meditation system of the speaker, or his teacher, can be considered to be *vipassanā*. Such insinuation is pure nonsense and leads to narrow-mindedness and confusion. There are, in fact, numerous approaches to *vipassanā*, and *ānāpānasati* is one of the most important. In fact, of the many approaches, *ānāpānasati* surely has the best claim to being Lord Buddha's approach. No other system is detailed in the suttas, whereas *ānāpānasati* has its own sutta, is partially discussed in the two *satipaṭṭhāna* suttas, and is prominent in the *Vinaya-piṭaka* and the *Saṁyutta-nikāya* as well. Such claims, however, are not the point. The sole point is whether a particular approach, when practiced correctly, brings a final end to *dukkha*. Such proof will be found in practice and realization rather than in sectarian arguments.

SANGHA

A growing number of people are practicing *ānāpānasati* in some form, as well as other kinds of meditation, but do not always have regular access to qualified teachers. Everyone shares in the same joys and difficulties that you meet with in your practice. To join with some of the many meditators—they are everywhere, even in your area—to form a sitting group will be of great benefit to you, not to mention to the wider community. Sitting groups need not be large. It isn't necessary that you be "Buddhists" or that everyone practice in the same way, as long as you all sit quietly. The important things are mutual friendship, respect, and support, and that the group meet regularly, say, once a week. Such groups can help keep you going when times are rough or your spirit is weak. Further, they are a source of the community or sangha that we all need, especially in our hyper-individualistic, alienated modern societies. Imagine what the world would be like with meditation groups everywhere cultivating peace, compassion, and wisdom!

I hope that you are able to use this information. I have presented it as clearly as I am able. Please study it carefully; you may find that more than a few readings are necessary. Think it through sufficiently. Then, most importantly, try it. By practicing, your understanding of these instructions will grow. You will need to make adjustments, but for the most part those adjustments will be in your own understanding and application rather than in Ajahn Buddhadāsa's instructions. Try to follow his advice as well as you are able. Avoid mixing it with things you hear from meditators using other systems. With patience, dedication, and wisdom allow this practice to deepen and lead to the understanding of non-attachment and the realization of the end of *dukkha*, the supreme peace and freedom of *nibbāna*.

Mindfulness with Breathing Discourse

(Ānāpānasati Sutta)[20]

INTRODUCTION

I have heard thus:

At one time the Exalted One[21] was staying near Sāvatthī,[22] in the mansion of Migāra's mother in the Eastern Grove, together with many widely known elder disciples: Venerable Sāriputta, Venerable Mahā-Moggallāna, Venerable Mahā-Kassapa, Venerable Mahā-Kaccāyana, Venerable Mahā-Koṭṭhita, Venerable Mahā-Kappina, Venerable Mahā-Cunda, Venerable Revata, Venerable Ānanda, and other widely known elder disciples.

At that time those venerable elders taught and trained the new bhikkhus. Some of the elders taught and trained ten bhikkhus, some of them taught and trained thirty bhikkhus, and some of them taught and trained forty bhikkhus. Those new bhikkhus, when taught and trained by the elders so, understood that which is lofty and excellent more than ever before.

During that time the Exalted One was sitting in the open surrounded by the community of bhikkhus on the observance day of the fifteenth, the full moon night, of the last month of the rains residence.[23] The Exalted One surveyed the calm and silent assembly of bhikkhus, then spoke:

"Bhikkhus, we are certain of this way of practice. Bhikkhus, we are convinced by this way of practice. Bhikkhus, for this reason you should summon up even more energy for attaining the unattained, for reaching the unreached, for realizing the unrealized. I will wait here at Sāvatthī until the fourth and final month of the rains, the blossoming time of the white lotus (komudī)."

The bhikkhus in the countryside came to know that the Exalted One would remain at Sāvatthī until the fourth and final month of the rains, the blossoming time of the white lotus. They streamed continuously into Sāvatthī in order to attend upon the Exalted One.

Further, the venerable elders taught and trained the newly arrived bhikkhus in great measure. Some of the elders taught and trained ten bhikkhus, some of them taught and trained twenty bhikkhus, some of them taught and trained thirty bhikkhus, and some of them taught and trained forty bhikkhus. Those new bhikkhus, when taught and trained by the elders so, understood that which is lofty and excellent more than ever before.

Now, at that later time, the Exalted One was sitting in the open surrounded by the community of bhikkhus on the night of the full moon observance day of the fourth and final month of the rains, the blossoming time of the white lotus. The Exalted One surveyed the calm and silent assembly of bhikkhus, then spoke:

THE COMMUNITY OF BHIKKHUS

"Bhikkhus, this community is not at all worthless. This community is not a failure in the least way. This community is established in the pure essence of Dhamma. Bhikkhus, this community is worthy of gifts, is worthy of hospitality, is worthy of offerings, is worthy of homage, and is a field more fertile than any other in the world for the cultivation of merit.

"Bhikkhus, this community of bhikkhus is an assembly such that people who make small offerings to it receive much and people who make large offerings receive even more. This community of bhikkhus is an assembly most difficult to find in this world. This community of bhikkhus is an assembly worthy of people packing up provisions and walking great distances to come and observe it.

"Bhikkhus, living in this community are bhikkhus who are worthy ones (*arahants*) without eruptions (*āsāvas*),[24] who have lived the sublime life, have done what is to be done, have dropped all burdens, have attained their purpose, have ended the fetters to existence,[25] and are liberated through right understanding. Bhikkhus such as these are living in this community of bhikkhus.

"Bhikkhus, living in this community are bhikkhus who are non-returners through having ended the five lower fetters, who are spontaneously arisen,[26] who will realize perfect coolness in that existence and by nature will never return from that world. Bhikkhus such as these are living in this community of bhikkhus.

"Bhikkhus, living in this community there are bhikkhus who are once-returners through having ended the three fetters[27] and lessened lust and hatred, who will come back to this world only once and then will put an end to *dukkha*. Bhikkhus such as these are living in this community of bhikkhus.

"Bhikkhus, living in this community are bhikkhus who are stream-enterers through having ended the three fetters, who by nature never will fall into evil again and are certain of future awak-ening. Bhikkhus such as these are in this community of bhikkhus.

"Bhikkhus, living in this community are bhikkhus who dwell devoted in practicing the cultivation of the four foundations of mindfulness (*satipaṭṭhāna*). Bhikkhus such as these are living in this community of bhikkhus.

"Bhikkhus, living in this community are bhikkhus who dwell devoted in practicing the cultivation of the four right efforts...[28]

...bhikkhus who dwell devoted in practicing the cultivation of the four bases of success...[29]

...bhikkhus who dwell devoted in practicing the cultivation of the five faculties...[30]

...bhikkhus who dwell devoted in practicing the cultivation of the five powers...[31]

...bhikkhus who dwell devoted in practicing the cultivation of the seven factors of awakening...[32]

...bhikkhus who dwell devoted in practicing the cultivation of the Noble Eightfold Path...[33]

...bhikkhus who dwell devoted in practicing the cultivation of friendliness (*mettā*)...

...bhikkhus who dwell devoted in practicing the cultivation of compassion (*karunā*)...

...bhikkhus who dwell devoted in practicing the cultivation of sympathetic joy (*muditā*)...

...bhikkhus who dwell devoted in practicing the cultivation of equanimity (*upekkhā*)...

...bhikkhus who dwell devoted in practicing the cultivation of the non-beautiful...[34]

...bhikkhus who dwell devoted in practicing the cultivation of the experience of impermanence (*aniccasaññā*). Bhikkhus such as these are living in this community of bhikkhus.

"Bhikkhus, living in this community are bhikkhus who dwell devoted in practicing the cultivation of mindfulness with breathing (*ānāpānasati*)."

MINDFULNESS WITH BREATHING

"Bhikkhus, *ānāpānasati*, which one has developed and made much of, has great fruit and great benefit. *Ānāpānasati*, which one has developed and made much of, perfects the four foundations of mindfulness. The four foundations of mindfulness, which one has developed and made much of, perfect the seven factors of awakening. The seven factors of awakening, which one has developed and made much of, perfect insight knowledge and liberation.

"Bhikkhus, how does *ānāpānasati*, which one has developed and made much of, have great fruit and great benefit?

"Bhikkhus, a bhikkhu within this training (*dhamma-vinaya*), having gone into the forest, to the base of a tree or to an empty dwelling, having sat cross-legged with his body erect, securely maintains mindfulness (*sati*). Ever mindful, that bhikkhu breathes in; ever mindful, he breathes out."

FIRST TETRAD

(1) "While breathing in long, he fully comprehends, 'I breathe in long.' While breathing out long, he fully comprehends, 'I breathe out long.'[35]

(2) "While breathing in short, he fully comprehends, 'I breathe in short.' While breathing out short, he fully comprehends, 'I breathe out short.'

(3) "He trains himself, 'Thoroughly experiencing all bodies, I shall breathe in.' He trains himself, 'Thoroughly experiencing all bodies, I shall breathe out.'[36]

(4) "He trains himself, 'Calming the body-conditioner, I shall breathe in.' He trains himself, 'Calming the body-conditioner, I shall breathe out.'"[37]

SECOND TETRAD

(5) "He trains himself, 'Thoroughly experiencing *pīti*, I shall breathe in.' He trains himself, 'Thoroughly experiencing *pīti*, I shall breathe out.'

(6) "He trains himself, 'Thoroughly experiencing *sukha*, I shall breathe in.' He trains himself, 'Thoroughly experiencing *sukha*, I shall breathe out.'

(7) "He trains himself, 'Thoroughly experiencing the mind-conditioner, I shall breathe in.' He trains himself, 'Thoroughly experiencing the mind-conditioner, I shall breathe out.'[38]

(8) "He trains himself, 'Calming the mind-conditioner, I shall breathe in.' He trains himself, 'Calming the mind-conditioner, I shall breathe out.'"[39]

THIRD TETRAD

(9) "He trains himself, 'Thoroughly experiencing the mind, I shall breathe in.' He trains himself, 'Thoroughly experiencing the mind, I shall breathe out.'[40]

(10) "He trains himself, 'Gladdening the mind, I shall breathe in.' He trains himself, 'Gladdening the mind, I shall breathe out.'[41]

(11) "He trains himself, 'Concentrating the mind, I shall breathe in.' He trains himself, 'Concentrating the mind, I shall breathe out.'[42]

(12) "He trains himself, 'Liberating the mind, I shall breathe in.' He trains himself, 'Liberating the mind, I shall breathe out.'"[43]

FOURTH TETRAD

(13) "He trains himself, 'Constantly contemplating impermanence, I shall breathe in.' He trains himself, 'Constantly contemplating impermanence, I shall breathe out.'[44]

(14) "He trains himself, 'Constantly contemplating fading away, I shall breathe in.' He trains himself, 'Constantly contemplating fading away, I shall breathe out.'[45]

(15) "He trains himself, 'Constantly contemplating quenching, I shall breathe in.' He trains himself, 'Constantly contemplating quenching, I shall breathe out.'[46]

(16) "He trains himself, 'Constantly contemplating tossing back, I shall breathe in.' He trains himself, 'Constantly contemplating tossing back, I shall breathe out.'"[47]

"Bhikkhus, this is how *ānāpānasati*, which one has developed and made much of, has great fruit and great benefit."

THE FOUR FOUNDATIONS OF MINDFULNESS (*SATIPAṬṬHĀNA*)

"Bhikkhus, how does *ānāpānasati*, which one has developed and made much of, perfect the four foundations of mindfulness?

"Bhikkhus, whenever a bhikkhu (1) while breathing in long fully comprehends: 'I breathe in long'; while breathing out long fully comprehends: 'I breathe out long'; or, (2) while breathing in short fully comprehends: 'I breathe in short'; while breathing out short fully comprehends: 'I breathe out short'; or, (3) trains himself: 'Thoroughly experiencing all bodies I shall breathe in...shall breathe out'; or, (4) trains himself: 'Calming the body-conditioner I shall breathe in...shall breathe out'; then that bhikkhu is considered one who lives constantly contemplating body in bodies, strives to burn up defilements, comprehends readily, and is mindful, in order to abandon all liking and disliking toward the world.[48]

"Bhikkhus, I say that the in-breaths and the out-breaths are certain bodies among all bodies. Bhikkhus, for this reason that bhikkhu is considered one who lives constantly contemplating body in bodies, strives to burn up defilements, comprehends readily, and is mindful, in order to abandon all liking and disliking toward the world.

"Bhikkhus, whenever a bhikkhu (5) trains himself: 'Thoroughly experiencing *pīti* I shall breathe in...shall breathe out'; or, (6) trains himself: 'Thoroughly experiencing *sukha* I shall breathe in...shall breathe out'; or, (7) trains himself: 'Thoroughly experiencing the mind-conditioner I shall breathe in...shall breathe out'; or, (8) trains himself: 'Calming the mind-conditioner I shall breathe in... shall breathe out'; then that bhikkhu is considered one who lives constantly contemplating feeling in feelings, strives to burn up defilements, comprehends readily, and is mindful, in order to abandon all liking and disliking toward the world.[49]

"Bhikkhus, I say that attending carefully in the mind to in-breaths and out-breaths is a certain feeling among all feelings. Bhikkhus, for this reason that bhikkhu is considered one who lives constantly contemplating feeling in feelings, strives to burn up defilements, comprehends readily, and is mindful, in order to abandon all liking and disliking toward the world.

"Bhikkhus, whenever a bhikkhu (9) trains himself: 'Thoroughly experiencing the mind I shall breathe in...shall breathe out'; or, (10) trains himself: 'Gladdening the mind I shall breathe in...shall breathe out'; or, (11) trains himself: 'Concentrating the mind I shall breathe in...shall breathe out'; or, (12) trains himself: 'Liberating the mind I shall breathe in...shall breathe out'; then that bhikkhu is considered one who lives constantly contemplating mind in the mind, strives to burn up defilements, comprehends readily, and is mindful, in order to abandon all liking and disliking toward the world.[50]

"Bhikkhus, I do not say that *ānāpānasati* is possible for a person who has straying mindfulness and lacks ready comprehension. Bhikkhus, for this reason that bhikkhu is considered one who lives constantly contemplating mind in the mind, strives to burn up defilements, comprehends readily, and is mindful, in order to abandon all liking and disliking toward the world.

"Bhikkhus, whenever a bhikkhu (13) trains himself: 'Constantly contemplating impermanence I shall breathe in...shall breathe out'; or, (14) trains himself: 'Constantly contemplating fading away I shall breathe in...shall breathe out'; or, (15) trains himself: 'Constantly contemplating quenching I shall breathe in...shall breathe out'; or, (16) trains himself: 'Constantly contemplating tossing back I shall breathe in...shall breathe out'; then that bhikkhu is considered one who lives constantly contemplating Dhamma in *dhammas*, strives to burn up defilements, comprehends readily, and is mindful, in order to abandon all liking and disliking toward the world.[51]

"That bhikkhu looks on with perfect equanimity because he has seen with wisdom the abandoning of all liking and disliking toward the world. Bhikkhus, for this reason that bhikkhu is considered one who lives constantly contemplating Dhamma in *dhammas*, strives to burn up defilements, comprehends readily, and is mindful, in order to abandon all liking and disliking toward the world.

"Bhikkhus, this is how *ānāpānasati*, which one has developed and made much of, perfects the four foundations of mindfulness."

THE SEVEN FACTORS OF AWAKENING (*BOJJHAṄGA*)

"Bhikkhus, how do the four foundations of mindfulness, which one has developed and made much of, perfect the seven factors of awakening?

"Bhikkhus, whenever a bhikkhu is one who lives constantly contemplating body in bodies[52]…is one who lives constantly contemplating feeling in feelings…is one who lives constantly contemplating mind in the mind…is one who lives constantly contemplating Dhamma in *dhammas*, strives to burn up defilements, comprehends readily, and is mindful, in order to abandon all liking and disliking toward the world; then the *sati* of that bhikkhu thus established is natural and unconfused.

"Bhikkhus, whenever the *sati* of that bhikkhu thus established is natural and unconfused, then the mindfulness enlightenment factor (*sati-sambojjhaṅga*) is engaged by that bhikkhu; he develops it further and finally its development in him is perfected. That bhikkhu, when mindful in such a way, selects, takes up, and scrutinizes these *dhammas* with wisdom.

"Bhikkhus, whenever a bhikkhu is mindful in such a way, selects, takes up, and scrutinizes these *dhammas* with wisdom; then the investigation of the *dhammas'* factor of awakening (*dhamma-vicaya-sambojjhaṅga*) is engaged by that bhikkhu; he develops it further and finally its development in him is perfected. When that bhikkhu selects, takes up, and scrutinizes these *dhammas* with wisdom, unwavering effort is engaged by him.

"Bhikkhus, whenever unwavering energy is engaged by a bhikkhu who selects, takes up, and scrutinizes these *dhammas* with wisdom;

then the energy factor of awakening (*viriya-sambojjhanga*) is engaged by him; he develops it further and its development in him is perfected. When energy is engaged by that bhikkhu, non-sensual *pīti* arises.[53]

"Bhikkhus, whenever non-sensual *pīti* arises in the bhikkhu who has engaged energy, then the contentment factor of awakening (*pīti-sambojjhanga*) is engaged by that bhikkhu; he develops it further and its development in him is perfected. When that bhikkhu's mind is contented, both body is calmed and mind is calmed.

"Bhikkhus, whenever both the body and the mind of a bhikkhu who is contented are calm, then the tranquility factor of awakening (*passaddhi-sambojjhanga*) is engaged by him; he develops it further and its development in him is perfected. When that bhikkhu's body is calmed, there is joy and the mind becomes concentrated.

"Bhikkhus, whenever the mind of a bhikkhu whose body is calmed and who is joyful becomes concentrated, then the concentration factor of awakening (*samādhi-sambojjhanga*) is engaged by that bhikkhu; he develops it further and its development in him is perfected. That bhikkhu looks upon that concentrated mind with perfect equanimity.

"Bhikkhus, whenever a bhikkhu looks upon that concentrated mind with perfect equanimity, then the equanimity factor of awakening (*upekkhā-sambojjhanga*) is engaged by that bhikkhu; he develops it further and its development in him is perfected.

"Bhikkhus, this is how the four foundations of mindfulness, which one has developed and made much of, perfect the seven factors of awakening."[54]

KNOWLEDGE AND LIBERATION

"Bhikkhus, how do the seven factors of awakening, which one has developed and made much of, perfect knowledge (*vijjā*) and liberation (*vimutti*)?

"Bhikkhus, a bhikkhu in this training develops *sati-sambojjhanga*, which depends on *viveka* (solitude, aloneness), which depends on *virāga* (fading away), which depends on *nirodhā* (quenching), which leads to *vossagga* (dropping away, letting go).[55]

"He develops *dhammavicaya-sambojjhanga*, which depends on *viveka*, on *virāga*, on *nirodhā*, and leads to *vossagga*.

"He develops *viriya sambojjhaṅga*, which depends on *viveka*, on *virāga*, on *nirodhā*, and leads to *vossagga*.

"He develops *pīti-sambojjhaṅga*, which depends on *viveka*, on *virāga*, on *nirodhā*, and leads to *vossagga*.

"He develops *passaddhi-sambojjhaṅga*, which depends on *viveka*, on *virāga*, on *nirodhā*, and leads to *vossagga*.

"He develops *samādhi-sambojjhaṅga*, which depends on *viveka*, on *virāga*, on *nirodhā*, and leads to *vossagga*.

"He develops *upekkhā-sambojjhaṅga*, which depends on *viveka*, on *virāga*, on *nirodhā*, and leads to *vossagga*.

"Bhikkhus, this is how the seven factors of awakening, which one has developed and made much of, perfect knowledge and liberation."[56]

After the Exalted One had spoken, the bhikkhus were contented and rejoiced at the Exalted One's words.

Notes

1. In some contexts, *dhamma* merely means "thing"; in this instance, we do not capitalize it. However, when *Dhamma* refers to "the secret of nature for developing life," then to distinguish it from *dhamma* as "thing," we have capitalized it.

2. The Thai word *kuab-kum* is used throughout this book. It can be translated "to regulate; to control or confine; to master; to oversee, supervise, or superintend." When one of these translations appear, all of the rest should be understood. In all cases, *kuab-kum* depends on *sati* and wisdom, never on force or willpower.

3. The *wat* is the traditional place for Thai travelers to rest and sleep, but nowadays it is no longer used by merchants and government employees, who prefer hotels with their modern amenities.

4. At Suan Mokkh, to the right and past the *hin kong*, where Ajahn Buddhadāsa lectured, this theater is one of the many vehicles for sharing Dhamma. It not only contains relief sculptures copied from the oldest Buddhist shrines in India that tell the life of the Buddha but also many Dhamma paintings from various Buddhist traditions.

5. The fundamental dualism that distracts us from the middle way and causes us to become caught up in attachment, selfishness, and *dukkha*.

6. Even those who use kneelers and chairs must strive to follow these principles: stability, weight evenly distributed, and spine straight.

7. The *ānāpānasati* form of *prāṇayāma* is not an overt or forced "control" of the breath. It is a subtle and patient guide or regulator, a feather rather than a hammer.

8. However, this is not yet the highest degree of control.

9. See chapter four.

10. The *hin kong* lecture area is covered by sand and is full of trees, rocks, and boulders. It is to these boulders that Ajahn Buddhadāsa refers here.

11. See Ajahn Buddhadāsa's *Practical Dependent Origination* (Bangkok: The Dhamma Study and Practice Group, 1992) and forthcoming translations on the subject. See also P. A. Payutto, *Dependent Origination: The Buddhist Law of Conditionality* (Bangkok: Buddha-Dhamma Foundation, 1994).

12. The reader can find a full translation of this sutta on pp. 113–122.

13. *Dhammapada*, 184.

14. The *Mahāsatipaṭṭhāna Sutta* (D.ii.22) and the somewhat shorter *Satipaṭṭhāna Sutta* (M.i.10), which follows the same pattern as the *Mahā* but is less detailed and extensive.

15. Whether these methods are correct and useful, or not, is not at issue here.

16. These quoted paragraphs are from a retreat talk given by Ajahn Buddhadāsa on 5 April 1987.

17. Ibid.

18. From a retreat talk given by Ajahn Buddhadāsa on 5 May 1987.

19. From the talk of 5 April 1987.

20. The translator is not well-versed in Pali. This rendering is based on Ajahn Buddhadāsa's translation from Pali to Thai and his line-by-line explanation of that translation. Previous English translations by I. B. Horner, Bhikkhu Ñāṇamoli, and Bhikkhu Nāgasena have been consulted as well.

21. *Bhagavā*, a frequent epithet of the Buddha, was a common form of address in India. Buddhists, however, reserve it for the Buddha. It is often translated as "Blessed One."

22. Then the capital of the kingdom of Kosala, which was located between the Himalayas and the Ganges River, Sāvatthi was the geographical center of the Buddha's teaching during his lifetime. He spent twenty-five of forty-five rains residences there.

23. The third month of the four-month-long rainy season.

24. Conditions that ferment in and flow out or erupt from the mind's depths. Usually given as three: *kāmāsava*, eruption of sensuality; *bhavāsava*, eruption of becoming; and *avijjāsava*, eruption of ignorance.

Sometimes a fourth is added: *diṭṭhasava*, eruption of views. The ending of the *āsāvas* is synonymous with perfect awakening. (Other translations are "cankers, taints, influxes.")

25. The ten *saṁyojana* that bind beings to the cycles of becoming are personality belief, uncertainty about the path, superstitious use of rituals and practices, sensuous lust, ill will, lust for fine material existence, lust for immaterial existence, conceit, restlessness, and ignorance.

26. *Oppātika,* born instantly and fully mature without going through the process of conception, gestation, infancy, and childhood—that is, instantaneous mental birth (not necessarily "rebirth" in the conventional sense).

27. The first three of the ten *saṁyojana.*

28. The four *sammappadhāna* are: (1) the effort to prevent or avoid unwholesome states that have not arisen; (2) the effort to overcome or abandon unwholesome states that have arisen; (3) the effort to develop wholesome states that have not arisen; and (4) the effort to maintain wholesome states that have arisen.

29. The four *iddhipāda* are: *chanda*, love of duty; *viriya*, effort in duty; *citta*, thoughtfulness regarding duty; and *vimaṁsā*, investigation of duty through practicing Dhamma.

30. The five *indriya* are: *saddhā*, confidence, faith; *viriya*, effort, energy; *sati*, mindfulness; *samādhi*, concentration; and *paññā*, wisdom.

31. The five *bala* have the same names as the five *indriya*, but function differently. The five *bala* function as powers that provide the strength needed to overcome and withstand their opposites (i.e., lack of confidence, laziness, carelessness, distraction, and delusion.) The five *indriya* are the chief sovereign or controlling faculties that lead each group of *dhammas* as they deal with their opposites (e.g., lack of confidence).

32. The seven *bojjhanga* are: *sati*, mindfulness; *dhammavicaya*, investigation of dhamma; *viriya*, effort; *pīti*, contentment; *passaddhi*, tranquility; *samādhi*, concentration; and *upekkhā*, equanimity. They are discussed in detail later in the *Sutta.*

33. The *ariya-aṭṭhaṅgika-magga* consists of right understanding, right aspiration, right speech, right action, right livelihood, right effort, right mindfulness, and right concentration.

34. *Asubha-bhāvanā* is used to counteract and overcome lust.

35. The words "fully comprehends" mean that there is *sati-sampajañña* (mindfulness and ready comprehension) with every moment of noting the in-breaths and out-breaths in all their aspects.

36. "Bodies" (*kāya*) refers to the breath in its aspect of conditioning the flesh-body. "Experiencing all bodies" *(sabbakāyaṁ paṭisaṁvetī)* refers to directly knowing the breath's characteristics—such as short or long, coarse or fine, calm or agitated—knowing how it conditions the flesh-body, knowing its natural processes of change, and knowing other relevant details about the breathing.

37. As the breath is calmed and refined, the conditioning of the body is calmed, and the mind becomes calm and concentrated to the extent, finally, of *jhāna*.

38. Know how feelings (*vedanā*), especially the pleasant ones, condition the mind with every breath.

39. Be able to decrease the ability of the feelings to condition the mind. Decrease their conditioning of the mind until there is nothing that is conditioning it, that is, there is no feeling, no perception (*saññā*), and no thought (*vitakka*) at that time.

40. Know the exact state of mind at that moment, whether it is spotless or darkened, calm or agitated, prepared to work (contemplate Dhamma) or not ready, or whatever state may arise.

41. Be able to amuse the mind with Dhamma in various ways.

42. Expertly observe the qualities and extent of the mind's *samādhi*.

43. Observe the qualities and extent of the mind's freedom from attachment.

44. With every breath, use the correctly concentrated mind to contemplate impermanence continuously, until realizing the unsatisfactoriness, selflessness, voidness, and thusness of all conditioned things.

45. With every breath, examine the state of the mind being disenchanted with, weary of, and dispassionate toward the things it has desired and grasped.

46. Examine the ceasing of attachment and realize it as being *nibbāna*, the ceasing and quenching of *dukkha*, then cherish it as the mind's regular object.

47. Realize that all conditioned things have been freed from attachment. This condition arises in the moments of path (*magga*) and path fruition (*phala*).

48. "Contemplating body in bodies" means seeing the truth of bodies directly within bodies themselves and seeing all the components of the body as being small bodies within the collective body. The breath is one body. It conditions all kinds of bodies, whether physical or mental, beginning with the flesh-body up to the joy of *jhāna*. Contemplate these bodies until there is no more attachment to any of them.

49. Contemplate feelings in the same way that bodies have been contemplated. Contemplate *pīti* and *sukha* until there is no attachment to any feelings anywhere.

50. Contemplate the mind in the same way as bodies and feelings were contemplated, until there is no attachment to any mind states.

51. Contemplate the truth of Dhamma in all things (*dhammas*) until there is no attachment left to any *dhamma*, from the lowest to the highest, including *nibbāna*.

52. The original Pali explains how all seven factors can develop upon each one of the four foundations of mindfulness, with each foundation considered separately. Here, for the sake of brevity, we have grouped all four foundations together.

53. This *pīti* is pure and associated with Dhamma; it has nothing to do with the physical senses. Such *pīti* occurs during *jhāna* and while realizing Dhamma.

54. The *bojjhaṅga* develop as follows. Mindfulness fixes on a specific thing, and investigation of *dhammas* examines it in detail, with energy and effort, until contentment arises. Then, the mind calms until it becomes tranquil and is concentrated in contemplating the object. Equanimity firmly and unwaveringly watches over and guards that concentration, and the penetration of and awakening to Dhamma continues by itself until complete.

55. Here *vossagga* means no longer becoming attached to previous objects of attachment, because the mind is disenchanted with them and now inclines toward the quenching of *dukkha*, namely, *nibbāna*. *Viveka*, *virāga*, *nirodha*, and *vossagga* are synonyms of *nibbāna*.

56. *Vijjā* is the insight knowledge of the path (*magga-ñāṇa*) that follows

upon the insights experienced through the practice of ānāpānasati. Its function is to penetrate thoroughly and destroy ignorance (*avijjā*). *Vimutti* is insight knowledge of fruition (*phala-ñāṇa*), the result of the path having done its work of clearing away *avijjā*. It is the mind's direct experience of being liberated from *dukkha*.

Glossary

AN ABUNDANCE OF PALI TERMS are used in this manual. This reflects Ajahn Buddhadāsa's advice that sincere student-practitioners of Buddhism should be familiar with the most important Pali terms and their correct meanings, for they offer a precision, clarity, and depth that English equivalents may lack. Most of the terms used here are explained within the text. This glossary is provided for easy reference and additional information. We also include some key English terms so that they may be checked with their Pali equivalents. As we have followed Ajahn Buddhadāsa's explanations, some of the translations and definitions found here may differ from those found in other books. Thus, to make the most of this manual, you need to understand how Ajahn Buddhadāsa uses these terms. Even those who have studied Pali may find some helpful insights here.

Both Pali and English terms are listed in alphabetical order according to the English language. Pali terms are defined and explained. When appropriate, we cite textual passages in which specific terms are discussed. Spelling is according to standard Thai usage (see *Dictionary of Buddhism*, Phra Rājavoramuni [P. A. Payutto], Bangkok: Mahāculalongkorn Rājavidayālai, 1985). English terms are not defined. You can find their meaning under the given Pali equivalent. In any case, it is important that you be wary of English terms found here and elsewhere. They seldom correspond exactly to the Pali terms they are meant to translate, and they often carry inappropriate connotations. It is always best to learn the Pali terms and their proper meanings. Terms that appear only once or are of minor importance may not be included in this glossary. All Pali terms used in the explanations below are themselves also explained in their own glossary entries.

Ācariya. Teacher, master.

Ādīnava. Penalty, disadvantage, peril, harm: the hook within the bait (*assāda*); the lowly, harmful, negative, or wicked aspect of something.

Āna. In-breath, inhalation, breathing in. The corresponding verb is *assasati,* to breathe in.

Ānāpānasati. Mindfulness with breathing in and out: to note, investigate, and contemplate a *dhamma* (thing, fact, truth) while being mindful of every in-breath and out-breath. In the Buddha's complete system of *ānāpānasati*, a natural progression of sixteen lessons or *dhammas* are practiced in order to explore fully the *satipaṭṭhāna* and realize liberation.

Anattā, anattatā. Not-self, selflessness, non-selfhood: the fact that all things without exception, including *nibbāna*, are not-self and lack any essence or substance that could properly be called a "self." This truth does not deny the existence of "things" (see *dhamma*) but denies that they can be owned or controlled or be an owner or controller in any but a relative, conventional sense. *Anattā* is the third fundamental characteristic of *sankhāra*. *Anattā* is an inevitable result of *aniccaṁ*. All things are what they are and are not-self. *Anattā* is more or less a synonym of *suññatā*.

Aniccaṁ, anicca, aniccatā. Impermanence, instability, flux: conditioned things are ever-changing, in ceaseless transformation, and constantly arising, manifesting, and extinguishing. All concocted things decay and pass away. This is the first fundamental characteristic of *sankhāra*.

Anupassanā. Contemplation: sustained, nonverbal, nonreactive, uninvolved, even-minded scrutiny of a *dhamma*, the essence of meditation. The four *satipaṭṭhāna* are the necessary objects of contemplation, thus: *kāyānupassanā*, contemplation of body, *vedanānupassanā*, contemplation of feeling, *cittānupassanā*, contemplation of mind, *dhammānupassanā*, contemplation of Dhamma. True *anupassanā* arises from *vipassanā* (insight).

Apāna. Out-breath, exhalation, breathing out. The verb form is *passasati*, to breathe out.

Arahant. Worthy one, fully awakened being, perfected human being: a living being completely free and void of all attachment, *kilesa*, self-belief, selfishness, danger, and *dukkha*. To speak of such a one in terms of entering *nibbāna* or not, as is done in Mahāyāna polemics, is a misunderstanding of the Buddha's teaching.

Ariya-sacca. Noble truths: there are four that together are one truth, namely: *dukkha*, the cause of *dukkha*, which is craving, the end of *dukkha*, which occurs when craving ends, and the path of practice that leads to the end of *dukkha*. The *arahant*, the truly enlightened being, has penetrated these truths thoroughly.

Assāda. Bait, charm, attractiveness: the tasty morsel hiding the hook (*ādīnava*): the lovely, satisfying, infatuating, positive quality of something.

Attā. Self, ego, (Sanskrit, *atman*): the instinctual feeling and illusion (mental concoction) that there is some personal, separate "I" in life. Although theories about self abound, all are mere speculation about something that exists only in our imagination. In a conventional sense, the *attā* can be a useful concept, belief, or perception, but it ultimately has no validity. That conventional "self" is not-self (*anattā*). No individual, independent, inherently self-existing, free-willing substance can be found anywhere, whether within or without human life (the five *khandhas*) and experience.

Attachment. *Upādāna.*

Avijjā. Not-knowing, ignorance, wrong knowledge, foolishness: the lack, partial or total, of *vijjā* (correct knowledge). *Avijjā* has two levels: the lack of knowledge that comes with birth, and the wrong knowledge conditioned and accumulated later.

Āyatana. Sense media, connecters: there are two aspects or sets of *āyatana*, internal and external. The internal *āyatana* are the eyes, ears, nose, tongue, body, and mind (mental-sense): that is, the six sense doors, the sense organs, and their corresponding portions of the nervous system. The external *āyatana* are forms, sounds, smells, tastes, touches, and mental-concerns: that is, the concerns or objects of sensory experience. *Nibbāna* is described as an *āyatana*, an unconditioned *āyatana*.

Bhāvanā. Development, cultivation, meditation: to produce or make happen. In particular, to cultivate skillful, wholesome qualities of mind. The term *citta-bhāvanā* (mental development) is preferable to the vague and often confusing "meditation." The Buddha mentioned four *bhāvanā: kāya, sīla, citta,* and *paññā.*

Body. *Kāya.*

Bojjhaṅga. Factors of awakening, enlightenment factors: these seven mental factors must be perfected, in succession, for the mind to be liberated. First, *sati* (mindfulness) fixes on a certain *dhamma.* Then, *dhamma-vicaya* (analysis of *dhamma*) investigates that thing subtly, precisely, and profoundly. Next, *viriya* (effort, energy) arises, which leads to *pīti* (contentment). Then, the mind develops *passaddhi* (tranquility) because of that contentment, such that there is *samādhi* (concentration) in the contemplation of that *dhamma.* Lastly, *samādhi* is continuously and evenly guarded by *upekkhā* (equanimity) as the truth of that *dhamma* and all Dhamma is penetrated and realized.

Buddha. The Knowing, Awakened, Fully Blossomed One, especially the Perfectly Self-Awakened One (*sammāsambuddha*). Specifically, Buddha refers to the historical prophet under whom Buddhism was founded, otherwise referred to as *Bhāgavā* (Blessed One) by followers and Samana Gotama by others. Generally, any arahant is also a buddha, that is, one who is awakened from ignorance and the sleep of egoism. Finally, a buddha is the ultimate potential of all human beings. The primary qualities (*guṭa*) of a buddha are wisdom, purity, and compassion.

Citta. Mind, heart, consciousness: all aspects, qualities, and functions of the living being that are not material-physical. In a more limited sense, *citta* is the consciousness-potential when it "thinks." *Citta* is also used to name that which is defiled by *kilesa* and realizes *nibbāna*. Further, *citta* is the maker of *kamma* or doer of actions and receives the fruits of those actions; that is, *citta* is the creator of all that we do and experience. *Citta* requires a physical structure, the body, and functions together with it. (Compare with *mano* and *viññāta*.)

Citta-sankhāra. Mind-conditioner: the *vedanā* that conditions and concocts the *citta*.

Concentration. *Samādhi*, calm-collectedness.

Craving. *Taṭhā*, foolish desire, blind want.

Defilement. *Kilesa*: namely, greed, hatred, and delusion.

dhamma. Thing, nature, things: both conditioned phenomena and unconditioned noumenon.

Dhamma (Sanskrit, *Dharma*). Truth, nature, law, order, duty: the secret of nature which must be understood in order to develop life to the highest possible purpose and benefit. The four primary meanings of *Dhamma* are nature, the law and truth of nature, the duty to be performed in accordance with natural law, and the results or benefits that arise from the performance of that duty.

Dhamma-jāti. Nature: that which exists within itself, by itself, of itself, and as its own law. *Dhamma-jāti* encompasses all things, both human and non-human.

Dosa. Hatred, ill-will: the second category of *kilesa*; includes anger, aversion, dislike, and all other negative thoughts and emotions; characterized by the mind pushing away an object.

Dukkha, dukkham. Stress, suffering, misery, unsatisfactoriness, pain: literally, "hard to endure, difficult to bear." In its limited sense, *dukkha* is the quality of experience that results when the mind is conditioned by *avijjā* into craving, attachment, egoism, and selfishness. This feeling takes on forms such as disappointment, dissatisfaction, frustration, agitation, anguish, dis-ease, despair—from the crudest to the subtlest levels. In its universal sense, *dukkham* is the inherent condition of unsatisfactoriness, ugliness, and misery in all impermanent, conditioned things (*sankhāra*). This second fundamental characteristic is the result of *aniccam*: impermanent things cannot satisfy our wants and desires no matter how hard we try (and cry). The inherent decay and dissolution of things is misery.

Ego. *Atta.*

Ekaggatā. One-pointedness: to have a single peak, focus, or pinnacle. The state in which the flow of mental energy is gathered and focused on a single object, especially an exalted one, such as *nibbāna.*

Emancipation. *Vimutti.*

Feeling. *Vedanā,* feelings. (Note: Sometimes the word "feeling" can denote other things that are not *vedanā,* such as "mood, emotion, or tactile sensation.")

Idappaccayatā. The law of conditionality (or causality), the law of nature: literally, "the state of having this as condition." All natural laws can be seen in *idappaccayatā.* Because all creation, preservation, and destruction occurs through this law, it can be called the "Buddhist God."

Jhāna. Peering, contemplation, absorption, meditation: one-pointed focus of the mind on an object, for the purpose of developing tranquility, or on impermanence, for the purpose of developing insight. *Jhāna* is understood as both an activity of the mind (focusing, peering, looking intently and deeply) and the results of that activity. These results are of two types: (1) the *rūpajhānas,* the *jhānas* dependent on the forms of material objects, mental absorption into objects of finer materiality; and (2) the *arūpajhānas,* the *jhānas* dependent on immaterial or formless objects. The *jhānas* are listed below. The first four are the *rūpajhānas,* and the second four are the *arūpajhānas.*

paṭhama-jhāna, which has five factors: noting (the object), experiencing (the object), rapture, joy, and one-pointedness.

dutiya-jhāna, which has three factors: rapture, joy, and one-pointedness.

tatiya-jhāna, which has two factors: joy and one-pointedness.

catuttha-jhāna, which has two factors: equanimity and one-pointedness.

ākāsānañcāyatana, which is the experience of infinite space.

viññāṭañcāyatana, which is the experience of infinite consciousness.

ākiñcaññāyatana, which is the experience of infinite nothingness.

nevasaññānāsannāyatana, which is the experience that is neither-experience-nor-nonexperience.

These eight levels of successively more refined *samādhi* are very useful but are not necessary for the successful practice of *ānāpānasati*.

Jhānaṅga. Factors of *jhāna*: the functions or qualities of mind that exist within *jhāna*. In the first *jhāna* there are five factors: *vitakka*, noting the object or *nimitta*; *vicāra*, experiencing the object; *pīti*, rapture, contentment; *sukha*, joy; and *ekaggatā*, one-pointedness. The other *jhāna* have successively fewer factors. (See *jhāna*.)

Kalyāna-mitta. Good friend, noble companion: a spiritual guide and advisor.

Kāma. Sensuality, sexuality: strong desire and its objects. Seeking and indulging in sensual pleasures; not to be confused with *kamma*.

Kamma (Sanskrit, *karma*). Action: actions of body, speech, and mind arising from wholesome and unwholesome volitions. Good intentions and actions bring good results; bad intentions and actions bring bad results. Unintentional actions are not *kamma*, are not Dhammically significant. *Kamma* has nothing to do with fate, luck, or fortune, nor does it mean the result of *kamma*.

Kāya. Body, group, collection, heap, squad: something composed of various elements, organs, or parts. Generally used for the physical body; refers to either the whole body or its parts ("breath-body" and "flesh-body").

Kāya-sankhāra. Body-conditioner: the breath, which conditions and influences the body directly. (Also can be translated "body-condition.")

Khandha. Aggregates, groups, heaps, categories: the five basic functions that constitute a human life. These groups are not entities in themselves; they are merely the categories into which all aspects of our lives can be analyzed (except *nibbāna*). None of them are a "self," nor do they have anything to do with selfhood, nor is there any "self" apart from them. The five are *rūpa-khandha*, form aggregate (corporeality);

vedanā-khandha, feeling aggregate; *saññā-khandha*, perception aggregate (including memory, recognition, discrimination, evaluation); *sankhāra-khandha*, thought aggregate (including emotion); and *viññāta-khandha*, sense consciousness aggregate. When they become the basis for attachment, the five become the *upādāna-khandha*.

Kilesa. Defilements, impurities: all the things that dull, darken, dirty, defile, agitate, stress, and sadden the *citta*. The three categories of *kilesa* are *lobha, dosa,* and *moha.*

Lobha. Greed: the first category of *kilesa*; includes erotic love, lust, miserliness, and all other "positive" thoughts and emotions; characterized by the mind pulling in an object. See *rāga.*

Loka. World: that which must break, shatter, and disintegrate.

Lokiya. Worldly, mundane, worldly conditions: to be trapped within and beneath the world; to be of the world.

Lokuttara. Transcendent, above and beyond the world, supramundane: to be free of worldly conditions although living in the world.

Lust. *Rāga.*

Magga. Path, way: the Noble Eightfold Path, the middle way out of all *dukkha.*

Magga-phala-nibbāna. Path, fruition, and *nibbāna*: this compound refers to the three activities that occur in rapid succession in the realization of Dhamma. *Magga* (path) is the activity of *vipassanā* cutting through defilements. *Phala* (fruit) is the successful completion of that cutting, the result of *magga*. *Nibbāna* is the coolness that appears once the defilements are cut. (Although these three terms appear separately throughout the Pali texts and are commonly grouped in the commentaries, their compound is found only in Thai.)

Mahaggatā. Superiority, great-mindedness: a superior, better than usual state (of mind).

Mano. Mind-sense, mind: the name given to the consciousness-element when it feels, experiences, knows, and is aware; mind as inner *āyatana* (sense organ). (Compare with *citta* and *viññāta*.)

Māra. Tempter, demon, devil; literally, "killer of goodness": often personified, the real tempters and murderers are the defilements.

Mind. *Citta* or *mano* or "*viññāṭa*," depending on the aspect referred to.

Mindfulness. *Sati.*

Moha. Delusion: the third category of *kilesa*; includes stupidity, fear, worry, confusion, doubt, envy, infatuation, hope, and expectation; characterized by the mind spinning around its object.

Nibbāna. Coolness: the ultimate goal of Buddhist practice and the highest achievement of humanity, beyond birth and death, good and evil. *Nibbāna* manifests fully when the fires of *kilesa*, attachment, selfishness, and *dukkha* are completely and finally quenched. *Nibbāna* is to be realized in this lifetime and should never be confused with death.

Nibbuto. Coolness, one who is cooled: a coolness that occurs when, either spontaneously or through correct Dhamma practice, the *kilesa* subside temporarily. *Sāmāyika-nibbāna* (temporary coolness) and *tadanga-nibbāna* (coincidental coolness) are types of *nibbuto*.

Nimitta. Image, sign, imaginary object: in the context of *ānāpānasati* practice, *nimitta* refers to a mentally created image that arises out of concentration upon the guarding point and that is used to develop *samādhi* further in step four. There are three stages: the initial image; images manipulated as a training exercise; and the final image, which is neutral, refined, and soothing, and used as a basis for *jhāna*.

Nirodhā. Quenching, cessation, extinction: a synonym for *nibbāna*, the end of attachment and *dukkha*. In Buddhism, *nirodhā* always refers to the cessation of ignorance, clinging, and *dukkha*, not to the death of the human being. The lesson of step fifteen.

Nivaraṭa. Hindrances, obstacles: semi-defilements that get in the way of success in any endeavor, especially mental development. The five hindrances are *kāmachandha*, sensuousness; *vyāpāda*, aversion: *thīnamiddha*, sloth and torpor; *uddhacca-kukkucca*, restlessness and agitation; and *vicikicchā*, doubt. (Do not confuse *nivaraṭa* with *nirvāna*, the Sanskrit *nibbāna*.)

Paññā. Wisdom, insight, intuitive wisdom: correct understanding of the truth needed to quench *dukkha*. *Paññā* is the third *sikkhā* (training) and the beginning of the Noble Eightfold Path. *Paññā* (rather than faith or willpower) is the characteristic quality of Buddhism.

Paṭicca-samuppāda. Dependent co-origination, conditioned co-arising: the profound and detailed causal succession, and its description, that concocts *dukkha*. Because of ignorance (*avijjā*), there is concocting (*sankhāra*); because of concocting, there is sense consciousness (*viññāta*); because of sense consciousness there is mind and body (*nāma-rūpa*); because of mind and body there is sense-media (*salāyatana*); because of sense-media there is sense-contact (*phassa*); because of sense-contact there is feeling (*vedanā*); because of feeling there is craving (*taṭhā*); because of craving there is attachment (*upādāna*); because of attachment there is becoming (*bhava*); because of becoming there is birth (*jāti*); because of birth, there is aging and death (*jāra-māraṭa*); and thus arises the entire mass of *dukkha*.

Paṭinissagga. Throwing back, giving up, relinquishment: to stop claiming things as "I" and "mine," and return them to Dhamma-Nature. The lesson of step sixteen.

Phassa. Contact, sense experience: the meeting and working together of inner *āyatana*, outer *āyatana*, and the *viññāna* dependent on them: for example, eye, form, and eye-consciousness. There is *phassa* when a sensual stimulus has a sufficient impact upon the mind to draw a response, either positive or negative, beginning with *vedanā*. There are six kinds of *phassa* corresponding to the six senses.

Pīti. Contentment, satisfaction, rapture: the excited happiness (pleasant *vedanā*) that arises when one is successful in something. *Pīti* is the lesson of step five.

Prana (Sanskrit), *paṇa* (Pali). Breath, life force, life: that which sustains and nurtures life.

Praṇāyāma (Sanskrit). Control of the *prana*, breath control.

Rāga. Lust: desire to get or have. *Rāga* can be sexual or sensual, material, and immaterial, depending on its object. (See *lobha*.)

Sacca. Truth.

Sacca-dhamma. Truth, fact, reality.

Samādhi. Concentration, collectedness, mental calmness and stability: the gathering together, focusing, and integration of the mental flow. Proper *samādhi* has the qualities of purity, clarity, stability, strength, readiness, flexibility, and gentleness. It is perfected in *ekaggatā* and *jhāna*. The supreme *samādhi* is the one-pointed mind with *nibbāna* as its sole concern or object. *Samādhi* is the second *sikkhā*.

Sampajañña. Wisdom-in-action, ready comprehension, clear comprehension: the specific application of *paññā* as required in a given situation.

Sangha. Community: the community of the Buddha's followers who practice thoroughly, directly, insightfully, and correctly. *Sangha* includes lay women, lay men, nuns, and monks.

Sankhāra. Conditioned thing, concoction, phenomenon, formation: anything depends on other things or conditions for its existence. There are three aspects of *sankhāra*: concocter, conditioner, the cause of conditioning; concoction, condition, the result of conditioning; and the activity or process of concocting and conditioning.

Santi. Peace, spiritual tranquility.

Sāsanā. Religion: the behavior and practice that binds the human being to the supreme entity (whatever we name it).

Sati. Mindfulness, recollection, reflective awareness: the mind's ability to recall, know, and contemplate itself. *Sati* is the vehicle or transport mechanism for *paññā*; without *sati*, wisdom cannot be developed, retrieved, or applied. *Sati* is not memory, although the two are related. Nor is it mere heedfulness or carefulness. *Sati* allows us to be aware of what we are about to do. It is characterized by speed and agility.

Satipaṭṭhāna. Foundations or applications of mindfulness: the four bases to which *sati* must be applied in mental development. Life is investigated through these four subjects of spiritual study: *kāya, vedanā, citta,* and Dhamma.

Sikkhā. Training: the three aspects of the one path, of the middle way. All Buddhist practices fit within the three *sikkhā*: *sīla, samādhi,* and *paññā*.

Sīla. Morality, virtue, normality: verbal and bodily action in accordance with Dhamma. Much more than following rules or precepts, true *sīla* comes with wisdom and is undertaken joyfully; its essence is non-harming of others and oneself. The first *sikkhā*.

Sukha. Joy, happiness, bliss: literally, "easy to bear"; tranquil, soothing, pleasant *vedanā*. *Sukha* results from *pīti*, which stimulates, and is the lesson of step six.

Suññatā. Voidness, emptiness: the state of being void and free of selfhood, soul, ego, or anything that could be taken to be "I" or "mine"; also, the state of being void and free of defilement.

Tanha. Craving, blind want, foolish desire: the cause of *dukkha* (second *ariya-sacca*), not to be confused with "wise want" (*sammā-sankappa*, right aspiration). *Tanha* is conditioned by foolish *vedanā* and, in turn, concocts *upādāna.*

Tathatā. Thusness, suchness, just-like-thatness: neither this nor that, the reality of non-duality. Things are just as they are (impermanent, unsatisfactory, and not-self) regardless of our likes and dislikes, suppositions and beliefs, hopes and memories.

Upādāna. Attachment, clinging, grasping: to hold onto something foolishly, to regard things as "I" and "mine," to take things personally.

Vedanā. Feeling, sensation: the mental quality that colors sense experiences (*phassa*). There are three kinds: *sukha-vedanā*, pleasant, nice, agreeable, delicious feeling; *dukkha-vedanā*, unpleasant, disagreeable, painful feeling; and *adukkhamassukha-vedana*, neither-unpleasant-nor-pleasant, indeterminate feeling. *Vedanā* is conditioned by *phassa* (sense contact). If *vedanā* arises through ignorance, it will concoct craving. If *vedanā* arises with wisdom, it will be harmless or beneficial. This subtle activity of mind (not physical sensation) is not emotion, nor is it the more complicated aspects of the English word "feeling." (Sometimes the word "feeling" must be used to translate Thai and Pali words other than *vedanā*.)

Vijjā. Knowledge, insight knowledge, wisdom: correct knowledge about the way things really are. Its perfection destroys *avijjā*. Synonymous with *paññā.*

Vimutti. Emancipation, deliverance, liberation, release, salvation: becoming free of all attachment, *kilesa*, and *dukkha*, and realizing *nibbana.*

Viññāta. Sense-consciousness: knowing sense objects or concerns through the six sense doors (eyes, ears, nose, mouth, body, mind). *Viññāta* is the fundamental mental activity required for participation in the sensual world (*loka*); without it there is no experience. Modern Thai uses of *viññāta* include "soul" and "spiritual," which, however, are meanings not found in the Pali term. (Compare with *citta* and *mano*.)

Vipassanā. Insight: literally, "clear seeing"; to see clearly, distinctly, directly into the true nature of things, into *aniccaṁ*, *dukkhaṁ*, and *anattā*. *Vipassanā* is popularly used to refer to the practice of mental development for the sake of true insight. It is important not to confuse the physical posture, theory, and method of such practices with true realization of impermanence, unsatisfactoriness, and not-self. *Vipassanā* cannot be taught, although methods to nurture it are taught.

Virāga. Fading away, dispassion, un-staining: the breaking up, dissolving, and disappearing of *rāga*, of attachment. The lesson of step fourteen.

Viveka. Spiritual solitude, aloneness, seclusion: to be undisturbed in quiet solitude and mindfulness. There are three kinds: (1) *kāya-viveka*, physical solitude, when the body is not disturbed; (2) *citta-viveka*, mental solitude, when no defilements disturb the mind; and (3) *upādhi-viveka*, spiritual solitude, freedom from all attachment and all sources of attachment, that is, *nibbāna*.

Vossagga. Tossing back, relinquishment: the natural giving away of everything by the liberated mind. Synonymous with *nibbāna* and the same as *paṭinissagga*.

About the Author

BUDDHADĀSA BHIKKHU (Slave of the Buddha) went forth as a *bhikkhu* (Buddhist monk) in 1926 at the age of twenty. After a few years of study in Bangkok, he was inspired to live close with nature in order to investigate the Buddha-Dhamma as the Buddha had done. Thus, he established Suan Mokkhabalārāma (The Grove of the Power of Liberation) in 1932, near his hometown in Southern Thailand. At that time, it was the only forest Dhamma center in the region, and one of the few places dedicated to *vipassanā* (mental cultivation leading to "seeing clearly" into reality). Word of Buddhadāsa Bhikkhu and Suan Mokkh has spread over the years, and Buddhadāsa Bhikkhu's life and work are considered to be among the most influential events in the Buddhist history of Siam. Here, we can only mention some of the more memorable services he has rendered to Buddhism.

Ajahn Buddhadāsa worked painstakingly to establish and explain the correct and essential principles of pristine Buddhism. That work was based on extensive research of the Pali texts (canon and commentary), especially of the Buddha's Discourses (*sutta-piṭaka*), followed by personal experiment and practice with these teachings. From this, he uncovered the Dhamma that truly quenches *dukkha*, which he in turn shared with anyone interested. His goal was to produce a complete set of references for present and future research and practice. His approach was always scientific, straightforward, and practical.

Although his formal education was limited to seven years, in addition to some beginning Pali studies, during his lifetime he was given seven honorary doctorates by Thai universities. Numerous doctoral theses have been written about his work. His books, both written and transcribed from talks, fill a room at the National Library and influence all serious Thai Buddhists.

Progressive elements in Thai society, especially the young, have been inspired by his wide-ranging thought, teachings, and selfless example. Since the 1960s, activists and thinkers in such areas as education, social welfare, and rural development have drawn upon his teaching, advice, and friendship. His work helped inspire a new generation of socially concerned monks.

He studied all schools of Buddhism and all the major religious traditions. This interest was practical rather than scholarly. He sought to unite all genuinely religious people, meaning those working to overcome selfishness, in order to work together for world peace. This broad-mindedness won him friends and students from around the world, including Christians, Muslims, Hindus, and Sikhs.

Not long before his passing, he established an International Dhamma Hermitage, where courses introducing foreigners to a correct understanding of Buddhist principles and practice are held in English at the beginning of every month. Retreats in Thai are organized for the latter part of each month. Further, he hoped that meetings would be organized for Buddhists from around the world to identify and agree upon the "heart of Buddhism." Finally, he wanted to bring together all the religions to cooperate in helping humanity.

In his last few years, he established some new projects for carrying on the work of serving Lord Buddha and humanity. One is Suan Atammayatārāma, a small training center for foreign monks in a quiet grove near the International Dhamma Hermitage. The guidelines he laid down for this center aim to develop "Dhamma missionaries" who are well versed in the Buddha's teaching, have solid experience of *vipassanā*, and can adapt the Buddha-Dhamma to the problems of the modern world.

Another sister project is Dhamma Mātā (Dhamma Mothers). Society is suffering from a lack of qualified women spiritual teachers; they exist but are not given adequate recognition. Dhamma Mātā aims to raise the status of women by providing them better opportunities and support in Buddhist monastic life and meditation practice. The hope is that there will be more women who can "give birth to others through Dhamma."

Ajahn Buddhadāsa died at Suan Mokkh on 8 July 1993. The work of Suan Mokkh continues as before, according to the law of nature.

Other Books by the Author

Handbook for Mankind
Theravāda Buddhist religious experience in modern terms one need not be afraid to think about. An overview of the whole of Buddha-Dhamma: basic concerns, morality, meditation, insight, and the fruits of practice.

Keys to Natural Truth
Five talks dealing with fundamental issues of Dhamma understanding and practice. Offers key perspectives with which to sort out the essential teachings from cultural admixtures.

Heartwood of the Bodhi Tree
A practical explanation of voidness—the heart of both the Theravāda and the Mahāyāna—as it is used in the Buddha's original teaching. (Boston: Wisdom Publications, 1995)

Buddha-Dhamma for Students
Direct, clear replies to common questions asked by thinking people when they seriously examine Buddhism. Issues covered include emptiness, *kamma*, rebirth, suffering, lay practice, the enlightened being, and *nibbāna*.

First Ten Years in Suan Mokkh
Account of the founding and early years of Thailand's most unusual and influential forest monastery. Full of lessons and insights directly from nature, including thoughts on establishing practice centers and one's own practice.

Practical Dependent Origination
A fresh look at the crucial teaching of dependent origination. Reasons why the traditional interpretations are unlikely to be the Buddha's intention. How to understand and practice dependent origination today, for liberation in this life.

Dhammic Socialism
Controversial essays exploring what a Dhamma-based society and economy might be like. Politics and economics viewed from the perspective of non-attachment and inter-relatedness.

Me and Mine
Collection of revised and condensed translations covering the broadest spectrum of Ajahn Buddhadāsa's teaching so far available in English.

Christianity and Buddhism
A Buddhist scholar and meditation master looks for practical nourishment in the Bible. In doing so, he challenges both Christian and Buddhist dogmatism.

*For further information on these publications produced in Thailand, contact
Suan Mokkh, Ampoe Chaiya, Surat Thani, 84110, Thailand.*

About the Translator

SANTIKARO BHIKKHU has lived at Suan Mokkh since 1985. Having arrived with a Thai language background from four years of service in the U.S. Peace Corps, he was soon put to work translating. When Ajahn Buddhadāsa began giving lectures to foreign retreatants, Santikaro Bhikkhu was trained to render these lectures into English. His ability to do so was aided by Ajahn Buddhadāsa's advice and support. The Venerable Ajahn found this kind of practice and service beneficial for himself after he founded Suan Mokkh, so he encouraged others to try it. He frequently discussed the mechanics of translating and the subtleties of English with the translator, in addition to clarifying Dhamma points about which the translator was unsure. Santikaro Bhikkhu is now acting Abbot of Suan Atammayatārāma.

WISDOM PUBLICATIONS

WISDOM PUBLICATIONS is a non-profit publisher of books on Buddhism, Tibet, and related East-West themes. We publish our titles with the appreciation of Buddhism as a living philosophy and the special commitment of preserving and transmitting important works from all the major Buddhist traditions.

If you would like more information or a copy of our mail order catalog, and to keep informed about our future publications, please write or call us at: 361 Newbury Street, Boston, Massachusetts, 02115, USA. Telephone: (617) 536-3358; fax: (617) 536-1897.

The Wisdom Trust

AS A NON-PROFIT PUBLISHER, Wisdom Publications is dedicated to the publication of fine Dharma books for the benefit of all sentient beings and dependent upon the kindness and generosity of sponsors in order to do so. If you would like to make a contribution to Wisdom to help us continue our Dharma work, or to receive information about opportunities for planned giving, please contact our Boston office.

Thank you so much.

Wisdom Publications is a non-profit, charitable 501(c)(3) organization.

About the Author

Robert Taibbi, LCSW, has 36 years' experience, primarily in community mental health, as a clinician, supervisor, and clinical director. He is the author of *Doing Family Therapy: Craft and Creativity in Clinical Practice*, now in its second edition and recently translated into Chinese and Portuguese, and *Clinical Supervision: A Four-Stage Process of Growth and Discovery*, as well as several book chapters and over 150 magazine and journal articles. He has served as teen advice columnist for *Current Health* and as a contributing editor to *Your Health and Fitness*, and has received three national writing awards for Best Consumer Health Writing from the Health Information Resource Center. Mr. Taibbi provides training nationally on couple and family therapy, treatment of emotionally disturbed children and adolescents, and clinical supervision. He is currently in private practice in Charlottesville, Virginia.

Preface to the Paperback Edition

Since the hardcover edition of this book was published, I've found myself paying even closer attention to what happens in the room as I work with couples. Some of this has undoubtedly been instinctive—sort of like the way you tentatively bite down on a new dental filling or crown, wondering how solid it really is. I've been doing much the same, I think, with my own thinking: "biting down" on my own theories and techniques, continuing to check on how well they stand up to everyday clinical practice.

I've also been observing my clients and learning new things from them. The first thing is how layered the therapy process with couples really can be. I make a distinction in the book between the skills that partners need—in communication, in empathy, in assertiveness—in order to be truly heard by each other, and the deeper "core dynamics" reflecting the reactivation of childhood wounds or poisons that contaminate their current relationship. What I've come to appreciate is how important the skills are and how tenacious and powerful the core dynamics can be. The ability to assess skills and change the process in the room is essential for keeping the couple on the conversational road and out of the ditches, so they can reach the destination that is the goal of the discussion. Similarly, the ability to quickly identify the core dynamics of the couple—the way they both instinctively trigger and then fuel the replication of lifelong feelings of unappreciation or abandonment, control or criticism—and then to help them reverse and heal these is essential to assuring the long-term health of the relationship.

I've also noticed in the past couple of years that the motivations of those seeking couple therapy are gradually changing. Yes, there are still those who come in crisis, who are looking to play "courtroom" and have you decide who is right and wrong, or who are looking for permission to get divorced. But there are now others: those who have been dating, are beginning to consider marriage, and who are preemptively seeking to put issues to rest; those who identify themselves as having little conflict, but also little in common; and those who are looking for change, not only for the kids' sake, but for their own. Although it's easy to think that this is perhaps a mere sign of the times—that therapy is cheaper than divorce—it seems also driven by a growing awareness and belief that proactively dealing with problems, rather than just enduring them, is not a bad idea.

In addition to tracking my clinical work, I've recently been providing more training—in teleconferences, via webcams, and in day-long workshops—on doing couple therapy. Not only have these opportunities been invaluable to me in further clarifying my own thinking, but they have reinforced something I mentioned in my first preface: namely, that many clinicians feel untrained, even today, in couple work. They come to the workshops because courses in couple therapy were not available in graduate school; they have marched ahead, armed with whatever they can get (books, tapes, trainings) and in spite of their hesitations and fears, into the fray. What they are often explicitly seeking are practical tips and techniques, but they are also implicitly seeking a confirmation of their sense that couple work is a unique type of therapy with a unique mindset.

Moreover, I've appreciated the feedback that I have received from readers and reviewers alike on this book. This book is meant to be user-friendly and to give readers readily applicable tools for thinking about and doing couple therapy. It deliberately does not have scores of references; it is not meant to be an all-comprehensive, survey-like text. Rather, it is designed to be a practical introduction and everyday guide to this particular type of therapy for students and for more experienced clinicians who are new to the work.

That being said, you'll find topics (e.g., sexual therapy) where few details seem to be provided. This is not intended to minimize the skills that may be needed, but rather to encourage you to seek additional material or training. Similarly, you'll find among your own cases that there are times when you'll want supervisory input—when ethical issues may arise, for example, or when you have to decide whether to put your focus on one or both individuals or on the partners as a couple. Seek out this support. It's easy when you are doing couple therapy for personal considerations to overlap, or for you to feel the pinch of being caught in the triangle. You'll need another hand to keep you balanced and thinking clearly.

Finally, I want to restate something else I said in the first preface: I hope that this book and its reflective questions will make you curious about yourself, your clinical style, your fears, and your passions. I hope that you will allow yourself to discover yourself through the couples you work with, to appreciate the sometimes fragile sculptures that are our lives, and to realize how these sculptures are ultimately shaped by the sum of our relationships.

Preface

I started doing couple therapy in my first job after graduate school and found it more than a bit intimidating. Many of the couples I saw were people like me: folks in their 20s with or without kids, having many of the same arguments I was having with my own wife—stupid squabbles over laundry, tracked-in mud, whose parents to visit at Christmas. Other couples I saw were older, more like my parents, and it was awkward on both sides. I wore a suit and tried to sound professional with my vast 6 months of experience, and they did their best, I imagined, to keep from wincing or laughing throughout the session, stuck talking to this kid who had no idea what it was like to sustain a relationship for a couple of decades.

Most of my professional training had been with individuals and families. In the field and in graduate programs at the time, couple therapy was like some distant relative who shows up suddenly for Christmas dinner and whom no one knows quite what to do with. Individuals and families seemed easier to me. Individuals provided an intimacy, and the focus was simple, while families seemed to run on their own momentum; my tasks with them seemed to be more that of jump starting and traffic directing. Couples combined the worst of both—less intimacy and control, less natural momentum—and often left me feeling, like them, stranded.

After many years of doing child and family work, supervision, and administration in mental health centers, I moved into private practice. I was professionally restless, looking for new clinical adventures, and returning to couple therapy seemed to aptly fit the bill. The field had changed over those years and I had changed along with it. The accumulating research on successful relationships now provided clues as to what worked and what didn't. My own decades of married life helped me understand what those older couples knew so well years before—just how hard it can be to stay together and work problems out. It requires more than just a commitment to hang in there through thick and thin, though for many couples such tenacity is the last strand of the steadily fraying emotional cord holding them together. Couples, I realized, needed help with life's challenges: communicating in a way that didn't just mimic their parents; realizing how one spouse's problems can spill over to the other spouse; acknowledging how new babies or outrageous teens can wear a couple down and take a toll on the relationship; appreciating how old age arouses fears that they thought belonged to the world of their parents or grandparents and somehow they would magically never reach.

Intimate relationships are the building blocks not only of families, but in many ways of one's identity. We're all shaped as much from the outside in as from the inside out, and it's our close relationships that have the capacity to shape us the most. These relationships become our training ground, continuing the process started by our parents. By learning to navigate our primary relationships we learn to navigate our larger world and, eventually, ourselves. In that light, I realized that couple therapy wasn't some distant relative after all, but was the examination of an elemental relationship around which everything else in a person's life is often built.

One of the purposes of this book is to help new clinicians, as well as experienced clinicians who are new to couple work, to know the terrain and not feel lost. The book offers a clinical map for treating couples that I lacked when starting out, one you can refer to as you need. In it are basic skills and techniques, as well as steps you can take when couples remind you too much of yourself or your parents, or present a problem that is foreign to your own experience, and you feel stuck. There are suggestions and case illustrations to help you move together with the couple through the layers of treatment—from presenting problems and assessment, to skill building and resolution of core issues, to successful termination.

The other goal, one that runs through much of my writing, is to help you realize that although skills are important, therapy, unlike computer repair or plumbing, is not a straightforward process. There is room for creativity—the more the better—and there are many roads to the same destination. What is often most effective with any given couple is the approach that combines their needs with your unique style and talents. Like a good relationship, like good art, good therapy is therapy that represents most fully who you are.

I find myself talking in this book about the clinician's need for courage and leadership. Doing this work entails working at the edge of your comfort zone and in unpredictable situations. But this edge, this flying by the seat of your pants that can make the therapy process so intimidating for new clinicians, is also what makes it so invigorating. This likelihood of therapy arousing both anxiety and exhilaration in you is particularly true with couples, where the therapist is one point of a triangle, where balance is essential, and where you see the rubbing together of lives enacted directly before you. Courage and leadership are essential because they are the antidotes to the couple's fear and stagnation. They enable you to help couples see what is possible by helping them interact in new ways. By creating this experience of change, you, in essence, become the midwife to a new vision of themselves and each other.

I hope this book, and the reflective questions I offer, will make you curious about yourself, your fears, and your passions. Curiosity, fear, and passion are the raw materials out of which we create the fragile sculpture that is our life. Couple therapy gives us the wonderful opportunity to be part of shaping the sculpture that is the couple's relationship, and through the work and process the couple, in turn, helps us shape our own. We are, it is said, the sum of our relationships. By helping one or two of us succeed, we all succeed as well.

Contents

Chapter 1

Into the Fray
Theoretical Foundation and Overview

Ellen sits at the edge of her seat, her arms folded across her chest, her coat bunched up against her, and looks directly at you. Her husband, Tom, sits diagonally across from you and her, looking at the floor.

You take a deep breath. "I want to thank you both for coming in," you say, glancing at each of them. "I know, Ellen, that we talked briefly on the phone on Monday, but didn't have time to go into details. The only thing I know is that the two of you have been separated about a week."

"He left! Up and walked out." Ellen's eyes are now bulging, her face is getting red, yet you notice tears in the corner of her eyes. "Out of the blue." She pulls her arms closer to chest.

"It sounds like this was a shock to you," you say in calm voice. Ellen nods.

Tom is still looking at the floor. "How do you feel about being here, Tom?" You want to connect with him before this goes any further.

"It's pretty strange." He looks up at you. His voice is quiet, his tone is restrained, maybe depressed.

"Yes, I bet it is. How long have you been married?" Again, you try and keep your voice calm—calmness is one of the best antidotes to the anxiety that clients bring to therapy.

"Twelve years," says Tom. He's back to looking at the floor.

"Do you have any kids?" you ask, looking between them.

"Two beautiful children," says Ellen, punching out the words. "I just don't understand why he is doing this." Her face is getting red again, she's tearing up. "I don't understand. How could he do this?" she asks,

1

her voice getting louder. "How can you walk away from your wife and kids just like that, after twelve years!"

Tom grips the chair tighter and sighs.

Ask any sailor what it takes to navigate a voyage, and he will tell you that you need to have basic sailing skills, know your boat and the waters, be able to read the wind and the weather, and trust your instincts. Whether it's making the subtle adjustments that keep you on course, or knowing when it's time to lower your sails and stay put, it's the ability to bring together all this knowledge that determines success.

Couple therapy is much the same. You need confidence in yourself and your clinical skills. You need to be able to rely upon your theory as a foundation, but also understand and manage the specific forces that shape each therapy and journey—the gale of the crisis, the undertow of the past, the moment-to-moment changes in the emotional climate, or the normal life cycle stresses that can suddenly blow a couple off course. You need to be able to recognize the signs and symptoms of danger and anticipate the challenges in order to make the corrections that will help bring the couple back on track.

A DIFFERENT THERAPY

Couple therapy is not like individual therapy. Individual therapy is a smaller world—just you and the client. Your focus can be simple and direct. The process seems easier to control. There is one voice to listen to, one side to take. The client's motivated—"I need help with this problem, this worry, this issue, these emotions"—and even when he is not ("The judge ordered me to come; I don't know why"), it doesn't take much effort to determine who has and what is the problem. At its best, individual therapy is like a heartfelt conversation at a coffee shop with someone you know well, one that often goes deeper than ordinary life, that makes the therapy experience profound and rewarding.

Couple therapy, in contrast, can seem more like a two-ring circus, with each of the partners doing his or her own act for the therapist. Instead of the one voice and one side you have two. While one is enthusiastically motivated for therapy, the other is likely to be as enthusiastically ambivalent. What do they want? Change? Maybe, as long as their partner does most of the changing. But one thing they want for sure is validation and absolution. If they haven't gotten this at home, maybe you, the therapist, will provide it; you will tell them who is right and wrong. Your job is to listen to each partner, but to also step back and look at the interaction between them; to understand them as individuals, but understand even more their relationship to each other. Rather than relaxing into the conversation, you're more likely to always be a bit on edge, always looking out of the corner of your eye to see what happens next. You're always engaged in a balancing act.

And this balancing act is what perhaps makes couple therapy most different from individual therapy. If you've ever gone out together with two other friends you know how awkward a threesome can be. In contrast to a dyad, a threesome often feels cumbersome and messy. There's always the danger of someone feeling left out, someone dominating the other two, two dominating one, someone not getting enough attention or too much attention or running the show.

In the therapy session you're faced with similar juggling—not letting Ellen get too far into a rant or into her despair and pushing Tom onto the emotional sidelines; not spending too much time with Tom and having Ellen feeling excluded and resentful; not taking over the conversation yourself and shutting them both down, or causing them to join forces and gang up against you. To manage the session well you need to lead and listen, and provide the emotional ballast that allows them to feel a little safer to talk about things that matter to them. By the time they walk out of your office both need to know that their sides have been heard, that their emotions have been respected and understood. Successfully establishing and maintaining the therapeutic alliance becomes critical.

The challenge can feel even more daunting when the emotional intensity is high and so close up. It can make some therapists anxious, cause them to question their ability to manage a relationship, and keep them away from doing such work. When a couple like Tom and Ellen break into full-tilt argument as soon as they sit down, or a couple announces that coming to see you is their "last chance" to make it work, even the most seasoned clinician can feel intimidated. And if you happen to be less clinically experienced, are uncoupled yourself ("Are you married?" they ask), are having trouble in your own relationship, or are much younger than your clients (so that it feels like you are looking in on the secret dark side of your parents' marriage), it can feel emotionally overwhelming at times. Your own countertransference, always sitting right there, gets stirred.

If all this isn't enough to make you think twice about taking this on, there is one additional challenge to face, namely, helping the couple transform their relationship, not simply put out the fire. Your role as therapist should be more than just that of a referee who helps them settle the fight of the week. Instead you want to learn what they do that creates the argument and change it so that they have fewer arguments in the future. You want to offer them a vision of a different type of relationship, one that is more honest, more intimate, more organic. You want to help them see and move toward the wider possibility of being more of who they are as individuals, not less, by the combining of their lives. You want to help them realize that by the intermingling of their lives, they can help each other discover who they are as individuals and as a couple.

LAYING THE FOUNDATION: THEORY

Couple therapy has historically been a stepchild of sorts in the therapy field, in which individual and family therapy models have been adapted and applied to it. Traditionally couples relied upon their doctors or their ministers to help them with their relationships. The first professional marriage counseling center wasn't established until 1930, and for the next several decades couple work was incorporated into psychoanalytic models. In the late 1950s early family therapists began writing about marital therapy from a communications framework. It has been in the last 10–15 years that therapists/researchers such as John Gottman,[1] the developer of the Marriage Laboratory, and Susan Johnson, the codeveloper of emotionally focused couple therapy,[2] have looked more closely at the unique dynamics of happy as well as unhappy couples to unravel what works and apply these findings to shaping the therapy process.

The model that we will be using is an integrative one drawn from five major perspectives. At its heart we will look at couple therapy from a family systems perspective, with its notion that problems arise from the interaction between the partners, rather than just from within the individuals themselves, and are held in place by the behavioral patterns that they jointly create. This perspective assumes that the patterns are often more powerful than personalities, and that by interrupting dysfunctional patterns, and helping the couple recognize them, the thera-

---

[1]Gottman has several popular books that discuss his research and approach: Gottman, J., & Silver, N. (2004). *The Seven Principles for Making Marriage Work.* New York: Orion; Gottman, J., et al. (2007). *Ten Lessons to Transform Your Marriage.* New York: Three Rivers Press.

[2]For more on Johnson's approach see Johnson, S., & Johnson, S. M. (2004). *The Practice of Emotionally Focused Couple Therapy: Creating Connection.* New York: Routledge.

pist can enable more functional communication and behavior to take their place.

A subset of such systems thinking is Murray Bowen's useful notion of *differentiation*—moving away from the reactivity and blame of undifferentiated relationships and toward the increased individual responsibility and proactivity of differentiated relationships.[3] The aim is to help both partners worry less about what the other is or is not doing and instead focus on their own openness and honesty. The more they can do this, not only are the dysfunctional patterns broken, but interactions become less defensive, more genuine.

Effective couple therapy is also behavioral and action oriented. In contrast to the insight-oriented approaches of the psychodynamic tradition, couples are encouraged to change their relationships by *doing* something different—in their communication, their physical behavior, at home, in the session—again as a means of breaking old dysfunctional patterns and creating new patterns. The truth is that if you continue doing what you are doing you will likely continue feeling the same way; change what you do and your emotions will change as well. In line with such thinking is educating couples and helping them develop new skills. This is similar to the work of Gottman, who initially focuses on helping couples master new and more effective means of communication.

But as Susan Johnson has pointed out in her research on couple therapy, new behaviors and skills can often only go so far. The therapy needs to be experiential. In order to truly propel them out of the dysfunctional patterns and help them solidify behavioral change, couples need to have a new emotional experience. This experience happens in the room, in the clinical process. As we will be discussing throughout, while one of the jobs of the therapist is to stop the dysfunctional patterns and change behaviors, another crucial one is to change the emotional climate by asking the difficult questions, deepening the communication, and moving the couple into areas that, because of their own anxiety, they stay away from. This requires courage on the part of the therapist—a sensitive but unflinching willingness to bring underlying problems and emotions into the open.

While good couple therapy is primarily present, action, and process focused, it does acknowledge the power of the past, specifically reactivation in the present of old childhood wounds.[4] These are what

---

[3]For more information on Bowen's theory see Bowen, M. (1978). *Family Therapy in Clinical Practice.* New York: Jason Aronson.

[4]In his Imago approach to couples Harville Hendrix centers much of his work on such healing of childhood wounds. Like Gottman, he has several popular books for the gen-

often create the sticking points in the change process, instances where the couple, in spite of your efforts to push them out of their behavioral ruts, continues to fall back. Rather than approaching history as a psychodynamically based therapist might, developing insight and making this work the focus of the treatment, my approach is more pragmatic—breaking through behavioral impasses by seeing them as signals that it is time to dig deeper and unearth the childhood wounds that may be holding the behaviors in place. The goal is to help the individuals step back and separate out past from present, help them each ask for and receive in the present relationship what they could not in the past. This allows them to both begin to heal these old wounds and move forward in their relationship.

Finally, overarching these clinical perspectives is a developmental one. We are shaped not only by our individual pasts and current interactions, but also by the personal challenges of adjusting to the life cycle, as well as the couple's challenges of adjusting to the family life cycle. New parents, for example, need to navigate the shift from focusing on themselves as a couple to the roles and responsibilities of childrearing, just as many older, empty-nest couples are forced in the opposite direction, that of making the transition from being largely preoccupied as parents to once again rediscovering and refocusing on themselves as a couple. If you can anticipate the challenges and recognize the common problems of each stage you can help the couple do the same—understand better the terrain around and before them, see the larger context, be less reactive and blaming and more proactive and self-responsible.

This theoretical foundation, then forms, the basis for assessment and treatment goals—looking for dysfunctional patterns and ways to stop and change them; assessing communication skills and teaching ways of making them more effective; closely tracking the process and shaping it in order to draw out new emotions and challenge old perspectives; uncovering old wounds that stop progress and signal a need for healing, and placing all these elements within a developmental context. We can think of couple therapy as moving through layers—from the presenting problem to the underlying issues, from the surface emotions to those that lie below, from the present to the past and back again. This is an active form of therapy that encourages the approaching of anxiety, that focuses more on process than content—on doing more than focusing on insight. It is one that supports individual clarity, action, and responsibility.

---

eral public. A good starting point for his approach is Hendrix, H. (2007). *Getting the Love You Want*. New York: Holt Paperbacks.

GETTING CREATIVE

One of the goals of this book is to help you know how to navigate a course through the often choppy waters of couple therapy. We'll discuss the basic skills you need to steer the session process and stay balanced, help you recognize the signs and symptoms of coming emotional turmoil and power struggles, and explore the developmental currents that can push even the most stable relationships off course. But this is just part of the picture. Good therapy is also creative and flexible, not one-size-fits-all. As the research shows, there are many approaches to effective treatment, and often, with any one couple, many forks along the therapeutic road.[5] Successful couple therapy is that which can best fit the expectations, needs, and personalities of the couple.

It needs to fit you as well. The biggest variable determining therapeutic success is, in fact, you: you working at your best, defining and following an approach that fits your personality and therapeutic philosophy, using yourself creatively, energetically, honestly—so that your clients can learn to do the same.

This is the other goal of this book—to stimulate your thinking about what you do and how you work best. To make you curious not only about the dynamics of the couple, but about yourself, and you as part of those dynamics. The model that we discuss can provide a foundation upon which you build, but it hopefully will also serve as a template against which you can compare your own thinking. The questions at the end of each chapter offer you an opportunity to reflect on your own values and theories and the influence of your own past, and discover how they all entwine into a therapeutic process that is uniquely your own.

As Buckminster Fuller, the visionary architect, once asked, what is it that you need to do that no one else can do because of who you are? This question is probably one of the most important ones you can ask yourself as you begin and evolve into your work. It is an excellent starting point for building a therapeutic style, as well as for helping couples define who they are as individuals and as a couple. Long-term success in therapy and in relationships is not necessarily about the ability to hold tight to one path, but rather the courage and flexibility to shift gears and explore others that can take you where you want and need to go.

---

[5]See Hubble, M., et al. (1999). *The Heart and Soul of Change: What Works in Therapy.* Washington, DC: American Psychological Association; for a good summary of research studies in the field also see Nichols, M., & Schwartz, R. (2008). *Family Therapy Concepts and Methods, 8th Edition.* Boston: Allyn & Bacon.

STARTING POINTS

All this brings us to some foundational ideas and assumptions that we can use as a starting point for our voyage together. As you read through this list, compare and contrast these assumptions with your own. See if you can begin to identify your own core beliefs:

The Power Is in the Process

Harville Hendrix once said that most marriages are doomed to fail in the way most of us think about them. In our own relationships, we tend to create a vision at the start based upon outcome goals—we want to have that three-bedroom house with the white picket fence, we'll have 2.3 kids, we'll have sex twice a week, we'll visit my mother on Sundays. But in the real world, while we may strive to successfully reach our goals, the outcomes are never guaranteed. The house, for example, may be suddenly and unexpectedly destroyed in a hurricane; we find out we are infertile and can't have our own kids; one of us is in a car accident and becomes a quadriplegic; my mother remarries and moves to Florida. We have no absolute control over the product of our labors.

What we can control, however, and set successful goals about, says Hendrix, is the process—what we do when the house is lost, how we talk about the changes we face, how we respond when we are sexually frustrated, support each other when we face a loss. If we have the means to listen, support, discuss, decide, we can successfully negotiate the challenges that life brings to our relationship. This, after all, is where life lives. This is where the true melding of our lives together takes place. Here in the moment, here in our response.

As a therapist you are powerless to shape what happens outside the therapy room. Trying to do so only handicaps you. You are in danger of becoming a manipulator, whom the couple can only comply with or resist. It distracts them, and you, from what happens in the session. Your only power is in the session, in the moment, with the couple. This is what you need to focus on, and help them to do the same.

You want to worry less about the content, *what* the couple talks about, and more about the process—*how* they talk. This is a difficult shift for couples, and even clinicians, to make. When a couple is arguing over whether the bill got paid on Tuesday or Wednesday, it is about helping them see that whether is it Tuesday or Wednesday is really not important. The problem isn't in the facts but how they talk about them. They are each throwing up more evidence in to order to feel better by proving they are right, and feeling angry and defensive. The content is merely fuel for their emotions.

Rather than getting lost in the content or focused on who is right and wrong, they instead need to recognize that their emotions are escalating and that the conversation is turning into a power struggle and ultimately getting nowhere. They need to learn how to talk about a difference of opinion without getting into a fight. If they can master this, and learn to see the dysfunctional patterns that you see as they arise, they can learn to transform their relationship.

People Naturally Grow and Change

"We must give up the life we planned," said Joseph Campbell, the world-famous mythologist, "so as to have the life that is waiting for us." Rather than building a life, we discover it. Rather than the hold-steady march to outcomes, life is the more gentle unfolding of growth and change. The challenge that every couple faces is that of remaining open to discovery, accepting the inevitability of change, and successfully adjusting the relationship to accommodate it. Your job, as a clinician and outsider, is to get the subject of change on the table. You not only want to help couples articulate the changes they see within themselves and within their relationships, but help them see these changes as an opportunity for growth rather than a threat.

That said, the foundation of any clinical plan is individual empowerment. Relationships get stuck because the people do. Rather than being clear and bold, they mumble. Rather than fighting for what they really want, they bite their tongues, give up, give in, or go along, only to have their resentment leak out later in less functional ways. The good process is the honest process. The good relationship is one where both people can be who they are, can feel that the other supports their dreams, and where both are committed to their growth as individuals and as a couple. To give up important parts of either person for the relationship, or give up important parts of the relationship for either one, creates the emotional potholes that both will invariably fall into. Part of their struggle, of course, and your challenge, is helping them decide which of those parts are most important, and helping them define their own priorities and needs.

The Solutions Are in the Holes

You probably have met parents who feel frustrated with their children when their ways of parenting and coping emotionally have reached their limits. The father, for example, who used spankings or time-outs as a way of containing his 7-year-old suddenly finds himself hamstrung when the same child 9 years later is 6 feet, 2 inches and weighs 180 pounds.

Similarly, the couple is handicapped when one spouse only deals with conflict by withdrawing or giving in, or the other by getting enraged when really he or she is terribly hurt and sad.

To say that the solutions are in the holes is to say that one of the keys to meeting the challenges of life lies in moving outside your comfort zone. To paraphrase Albert Einstein, you cannot solve a problem with the same mind-set that you used to conceive of it. Only by learning to take risks can couples become more emotionally and psychologically flexible, and better able to weather the stresses and strains of life. Only through such risk taking can they not only develop the different mind-set that Einstein is talking about, but discover the process of changing their mind-sets themselves.

What this means for you as a clinician is that you are constantly looking for what is not in the room—topics never talked about, emotions not expressed, sides of personalities never shown. This is what you want to guide the couple toward. It is here that those untapped parts of themselves are stored. By your own role modeling, by your encouragement and support, you want to help them to become more curious than afraid. You want to show them that they cannot only learn to approach their anxiety and survive, but discover something new and valuable.

Problems Are Bad Solutions

We are made up of emotional and cognitive layers, some of which always seem to be just beyond our awareness or reach. What we often see as a problem in others, in a relationship, even within ourselves, is really just a bad solution to something else beneath it.[6] The most obvious example, perhaps, is addiction, where the dependence on alcohol, work, or sex is a bad solution to feelings of depression, impotence, or rage. But it's also true for affairs or violence or passivity—ways of coping with underlying emotions too difficult to tackle directly. When a couple presents the problem that is driving them crazy (Maria's nagging, Luis's criticism and control), you turn their attention to the unacknowledged emotional problem—their underlying anxiety, fear, hurt—that is the real concern. This doesn't mean you don't help them change their behavior—you do—but you also help them realize that what seems simple is really more complex.

---

[6]The team at the Mental Research Institute (MRI) in Palo Alto founded their whole approach to therapy on this principle. For more information see their classic work: Watzlawick, P., et al. (1974). *Change: Principles of Problem Formation and Problem Resolution.* New York: Norton; Weakland, J., & Segal, L. (1982). *The Tactics of Change: Doing Therapy Briefly.* San Francisco: Jossey-Bass.

A corollary of this perspective is that people are usually doing the best they can. Yes, there are evil people in the world, but by and large, we assume that people are not by nature malicious. When someone is being manipulative or critical, they are not struggling with you but more with themselves. If you can adopt this point of view as a therapist—and help couples to do the same—you and they are more likely to be compassionate than defensive. You and they can set boundaries without engaging in power struggles. By looking at problems as solutions, you are helping to create the change that Einstein says we need.

Advocate for the Relationship

Our cultural values shape what we do, and they, like our relationships themselves, change over time. In the late '70s and early '80s, for example, divorce was popular. The needs of the individual were seen as more important than the relationship; if you could be all you could be and be in the relationship, fine; if not, move on. Lately there's lots of talk about the marriage preservation movement and making the relationship the priority. It's hard not to get caught up in the shifting tides. What's important is being clear in your own mind and with the couple in order to help them to do the same.

Here is a shorthand way of looking at various types of relationships:

$$\frac{1}{2} + \frac{1}{2} = 1$$
$$1 + \frac{1}{2} = 1\frac{1}{2}$$
$$1 + 1 = 1 + 1$$
$$1 + 1 = 1 + 1 + 1$$

What does this all mean? In the first line $\frac{1}{2} + \frac{1}{2}$ refers to two people who may be deficient in various ways but lean on each other's strengths. By doing so they together become one stronger unit better able to cope in the world. Next, $1 + \frac{1}{2}$ refers to couples where one person is psychologically stronger, the other less so, and in their coming together reflect the unbalanced combination of the two. The third sum, $1 + 1$, refers to two people with similar psychological strengths who come together and essentially stay the same, that is, two people living together who remain individually strong but share little within the relationship. Finally, the last refers to two people who are balanced and individually strong but have also created something else—the two has become three, and the third is the relationship between them that they share and nurture.

One way of looking at couple therapy, in contrast, for example, to individual therapy, is this last formula—which says that the third client always in the room is the relationship itself. You become an advocate not in terms of pushing couples to stay together, but more in the way that you might advocate for a child in family therapy. Like a child, the relationship is an offspring of both of them. Your job is to help them appreciate the relationship's needs and personality, realize their responsibility to nurture it, and give it voice when one or both of the partners are blinded in the moment by their individual needs. Whether or not they decide to stay together, by understanding how the relationship has unfolded through their mutual contributions, they are able to have a more balanced view of the relationship process.

We'll be returning to these principles and assumptions throughout our voyage together. Again, compare and contrast these principles with your own. By being clear you have a foundation you can return to, a sense of direction so that you keep moving forward rather than getting lost in the maelstrom of the couple dynamics.

CHARTING THE COURSE

The book is divided into three sections. In the first section (Chapters 2–8) we look at the foundational structure of couple therapy, the basic skills and concepts that you need to successfully navigate doing couple therapy—managing opening sessions, doing assessments, developing initial goals and treatment plans for the most common presenting problems. We also discuss building communication skills, dealing with crises and anger, uncovering core dynamics and clearing away family-of-origin issues that can arise and block progress, and handling the power issues of children, sex, and money. Along the way you will find brief vignettes, and various exercises and questions to help you increase your skills and clarify your style.

In the second section (Chapters 9–13) we look at specific challenges that couples face as they move through the adult life cycle—newlyweds, couples with young children, and then teenagers, the empty nest, the remarried and elderly couple. We talk about the dangers of failing to renew the relationship contract, about how to revitalize the stale couple. We discuss the problems you're likely to see and discuss through longer case examples how to apply your skills to these particular issues.

Finally in the third section (Chapters 14 and 15) we'll discuss ways of repairing relationships when only working with one partner, look at how the couple can help the individual, and conclude with a final chapter on nuts and bolts of practice and good self care. By the time we finish our voyage together it is my hope that you will know how to navigate the back bays and channels of couple therapy, be better able to define your own style, and, most of all, believe that your approach is the best one for you.

Looking Within: Chapter 1 Exercises

As mentioned, you will find at the end of each chapter questions and exercises relevant to that chapter. They are ways of helping you connect to the material personally—by considering your own history and experience, your own values, your ways of approaching problems, your own vulnerabilities and strengths. Please try them, especially those that seem more difficult, to see what you may discover about yourself, and to become more aware of how your personal self shapes your professional work.

1. Write out your own theoretical orientation regarding couple therapy. What do you change in couple therapy? How, specifically, do you bring about change? What is your role? How is it in line with or different from other therapeutic work that you do?

2. What are your own assumptions about clinical work? What personal values influence your work?

3. Think back to times that you have been involved in a three-person triangle. What role do you tend to take—leader, follower, mediator? How may that carry over to your clinical work?

4. What intimidates you most about doing couple work? Why? What types of support do you need to feel less anxious, more secure?

5. What biases about gender might you bring with you to couple therapy—that women complain too much, for example, or that men are too cold or silent?

Chapter 2

The Basics
Clinical Goals and Tasks

"We always argue about the kids."

"My husband is threatening to leave."

"We don't ever talk. We don't seem to have anything in common."

"My wife told me she was having an affair. We are here to see if we can work things out."

"We never have sex anymore."

"After our last fight the judge and my lawyer told us we need to come here and talk to you."

There are many reasons why couples come for therapy. Some are clearly at the edge. A precipitating event—a violent argument, an affair, a decision by one partner to separate—threatens to collapse the entire relationship or has become the last straw. Others come not because they have hit bottom, but because they worry that they are gradually moving toward it—partners who feel that they have little in common and who dread those long weekends when their children are away at sleepovers and they're left together alone in an empty house. And then there are those couples who come but are questioning the whole idea of therapy itself. Their doctor referred them, the judge ordered them, and they are skeptical, angry, or going through the motions. They think that what goes on between them is really none of your business.

Whatever reasons bring them to your door, your initial goal is always the same. You want to provide the safe space—literally and psychologically—for them to explore themselves and their relationship with each other. Yes, in their own minds they may be seeking something else—the ideal parent who will listen to their side of the story and help them put an end to the squabbling, or the judge who will say who is right, who is wrong, who needs to change, whether things are hopeless. The one who has one foot out the door may be seeking your permission to put the other foot beside it and to shut the door on the way out. One may want you to fix the other—to make him speak and engage, to make her want sex or stop nagging. They may want you to throw them a line that keeps them from tumbling off into a crisis, but once you pull them back from the edge, they are eager to leave.

They may be seeking any or all of these, but you want to offer them something else, something more. Couple therapy is not couple mediation. Your interest is not in merely helping them cobble together an agreement—what time their daughter Katie should go to bed, how often they should make love—so they can end the frustration or get their partner off their back. You want to help them think bigger—to define what they would ideally like to be different in their relationship and in themselves. You want to help them see how their actions and reactions interlock to form what they call "the problem." You want to change the emotional climate, in the room and between them, and rather than giving them the black/white simplicity that they yearn for, provide them with the opportunity to wrestle with their problems and discover what lessons they may offer. You want to create a safe space so that they can paradoxically risk not feeling safe and thereby learn to grow.

To do all this you're going to be paying close attention to balance, process, and empowerment. These principles are like the ballast of the ship that helps you and the therapy to stay centered and focused. In this chapter we discuss how these principles are translated into essential tasks that you can integrate into your own therapeutic style. We begin by first talking about the Basic Four—core tasks and concepts that form the meat and potatoes of all sessions, and that you can always return to when you feel like things are going off course. Next we discuss in detail two foundational models—the drama triangle and the relationship rollercoaster—that not only provide you with a framework for setting clinical goals and tasks but help the couple to view their problems in new ways that offer hope. Finally, we conclude the chapter with questions for reflection.

THE BASIC FOUR

When you feel overloaded by information, emotionally rattled, or unsure in what direction to go, the Basic Four are what you come back to get grounded. If you can do these and nothing else, you will be providing the solid foundation for couple change and problem solving. We'll take them one by one:

Demonstrate Leadership

Doing couple therapy is not for the timid. Couples who come in emotionally burned out or mired in ambivalence need your energy and direction to get them out of their sluggishness; without it you all will end up psychologically napping. Couples who come in in crisis, are angry, or have strong personalities need you to be the powerful counterforce. If you aren't, the couple will wind up doing exactly what they do at home and leave feeling the same—angry, frustrated, or lonely. They will quite rightfully think that they could stayed home and done the same thing for free.

Therapy works when the therapy space feels safe. Beth can say aloud that she always feels criticized, Manuel can say that he is worried that he is letting the family down by working at his low-paying job—and they both know that you are there to keep things from getting out of control, can protect them from retaliation, keep them both from going down that same familiar path. To do this you need to demonstrate leadership and stay in charge of the process in the room.

This does not mean that you are the micromanager, always in control. Just as you don't want couples to go on and on as if you were not in the room, you don't want to swing in the other direction and expect them to wait and respond only to your questions. This may help you contain your own anxiety, but it's not good therapy. Leadership is about creating balance. You shape, much like an orchestra conductor might, the conversation and the anxiety so that it unfolds in a way that is different and productive, rather than the same and destructive. With your leadership couples can move, individually and together, toward the new emotions and behaviors that they were afraid of or incapable of approaching before.

Your leadership is yours to lose. As a professional and an outsider to the relationship, your observations and suggestions carry weight. Whether they initially see you as the judge, the mediator, the sage, they come expecting something from you. What you provide usually doesn't need to be grand and dramatic: helping them see the problem in a new way, or simply getting their side of the story heard; helping them stay on track by helping them see how and when they get off track—these are often good starting points. But you need to take charge, step up, and be active.

Stop the Dysfunctional Process

Every time Eric starts to talk his wife, Helen, interrupts him.

Jane and Wilson go off into a heated argument over whether their last argument was on Wednesday or Thursday night.

Colin begins another lecture about why he thinks their son needs to do his homework right after school; his wife, Tamara, gets quiet and has a glazed look.

While you want to watch what unfolds long enough to identify the pattern, but you don't want a couple to continue replicating their dysfunctional process without intervening. So step in: "Helen, hold on a second; please give Eric a chance to finish what he was saying" or "Eric, Helen is interrupting you; is that okay with you?" "Jane and Wilson, you both seem to be going around and around over a minor point—what is it that you most want each other to understand?" "Hold on, Colin. It seems like you are trying hard to get Tamara to understand why you think this is important, but Tamara, you're quiet; I'm wondering what you are thinking and feeling right now."

By stopping the dysfunctional process and describing what you see, you are doing several things at once: You're asserting your leadership, taking an active role, showing that while you are attentive to what everyone is saying, you are interested in keeping them from falling into the same unproductive ruts. By remaining calm, you are helping them feel safe, and encouraging them to take the risk of being more open and honest.

Susan Johnson views dysfunctional patterns like these as the mutual enemy that the couple needs to join against. She's right. These patterns lead them over time toward the same stalemates, negative feelings, and sour results, and truly are more powerful than their individual personalities.

By interrupting couples' interactional patterns, you are creating for them the opportunity to move in new directions. You're also helping them become more aware of the process—how what is happening right then between them is different than the content that they are so fixed upon and get so lost within. When you stop and describe their "It was

Tuesday, it was Wednesday" escalating banter, they can begin to recognize that the issue isn't what day it was, but rather that they are feeling frustrated right there and then. They can begin to see how the flow of the interaction, or the lack of it, is really the source of the problem between them. By learning to recognize in the moment when their conversations are going off track, they are mastering an essential skill that can help them navigate their relationship over the long term.

You probably remember when you first were learning to drive and the way the car veered from one side of the road to the other—you were constantly overcorrecting the steering. In many ways the skill of steering a conversation is similar to the process of learning to steer a car. With practice, you learned to look at the road ahead rather than intuitively staring at the hood or watching your hands. With experience you gradually learned how to make the microadjustments of the steering wheel in order to stay centered on the road.

What you learned to do with a car physically, you want to help couples do verbally: to look ahead and keep in mind the ultimate direction of the conversation, rather than myopically getting caught up in their own emotions and content; to learn to make microadjustments in the conversation ("You just made a face and seem to be getting angry—did I hurt your feelings?") so they can stay on the conversational road and avoid winding up in the same old emotional ditch.

You are like the driving instructor in the front seat next to them. When the conversation begins to go off course, when they begin to get defensive and repetitive, let them go a bit and see if they can self-correct. If they can and the conversation is going well—if the couple can stick to the topic, if they are able to break new emotional ground, if the content is honest and heard—sit back, look at the floor, keep out of their way. But if neither is being heard, if they are using words only to fuel emotions, if the process is falling into a power struggle and becoming destructive, step on your brake and stop it.

Again, balance is important. You don't, for example, want to always be holding up your hand to Helen so that Eric can talk—Helen will feel picked on and think you are taking sides against her. Similarly, you need to be careful about interrupting Jane and Wilson too much. If they get too frustrated, or see what you're doing as controlling and annoying, they may gang up against you in the room, badmouth you in the hall on the way out, or see you as a traffic cop and become dependent on your intervention.

Stop the destructive dysfunctional process, but stay aware and connected to each person. If Helen makes a face when you hold up your hand, respond to it—"Helen, do you feel like I'm giving you a hard time?" Explain what you are doing—"It's probably easier for me as an outsider watching you both to see where your communication goes off course. I want to help you recognize when this happens so that you don't both keep falling into the same ruts." Then make sure you intervene when Eric gets too loud or too preachy toward Helen.

Draw Out and Label Emotions

Most couples will need your help in breaking new emotional ground. The dysfunctional process is not only dysfunctional because it is abusive, defensive, or vague, but also because it is repetitive, restricting, and familiar. Your job is to change the communication, to stir the emotional pot. You're moving toward the holes, looking for what they are not saying. This is where their anxieties and ultimately the solutions lie. By uncovering new emotions you are not only changing the emotional climate in the room, you are helping couples to experience something new, which, in turn, can open doors to new behaviors.

How do you draw out these new emotions? Here are some specifics:

Make Language More Specific and Complete

"Helen, you said you get upset? What do you mean by upset?"

"Eric, you started to say 'I remember when' but then didn't finish your sentence. What do you remember?"

"Jane, you said that wasn't true. What's the *that* that you are referring to?"

Vague terms and incomplete sentences are often unconscious protection against strong emotions that lie beneath. When you ask clients to be more precise in their language, they usually become more clear in their emotions, which in turn creates further depth to the story and its understanding.

Ask about and Label "Missing" Emotions

We all have our own emotional range—the number of different emotions that we can feel and identify. We all have certain emotions that are easier to express than others: Some people, for example, who are afraid of anger pout and withdraw and show hurt, while those who are afraid to be vulnerable may only show anger. In order to change the emotional climate in the room, you need to draw out the other, "opposite" emotions that aren't being expressed.

If Bill is launching into an angry tirade, ask him what is he most worried about. If Susan snaps back at Bill, ask Susan if her feelings were just hurt. If Clarisse at once gets quiet and teary, wonder aloud if she ever feels frustrated or angry about what her husband is saying. Clients will usually respond positively and emotionally move in that direction—Bill will talk about his worry, Susan about her hurt, Clarisse about her anger. But even if they don't, if they seem puzzled or vague, you are seeding the idea for both that there may be more lying below the surface.

Cut Through the Verbiage

You really can't overtalk as long as your talking is clear and honest— explains your intentions, corrects a misunderstood remark, apologizes for a hurtful comment—and allows you to stay out of the ruts and on the road. This is different from the other type of overtalking, which is essentially about reducing anxiety. There are some therapists who tend to do this. They fall into a comfortable, familiar teaching role, or because of their own anxiety—with silence, with emotions, with their performance, with anxiety itself—are constantly stepping in to interpret or direct. They rationalize what they are doing, and such behavior can be seductive, enabling them to both feel important and keep their anxiety at bay. Couples can do the same—rather than taking the risk of clearly stating their own emotions and needs, they overtalk by repeating themselves, stacking fact upon fact, but emotionally going nowhere. When you see this happening, help the couple out by encouraging them to be direct and clear: "Allen, I think I understand what you are saying, but what is your point?" "Beth, you are describing a lot about what happened, but what is it that you want Jesse to understand about how you feel?" Questions like these pull the conversation out of the rut and onto more solid and productive ground. They encourage the couple to keep moving forward rather than staying stuck in their comfort zone.

Model and Insert Good Communication

There are times when it is helpful to restate what one partner is saying and include clear, assertive statements that change the emotional climate, provide a summary, and model better communication. If Bill's angry tirade about Susan's cavalier use of money, for example, results in only snappy responses by Susan, you could intervene and break the cycle by saying something like: "Susan, I wonder, if Bill came to you and said that he was really worried about the budget and the debt on your credit cards, what would you say?" or "Bill, if Susan said to you, 'Bill, every time you start talking about the budget, I just start to feel scolded and more like a child than a partner,' what would you say?"

You are interrupting the pattern, demonstrating more effective communication, and changing the emotional climate by your words and tone. If you are clear, assertive, and nonemotional, what you'll generally hear in response is "That would be great if he or she said that" or "Is that how you feel—are you worried?" or "Is that true, do you feel like I am scolding you?" The conversation moves out of the defensive rut that it is in and allows underlying issues to come to the surface.

Identify Similar Emotions

Couples entering therapy are often most sensitive to their differences. He, for example, wants to ground their teenager, who is acting out, while she wants their teenager to see the natural consequences of his actions. Or both partners are aware of how much they are trying to do to show the other that they care—he by working hard, she by being affection-ate—but both feel that their efforts are never appreciated and that the other does little for them. Instead both hear only resentment and criti-cism, and arguments ensue over who did what for whom. Their focus on their differences keeps them from seeing what they have in common.

What they share is the same underlying feeling and goal—both, in fact, are worried about their teenager, both are trying very hard to show that they care and feeling underappreciated. If you can cut through arguments and help them both hear that while their behaviors may be different, their emotions and intentions are the same, the problem is reshaped. Helping them see that they both feel exactly the same helps them empathize with each other. Rather than only seeing themselves standing on opposite shores, they realize they are, in fact, both emo-tionally in the same boat.

Ask the Hard Questions

When teaching suicide prevention, it is stressed over and over to par-ticipants that when they see the warning signs of suicide, they need to turn the corner and clearly ask the person at risk whether he or she has thought about suicide. When you explicitly ask the question the suicidal person knows that you are seriously concerned about his or her level of pain and, unlike a lot of people, are not afraid to talk about his or her deepest thoughts. This helps the suicidal person relax and open up, and enables you, as the helper, to clearly know what you are dealing with; it is on the table. The worst that can happen if you ask is that the person will say no, I would never think of hurting myself. You then know you are free to move the conversation in a different direction.

The reason this is emphasized in the training is that such a bold asking of the question seems emotionally counterintuitive to many people. Instinctively most folks are afraid that if they say the word suicide the person will actually get more upset or depressed, not less; somehow you may seed the idea and inadvertently encourage the person to move toward suicide, when, in fact, the opposite is true. It's the helper's assumptions and anxiety that get in the way of helping.

Couples often make the same assumptions and do the same avoidance. Harriet worries that Sam's depression could really make him suicidal; Sam worries that Harriet's drinking could get her fired from her job; both worry that if things keep going the way they are they will wind up divorced. But they shy away from saying any of this because each thinks the other will take it the wrong way and it will only make matters worse, or cause the feared situation to happen. Instead, they walk around on eggshells; they nudge each other to change without saying why, and then feel frustrated when no change occurs.

Your job is to ask the hard questions—to say what they may be thinking but are afraid to say themselves. As the outsider you're like the child in the fairy tale of "The Emperor's New Clothes" who is the only one in the crowd to say aloud that the emperor is in fact wearing nothing. Your neutral role allows you to say what you see:

> "What is your fear if things keep going the way they are and nothing changes?"
>
> "Are you afraid that your husband might have another affair?"
>
> "Are you worried by your wife's drinking?"

You ask about suicide, potential violence, divorce. You can put words to the emotions that are unspoken. Again the worst that happens is that they will say no, that's not the worry. But bringing it up makes the bottom lines more clear. The topic is on the table. You know where you stand and what is a priority.

Separate Shoulds from Wants

Couples who come to see you are torn—between their commitment and sense of obligation to their lives as they are and the desire for something different. The conflict gets played out in the complaints and arguments between them—about sex, for example, or nagging over laundry—but often this is merely an external representation of an internal struggle that they can't articulate. It's the classic shoulds versus wants split. The shoulds in their head keep them locked into patterns that may no longer fit who they are; the wants tell them about parts of themselves that have been pushed to the sidelines. The shoulds demand appreciation and similar sacrifice from the other; the wants are generous and require no payback.

When they say how hard they work on their jobs, how they have to do everything for the children, or expend enormous amounts of time cooking healthy meals for the family, ask if that is something they want to do. This introduces the notion that they can make choices and exercise self-responsibility rather than going on autopilot or falling into a martyr role. The wants become the basis for a new vision for their lives.

These are just some of the ways you have of raising underlying issues and changing the emotional climate in the room. Again you're looking for the holes, pushing the couple to take conversation once sentence further, putting words to nonverbal cues that they have long habituated to. You are making the unspoken the doorway to change.

Be Honest

The movie version of honesty is dramatic. The camera moves in for a close-up, the heroine turns and says, "To be honest, Frank, I never did love you." The music swells. Frank looks stunned. Finally the emotional dam is broken and the Truth spills out.

Couples often think of honesty in a similar way—as blurting out resentment, fear, or regret when fed up enough, stressed enough, drunk enough. But real honesty is something else and more rare. It is the subtle matching of words with intention and emotion in the moment. It is the foundation of integrity, and the most basic of the Basic Four. When you can't make sense of what Mia is saying, when you feel discouraged because Denelle and Rashan once again have "forgotten" to do the homework you assigned, when a couple asks whether it is fair that their grown son lives in the basement and doesn't contribute a lick of money to the household expenses, you say what you think and feel in the moment. You say you are confused, discouraged, or have no clear idea of what to say, rather than pressuring yourself to figure it all out or have the right answer.

This type of honesty takes focus, mindfulness, courage. It requires that you stay close to yourself, to pay attention and give voice to your own emotions and intuitions as you do to the couple's. Rather than continuing, like the couple, to ignore the emotional elephant in the room, you point it out. You keep your hand on the process in the room, and if you believe that things have gone off course—in the room, in the treatment—you say it and demonstrate leadership in setting it right once again.

Your doing this enables the couple to learn to do the same. You're showing them how, in the microinteractions between them, problems are formed. When Denelle says she is fine while her head subtly shakes a no, you stop her, say what you see, and encourage her to take the risk to match words and thoughts. You're empowering her to be honest, right there and then, so she can have the experience of being authentic and Rashan can get to know his wife as she really is. Yes, she may brush you away at first. But if you gently persist, and model this way of being, she will learn to pay attention to her inner self, rather than staying fixated on what she thinks she may see in the face of her husband. With your support she can learn to respond more authentically.

Honesty is what you always return to when you feel overwhelmed or stuck.

As mentioned above, the Basic Four form the core of couple work. They allow you to help a couple see the relationship from a new and expanded perspective. Everything else you may do builds on these. If you can master them, you'll have a solid foundation for treatment.

Let's turn now to two foundational models that can give you a lens through which you can view the couple's challenges.

THE DRAMA TRIANGLE

The drama triangle, also known as the Karpman triangle, was developed by psychiatrist Steven Karpman in the early 1970s and in many ways it is a graphic representation of Bowen's concept of differentiation.[1] It's a

---

[1] For more information on the theoretical foundations of the drama triangle see Steiner, C. (1994). *Scripts People Live: Transactional Analysis of Life Scripts*. New York: Grove Press; James, M., & Jongeward, D. (1996). *Born to Win*. Reading, MA: Addison-Wesley.

useful tool for describing the patterns couples seem to be in, as well as mapping out overall goals of treatment. Here is a visual representation:

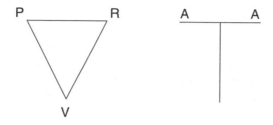

The triangle represents the relationship between two people. The P, R, and V represent different roles that the people can play—not the people themselves, but roles. The roles interlock and there is always someone on top who seems to have more power, and someone on the bottom. The relationship moves about in a circle as follows:

The person in the R position is the rescuer. The person in that role essentially has "nice guy" control. He hooks into the V or victim. The person in that role feels overwhelmed at times. He feels that problems are falling down on his head. The rescuer steps in and says, "I can help you out. Just do what I say, everything will be fine." Oftentimes couples will begin their relationship in some form of this dynamic. They psychologically cut a deal: The rescuer says, "I will agree to be big, strong, good, and nice"; the victim says, "I will agree to be overwhelmed and unable to manage." Everyone is happy. The rescuer feels needed, important, and in charge. The victim has someone to take care of him.

And it works fine, except every once in a while one of two things happens. Sometimes the rescuer gets tired of doing it all. He feels like he is shouldering all the responsibilities and like the victim is not pulling his weight, not giving anything back, not appreciating what the rescuer is doing. The rescuer gets fed up, angry, resentful. Bam! He shifts over to P, the persecutor role. He suddenly blows up, usually about something minor (laundry, who didn't take out the trash), or acts out—goes out and spends a lot of money, goes on a drinking binge, has an affair. He feels he deserves it. Look, after all, he says to himself, at what I've been putting up with. The message underneath the behavior and anger that usually does not come out very clearly is: "Why don't you grow up?! Why don't you take some responsibility?! Why do I have to do everything around here?! Why don't you appreciate what I am doing for you?! This is unfair!" The feeling of unfairness is a strong one.

At that point the victim gets scared and moves up to the R position, tries to make up and calm the waters. "I'm sorry," he says. "I didn't

realize how you felt. I really do appreciate what you do. I'll do better."
Then the persecutor feels bad about whatever he did or said, goes down
to the victim position, and gets depressed. Then they both stabilize and
go back to their original positions.

The other thing that happens sometimes is the victim gets tired of
being the victim. He gets tired of the other one always running the show,
always telling him what to do. He gets tired of being looked down on
because the rescuer is basically saying, "If it wasn't for me, you wouldn't
make it." Every once in a while the victim gets fed up and—bam!—
moves to the persecutor role. Like the rescuer, the victim in this role
blows up and gets angry, usually about something small, or acts out.
The message underneath that doesn't get said is "Why don't you get off
my back! Leave me alone, stop controlling my life! Back off, I can do
things myself!" The rescuer hears this and moves to the victim position.
He says to himself, "Poor me, every time I try to help, look what I get."
The persecutor then feels bad about whatever he did or said and goes to
the rescuer position, saying something like "I was stressed out, off my
meds, tired from the kids. I'm sorry." And then they make up and go
back to where they originally were.

While everyone gets to move among all the roles, often one person
will fit more comfortably in one role than another. This has to do with
personality, upbringing, and learned ways of coping. The rescuer as a
child was often an only child, oldest, or grew up in a chaotic family.
He usually did not have many buffers between him and his parents,
and learned early on that he could avoid getting in trouble and avoid
conflict by being good: "If I can stay on my toes and just do what my
parents (and teacher) want me to do all the time, I won't get in any hot
water." This type of person learns to be very sensitive to others as a
means of survival. He develops good radar and can pick up the nuances
of emotions. He is hyperalert, spends all his energy surveying the environment, and stays on his toes, ever ready to do what the parents want.
Essentially he takes the position of "I'm happy if you're happy, and I
need to make sure you are happy." He gets rewarded for being good and
his head is filled with shoulds.

What works for the child, however, doesn't necessarily work so well
for the adult. Now the world is bigger. Rather than just two or three
important people to pay attention to, the rescuer adult has many more—
the boss, the IRS, the president of the local Rotary Club or VFW. He
now feels pulled in a lot of directions, stretched thin, as he scrambles to
accommodate what he thinks others want from him. He easily feels like
a martyr, he is always at risk of burnout.

He also has a hard time knowing what he wants. Because he spent so much of his energy as a child looking outward and doing what others wanted, he never had the opportunity to sit back and decide what he wanted. Wanting, unlike following shoulds and rules, is a feeling, and he is often not aware of what he is feeling. As an adult, if he is asked, "But what do you want?" he hesitates and gets stuck. He worries about making the right decision, about not offending anyone in his life or the critical voice in his head.[2]

He also has a hard time with anger and conflict (which is why he became good in the first place) and tends to stuff anger down until he gets fed up and begins to gag on it. Then he blows up, and because he is so uncomfortable with it and it creates so much drama, he feels like his worst dream has come true. He feels guilty and shoves it all back down again, only to have it build up again.

The victim, in contrast, was, as a child, often the youngest in the family, was overprotected as a child by parents or had older siblings who stepped in and took over all the time when he was stuck with a problem. What he missed in growing up were opportunities to develop the self confidence that comes from learning to manage problems on your own. Now, as an adult, he easily gets overwhelmed, feels unconfident, anxious. To handle these feelings he looks to the rescuer, who takes over and helps him feel better.

The persecutor as a type is the evil twin of the rescuer. Whereas the rescuer controls by being good and nice, the persecutor is angry, critical, and blaming. This is the abuser, and obviously some couples start with this persecutor–victim relationship, playing out childhood models and roles. The persecutor learned early on, "When I get scared I get tough. If I can negatively control everything going on around me, no one can sneak up behind me and get me."

The A stands for adult and is similar to Bowen's differentiated self. This person is not in a role, is more complete, proactive rather than reactive, self responsible rather than blaming, and is outside the triangle. Adults are peers; they are on the same level in terms of power. The adult says, "I'm responsible for what I think, do, say. If something bothers me, it is *my* problem. If you can do something to help me with *my* problem, I need to tell you, because you can't read my mind. If you decide not to help me, I'll need to decide what I'm going to do next to

---

[2]Actually, you can apply this model to one's internal dialogue as well, substituting different voices or subpersonalities for the roles. Those prone to depression, for example, often see themselves in the victim position, always at the mercy of the P, or critical voice that constantly judges and criticizes what they do, or the R, or the controlling voice that constantly hands them a list of shoulds that need to be followed. Either way they feel oppressed.

fix my problem. Similarly, if something bothers you, it is *your* problem. If there is something I can do to help you with your problem, you need to tell me. And if I decide not to help you with *your* problem, you can work it out. You may not handle it the way I might, but you can do it. I don't need to take over."

Two of the problems the rescuer and victim have in their relationship is that they do expect a lot of mind reading—you should know what is going on or how to help without my having to say so—and then feel frustrated or disappointed or angry when the other does not do it. They also have a distorted sense of responsibility: The rescuer tends to be overresponsible—your problems are my problems, I'm happy if you are happy, and it is my job to make sure you are happy. In the attempt to "make" the victim happy, the victim over time begins to feel pressure and control, which sets up the explosion. Similarly, the victim tends to be underresponsible: my problems are your problems—I expect you to fix them, and I either have to wait or manipulate you into doing so.

The adults, in contrast, are clear about who has the problem. This is represented by the vertical line running between them. If you feel it, it's yours. This is a key concept, one invaluable for couples to understand and incorporate. By being aware of who has the problem, the individuals can avoid the defensiveness, anxiety, control, and manipulation of couples caught in the triangle. They also can be more intimate. The problem the rescuer and victim face in their relationship is that the roles, which are not the people themselves but only parts of them, keep them stuck. The rescuer cannot let down his guard or get too vulnerable because he is afraid that the victim will not be able to handle it. Similarly, the victim cannot ever get too strong because the rescuer will feel threatened and out of a job. The long line between the victim and rescuer is real. It represents the emotional distance between them. The adults don't have this problem. Both can be responsible and strong, and yet honest and vulnerable. They can take risks, are not locked in roles, and, hence, can be more open and intimate.

Two people can obviously be in this pattern for a long time—seemingly getting along, suddenly having some acting out or emotional explosion, making up, returning to their roles, and repeating the pattern over and over again. Sometimes, particularly for the rescuer, it will continue until it eventually drops from the weight of it all—he gets a heart attack or has a psychological breakdown, and everyone is surprised and afraid. What can also happen over time, and what often brings the couple into therapy, is that one person is either tired of going around the cycle or begins to outgrow the role he is in. Like any other pattern it takes two to play the game and as soon as one person begins to move toward the adult, the other gets scared and tries to pull him back in to keep it going.

For example, you may have a rescuer who gets tired of mopping up all the time and starts to pull away and better define boundaries and problems. The classic case of this is the codependent of an alcoholic. The wife, for example, begins to attend Al-Anon meetings and starts to tell her husband, "Jake, I'm not going to call up your boss for you on Monday morning and tell him you are sick. You can call him yourself. I'm not going to pick you up off the front lawn on Saturday night if you get drunk." The wife is stepping out of the triangle, and if Jake got drunk before, he is going to get rip-roaring drunk to try and hook his wife back in. If that doesn't work, Jake is likely to switch to one of the other roles: He may shift to the persecutor, get angry, and threaten divorce and a custody battle over the kids or cut off money; he may get nice and tell her how he is going to start going to AA meetings to appease her and bring her back.

Similarly, if the victim moves to the adult position, the rescuer feels threatened. This is often seen in the empty nest stage of marriage. The husband has more or less been in charge—making most of the big decisions, financially supporting the family—and then the kids begin to leave home. The wife starts to say something like "You know, Bill, I'm thinking of maybe going back to school. I never finished my degree because I stayed home with the kids, and now is a good time to do it. Maybe I'll go back into full time work. I think I'd like to get my own checking and savings account so I can have my own money and be more independent."

While Bill knows what to do when his wife is in the one-down position, he doesn't know what to do when she shifts. Generally the first thing Bill will instinctively do is be nice but try and talk his wife out of the changes: "Why do you want to go back to school now? You're 45 years old. What are you going to be able to do with a degree? It will cost us 30 grand for tuition, for what? You don't need to get a full time job. This is a time to take it easy. We don't need another checking account. It cost $10 a month in fees that we don't need to spend." "Stay put" is the message. If that doesn't work, Bill may shift to the persecutor role and get angry—"If you want to go to school, you find a way to pay for it. We're not taking it out of our retirement." Or Bill will move to the victim position and get depressed so his wife needs to stay home and take care of him.

Finally, you easily see this dynamic in abusive relationships. If the victim in a persecutor–victim relationship decides to move out of the triangle or out of the relationship and not be a punching bag anymore, the first thing the persecutor will do is more of the same. If he was angry, he is now going to get explosive. He will stalk her, hunt her down, emotionally abuse her, or beat her up. If that doesn't work, he may get nice. He will be calling you up for anger management and ask if you could call up his wife or girlfriend and tell her that he called about therapy, then not follow through. If that doesn't work, he may get depressed, even threaten to kill himself so she will come back into the relationship.

If all the jockeying around doesn't work, the person left behind has one of two choices. He may end the relationship and find someone else to play the corresponding role, someone else to control, someone else to take care of him. Or the person left behind can move toward the adult position too.

The challenges of both partners moving to the adult position are several. The natural feeling of the one left behind is that if you care, you'll stay in the triangle. If they both move, the partners need to develop new ways of showing that they care for each other. There will be a period of transition while these new ways are being created, and the new ways will not, at least for a while, feel as good as the old ways. There are also the challenges of learning new skills, especially for the one feeling left behind.

The reason the triangle is so strong and works so well is because the roles are complementary. Each sees in the other what he is unable to see in himself. The rescuer, for example, is not as nice or strong as he thinks, but sees his vulnerability and anger in the victim and persecutor. The victim is not as weak as he thinks, but projects his strength and anger onto the rescuer and persecutor. The persecutor is not as tough as he thinks but only sees his weakness and goodness in the victim and rescuer.

To be successful they each must learn to recognize and incorporate what has been left out. The rescuer needs to learn to recognize his wants and take the risk of not being good and overresponsible. He needs to learn how to recognize his anger and then use it for information about what he wants. He needs to experiment with letting go of control and resist the impulse to fix his own anxiety by taking over when the other is struggling. He needs to learn how to let down his guard, so he can learn to trust and be vulnerable and nurture in a genuine caring way, rather than out of fear and the need for control.

Similarly, the victim needs to build up his self-confidence—by taking risks and doing things on his own, by using the rescuer not as a rescuer but as a support. He needs to learn how to partialize problems—separate them into manageable chunks—so he doesn't feel so overwhelmed. Like the rescuer he needs to tap into his anger and use it to better define his boundaries and wants.

Finally, the abuser needs to recognize that his anger is a defense. He has to look for the softer emotions that he sees in the victim—the hurt, the sadness, the regret—in himself and beneath the cover of his anger. He also needs to shift his strength to one that is more generous, needs to find ways of being nurturing and allow himself to be nurtured by the other.

The drama triangle gives you a way of conceptualizing the dynamics of a relationship, gives you a possible explanation for why the couple is seeking help now, and lays out individual and couple treatment goals. It is a useful tool for sorting and connecting the bits of information the couple presents, and as we discuss in the next chapter, provides a format for assessing the relationship. Finally, because it is so common that there is a diagram to explain it, presenting this to a couple as a way of summarizing and framing their concerns and dynamics helps them feel normal, and less embarrassed. The diagram can stay in their minds, and you can refer back to it, or use the terminology—"John, it seems like you are rescuing"; "Maria's upset is her problem, not yours"—to help the couple see how the pattern invades their microprocess.

THE RELATIONSHIP ROLLERCOASTER

The relationship rollercoaster is our second foundational concept. Like the drama triangle it provides a useful explanation of the normal change process over time, suggests the sources of common problems, and points to treatment goals. It too is a helpful guide for assessment. The model goes as follows:

When two people meet and fall in love, it's usually due to the right mix of common and complementary interests and qualities. Steve and Megan, for example, may share the same sense of humor, both are politically liberal, but Steve is outgoing while Megan is shy. On the conscious level, they both instinctively weigh out the pros and cons of their respective similarities and differences—Steve sees Megan's quietness as intriguing and comforting, Megan admires Steve's ability to reach out to strangers, and somewhat enjoys his dragging her out to parties that she would never go to alone. There's a physical chemistry between them, and also a psychological one shaped by their childhood experiences and other dating relationships.

But their chemistry is also shaped by the present. At the particular moment they meet they each have something at the top of their list of needs. Megan may have recently ended a relationship with a controlling, abusive boyfriend, or she may have had a depressed, withdrawn father; what she appreciates the most is Steve's gentle humor and support. Steve's mother may have recently died, and Megan's quietness reminds him of her and allows him to open up and grieve. They may or may not be fully aware of these needs at the time, may not be able to fully articulate what they feel, but later if you ask the question about what most attracted them to each other, these are the elements they will usually claim.

And so they get married. They unconsciously make a contract with each other, saying, in effect, that I will give you this (my outgoingness, my energy and humor) if you give me that (your quiet support).[3] In the first year of marriage, they work out routines and rules about how they will live together, how they will handle differences and conflicts, who will be in charge of what, who will lean and when. Sorting this all out and the jockeying around power can be stressful and difficult—battles over toothpaste tubes left uncapped, garbage not taken out, who is in charge of the laundry, and who decides when, how, and who will do it. But if they can work through all these, after about 6 months or a year, they settle into routines and roles. They work together to carry out their vision of their relationship: They work their two jobs and save up money to buy a house. They have a child or two. Megan decides to stay home or work part time while Steve commutes to the city and works on climbing up the career ladder. Everything is fine.

But then things begin to change. By year 5, 6, or 7 there is a shift. Perhaps the couple find themselves moving into parallel lives. Steve is working until 8:00 most nights, while Megan spends Saturdays going shopping or visiting her mother. The time they spend together often seems boring or too routine. What was most attractive now turns into an annoyance. Steve's outgoingness now seems to Megan like a distraction, his humor now seems to slide into a cruel sarcasm, while Megan's quietness now seems to Steve like indecision, a passivity that is driving him crazy. There is tension—they argue over the kids, or money, or in-laws—and the arguments rarely lead to a true understanding or solution. Each "tries" and gives in for a time, only to collapse in frustration, or they silently agree to emotionally just sweep the issue under the rug. Things are not working as well as they used to. Both sense a growing gap—between the routines and rules and even the vision that they hammered out at year one and who they are now as individuals.

---

[3]Clifford Sager has written extensively on conscious and unconscious contracts as the foundation of couple relationships and their treatment. For more information see Sager, C., & Hunt, B. (1981). *Intimate Partners: Hidden Patterns in Love Relationships*. New York: McGraw-Hill.

What has happened is that the relationship contract has run out because the relationship has been successful. They gave each other what they needed and filled the emotional holes. Steve no longer misses his mother or needs one; Megan, thanks to Steve, is no longer so timid or fearful. They both have changed; something else is now at the top of their need list. They each feel cramped within the box of the life they have created and are living.[4]

One way to visualize this process is to imagine the start of the relationship as a move into a large empty house. The couple is free to decorate it and use it as they like, and this is what they do in that first year. But over the years the rooms get filled with psychological junk—unvoiced resentments, arguments that are never resolved, hurtful, situations and events from which the couple never really healed. As a room gets filled, the couple unwittingly chooses to simply close the door to the room rather than clearing it out. They do this over and over through the years until one day they find themselves living in the entranceway near the front door, talking only about the kids or the weather.

This is the point where some couples decide to divorce.[5] Because the house that is their relationship has grown too small and cramped, it's easy to think that moving out and starting over in a new empty one would solve the problem. Others too frightened to take this step try and distract themselves from their emotions. Steve may take a promotion that takes him out of town 3 days a week; Megan may find herself in an affair with the neighbor across the street; both may decide that it is time to get another dog or buy that cottage on the lake and spend the weekends teaching the kids to water ski. Or they may focus on a comfortable problem—they become child centered and both worry about Tommy's school performance or ask Megan's newly divorced sister and her kids to come live with them.

And this distraction works at least for a while. But then the kids get older—Tommy goes off to college, Megan's sister moves out. The couple faces the changes of the empty nest and empty house. They find themselves staring at each other from across the room and panic sets in. Again the notion of divorce looms. Steve faces a midlife crisis and decides he really hasn't been happy for a long time. He resents the pres-

---

[4]Research in adult development supports these periods of transition. For classic writings in this area see Sheehy, G. (1984). *Passages: Predictable Crises of Adult Life*. New York: Bantam; Scarf, M. (1988). *Intimate Partners: Patterns in Love and Marriage*. New York: Ballantine Books.

[5]According to a report issued by the U.S. Census Bureau in 2005, first marriages that end in divorce last an average of 7.8 years.

sure that he has been feeling from Megan to succeed. He wants to quit his job and sail solo around the world. Megan decides it is time to get back into her career, and she wants to go get her degree or go after that high-powered job in Chicago. And they battle or don't and instead move further apart into their own parallel lives. Or they may distract themselves once again—pulling in grandchildren or foster children, or getting more dogs to fill the space between them.

Or they come in for counseling. They tell you they are talking about divorce or feeling like the relationship is stale and empty. They individually realize that large chunks of themselves have been pushed to the back corners of their lives. Their early dreams have withered and they are seeking to reconnect with them once again. You want to help them to discover and say what they each want, unleash their imaginations to reenvision their present and future. But most of all you want to encourage them to go back down the hall and up the stairs. In order to revitalize and open their relationship they need to clean out the rooms that were closed off so many years ago.

It's easy to see overlap between this developmental model and the drama triangle, different perspectives on the notion that the initial success of the relationship in meeting individual needs leads to a natural change in these needs over time. Both point to the challenge facing every relationship, namely, having ways of changing the relationship to keep step with the changing individuals. This requires a couple to be honest, to understand the processes that limits them, the patterns that constrain them. It requires that both partners be empowered to be who they are rather than simply replicating the old roles and coping styles of their childhood. If they don't learn to do this, there is a high probability that they will find themselves in the same place 8 or 15 years later and thinking of divorce. But if they can stay and work to bring the contract up to date, learn the skills that allow them to stay closer to their lives and handle problems as they arise, rather than continuing to fill the rooms and close the doors, they can be successful over the long haul.

SETTING THE FOUNDATION

We've now laid the foundation for doing couple therapy and highlighted your role in shaping the process in the room and understanding some of the challenges that bring the couple to your office. In the next chapter we look at the specifics of starting treatment, defining and redefining the problem, setting goals, and engaging the couple.

Looking Within: Chapter 2 Exercises

1. Practice becoming more aware of process and patterns. As you sit in a staff meeting or gather together with your friends, try sitting back and noticing not what is said, but the patterns of interaction—the roles that various people take, the ways that folks predictably respond to each other, the ways each copes with his or her anxiety or manages conflict. See if you can step back even further and see your own patterns in the interaction.

2. Experiment with honesty. Try matching your words, thoughts, and feelings as closely as possible as you talk with your spouse or a friend, as you meet with a colleague over lunch. Try not telling a lie for a day and see what happens and what it feels like.

3. Attune yourself to nonverbal communication. Pay attention to the way a friend sighs or rolls her eyes or laughs away a serious statement. See what happens when you pick up on it and comment on it, rather than ignoring it or focusing only on words.

4. Sensible risk taking prepares you for leadership and honesty. Increase your self confidence by deliberately deciding to do something against your own grain—speak up rather than staying quiet, be quiet rather than speaking up. Take on a physical challenge—a long hike, a ropes course—to confront your fear or reluctance in a new way. Try letting go of your routines for a day and follow your wants rather than your shoulds.

5. Think about the drama triangle. How do you see it playing out in your own life? In your parents' lives? How have your roles and relationships changed over time? What would it take for you to move toward the adult position in your relationships?

6. Think about the relationship rollercoaster. What most attracted you to your partner or those close to you? What rooms have you closed off between you, or within yourself?

Chapter 3

Beginnings
Presentations, Assessments, and Goals

"A beginning is the time for taking the most delicate care," says Frank Herbert in his book *Dune*, and he's right. While the motivations, expectations, and goals vary from couple to couple, your challenge in those first sessions is essentially the same—to help them feel heard and safe, to help them see that sitting in a room with you and talking about their lives can be an effective way of quelling a crisis or creating a life that can be better. You want to get them on board and motivated to continue.

While this is the explicit goal of any starting therapy, the challenge is greater when doing couple therapy. As mentioned earlier, you lack the intimacy so accessible in individual therapy; you are not facing worried and motivated parents in family therapy who are rallying around a child. Instead here you are, a stranger peering into the bedroom of their lives, causing them to feel vulnerable and exposed. And they are likely to be on different pages. If one partner is convinced that therapy can offer a solution, the other is likely to be thinking that this is really not such a good idea.

The struggles of the couple relationship are, not surprisingly, reflected in the coming to therapy itself. As noted couple therapist William Doherty has said, there is always one partner who is "in" and one who is "out" in terms of commitment to the relationship, working on the problems, and seeing someone like you to help them do it. This reluctance, resistance, or mere going along creates an imbalance from the start. If the therapy is to continue, you need to correct the imbalance as quickly as possible so both are engaged.

In this chapter we discuss what to look for and think about during the first few sessions—common couple presentations, session goals, assessment—as well as what to do and to avoid doing: all the ingredients for creating that good start.

COUPLE PRESENTATIONS: THE TOP SIX

While each couple's concerns are unique, their presentations to you can be grouped into several discrete patterns, each with its own challenges. Here are the six most common ones:

The Crisis Couple

> *Hank and Paula have argued before but last Saturday night it turned physically violent.*
>
> *Tom got fired from his job, again, and for Julia it is the last straw.*
>
> *After 12 years of marriage David told Suzanne that he is gay and wants a divorce.*

Couples in crisis. For one or both of the partners reality has suddenly shifted. The fabric of the relationship itself seems in tatters. Emotions are running high. One person is crying or angry, the other apologetic, or defensive, or guilty. One feels like a victim and sees the other as the perpetrator and may be pummeling the other for answers. They want to battle in your office, or may sit there bewildered and stunned. You are at this point a firefighter. Your job is to turn down the heat in the room, move them beyond their shock. You want to help them put the crisis in a larger context, help them see that what seems sudden or drastic is actually the product of more subtle, ongoing dynamics.

The Stale Couple

They are tired of going around and around with each other about how to handle the kids and never getting anywhere. Or they feel disconnected, each in his or her own separate world, or feel bored, have little to say, and are never intimate. They may have been married a long time and feel like they are just going through the motions. They're not angry as much as exhausted. They feel like they have tried to make things better but have run out of ideas. At least one of them thinks that maybe you have some answers.

You can feel the lethargy or frustration in the room. Rather than putting out a fire, you need to heat them up—to get them to talk about their regrets, their resentments. You want to replace detachment with emotion, the superficial with the honest. You wonder if they have reached the limits of their skills. You wonder why they are afraid to speak up, why they are deciding to tackle this now when it is obvious that the situation has been going on for some time. You want to help them break the long-standing patterns, help them not just do something different but feel something different so they can believe that things can change.

The Fix-My-Partner Couple

"Janet and I used to have sex all the time before we married; now we rarely have it."

"Tyrone never talks. I feel like I am living alone."

"Emily nags all the time. It is driving me crazy."

One partner drags in the other for you to fix. It's less about couple therapy and more about seeing you as a repair shop. These situations are like those in family therapy where the parents at the first session literally drop off the 8-year-old for you to straighten out while they wait out in the car. The "broken one" comes along because he or she is compliant or feels guilty, and thinks maybe the other is right. There's a one-up and one-down stance in terms of power.

You are susceptible to two dangers in these situations. One is that you go along with the presentation and side with the person in power. You pull Janet aside to find out why sex is so difficult for her, or Tyrone to find out why he won't talk, or Emily to see why she nags. In their minds you become another powerful person, albeit a kinder one, telling them that they need to shape up. They may follow your lead and talk about the other's complaint, but you have succeeded in perpetuating the dynamic and fueled the more powerful partner's fantasies that he or she is just fine. The other danger is that you side with the victim. You feel sorry for pushed-around Janet, Tyrone, or Emily. You find yourself taking on their battle while they watch quietly in the corner.

As a couple therapist you want to stay balanced and focused on the couple. Rather than thinking in a linear, problem–solution fashion, as they do, you want instead to think in a circular way—not how to fix the one with the problem, but how the interplay between them, the process, creates and sustains the problem. Rather than worrying about how to make Janet more sexual, focus instead on helping her move, in terms of the drama triangle, out of the one-down position and into the adult position. Explore whether this is really a problem for Janet herself, or how as a couple other problems or patterns may have lowered the overall level of intimacy. Instead of suggesting there is something wrong with Tyrone's ability to verbalize, wonder aloud with him if there is anything his partner does that makes him feel unsafe or unheard. Explore with Emily what she feels her husband doesn't really understand about her and her feelings, and what emotionally drives what he considers nagging.

Your goal is to empower the "problemed" partner to speak up and give his side of the story, his vision of the relationship without speaking for him. You want to help the partner in power to become curious about his role, begin to see that his response may actually contribute to the problem rather fixing it. Direct your focus toward changing the process in the room rather than, like the couple, getting stuck on the content.

This presentation is different, however, from those in which one partner openly acknowledges that he or she is struggling in a particular area, and the other is sincerely looking for ways to help. Brian, for example, may have a history of bipolar illness and is worried about the stress of starting a new job. Or Colleen may have a history of eating disorders and the stress of the new baby is igniting old patterns of bingeing and purging. Here both partners show up, actively agree on the problem, and are seeking your help in best providing support for the relationship. They are like the couple facing their child's heart transplant, and their motivation is caring, rather than frustration and power. In contrast to the true fix-my-partner couple, your focus is not on rebalancing power, but helping one partner best help the other move through a difficult situation.

The Fine-Tuning Couple

Nora and Armand are getting married in a few months, and both find that they don't know what to do when they get emotionally deadlocked on an issue. Sal and Kate feel that they have a fairly strong relationship but realize that they have built much of their relationship around the kids. Now that the kids are leaving for college they worry that they might each spin off into their own separate worlds.

While these types of proactive, anxiety-approaching couples seem to be a minority of those seeking therapy, they are out there and seem to fit the clinician's ideal. They are not in crisis or apathetic, but equally motivated. Therapy for them is a first line of defense and they come to you seeking ways of getting over a challenge in the relationship. They are asking for new skills or tools, seeking a safe place to unravel what is concerning, but not incapacitating their relationship.

And that's what you do—help them improve their communication, provide the safe environment, and guide them toward taking their conversations one step deeper. Offer on-the-spot coaching to help them talk through a particularly thorny issue, give homework that helps put new skills into action, recommend a self-help book for them to work through together. They will come a few times or come every few weeks for a few months. They'll try out the new skills, feel less anxious or more equipped, and come back later if they run into trouble.

The Problem-with-Children Couple

Couple problems are sometimes hidden behind a smoke screen of other family issues. One of the most common presentations is that of parents who come in asking about ways of getting their child to bed on time or dealing with a defiant teen. By the second session they have dropped this focus and are zeroing in one partner's Internet addiction, or when you ask more questions about their relationship you find them openly spilling out a host of problems.

What the couple is doing in these cases is using the parenting issue as a way of testing the therapeutic waters. They want to see if your style is compatible with theirs, whether they feel comfortable enough and/or whether you seem knowledgeable enough to handle the more sensitive issues of their relationship. If they feel like it is a good fit, they move on to their real concerns.

The No-Problem Couple

If the fine-tuners are a good example of being anxiety-approaching and proactive, the no-problem couples are an example of the opposite— anxiety avoiding, reactive, and unwilling or unable to see the problems between them. Often these are couples who are referred by an agency— social services, for example, who want the couple to have counseling before the children will be returned from foster care—or the court, which has stepped in yet again after a volley of charges and counter-charges for domestic assault. Often their relationship is built around a you-and-me-against-the-world stance. They may not get along well together, but they feel like they've got each other's back covered. They stand united against the outside world, which they see as interfering, dangerous, or out to get them.

In your office they minimize the problems—sure, Jeff shouldn't have pulled out the knife, but he was drinking vodka, which he rarely drinks, and really didn't intend to use it. Sandra shouldn't have locked Jonathan out of the house again, but she knew he was in "one of those moods" and she had a hard day and didn't want to deal with it. The agency or the court made a big deal about nothing. Everything is okay now, they are getting along just fine. They really don't see any point in coming to see you.

This is a case where they see you as another one of "them" who they distrust and see interfering in their lives. The party who has the problem—the agency, the court that referred them—is not in the room. Start by getting them in the room—have the lawyer or the social services caseworker come to the next session and explain why he or she wants them to attend counseling, and the consequences for not doing so. Say to the couple that you are ready to help them, whatever they want to work on, even if it is just getting the referring agency workers off their back. The core clinical issue is gaining trust. Any one-up stance on your part only heightens their resistance.

Rather than getting lost in discussions about the means—whether or not to do therapy—stay focused instead upon the community's priorities and goals: that they need, for example, to stop their violent arguments if they want to get their kids back or avoid going to jail. Therapy is one way of helping them do that, but, you say, you, and usually the community, are open to others. Help them come up with creative alternatives if they are against therapy; help them be proactive rather than victims of the system. If they decide not to continue therapy, offer to write a letter explaining their decision. Avoid the power struggle and avoid overworking.

You'll find most couples fitting into one of these presentations. Recognizing them can give you a start on what to look for and what to avoid. Let's turn now to your clinical goals for these early sessions.

IN THE BEGINNING: GOALS

Whenever you've been to see a new physician, you probably have a distinct impression of what made the experience a good or bad one. In a good experience the doctor seemed focused rather than distracted, asked what you were most worried about, and listened to your questions and concerns, rather than running you through a list of questions or symptoms. He or she talked about treatment options, rather than pushing you toward one. Though initially nervous, you relaxed. By the end of the appointment you left feeling that you were in capable hands and this doctor was the right person to help you.

Couples seeing you for the first time are looking for that same experience. The process may be new and unfamiliar to them, and they want to feel relaxed and feel that you understand what they are struggling with. They want to know what can be done, and whether you are the right person to provide it. You want to answer the questions, help them feel safe, and leave them with a realistic sense, not only of how this will work, but that it can help. Here are the goals you'll want to focus upon:

Establish Rapport

This is the starting point, of course, of all therapies. The challenge with couples is making certain that you connect with both of the partners, not just one. Say "Can you tell me why you are here?" then be quiet and listen intensely. Ask them to talk one at a time and block interruptions by the other. This creates a safe forum, and is what each of the partners has often been missing the most. Generally clients have thought a lot about what they want to say, so let them say it. Nod, reflect back their emotions—"Mary, you sound frustrated"; "Shamika, it sounds like you've been dealing with this problem for a long time"; "Eric, you sound angry even as you talk about it now." Give them the space to vent their feelings or say their thoughts aloud without criticism or judgment by you.

For couples who are hesitant, shy about jumping in, make small talk—ask Mary about her job, Eric about the kids; ask Shamika what she enjoys doing the most. Give them a chance to hear your voice and see you are an active, caring listener.[1]

Be sensitive to cultural and ethnic diversity. There are plenty of resources to help you learn about diversity—articles on gay relationships, books on the values and family structures of various ethnic and racial groups—and these can familiarize you with the qualities and characteristics of these various populations. But what is important to keep in mind about cultural, ethnic, or racial diversity is simply to keep it in mind. That is, don't ignore differences between you and the couple, because generally they won't. Approach differences with an air of curiosity and speak up about them: "Because I am not gay (or African

---

[1] There has been research in recent years to support the impact of these positive first impressions. See Hubble, M., et al. (Eds.). (1999). *The Heart and Soul of Change: What Works in Therapy*. Washington, DC: American Psychological Association.

American or Indian or Ethiopian or Muslim) myself, I wonder if you can tell me how you feel your lifestyle (culture, race, religion, etc.) has shaped your relationship." People are usually happy you brought it up and happy to tell you what they think. And even if they feel the differences are minimal, your question may stimulate their own curiosity about their values and priorities.

If you can, mirror their expressive styles and stances. If Tom seems emotional and Sandy is intellectual and logical, empathize with Tom's feelings ("It must seem frustrating at times"), while offering Sandy information and explanations to allay her anxiety ("I'm asking about this because the research shows ... "). If Tom leans forward with his elbows on his knees, subtly do the same, but sit upright like Sandy when talking with her. Watch for the subtle nonverbal clues to let you know how you are doing. If Tom rolls his eyes or looks away, if Sandy starts to challenge your research or crosses her arms against her chest, gently point out what you notice ("You seem like you don't agree") and go back to the starting point—be quiet and just let them talk until they again relax.

But remember that most of all you want balance. You want them to see that you are interested in the couple, not just the one who is more verbal or emotional. So don't let Sandy go on and on about herself or how she sees the problem while Tom stares at his shoes from across the room—you're probably only replicating what happens at home. Watch the time and make sure there's enough for him to be heard as well.

Determine What Is and Who Has the Problem

While some folks will be very clear about their concerns ("I always feel criticized"; "Our arguments have turned physically violent"; "He is always nagging me about the kids"), others are more vague—"We don't get along"; "We don't communicate well"; "He doesn't seem to care." When this happens, you want to clarify asking questions ("What happens when you don't get along? How do you feel? What do you do?" "What are you looking for to know that John cares about you?") or by observing the process in the room ("I notice you both are interrupting each other right now. Is that what happens at home? Is this what you mean by not communicating well?"). By uncovering the specific behaviors and emotions, you will begin to unravel the patterns within the process and better understand what needs to be changed.

Finding out who has the problem connects back to the drama triangle, the notion that whoever feels upset or believes there is a problem is the one who is ultimately responsible for solving it. If Jay feels that he and Suzanne don't have sex often enough, Jay's got a problem that Suzanne may or may not share. If Suzanne feels Jay is too critical, Suzanne's got a problem that ultimately she needs to deal with. By your drawing the lines of responsibility, you are moving each of them out of the triangle, out of the victim, persecutor, or rescuer role and toward an adult position. You sidestep the blame—who's right and who's wrong— and remove the power struggle.

Once you define who has the problem, you can then look at the reason for the frustration or anger, ways each can possibly help the other with his or her problem, or, best of all, explore whether their two individual problems are in fact linked. For example, you may say: "Suzanne, Jay says he is unhappy and frustrated by your sex life, and you say you are annoyed by his constant criticism. I wonder, if he were less critical, do you think you would feel better about the relationship? Might that make you feel differently about sex?" Or "Jay, Suzanne feels that you are critical all the time. Is there a connection between the criticism she seems to hear and what you describe as your frustration over the lack of physical contact? I wonder if each of you felt more cared about in the way you are each seeking it, would each of your problems begin to be resolved?"

Again, what you don't want is imbalance—that Suzanne's problem is more clear or more important than Jay's; that Jay is right and if only Suzanne fixed her problem with sexual intimacy, everything would be fine. If you have any thought that you may be leaving this impression by what you say or don't say, or suspect it by one person's nonverbal response, bring it up, check it out, and rebalance. Say, for example, "Jay, you are making a face. What are you thinking about what I just said?" or "Suzanne, I don't want to leave you with the impression that I'm siding with Jay against you." And if you feel things are unbalanced or unresolved after the session, give them a phone call to check and clarify.

Clarify Expectations

Each partner walks in with some expectation about you and the process—that you will tell them to get divorced, will decide who has the problem and will fix it, will teach skills, will provide a safe place for them to talk. If you don't know what they expect or don't meet their expectations, they will not come back. The easiest way to understand what they are seeking is to ask: "How did you think I could help?" "What did you most want to get out of our meeting today?" Again, make sure you hear from both partners.

Ask if they have been in some type of counseling or therapy before, individually or as a couple: "Yes," says Brad, "my parents dragged me into family therapy when I was a teenager and it was awful—all that happened is that I got blamed for an hour about screwing up"; or "We tried couple counseling for a few sessions last spring, but then dropped out. The therapist just sort of sat there and we essentially just said to her what we had said to each other at home." These responses and experiences tell you that you need to make sure Brad doesn't feel blamed, that you don't sit there and leave the couple hearing nothing new. If the couple has not been in therapy before they no doubt have something in mind gathered from friends' experiences, or from TV, however distorted it may be. They will automatically be matching these images against what is happening in the room.

You need to help them by clarifying your own expectations and style. Some of this will become clear to them as the session unfolds— how active you are, what types of questions you ask—and some of this you will explain: I'll be giving you homework; I'm interested in how you react to each other rather than who is at fault; I'm not going to tell you whether you should get a divorce, but will hopefully help you reach your own decision. By the end of the session you want to be sure that you all share the same vision of the therapy process.

Create Something New

The format and focus of the first session may vary based on the setting (a mental health clinic versus a private practice, for example) or the clinician's style and orientation (the use of formal assessment tools, for example, or the more reflective style of a psychodynamic practitioner). But regardless of settings or approach most clinicians would agree that even after one session the couple needs to walk out feeling differently than when they walked in—less anxious, more hopeful about the therapy process if not yet about the relationship, more clear about the clinician and approach even if they are not absolutely sure what will happen or how it will turn out.

It's useful to think of treatment actually beginning in the first session. You are observing but also changing patterns; you are actively listening but also changing the depth of their conversation through your questions and comments. You want to help the couple feel differently by the end of the session by creating something new for them to hear, think, and feel in the session. Here are some of the things you might do. We will be discussing them more fully in later chapters.

Change the Emotional Climate

Move toward the holes, what is not in the room. If they are angry, uncover the softer emotions—worry or sadness. If they are anxious, help them to calm down by listening or asking them to focus on their breathing. Generally, shifting the emotions of one partner will change the process between them.

Help Them Hear Something New about the Partner or the Relationship

While you may place some pressure on yourself to say something profound or moving, what often makes the biggest impact upon the couple is hearing something different from each other—how Frank really felt when his mother died, that Kelly was actually worried, not angry, when Tim left for the army, that Tom doesn't blame Grace for not getting the promotion at work. Uncovering new content will uncover new emotions, which in turn can change perceptions of the other and the relationship. So ask about personal dreams ("Wilson, did you always want to work in accounting?"), about what they remember most about the time they were dating, about common concerns and accomplishments ("As parents what makes you most proud of your son?"), about each other ("What is it that you feel Carl most misunderstands about you?"). Help them see that the other person is more complex than he or she seems, that underneath the familiar face of anger or indifference lie deeper emotions and memories.

Give Them a New Problem

The concept that problems are usually bad solutions to other problems means that the first step in fixing a problem usually means uncovering a new one: "You both are arguing about money, but I wonder if it's more a question of who's in charge"; "You're both talking about a lack of physical intimacy, but I sense there is a lack of emotional intimacy as well"; "John, you say that you don't feel like doing anything with Carol and the kids on the weekend, but from the symptoms you just described, I'm wondering if you are clinically depressed." Changing the problem and changing their view of the problem gives them new focus and new energy.

Normalize the Problem

It's easy for couples to blame themselves or their partners for problems or situations they feel they should have somehow avoided. By helping couples see their problems from a wider and common perspective—such as the drama triangle or developmental rollercoaster—you can reduce their anxiety and instill hope. Knowing, for example, that many couples have difficulties during the first months after the birth of a child, or that the transitions of the empty nest and retirement are normal, if stressful, challenges in the life of a relationship can help reduce the angst and pessimism. What they are experiencing is not abnormal but typical; what others have accomplished, they can too.

Teach a Skill

Help them see the process and patterns—"Bill, I notice that you are always interrupting Janice; see if you can try listening to what she is saying rather than thinking about what you want to say next"; "Carlos, it sounds like you are criticizing what Teresa is doing; try telling her what you are worried about instead"; "Pam, you seem to be getting upset; try to just focus on your breathing for a few moments and see if that helps you to relax." As one outside the system you can see what they cannot. Help them begin to recognize the patterns and change the behaviors in small ways.

Again, each of these strategies is a way of shaking up the system and changing how the partners feel about and see the relationship. It is the experience of change itself, however small, that instills hope that more change can follow. Rather than feeling stuck, they will feel more empowered. They will be more optimistic that therapy can help them achieve their goals.

ASSESSMENT

Along with making a solid connection with the couple and defining the presenting problems and the couple's expectations, your other focus during these initial sessions needs to be your clinical assessment. This will determine the goals and foci that are to follow. Obviously your own theoretical approach will shape the assessment itself—a psychodynamic approach, for example, will push you toward exploring childhood issues, a communication-based approach toward assessing their skills, a solution-focused approach toward mapping areas of success. Your model provides the frame within which you can organize what you see and hear.

The assessment model we are going to use looks at four major areas: skills, power, positives, and individual personalities and coping styles. We outline them here, and then discuss in the next chapter how to put the assessment into practice. Compare this model against your own.

Skills

Many clients unfamiliar with therapy associate it with a world of deep, dark individual pathology, unresolved childhood issues, or personality complexes—impressions gathered from the mass media. They brace themselves for what they imagine to be extensive excavation, the gradual, at times painful, peeling away of layers, a large investment of time and money.

Talking about skills is often a relief for such clients. It is more approachable, it sidesteps blame and guilt, it reduces anxiety. Couples can quite rightfully believe that if they master the new skills, they can begin to turn things around. And they can. There is a long tradition of behavioral approaches in couple work. They are the basis of the couple enrichment movement, and research has shown that couples who can learn new skills can successfully change their interactional patterns.[2]

So what skills do they need? The obvious communication skills include the use of I-statements, no name-calling or blaming, and the labeling of emotions, as well as the ability to actively listen—to understand what the other is saying and how he or she feels even if they don't agree—rather than interrupting, getting defensive, shutting down, and tuning out. By learning these skills couples can keep their conversations from escalating and becoming emotionally destructive.

But in some ways this is just the surface level of communication. The greater challenge and skill is helping couples not only to mind the rules, but to be acutely and actively aware of the process itself—to tell when it begins that the conversation is going off course, to realize when emotions are escalating and the discussion is moving toward a power struggle. They then need to be able to stop, repair, and change it, clarifying their intentions, apologizing for hurting feelings, saying how they feel in the moment—I'm getting frustrated, I feel confused. We're back to our analogy about steering a car. The couple needs to be able to look ahead while making the microadjustments as they go along to make sure the conversation stays on the road and out of the ditch.

This is often where couples get stuck. It essentially requires them to stay aware of two things at once—what both are saying and how both are saying it, to be aware of what they think, but also what they feel.

---

[2]In addition to the work of Gottman cited in Chapter 1 that extensively details communication skills, see also Bornstein, P., & Bornstein, M. (1986). *Marital Therapy: A Behavioral–Communications Approach.* New York: Pergamon Press. For a more cognitive-behavioral approach see Beck, A. T. (1988). *Love Is Never Enough: How Couples Can Overcome Misunderstandings, Resolve Conflicts, and Solve Relationship Problems through Cognitive Therapy.* New York: Harper & Row.

Again, their instincts are to fix emotions with content—to heap on more facts to bolster their argument rather than acknowledging their anger, to bring up a hurtful event from the past rather than acknowledging their own hurt. This is like flooring the gas when the car begins to get out of control.

They will need your help to slow the process down, step back, and see the patterns. You will need, especially in the beginning, to point out the process and the way things are going off course so they can become more sensitive and change it in the moment. They may also need your help to expand their individual skills as well—to feel a range of emotions and articulate them; to empathize with the other; to self-regulate, that is, to know that one is getting upset and calm oneself down. They are things that you can see in the room in the process. These are things that you can ask about directly—"Can you tell when you are feeling angry? Can you let Pete know?" "Margaret, you look sad; Paul, how do you feel when you see Margaret this way?" "Do you have ways of calming yourself down when you start to get upset?"

Finally, the arena of skills includes couple management and problem solving. Even the most skilled communicators will miscommunicate at times; even the most devoted couples will end up with unresolved arguments—that's human nature and to be expected. What is important is not what happened, but what happens next.

Are they able, once they have calmed down, to circle back and try again to discuss a problem? Or do they give up and sweep it under the rug for fear of stirring it all up again? Can they repair the relationship—apologize for hurting each other's feelings, they talk about the problems they had with talking? Can they solve the problems—discuss them without heavy emotion, make compromises while asserting their own needs, be pragmatic and try new behaviors, come back and evaluate and fine-tune them? Find out just how well the couple does in these areas by asking directly and observing.

Power

An imbalance in power will undercut communication every time. Even if Roger is able to talk openly and honestly with his friends and workmates, it doesn't matter if he feels he is constantly walking on eggshells or biting his tongue in his relationship with his wife, Sarah. If, following the drama triangle, one person is on top and the other on the bottom, the one on top is usually going to be controlling the conversations and the decisions.

How do you find out about the power balance? Ask how the couple makes decisions—about sex, money, the kids. Ask who usually gets his or her way and why. Ask if they find themselves feeling anxious or biting their tongues worrying how the other is going to respond. Watch who initiates the conversation in the room, who speaks for whom, whether one seems hesitant to speak up, if both can carry their weight in a conversation or argument. If you determine that the power is imbalanced, that they are likely locked into some form of the drama triangle, your goal will be to empower each of them to move out of their roles and into the adult position.

Positives

Sure, you are going to hear in the opening session that everything is negative—all about the problems, the blame, the criticism, the pessimism. But your prognosis and their sense of hope lies in what you may not hear, namely the positives of the relationship. Positive memories, positive emotions, positive comments are the ballast that keeps the relationship upright and prevents it, in difficult times, from sinking. See if you can help couples draw these out. Ask about the good times when they were dating, what they most liked about the other person when they first met. Are they able to shift gears or do they stay stuck in the anger and hurt of the moment? Are there good times they can look back to, or are all their memories laden with regret?

Do they compliment and thank each other, do they help each other destress and reconnect by talking about their day? Can they do what John Gottman calls "turning toward" rather than away—respond and engage when the other makes a comment ("Look at the sunset; isn't it wonderful!" and the other says, "It really is" rather than ignoring the comment and saying something critical)? Do they proactively create quality time as a couple—couple dates without the kids, gourmet sex, sharing common interests? Without these positives within the relationship either the stresses of life continue to build or they are forced to find all their stress relief from outside of it. If their best is some neutral zone—they're not fighting, the tension is less than it was—it becomes easy to feel that there is not much keeping them together. Moving them out of this negative or neutral ground means not only helping eliminate the problems but building in positive routines and habits.

Individual Personalities and Coping Styles

Each individual's personality shapes the relationship just as the relationship shapes the individual. The partner of someone with a borderline personality may feel like he can't do anything right or be hyperalert to the possibility of triggering an outburst of anger. A husband with obsessive–compulsive disorder (OCD) may leave his partner feeling isolated by his preoccupation, or driven to distraction by rituals and endless focus on details. A partner suffering from depression can emotionally drag the other down. Those with a history of addiction—to drugs, alcohol, Internet pornography—may leave the other always suspicious that they will slip back with no warning.

You want to know about these issues by asking about personal and family history of psychological problems, of past treatments. Sometimes these disorders may already be under control—the partner who is obsessing is already taking medication, seeing a therapist, and doing better; the addict truly is in active recovery, attending multiple support group meetings a week. But sometimes not—the person is not aware that his depression really is depression, the addict minimizes the addiction, the partner with the personality disorder tends to blame the other for her reactions.

The clinical issue you need to decide is whether the individual issues need to temporarily take priority over the couple's issues. If one partner is actively alcoholic, you may, for example, want to recommend that he put his energy into getting his addiction under control or at least get a separate addiction assessment before doing intensive couple therapy. Sometimes couple therapy can be woven into the other treatment—mild to moderate depression, for example, can be treated with medication that is started simultaneously with couple therapy; the person with OCD can continue to see the individual therapist while seeing you for couple work. For those with personality disorders, you may be able to use the couple therapy to help them see how their personality and behaviors shape the relationship process.

But in addition to these obvious individual issues are ones more subtle yet as important. If Margaret has a history of violence, for example, is it a generalized characterological response or limited to those few situations of extreme stress? Does one of the partners have a history of physical, sexual, or emotional abuse which triggers old reactions that ignite problems in the current relationship? Does Mark, for example, emotionally shut down and react more like a 10-year-old whenever Cynthia shows the slightest disapproval? Does Linda dissociate or avoid sex with her husband because of her past history of abuse?

Ask about their family of origin. Did the parents have a tumultuous marriage? Was there a divorce, violence, addiction? What role models did the individual have as a child with regard to close relationships, communication, men, and women? Looking back, what roles did each of them play in their families—the good oldest child, the babied baby, the loner, the rebel? Are these roles still being replicated in the present? What skills and strengths were developed by these experiences? What skills are lacking? How have these two pasts created the one present between the couple?

The good child, for example, may continue to cope with tension by being pleasing and overresponsible, playing the rescuer role of the drama triangle. His challenge will be to renounce some of that responsibility and deal with conflict in a more direct way. Similarly, the person who's witnessed a number of divorces will either be determined to break the pattern but lack the skills to do so, or may see divorce as an acceptable solution for difficult problems. That partner's bottom line and tolerance for conflict may be very different from that of a partner whose parents never divorced, and in fact rarely argued.

Finally, just as you do in the relationship, you're looking in the individual for positive qualities and coping styles to offset any negatives. An ability, for example, to tolerate anxiety, to take risks, to see mistakes as mistakes and not tragedies; an emotional flexibility—an ability to change one's mind without guilt, and allow others to change theirs without anger; a self-esteem that allows one to ask for help.

What you are creating for yourself and the couple is an inventory of strengths and weaknesses. You're mapping with the couple their developmental and historical changes—how the new mother, for example, now feels empowered and is less submissive to her husband than she was in the past, or how the husband decides to quit his job because his father never could—and helping the couple place these changes into the context of their presenting problems. By exploring the element of natural change in their lives, by stirring up old information and recombining it in new ways, they can connect the dots differently. With a new perspective on the present, they can create a new perspective on their future.

Again, what you look at most, how you go about the assessment process, will reflect over time your own style and clinical orientation. Some clinicians tend to be more interactional, pragmatic, and informal, with assessment and treatment unfolding together throughout the process. Other clinicians use a more structured process—gathering extensive histories through questionnaires, for example, or dedicating several sessions to a formal assessment process before officially talking with the couple about a treatment plan. Either approach is fine just as long as you are clear about your process and clear with the couple. Again, everyone's expectations need to match if you are all to get off on a good foot.

Our discussion of presentations, goals, and assessment lays a foundation for moving through the opening stages of therapy. Next we move on to putting these ideas into practice.

Looking Within: Chapter 3 Exercises

1. How strong are your own communication skills? How well are you able to use I-statements, make positive comments, stay aware of the process? What types of situations are apt to make you less assertive and more reactive, or trigger strong emotions?

2. Practice your ability to discern who and what is the problem. As you listen to conversations between friends, as you engage in your own relationships, be aware of times where the lines become muddied, where blame denotes a giving up of responsibility, where the problem is unclear.

3. Consider your own family of origin. What childhood impressions did you get about marriage, about conflict, about the nature of men and women? How have those impressions affected your view of your own close relationships and your work with clients?

4. Define your assessment model. Based upon your working theory, what information is most important for you to uncover early in the therapy process? Are you comfortable combining assessment and treatment, or do you prefer to gather specific information before moving on?

5. What types of couple presentations are most difficult for you? What types of individual problems? How do you tend to respond? What type of emotional or educational support do you need to handle these cases more effectively?

Chapter 4

Beginnings in Action

You know what you want to do—connect, determine who has and what are the problems, see and stop the dysfunctional patterns and process, leave the couple with something different from what they walked in with. It's time to put your knowledge into action. Do you feel nervous? Sure, a bit. They do too. If you focus on them, rather than how well you think you're doing, you and they should settle down within a few minutes.

In this chapter we will discuss the details of managing the beginning sessions as they apply to the six common couple presentations. We'll also talk about variations and clinical options.

THE INITIAL CONTACT

The way you initially make contact with a couple depends upon your own style and your work setting. In a large agency, for example, you may be handed an intake sheet from the assessment unit assigning a couple to outpatient treatment. The information may be minimal, a simple listing—marital problems, anger issues—or it may be extensive, with detailed personal histories on each partner. In a small agency or a private practice you may field the phone call yourself.

Many clinicians find that making some contact with clients before the first appointment is a good idea. Between the time they may talk to someone at intake and the scheduled appointment, couples, because of their own ambivalence and anxiety, can easily change their minds about coming in. A brief phone conversation helps them connect to you and ensure their follow-through. Not only do they have an opportunity to ask make-or-break questions that may be on their mind—"How much do you charge?" "Can you see us after 5:00 P.M.?" "Do you mind if we bring our 3-year-old?"—they can hear your voice and sense your support, dispelling some their fantasies about what you are like.

What do you say on the phone? Introduce yourself, ask if there is anything they have questions about before you meet. Sometimes they will ask about your clinical approach—are you psychodynamic, will you teach them communication exercises, will you see both of them together?—or you may want to just go ahead and give them a quick summary of your approach. They may ask how many times they will need to come in or how often. You may want to ask if their doctor or someone else referred them, or how else they got your name (phone book, etc.)—clues to their level of motivation, knowledge of you, and the need for possible coordination.

Ms. Jones, for example, says that she went to her family doctor for help because she was feeling depressed, and after talking with him about her marriage, he suggested couple therapy. Ask her how she feels about the referral. If she says that she doesn't understand why it is necessary, she thought he would just give her some medication, you may want to give her a quick idea of what therapy may do. You can also suggest that she call her doctor back and talk about the referral so she better understands why he thought the counseling might be helpful.

Some individuals will invariably begin to describe the problems on the phone—"Thomas and I had fight last week ... "; "My wife says she is leaving ... "; "We've not been getting along for some time and I thought that this might help.... " Let the person talk, be supportive, but resist asking a lot of questions. You don't want to start the therapy on the phone. If you do you'll unbalance the system.

If Ms. Jones, for example, starts telling you how explosive her husband was last week, resist getting details or making suggestions. If you do she may invariably be tempted to tell her husband that night exactly what you said, leaving her husband feeling that you may already be taking her side before he walks into the room. Instead say to Ms. Jones that it sounds like they have both been having a hard time (emotional support), you're glad that she called (reinforce her motivation), that you are looking forward to talking with them both next Wednesday and seeing if the three of you working together can make things better (focus on the couple and the process rather than who is right or wrong).

Clients may also say that their partner is claiming he may or may not come in, or that he doesn't want to talk with a woman, or he'll only come once, and so forth. Suggest that they be both honest and matter of fact in discussing the appointment—"I'd like you come because I think it could help us both; come this one time and we'll see if it helps." This "one-time" response helps make the process less overwhelming for the reluctant partner. It's your job, not the spouse's, to connect and to persuade the partner to continue. By the end of the phone call the client should be committed to coming, have a sense of your personality, and feel less anxious. You may have a better idea of the presenting issue and a clearer sense of the couple's motivation or the possible obstacles to connecting.

THE FIRST APPOINTMENT

You go out to the waiting room. Be on time so they feel from the outset that you are trustworthy and dependable. Shake hands, introduce yourself. Lead them back to your office, tell them to sit where they like, let them get comfortable.

It's helpful to think about the first session as divided into fourths: The opening and presentation of the problem; the exploration/assessment; the return; summary and closing. We'll take each one in order with variations among the types of presentations.

The Opening

How's the mood in the room? Stiff and awkward? Overly friendly and anxious? Tension ready to explode? Often the partners will complement each other: one eager, wide-eyed, and talkative, the other quiet, withdrawn, staring at his shoes.

You can start off by referring back to the intake or phone call to create some continuity. "I know you both came in last week for an intake appointment. What I received was a copy of the form that they filled out and it says here that you have been having some marital problems." Or "Mary, you and I talked on the phone Tuesday, and I know that I told you a bit about my background and approach. Alan, just to fill you in on what I told Mary.... " Start upfront, with openness and balance—don't leave Alan wondering what you talked about or even in the dark about the fact that you and Mary had talked.

If a couple seems tense, some clinicians will ask easy questions to break the ice and get the process rolling—"Do you have kids?" "Where are you originally from?" "What kind of work do you do, Alan?" (especially if Alan seems quiet and removed)—to get the couple used to your voice, to begin to make a connection. Other clinicians will launch right in—"Can you tell me why you are here?"

If the couple is in crisis, brace yourself for an emotional onslaught—"Harriet walked out two days ago"; "We had a fight and Ted pushed me." The tension that was building in the room explodes. One partner may cry, yell, point fingers. The other may sit quietly and look away, or interrupt and yell back.

Take a deep breath. If one of the partners is venting and the other has not interrupted, let it go. Make supportive statements, listen actively—"It sounds like Harriet's leaving was a real shock to you; the fight must have seemed very scary to you both"—and see if the person can begin to calm down. Let the person vent but don't let him go on and on. If the description of the one event starts to spin off into a host of others, raise your hand and ask the partner to hold on for a minute. Exercise leadership. You don't want this to turn into a 40-minute harangue that leaves the other partner feeling beat up and leaves you with no opportunity to balance it out.

Turn to the other partner and ask about what she thinks the problem is, and see what happens. She may be quiet because she is emotionally flooded and shut down. Ask how she feels—angry, frustrated, doesn't know. Usually she'll begin to tell her side of the story. You need to let her talk—this provides the balance—but you don't want to dwell on the details—"And what day did you say that was?" This only creates the impression that the content is important, that you are thinking like a judge or a cop. You're neither. You're interested in tracking the interactional patterns—"She did this and how did you feel? And then what did you do?" Or, "Harriet, Bob says he doesn't understand why you decided to leave Tuesday. What made you decide to?" Watch the process—is the other person listening or getting defensive and ready to counterattack?

If the couple begins to argue right there in the office, again take a deep breath. You have two options. One is to stop it then and there, ask them to talk one at a time, block further interruptions. The other is watch the process carefully and see how it unfolds: Are they able to stay on track or are they bringing up old wounds? Are they arguing over details, are they able to cut through the information and say how they feel? Is the process escalating? Are the emotions are getting more intense, is someone becoming more nasty and critical? Has someone felt overpowered and shut down, or can each hold his or her own? Is it turning into a power struggle where the point is lost, with each just trying to get in the last word, or are they able to turn it around and deescalate themselves?

If the argument is moving toward some resolution (though this is not likely), let it go. If it is escalating (more likely), you need to step in like a referee—"Bob, let Harriet talk; try not to interrupt"—or halt it altogether—"Okay, let's stop for a minute"—and hold up your hands. Don't let it continue, don't lose control of the process. If they continue to escalate and you can't get them to stop, separate them—"Hold it, everybody, let's take a break; Bob, could you go sit in the waiting room for a few minutes while I talk to Harriet and then I'll talk with you?"

Once they stop your goal is to begin to change the emotional climate: "Wow, is this what happens at home? It seems like you both know how to push each other's buttons and can get angry quickly." Ask questions about the bigger picture—"How long has this been going on?" "Has it gotten worse?" Ask about softer emotions—"What hurts your feelings?" "What scares you about her leaving?" A lot of couples get stuck in unproductive arguing because they lead with their defenses—they criticize and attack in response to feeling scared or hurt or lonely. Change the emotional climate by moving toward these underlying emotions.

The stale couple will likely be less volatile. Instead of anger and arguing you will sense distance, a lack of connection; they will discuss rather than argue. The goal is to get them talking in ways that they don't talk at home. What's said is less important than that it is more intimate. Move them away from detachment and ambivalence to something stronger, deeper—anger, sadness, regret, worry. Ask "What are you most concerned about?" "Do you feel lonely?" "Why do you think you both have drifted apart?" "What are you hoping for for yourself and your relationship in the future?" "What do you most regret?" See if the new communication can open a dialogue.

In the fix-my-partner couple, the dissatisfied partner will generally start—"Fred needs to do something about his anger"; "Emily doesn't ever want to have sex"; "Truman can't hold a steady job." The feeling in the room will be like that of a parent complaining about a child. You want to draw out the emotional issues beneath the complaint. You want to focus more on how the person feels—"What worries you most about Fred's anger?" "What do you miss most about not having sex with Emily?" "What bothers you about Truman's struggle with work?"—than on what the other is doing wrong. The problem at this point belongs only to the complainer; you don't want to collude in being the repairman.

Your attention then can turn to the "problemed" partner—how does he see the problem? Has he heard this before? (Yes, a lot.) Is it something that he is concerned about? What doesn't the partner understand about Fred's anger, Emily's sexuality, Truman's struggle with employment? What changes would he or she like in the relationship? The goal is to move beyond defensiveness, create a balance in power. If the "problemed" person seems unable to speak up and be assertive in the presence of the other partner, separate them so you can get a more honest impression of his or her view of the situation and the relationship.

For couples looking for fine-tuning and skill development, the atmosphere will be calm and perhaps academic. You want to ask about specifics and understand the larger context. If they want to learn communication skills, for example, what specific problems are they having communicating? Where do they get stuck? Why are deciding to get help now? What are they worried may happen if things keep going the way they are without change? As with the stale couples, you want to open up the communication and see how they respond. You want to explore any worries and concerns that lie below the surface.

The goals are similar for couples who present with parenting issues. Yes, they may need information and guidance on parenting. But if they are arguing about parenting and seek you out essentially to arbitrate for them, you want to wonder aloud what keeps them from resolving their differences themselves. Agree that it is important that as parents they be on the same page, but you'd like to help them overcome the obstacles that keep them from doing so. Ask about the way they make decisions and resolve problems in other areas so they know you are comfortable talking about other topics. Look for process and patterns. Help them see that the problems to be fixed are not only with their children, but right there in the relationship between them.

Finally, the no-problem couple will usually express their resentment at those who sent them, bewilderment about why they are there, or an indifference about the entire process. They may not understand what therapy is about, may not see the connection between their problems as a couple and other family or individual issues, may be united in what they see as outside authority. The initial goal is to clarify your role as a service provider, not an enforcer, demonstrate in the session how therapy works, and help the couple define possible issues they are willing to work on. If the referral process is unclear, suggest they talk with the referring agent (their attorney, the caseworker, the probation officer), who could be invited to the next session to clarify his or her concerns as a community representative.

You're always looking for holes, always pressing for underlying emotions, always observing and at times commenting on the process in the room.[1] By your questions and focus, you want the couple to see that you are less interested in facts and more interested in feelings; that what happens in the room and the patterns that unfold are just as important as what happens outside the room or in the past. Emotionally,

---

[1] Irvin Yalom's books are always a good way of becoming more sensitive to the process between therapist and client and learning how to think like a clinician in the moment. For examples see Yalom, I. (2006). *Love's Executioner.* New York: Harper Perennial Classics; Yalom, I. (2005). *When Nietzsche Wept.* New York: Harper Perennial Classics.

you want to be what the partner appears not to be—supportive if the other partner is critical, more assertive if the other partner is passive or withdrawn, curious if the other partner is indifferent, calm yet clear if everyone is angry.

By doing this you are providing subtle but important role modeling for each of them on new, more effective ways to interact. You are helping to create an experience that is different from what they normally experience, and by doing so not only change the emotional climate, but help them see that change itself is possible.

Exploration

Exploration flows from the opening. Once both have had their say and you know specifically who has and what are the presenting problems, it's time to explore the larger relationship landscape. What you actually ask will be guided by your clinical theory; your theory provides you with a map of the source for and ultimately the solutions to the couple's problems. Based upon the assessment model presented in Chapter 3, here are some questions you might ask about history and process. In the bracketed text is the underlying concept:

> *"Why do you think you are having the problem(s) you are having? How are you hoping that therapy will help?"* [Understanding personal theory and where they think the solution lies; clarifying their expectations]

> *"How did you first meet? What did you most like about each other? What do you appreciate about each other now?"* [Early history of relationship; ability to state positives in the relationship]

> *"How do you make decisions between you? Who is in charge of what? How are decisions made about children, money, sex?"* [Understanding the process and the power balance]

> *"If you have an argument, how does it usually go? How do you stop? Can you tell when it is turning into a power struggle? What is the worst a fight has ever gotten?"* [Ability to recognize patterns and process; ability to set limits on behaviors and self regulate; communication skills; extent of violence]

> *"Are you able to go back and try and talk again about the problem if it initially led to an argument? Can you apologize to each other? How do you make up?"* [Ability to approach anxiety and problem solve, rather than avoid and sweep under the rug; ability to reconnect and repair the relationship]

"When you look back on it, what did you need most from each other when you met? How are you a different person now than you were when you first met? How have your needs changed? What do you need most from each other, from your life now?" [Tracking developmental changes over time; separating the individual needs from those of the relationship]

"Do you ever feel like you are pulling more than your share of the responsibilities and the partner doesn't do enough or appreciate what you do? Do you ever feel like the other is too controlling? Do you sometimes get resentful, get fed up, get angry, or act out?" [Tracking drama triangle patterns and roles]

"What do you like to do together? What interests do you share? How has that changed over the years? How do you show that you care?" [Tracking positives and areas of mutual support; tracking developmental changes]

"How hard or easy is it for you to talk honestly and openly to each other about things that bother you? What causes you to hold back? Is there someone else who you are more open with and whom you turn to for support? Why? What makes it easier? What is that you feel your partner does not understand most about you?" [Risk taking, level of intimacy, obstacles to honesty]

"Do you have family, friends that you are close to?" [Outside sources of support]

"What were your parents' marriages like? How is yours similar or different? Any history of physical, emotional, or sexual abuse? How has this affected your own marriage?" [Childhood history and impact on marriage]

"Have you had difficult times in your relationship in the past? How did you get through them? Do you feel they left any wounds, did they make you stronger in some way? How is this time different from then? Have there been any major losses?" [Ability to deal with difficulties in the past and to find resources to do it again; any unresolved grief]

"Is there any family or individual history of depression, addiction, anxiety problems, major emotional illness? How were they handled? How do they affect your relationship? Are you getting treatment?" [Assessment of individual mental health issues]

"Have you been in individual, couple, or family therapy before? What did you think about it?" [Expectations of therapy]

"Is there anything else you would like to change about your family?" [Goals, larger family context]

"If things were to continue without changing, what do you think would eventually happen between you and within yourself?" [Goals, visions of the future]

This probably seems like a lot of ground, and you undoubtedly would not cover it all in the first session nor necessarily want to. If the couple is in crisis, you may use some of these questions only to change the emotional climate and expand their views of the problems. Some of these may naturally come up as the conversation progresses. If Sarah, for example, mentions how she is acting just like her mother did with her father, this may spark an exploration of the relationships of each set of parents. If Henry refers back to the time when he was jobless for several months, or the time their child was in a car accident, you may explore past crises and resolutions. If Olga complains about her mother's interference in her life or her father's history of depression, you may ask about mental health history and status.

Again, you are doing several things with this exploration. You are gathering information for your assessment. You are turning up the corners of the relationship to see what lies underneath. You are seeking to draw out other emotions, show how their settled worldview and theory may actually be different and more complex than what it seems. You are looking for new problems to replace the ones that they initially present, showing how problems may be bad solutions to other issues. You are giving them a taste of what therapy is about.

And along the way, of course, you are observing the process in the room. If they begin to squabble yet again about whose mother is more interfering, stop the dysfunctional process. If the language is vague, ask for specifics. If some new emotions begin to bubble to the surface, label them, support them, place them in the context of the larger relationship ("You are looking sad.... What do you do when you start to feel this way at home? What can Robert do to help you when you feel this way?"). You want them to feel something different, think about the problems in a new way.

The Return

Now that you have stirred the emotional and intellectual pot, it's time to circle back to the presenting problem. You need to connect all the new information about the relationship and in the room with the opening concerns. Here are some examples:

"Ellen, I understand how you are confused and angry about Tom's leaving. Tom, it sounds as if you have been feeling left out of the family and the relationship for a long time, but have had trouble explaining this to Ellen. It seems like you feel that things are never going to change, but Ellen is here with you today and saying that she wants things to be different for you, for you both."

"Jose, you feel that Teresa nags at you all the time and doesn't care about you, and Teresa, you feel that Jose doesn't listen to you or even show that he cares about you. You both seem to be feeling the same way, but show it in different ways. I'm wondering if you both can find ways to show each other that you care and feel cared about."

"You both seem to be able to speak up for yourselves, but have trouble keeping differences from turning into a power struggle that quickly gets out of control and hurts you both. One of the skills that it seems would be helpful for you and us to work on is recognizing when the discussion is off course or too emotional, and having some ways to stop and cool down."

"You both, like most couples, needed something from each other when you first met 10 years ago. Emily, you said that you liked Sam's ability to take charge, but now it seems to you like he is micromanaging you. Sam, you said that you liked the fact that Emily seemed to need you, but now you feel like she is a bit too dependent and not being responsible enough. It seems like you have both changed as individuals over the years together, and that you both need something different from each other than you did at the beginning."

"You both seem to agree that things between you changed a lot after Billy died. Ed, you got more involved with work, and Susan, you said you found yourself more irritable, depressed, and disconnected from Ed. I wonder if you both were struggling with your grief in your own ways and lost that connection between you."

"You both say you feel that your relationship has gone stale, that there is little you have in common, that you seem to be on parallel tracks. It also sounds like you don't have good ways of resolving problems when they come up and instead try and sweep them under the rug. I wonder if these unresolved problems and resentments have helped create the gap between you."

"The caseworker asked that you come for couple counseling and you feel like you don't need it. But you both have said that you argue a lot about the

kids and I wonder if the caseworker is concerned about how the kids may be affected by the yelling and tension. Would you both be willing to come back to see if we can work out ways you can handle the kids better together?"

"Mary, I can tell you are extremely upset and shocked about Todd's affair. And Todd, while you said at first that you don't know why you did it, that it just sort of happened, it also seems that you've had a hard time opening up to Mary—that you feel criticized if you begin to express some of your feelings, that what you most appreciated about the woman you had the affair with is that she was easy to talk to. Now that the affair is over and you are both here together, I wonder if you would be willing to work to together to better open the communication between you."

"You both said that you have been arguing a lot in the last few months about little things. And Gwen, you said that you feel nervous about your daughter going off to college in a few months. You both seem to have centered a lot of time and focus on being parents, and now that your daughter is leaving home you both are understandably worried about what it will be like to be alone together again after all these years. This is a common struggle for a lot of couples at this stage in their relationship. Your challenge, it seems, is discovering ways to reconnect as adults who care about each other rather than just as parents."

You can begin to see the process here—placing the presenting concerns into a larger context; showing how the patterns run on their own energy; normalizing developmental changes; redefining the problem and showing how one seeming problem is really a solution to another. The goal is to move away from the "who's right, who's wrong," the blame, the one person with a problem, to show how the problem is woven into the fabric of the relationship, how the underlying emotions that are not expressed or not heard are important.

You make the connections and then you wait to see what you hear next. Do they both agree? Does one agree while the other sits silently and shakes her head? This is a critical moment in the session process. You need to be sure there is agreement from both with your perspective. If you have changed the emotional climate, if the clients have felt understood, if your perspective addresses both of their concerns, then what you say will generally be accepted.

If, however, one or both of them is still emotionally upset or detached or feels unconnected to you, whatever you say may seem irrelevant or wrong and be dismissed. Pick up on their head shakes, detachment, questions, and invite them to express their reservations—

"Tim, you're shaking your head; do you feel like I am missing something here?" "Susan, you still seem upset. What are you thinking?" Backtrack. Let Tim or Susan talk and listen carefully. Restate what they are saying to be sure you understand and they know that you understand. See where their theory and yours diverge. Tie their concerns and emotions back into your formulation—"I understand that you are hurt and I believe that it's important that your feelings are dismissed. That's why I'm thinking it's important that.... " Now is the time to make sure that they feel that their presenting problems are understood and being addressed, that your relationship with each of them is solid. If you press on, override their objections, or ignore non-verbal indications of doubt, you're going to face ongoing resistance or they will drop out.

Summary and Closing

It's time to start to wrap things up. Again, with couples in serious emotional crisis you may wind up spending the entire hour hearing them out, putting out the emotional fires. Thank them for having the courage to come together and face this, get a commitment to come back and talk about the problems once more.

For less volatile couples, it's a question of laying out next steps. If you have not done so before, this is a good time to both get feedback about the session and clarify their individual expectations—"So how do you both feel about being here today?" "Did you hear anything that you had not heard before?" "Is this what you expected?" "What were you envisioning about the therapy process?" Again you're looking for any negatives ("I didn't hear anything I hadn't heard before") or any unrealistic expectations ("I thought we would just need to come this one time"). If one or both of them still seems ambivalent, try and talk it through if you have the time. Sometimes one of the partners had agreed to come this one time as a concession to the other, and has no intention of coming back. They may openly say so, and you can do your best to find out why, but may have little success in changing their minds. Others say they'll talk about it, or the spouse will say that she will come back even if he does not.

These can be awkward moments. You may feel like the couple is emotionally falling back at the close to where they were at the beginning of the hour. You can feel like you failed or missed something. Try not to be too hard on yourself. You did the best you could. Tell them you're fine with their taking the time to talk about it more at home, that you think this could be helpful, that if they have any questions they should feel free to give you a call. Make a note to yourself to follow up in a few days or a week at the most to see what they have decided.

But if the emotional climate has changed, the couple will usually be satisfied. Talk then about the overall treatment process—"I think this is a good idea that you came in. I would like to help you with this problem. I'd like us to meet once a week. How about we agree to five sessions then reevaluate?"

You can also talk about the next session. Many clinicians like to build in some individual contact at some point, and this is a logical time to do so: "I'd like to see you both individually for a session [or split a session between them] next time to help me better sort you out as individuals from you both together as a couple." If you feel that there was good momentum in the couple session that you would like to continue to build on, you may decide to put this off till later. If you had to separate the couple during the first session because they were too volatile or one was too overwhelmed, you need to decide with each of them if they both may be ready to meet together.

There's always the question about homework. Homework can be useful for several reasons: It helps the couple apply what is discussed in the office to their everyday lives in concrete ways; it allows you the opportunity to see what type of interventions may be most effective and better understand where the process breaks down; it gives you an impression of their response to your leadership and overall motivation for therapy. The actual assignment should obviously be linked to what was discussed in the session, will be linked to your theoretical frame, and should be simple enough for the couple to do successfully. For example: "Individually think about specific positive changes you would like in the relationship"; "Think about other specific areas of conflict that we need to discuss here"; "Make an effort to compliment and thank each other more over the course of the week"; "Try paying closer attention to the way your conversations go and see if you can tell when the discussion is going off course"; "Check in with yourself several times a day and simply ask yourself how you are feeling at that moment"; "Express aloud once or twice a day your mood, your emotions, so that the other knows what is going on inside you"; "See if you can try eating dinner together one night without the television on."

Make sure they understand the assignment and that they both agree to do it. If the following week you find out that they "forgot" to do it or didn't have the time, or that one proposed trying it and the other put it off, all this is grist for the mill and can be explored: "You had a hard time shutting off the TV during dinner; I wonder why." "Did you feel nervous about making conversation?" "You said you didn't have time to do the exercise: Did you feel anxious about doing it?" "Does the pace of your lives make it hard for you to have time together?"

If there is anyone you need to coordinate with—the probation officer or attorney, the referring family doctor—get signed releases before the couple leaves.[2] If you have any nagging doubts about the session— that you didn't really connect with the husband or that you felt you may have seemed like you were taking the wife's side, or the couple still seemed to be upset after they left—follow up. Write a short note or give them a call, even if it is to leave a message. Express your concern: "Tom, I realize that I didn't get a chance to talk with you as much as I did with Lois and hope you didn't feel left out; I appreciate your coming in; feel free to give me a call if you have any questions or concerns; I look forward to seeing you next week." These gestures often go a long way in solidifying or repairing the relationship, modeling a healthy process, and relieving your own anxiety.

SESSION 2

They come back. As mentioned above, some clinicians will use this time to continue with their more structured assessment process—after two or three sessions of couple and individual interviewing they will then sit down with the couple and propose their treatment plan. In most agencies or practices where there are time and caseload pressures, this formal multisession assessment is usually not practical for couples who are in crisis. Your second session often becomes the time to gather up emotional loose ends and information that you didn't get to in the first session. Meeting individually at this point may be useful though not essential.

If you do decide on an individual session, you can begin by linking back to the first session—"Did you have any questions or reactions to our sessions last week?" Often there is little, or only vague, response—

---

[2]There is the issue of legal testimony and therapy. Many clinicians provide some type of informational handout, mailed in advance of the first appointment or given when the couple comes in, that they are asked to read and sign. It usually talks about confidentiality, states the limitations on it (child abuse reporting, suicide/homicide risk), and may include a statement that the clinician will not testify in court in divorce hearings. While this is not legally binding, it is a clear statement that therapy is separate from gathering court evidence. Most clinicians will agree to write summary letters to attorneys but are clear with the client and attorney that therapy is not the same as a court evaluation for mental status, child custody, and so forth. If that is the purpose of the consultation, the clinician can refer the couple to someone who provides that service.

"No, nothing in particular, I thought it was helpful." Sometimes the answers are more specific—"I really liked that drama triangle that you showed us and have been thinking about it all week"; "I remember you asked if I ever felt I was holding back, biting my tongue—I've been paying attention to that this week and have actually caught myself doing it." Comments like this give you clues about issues the client is sensitive to as well as feedback about your impact. Again, if you were concerned that your emotional connection to the client after the first session was weak, or that the individual was still ambivalent, this is a good time to repair it—"So, John, I realized that I really didn't get a chance to learn a lot about you aside from your marriage. You mentioned you were a mechanic; how did you get into that type of work?" or "I couldn't tell how you were feeling when you left here last week; how do you feel about coming to counseling? Was this more Vicky's idea than yours?"

Tell them your own goals for the session—"I want to find out more specifically what you want to work on in therapy"; "I want to explore some individual history about yourself and your parents"; "I want to give you an opportunity to talk about anything that you didn't feel comfortable talking about in front of your husband."

This last statement opens the door to confidential information, to secrets. This is where you find that while the client is willing to come, he really doesn't think this is going to work, or that she has pretty much made up her mind that the relationship is over but is willing to give it a try for the sake of the partner. This is where you learn about their view of the partner's drinking, the depth of her depression, his Internet pornography addiction. This is where you learn about past physical abuse, current emotional abuse, or the client's own affair of 10 years ago.

What do you do with this information? Some clinicians believe in taking a clear, strong stand on this, namely, that they will keep no secrets. They feel that secrets undermine the relationship. Anything disclosed, such as affairs, will be shared, and they may say so at the beginning of the first session or at the beginning of this individual session, or even have it written down in a disclosure statement that the clients sign. Others take a less stringent stand. The issue is less about the information itself and more about the context. Why is the client mentioning it at all? Is she afraid to discuss the drinking in front of her partner for fear of his reaction? Is he afraid to talk about the depression because he is afraid that doing so will only make it worse? If it's a question of their anxiety, you can mentally walk them through it or offer to support them in a joint session where they can bring it up.

Sometimes it's not about the other but about themselves individually—"I'm mentioning this because though the affair was long ago, I still feel guilty at times." Or "I'm telling you about my sexual abuse as a child because I know it interferes with our sex life and Tom doesn't really understand why." Or "I'm mentioning my father's alcoholism because I realize I still have flashbacks about some of things he did when I was growing up." Knowing the context helps you decide what to do next—to talk further with the client to see what he believes may help him with his guilt; to help the client talk about her sexual abuse in a different way so that her husband understands and so they both can be more sexually satisfied; to explore the possibility to posttraumatic stress and see if individual therapy might be an important adjunct treatment.

And if you really believe that the information is linked to the current problems in the relationship, say so—"That helps me understand how you reacted last week; maybe it would help your wife to hear this" or "Tom was saying last week that he was unhappy with your sexual relationship; maybe he needs to hear this in a different way so he can better understand how you feel and support you." You and the client can then talk about acceptable ways of weaving this information into the treatment.

But if the client absolutely refuses to take the risk of disclosing such information at this time, there are still two ways to make use of the information. One is to apply it to the present: "Looking back on it," you ask Mark, "why do you think you had the affair 10 years ago? How does the affair represent needs that even now may not be getting met? Can we address those issues in the therapy?" The other is to look carefully at the process issues, namely, why secrecy at all? If withholding is the solution, what is the problem in the relationship now?

The answer to this question is often more important than the disclosure of any particular facts. The withholding is tied to issues of intimacy, risk taking, self-responsibility, fear. The issue less about what happened 10 years ago and more about a courageous honesty that is currently absent from the relationship. Repairing these underlying concerns, the breakdown in the relationship process, is what is important.

Apart from this more theoretical side to confidential information and secrets, there is often a more practical one. If, for example, a partner admits that he is currently having an affair, there is a real question on the table about the purpose and goals of couple therapy. You can't do couple counseling when someone is committed to two relationships, and the clinical issue becomes one of helping the individual define his priorities, needs, and options. Similarly, if one partner is concerned about addiction, there is the issue of raising the question in counseling, but also the issue of helping the person decide what she wants to do if the other person fails to acknowledge it as a problem.

If there are concerns about real danger—that a partner is afraid to speak up in joint sessions for fear of retaliation and abuse—then the question is what the client most wants help with. Certainly if the husband agrees that he has a problem with his anger, everyone is on the same page, and it can be managed. But if he denies there is a problem, what remains is to help the other spouse consider her options. Telling you is usually a cry for help, and you provide the reality check. The focus moves toward helping the abused partner emotionally and practically step out of the victim role rather than maintaining the magical thinking that if only she could "do better" the abusive partner would somehow change. Couple counseling becomes individual counseling.

Generally, however, these individual sessions are not so dramatic. They are an opportunity to fill in blanks in the assessment (psychological history, use of medications, insight into family-of-origin influences), strengthen the therapeutic relationship, and define individual and relationship goals. When you come back together with the couple, you can summarize your conversations, or better yet ask each partner to summarize for the other. You and they should at this point have a good idea of how the pieces that are the relationship fit together, and everyone should be in agreement about what the initial focus of the treatment will be.

INITIAL TREATMENT PLANS

Obviously the initial treatment plan is built around the presenting problem and the expectations of the couple. As mentioned above, you are always looking to expand the emotional range, to move the couple toward the holes and enable them to take risks, you are seeking to break the dysfunctional patterns and develop skills. Here are some common foci of the six common presentations:

The Crisis Couple

Managing the couple's emotional volatility is usually the first order of business. Hopefully you have been able to change the emotional climate within the first session. If the couple is so volatile that they are unable to control their own emotions within the session even with your leadership and intervention, see them separately until they can. The challenge is to move each of them away from simply blaming the other and toward recognizing how the process unfolds. You want to help them be less reactive and better able to regulate their own emotions.

Whether you are doing this individually or as a couple, your coaching needs to be specific, concrete, behavioral. If they get caught in the blaming and the anger, the goal is to stop the process in the room, to help them focus on themselves and calm themselves down, to stop fueling the conflict with the loading on of more content: "Please stop for a minute. You both seem to be getting upset and defensive. Can you tell that you're really not able to listen to each other, and that the conversation right now is turning into a power struggle?" Help them understand that it really does take two to make an argument, and that they each have a choice not to argue, that they can be responsible for themselves. You may have to do this several times to sensitize them to the process. You can slow the process down by asking them to summarize what the other said before they reply, or take turns listening and literally writing down what they each think the other is saying.

Help them map out a strategy for keeping the process from escalating at home. One effective technique is to help them decide on a nonverbal signal (throwing a dish towel in the air is a good one—verbal cues just add fuel to emotional fire) that either one can use when he or she senses the conversation is getting out of control. The thrown towel signals the stopping of the conversation. A timer is set for 30 minutes so everyone can calm down. If one partner continues to pick a fight, the other is instructed to do what he or she needs to do to separate and avoid the escalation. If after 30 minutes, one or both are still upset, the timer is reset for another 30 minutes.

It's essential that the couple understands that strong emotions and problem solving do not mix. They need to first put out the emotional fire, and only after they are emotionally flatlined can they try and discuss the problem. If emotions rise up again once the discussion starts, they need to again stop it. Sometimes they may need to wait until the next day. Stress to them that the delay is merely that—a cooldown period; it's not a way to sweep the problem under the rug and avoid dealing with it.

If a couple feels that emotionally they are not ready to do this at home, ask them to write down their feelings when they get upset and bring in problems that they want to talk about at the next session. Make sure you use the session to steer them through the process rather than taking on the role of arbitrator of the problem.

If the emotional fires can be contained, if the individuals are able to self regulate and handle their emotions relatively responsibly, you can focus more directly on the precipitating event, such as the sudden separation, the affair. While your initial goal is to provide a safe forum for each of them to voice their anger, guilt, and grief, you want to also help them put the crisis in a wider context. The separation or affair, for example, is a solution to another problem and you want to help them explore what lies beneath—the unmet needs, the unresolved conflicts, the ways each may have felt unappreciated, ignored, or overcontrolled by the other (the drama triangle). Again, helping them be more aware of the process ("I couldn't tell you how hurt my feelings were") is just as or more important than clarifying the content ("You said you didn't want to have any more children"). Again look for ways the problem is being replicated in the room (Ted becomes quiet rather than speaking up). Point out what you see and help them reshape their behaviors.

All three of you need to be clear about each partner's commitment to working on the relationship. Is the affair over, are they both willing to work hard in therapy for an agreed amount of time (say, 3 months) before making a decision about the marriage? If they are separated, what type and amount of contact are they willing to have? What needs to be changed most? What are the criteria for measuring change?

The Stale Relationship

As mentioned earlier, the stale marriage suffers from low-level, low-intensity unresolved conflicts, limited, routinized communication, lack of positive feedback, parallel lives with few shared interests. The initial focus is upon opening the system up—talking about and attempting to resolve the chronic issues, increasing the depth and range of communication, making deliberate efforts to engage and give each other positive feedback. The individuals can choose where they want to start, but the process goals are breaking the entrenched patterns and encouraging the couple to take emotional risks.

Teach them how to talk through areas of disagreement (the kids, the budget, sexual issues) there in the session, rather than ignoring them or giving up on the conversation too soon; help them recognize both good process and clear content; help them view anger as information rather than threat. Help them develop a vision of the type of relationship they would like to have. Press them to broadcast their emotions—to say how they are feeling throughout the day rather than internalizing or waiting to be asked—and to verbalize nonverbal expressions ("Sue, you are frowning; what's going on?") Help them discover new areas of interest by following their brainstorms and taking risks (sign up for the those tango lessons). Help them plan a Saturday afternoon of couple time, rather than retreating into their own computers or only shuttling the kids to soccer games. Help them say, hear, and do something new to invigorate the relationship.

The Fix-My-Partner Couple

Clarify who has the problem, rebalance the system, expand the conversation. Help the complainer talk about his side of the problem—what about it bothers him so much, what he is worried about, what the problem means in terms of the relationship. If Kim, for example, agrees that she has problems with sex or with spending money, the next step is to help her say exactly what type of support or changes she needs from her partner in order to be successful in changing her own behavior. If, however, she feels that it is not a problem—she is not worried because they have lots of money in savings—but feels intimidated to say so, support her in making her case. Once the power is more equal, who has the problem is more clear, and you can then help them both negotiate a solution from an adult position—"Kim, it sounds like you don't feel money is a problem." "John, what still worries you about it? What is it that Kim can do to help you with your worry besides doing what you feel she should do?"

The Fine-Tuning Couple

Ask them to bring in arguments from the previous week so you can help them learn how to listen and communicate clearly. Suggest that they go down to the local bookstore and look for a couples book that they like and offer to work through the exercises with them. Let them set the agenda, but don't be afraid to ask the hard questions to let them know that you are willing to explore deeper issues with them ("Tim, you seem particularly sensitive when Wendy disagrees with you—I'm just curious about why her comments affect you so strongly"). Point out the holes that you notice in the room: "I notice when you both talk about affection and intimacy you never mention sex—how come?" Invite them to expand their flexibility by moving into those areas

The Problem-with-Children Couple

If you find the couple quickly pushing the parenting issues to the side to focus on the relationship, you obviously have permission to march forward with them and begin to talk about communication, problem solving, and so forth. Don't, however, forget about the initial parenting concerns. If Matt and Heather, for example, shift the focus from trouble getting the kids to bed to openly saying that what really bothers them are their arguments about whose way of getting the kids to bed is best, go ahead and talk with them about the power struggle they seem to be having, but remember to circle back at some point to the concrete bedtime problem. There may be parenting information and skills you can help with in addition to the couple skills that they need to be successful.

Some struggling couples presenting with parenting issues, however, may have a more difficult time shifting the focus from their children to their relationship. While it may become more and more clear to you during the first few sessions or as part of your assessment that the children are just an arena for playing out their relationship problems, they resist openly discussing other aspects of their relationship. They are in fact replicating the problem in the room—they are managing the anxiety you stir up about the relationship by always turning the conversation back to the children.

The issue is one of fear. You need to move gently, yet clearly, and help them feel safe: "I'm really glad you both have decided to come in together to work out your concerns about the kids. I know you both are worried about their behavior and are particularly frustrated about these struggles over bedtime. I notice when you both start talking about it you seem to both get aggravated because the other one is not willing to go along with your way of handling it. I wonder if this is where you are both getting stuck in coming up with a solution?" Or "I notice that you both talk easily about the children, but when I ask questions about other aspects of your relationship, you both get quiet or seem to shift the conversation back to the children. I'm wondering why."

See if they agree with this and begin to open up. If they do, you can shift the focus to the power struggle between them. If not, help them see the connection between their relationship problem and their concern with the children: "Usually kids figure out how to play you against each other or get confused if you both are not on the same page. I'm thinking that if we can help you both move beyond the struggle you are having with each other and come to an agreement, the kids will be able to settle down." By building upon their mutual motivation to help their children, you can then shift the focus to the relationship, help them work together to set priorities and goals, and assure them you can create a safe environment for discussion and problem solving.

The No-Problem Couple

As mentioned above, you want to allow them to express their frustration or anger at the outside system and avoid the power struggle with them over who has the problem. Bring in the referral source to clarify his or her concerns or goals. Offer to help them work on anything they wish in order to build trust, and to acquaint them with the therapy process.

Because it is easy for them to see you as joined to an outside system that they resent, take the lead, but be sensitive to their distorted view of your own power. Thank them for their openness and provide plenty of positive feedback, especially when they are able to talk about themselves rather than blaming the system. Be careful not to work harder than them, and keep in mind you are providing a service that they are free to use or not.

This completes our discussion of opening moves and solid beginnings. In the next chapter we look at the heart of the work—helping couples resolve their presenting problems by changing the core dynamics.

Looking Within: Chapter 4 Exercises

1. What types of crisis situations would be most difficult for you to handle—those, for example, with a great deal of anger, those around certain topics such as affairs? What makes you sensitive to these emotions or issues? What skills or support would help you learn to manage these situations better?

2. How well are you able to talk about talking in your personal life? How well are you able to calm yourself down when you are upset? What triggers or situations make it particularly difficult for you to do so?

3. A brief guided-imagery sequence: Sit comfortably, close your eyes, take a few deep breaths, begin to feel relaxed. See if you can image in your own mind yourself as a young child. There is something wrong with you, you are emotionally upset—crying, worried; perhaps you are physically hurt. With you is one or both of your parents. Just watch to see what happens. What does your parent say or do? Watch how you respond.

We all leave childhood with our own notions of help and trust. What does this scene possibly tell you about what you learned about trusting others to help you, about your ability to ask for help rather than feeling that you must take care of yourself? Can you now as an adult lean on others, let them know what you need?

How do these attitudes affect your reactions to clients coming to you for help? Do you feel they should be more like you? Where do you draw that fine line between appropriately asking for help and seeming too needy, too whiney, not independent enough?

4. Think about creating your own introductory guidelines for clients. What information would you want to include? What would you like them to know about your own working style, your own values, your own limits? What is your own stance about revealing secrets?

Chapter 5

Clearing the Clutter
Improving Communication Skills

So you've gotten over the first challenges. The presenting problems and emotions are on the table. You've been able to build rapport with each of the partners. The couple is feeling more settled and beginning to see their problems in a broader context. They've made a commitment to continue, and you and they have some sense of the direction in which you all will be heading. You're ready to move into the core of the therapy. This is where you help them discover what holds their problems in place and find new ways to approach them.

One of the first questions you are curious about is why the couple can't solve this problem on their own. This leads to the problems in communication that you saw played out before you in the opening sessions—the difficulty expressing or containing emotions, the fueling the process with ever more content, the power struggles. This is what runs the conversation into the ditch and gets them stuck. You need to help them develop the skills and the awareness to steer the conversation so that it keeps moving forward, so that it is productive rather than destructive.

Doing exactly this is the focus of communication-based models of couple therapy, and sometimes this is enough to create positive changes in the relationship.[1] The couple learns to steer the conversation them-

---

[1] And some clinicians feel it should be enough. The positive psychology movement, with its strength-based approach, has reinforced what many behavioral clinicians have felt for a long time—that the goal of treatment should be eliminating the negative and teaching and building upon the positive. For examples see Seligman, M. (2004). *Positive Psychology*

selves. Beth and Mark learn to recognize that they are not listening, that they are getting defensive, that they are getting in their own way, and once they do, their own problem-solving skills are strong enough to carry them forward. You may provide information and coaching to help them approach and manage their problems differently—help them understand, for example, that their struggle to rediscover common interests is normal for couples whose children have left home; encourage them to deliberately make time for each other and experiment with exploring new activities. And they use the information, they do what you suggest, and they get out of the rut.

But often more is needed. Yes, Beth and Mark work hard to calm themselves down and listen, but when they try to put into place your suggestions, they get stuck. Or they have two good weekends out of town but then have another familiar fight over who's getting whose way. They come in discouraged, feeling like nothing can change, like therapy isn't working. They're angry again and ready to quit.

You need to look deeper. There's something wrong within the structure of the relationship itself. To use an analogy, the couple comes in and says there's something wrong with the flooring of their relationship; it seems uneven. Your first step is getting the clutter up—helping them listen and not overreact so you can see what is there. And sometimes that's all that's needed. Once the clutter is gone, you all realize that the problem turns out to be nothing, merely all the stuff they were stepping on and tripping over rather than picking up. But often even after you clear off the clutter with good communication, the unevenness is still there. You need to go deeper, look under the floor to see what is structurally wrong underneath.

If your first question is "What prevents the couple from solving their problem themselves?"—the clutter of communication problems—your next questions are "Why these problems and not others?" and "Why are they reactive to these issues?" Psychoanalytic couple therapy makes this the thrust of the work—to help the couple become curious about and explore why these problems and not others, to track these sensitivities and triggers back into the past so they can be unraveled from the present.[2] In traditional practice this form of couple therapy is long term.

---

in Practice. Hoboken, NJ: Wiley. Stuart, R. B. (2003). *Helping Couples Change: A Social Learning Approach to Marital Therapy*. New York: Guilford Press.

[2]For more information on psychoanalytic applications to couple therapy see Scharff, D., & Scharff, J. S. (1987). *Object Relations Family Therapy*. Northvale, NJ: Jason Aronson; Messer, S. B., & Warren, C. S. (1995). *Models of Brief Psychodynamic Therapy*. New York:

Our goals are more modest than those of psychoanalytic therapists. Where they may be interested in replacing the couple's psychological infrastructure, we are looking to repair the weak spot in the psychological flooring. When we see the couple get stuck in the same core pattern over and over, even when other aspects of the relationship have improved, it is then that we want to dig deeper and see what holds this particular pattern in place. Often there are old wounds that are being reactivated in the present. Our goal is to help the individuals cognitively and emotionally understand how they are projecting hurts from the past into the present, and then help them break the pattern by making specific behavioral changes in the present relationship. For many couples this becomes the focus of the therapy.

In this chapter and the next we are going to show how to move through these layers by following one case. We will start with the clutter—the communication issues—and talk about the techniques important to improving it. In the next chapter we'll also talk about the core pattern, and ways of repairing the present by understanding the past.

SARA AND ANN

Ann and Sara arrive for their third session. They have been together for 7 years, and they share parenting of Sara's 8-year-old daughter, Amy, from her marriage. They came in concerned about a painful argument they had, seemingly out of the blue, over disciplining Amy. While not physically violent, the argument was emotionally devastating for each of them. While we will be looking at multiple layers of this case, let's start with the first, the communication skills and patterns. We'll stop along the way to clarify the process and clinical thinking:

When asked what they want to talk about, Sara begins: "Ann and I had an argument, or rather started to have an argument over Amy's cleaning up her room. Ann was actually able to see that we were starting to escalate, and called a halt to it. Rather than stirring up the argument again we agreed to talk about it here today."

Ann starts: "Sara asked Amy to clean up her room on Saturday morning. Sara had to go to her office for a couple of hours and told me before she left what she asked Amy to do."

Guilford Press; Donovan, J. M. (2003). *Short-Term Object Relations Couples Therapy*. New York: Brunner-Rutledge; Solomon, S. (1992). *Narcissism and Intimacy*. New York: Norton.

"Yes," snaps Sara. "I told *Amy* to clean up her room, not you and Amy. I come home and find you helping her!"

"She asked if I could help her pick up all her clothes for the laundry. What's the big deal?"

"The big deal," says Sara, "is that you have done this before and we have talked about it. She's manipulating you. Her chores are *her* chores!"

"I don't do this all the time, and she's not manipulating me!" Ann sounds defensive and whiney. "It's okay for people to ask for help. I'm not doing it *for* her. Sometimes you're just too, too ... tough on her."

"She needs to learn responsibility, Ann! She needs to honor *my* requests!" Now Sara is getting red in the face and almost shouting.

What have you noticed so far? One positive thing is that they were able to be aware at home of the argument escalating and stop it. They are aware of the process, didn't get lost in the content, had self-control, took responsibility. They also decided to bring the discussion to therapy, an appropriate way of using the therapeutic process in the beginning of treatment, and a sign that they are able to return to problems rather than sweeping them under the rug.

We are seeing several issues being played out. One is their communication pattern, the other the whole question of who is in charge of Amy, and then why this issue is such an emotional one. We can begin to think about all of these, but obviously can only tackle one at a time. Just looking at the process we see that Sara quickly gets angry, and while Ann can push back a bit, she seems a bit overpowered by Sara. She becomes defensive, fueling Sara's anger even more.

It's time to intervene, to interrupt and slow down the conversation. You don't want to re-create what they do at home. When emotion threatens to outrun reasoning, you need to change the emotional climate in the room. We see that Sara is angry but don't fully understand the emotion beneath it. Let's ask about the softer emotion—the worry, the concern—to help her and the conversation move away from blame and anger at Ann.

"Hold on for a minute, please. Sara, you sound more and more angry, and Ann, it sounds like you're feeling defensive. Can you tell this is starting to unravel?" They both nod. "Sara, what worries you about Ann helping out Amy?"

Sara takes a deep breath, trying to calm herself down. "I'm worried that if Ann keeps doing this Amy's going to learn that she doesn't have to listen to me and as she gets older she is going to be out of control ... I guess I feel that Ann is undermining me as a parent."

"But you are just so tough on her!" *Ann is sounding angry again. She's not really hearing what Sara is saying, but instead getting defensive. We need to slow down the process again, move away from anger, back to worry.*

"Ann, did you understand what Sara said she's worried about?"

"Yes, but I'm a parent here, too. I don't want to be second fiddle!" Ann sounds angry and sad at the same time.

"But I don't want Amy thinking—"

"Fine," says Ann. "She's your daughter. Do what you want." She crosses her arms and looks away from Sara. Sara looks away as well and makes no move to close the gap.

They have reached their stuck point. You have a couple of options here. One is to point out the process in the room—"You both seem to have just got stuck. What's going on?" or "Ann, Sara, how are you feeling?"—and see if they can get back on track. You also can pick up on the parenting issue that Ann defines by her "second fiddle" statement—"Ann, what do you mean, 'second fiddle?'— and begin a clearer discussion of the parenting issue. You can also pick up on Ann's giving up and giving in. This is a concern, and this is what stopped the conversation. Rather than pushing back at Sara and being assertive in what she wants, she withdraws, seems resigned, and gives up.

There is an imbalance of power in the room and in the relationship—Sara seems more in control; through her anger she can overpower Ann and make her shut down. This may be a pattern around parenting, but may also spread to other aspects of the relationship, causing resentment and anger in Ann, a playing out of the drama triangle. You could change this pattern by going back to Sara's worry—moving toward the softer emotions again, making Sara less threatening, and making it easier for Ann to hear and understand Sara and move forward. Or you could approach it from Ann's side—help rebalance the process by gently pointing out what we see and encouraging Ann to move for- ward, to put into words what she is really feeling. All of these would work in that they would help them move beyond their stuck point and get the conversa- tion back on the road.

Finally, you could step back and clarify the bigger picture—the way the issues come together—and see if they can move toward adult positions and prob- lem solving. The advantage of the last is that it does three things at once— clarifies the issues so they both can see them more clearly, moves them toward problem solving, and, in the process, provides a therapeutic opportunity for Ann to be assertive and state what she wants. This also is a little less directive and helps reduce their dependency on the therapist. Let's try that.

"It seems that you're both talking about two separate problems— the parenting issue of what is best for Amy, which you both have differ- ent ideas about, and then the larger question of who is really in charge of Amy. Ann, even though you said you want to coparent, it seems like you just gave up and deferred to Sara. What do you want?"

What we are doing is asking Ann to use her emotions as information, to translate what she doesn't like into a clear assertive statement—this balances out the power in the relationship and in the room. What is absolutely important in approaching Ann is that we sound gentle and supportive. We already know that she is reactive to Sara's anger and criticism. If she hears criticism in our voice, we become another Sara and she will likely withdraw. So our tone of voice is what carries the message. If she were to bristle, sound defensive, shut down, we would know that we sounded accusatory and we would need to repair the relationship then and there—"Ann, I'm sorry if I sound critical. I really would like to know what you would like to handle differently—*as gently as possible. This provides modeling for Sara as well.*

"I guess I want us to be able to discuss this together without all the anger," says Ann.

Ann is moving forward, she is feeling supported.

"What's the *this*, Ann?"

Both for problem solving and good communication we want to encourage Ann to talk clearly.

"To be able to discuss how to best parent Amy."

This is a clear statement of what she wants. Ann sounds stronger.

"Ann, I'm not trying to leave you out. I do see you as Amy's parent, too." Sara sounds more calm. "When I see you giving in to Amy, being too easy on her, in my opinion, I guess I feel that I need to be more tough."

Sara's response is also clear: When you do _____, I feel _____. There is no blame or anger. Ann's clear statement and assertiveness has perhaps helped Sara become clearer and less angry herself. You could let them continue and see if they can stay on course. But Sara just said something important: she described a reason for her reactions—that Amy's leniency triggers her toughness. This polarization fuels the attack-and-withdraw cycle. It would be valuable to underscore this so they hear it.

"What you both are describing is a pattern that it is easy for parents to fall into—everybody gets polarized. The tougher one parent seems to get, the easier the other one feels she needs to be to balance it out. It sounds like you agree that you both want to be equal parents to Amy—yes?"

A normalizing statement puts their problem in a broader context and moves them further away from blaming. Clarifying their agreement is important before moving forward to the details. If Sara were to say that while she understands how Ann feels, she still wants to be in charge of Amy, we're back to working out that aspect of the parenting issue.

Keep in mind that whatever decision they arrive at is up to them. Your job is to help them express their positions nondefensively so they can hear each other.

STAYING FOCUSED ON GOALS

Let's stop here. You may be feeling that this is a lot to digest; we'll be breaking this down into specific techniques shortly. What's important is that you don't feel pressured to follow a clinical recipe. As you can see, there are a number of paths that could have been taken; the process is not linear but circular. You try and shape the conversation or make a point, and see what happens next—does the conversation move along more productively, has the emotional climate changed for the better, or is there no change, or a regression to more hurt and anger?

Instead of trying to follow a recipe, you want to stay focused on your clinical goals. The overriding one is helping the partners move to the adult position on the drama triangle. What this means is that each of them learns to take responsibility for what he or she thinks, does, and feels. As they do they move away from the overresponsibility of the rescuer and the underresponsibility of the victim, and abandon the abuse and blame of the persecutor. This self-responsibility translates into being nurturing without being controlling, being able to regulate your emotions, being able to be honest with others, not taking everything personally or having someone else's emotions constantly contaminate your own. In Bowenian terms, they become more differentiated—able to stop and think about how to respond, rather than reacting with reflex emotion. This is crucial for couple therapy because this is where the problems lie. Because of the closeness of the relationship the walls between self and the other are easily eroded. Responsibility is distorted. Dysfunctional patterns are shaping the relationship and are running on their own momentum.

In the early stages of treatment, as with Sara and Ann, your main goal is largely clearing away the clutter—keeping Sara and Ann, for example, from escalating by helping Sara say what she feels rather than attacking, by helping Ann speak up when her inclination is to shut up. You want to teach them communication skills, help them listen for the process, talk more honestly. You want to slow down the process in the session so you and the couple can begin to see and catch in the moment how their interactions and their emotions are coming together. You also want to coach them on how to slow down the process at home by focusing on their own feelings rather than what the other is saying, by agreeing to take time-outs to cool down when either one of them senses the discussion going out of control.

As the communication noise is reduced you will better be able to see patterns repeat and better define the core pattern—Sara's anger and Ann's withdrawal, for example—as well as underlying issues, such as

Sara's need for control, or Ann's sensitivity to being second fiddle. You want to be curious about the ways these issues may play into presenting problems, why the couple defines these problems rather than something else.

Finally, you want to help them be more flexible. This is really the key to their success. It's the old adage that you can't necessarily change how you feel, but you can change what you do. If you change your thinking or your behavior, your emotions will eventually follow. This is what skill building is about—learning ways of becoming more aware of and deliberately changing self-talk and ingrained behavior in order to change emotional states and break dysfunctional patterns. This is why you encourage couples to move out of their ruts. If they keep doing the same thing, they will keep feeling the same way.

Let's look at the individual and couple skills that can improve the communication in the relationship and reduce destructive arguments.

INDIVIDUAL SKILLS

If you have ever flown on a plane you've inevitably heard (and probably tuned out) the safety orientation that the flight attendants always give—the seat belts, the cabin lights, and, of course, the oxygen masks. And, they conclude, if you are traveling with young children, always put on your mask first and then help them with theirs.

This pay-attention-to-yourself-first idea applies in couple therapy as well. Rather than focusing on all the annoying things that their partners do, you want to help the individuals to pay attention instead to the ways they react and respond; you want to help them develop what Bowen calls *self-focus*. By focusing on themselves they have a better chance of representing themselves honestly and accurately. They will emotionally feel less entangled. They will be able to step back and out of the dysfunctional patterns and learn to see their own part in them.

This does not mean that you encourage selfishness, nor does it mean that you should interrupt couple therapy by shifting to a long stint of individual therapy. What's needed is shifting awareness, redirecting, and defining what is self and what is not. There are several ways you can promote this process. Here is a quick list of foundational individual skills that are valuable not only to couple relationships, but social relationships in general:

The Ability to Be Aware of and Label Emotions

We talked about this earlier as one of your basic tasks as leader of the therapeutic process, but the individuals need to be able to do this for themselves as well. While some clients are already able to do this well, others struggle. Some are able to feel their emotions but get easily flooded by them, either spewing them out or shutting down. At the other end of the spectrum are those who live only from the neck up; they think but have trouble feeling. And then there are those who can feel but can't identify. They always say they are upset and don't know what they are feeling except bad. Or they may be restricted to only one or two strong emotions, like anger or hurt, and have little awareness of or ability to identify the more subtle ones.

Partners are often complementary around emotions. Brad and Carrie fit this profile. In arguments Brad always wound up telling Carrie to calm down and think. He was frustrated by Carrie's emotionalism. From Carrie's side in such situations, Brad seemed controlling and parental. She criticized him for being too controlled. She constantly pushed him to open up. They were operating from two different systems.

The goal with such combinations is to stop the polarization and help them each move toward their holes and the middle ground. You could help Brad, for example, by picking up on nonverbal cues—the reddening of his eyes, a sigh. "I noticed you just sighed while Carrie was talking; could you tell how you were feeling?" You can also model through self-disclosure—"I was in a situation like that and I felt ... "—as well as by the gentle but steady use of feeling language—"Gee, that must have felt frustrating."

As was noted above with Ann, the key in doing this, or making any challenge successfully, lies in doing it differently than the partner. You don't want to sound like Carrie—critical or demanding. Intellectually it will seem like you are siding with Carrie, emotionally it will re-create the problem and cause the same reaction in Brad. You want to be clear but gentle. You want to explain what you are doing and place it in context of the individual's concern: "It seems difficult for you to tell how you are feeling sometimes. I wonder if it would be helpful for you to be able to do this better not so much because it is something that Carrie is demanding but because it ... " and link it to his concern—because he has a difficult time making decisions, because it creates an off-putting impression at work at times, and so forth. And then, like Ann, track closely what happens next. Brad tries to describe how he feels—good—or he gets defensive and says that he doesn't understand what the big deal is—bad. If he gets defensive, you need to fix the problem in the room and in your relationship with him before going any further.

As mentioned earlier, these less emotional, more analytical individuals often take the role of rescuers in the drama triangle. They are filled with shoulds, struggle to discern wants, and stuff emotions until they eventually explode. One effective homework assignment is to have them ask themselves several times a day simply how they are feeling. For the first couple of weeks they may have a difficult time determining much of anything. With practice, however, this will become easier. They can also be encouraged to take note of, and, ideally behaviorally act upon the slightest wisp of emotion—a slight annoyance over something their boss said that they then clarify with their boss, a sudden desire for a slice of cheesecake that they then get—further strengthening these internal connections.

For those other individuals who have no trouble feeling their emotions but have difficulty differentiating and labeling them, apply the same techniques with their weaknesses in mind. Give them vocabulary (frustration, worry, jealousy), pick up on the nonverbal cues (they sound angry but look sad) to help separate what feels to them like an overwhelming ball of undefined emotions.

The Ability to Use Emotions as Information

This is both a concept and skill. Ann was encouraged to use her hurt feelings not to simply withdraw, but as a starting point to articulate what she wanted changed in her relationship with Sara. Overly rational clients can be encouraged to approach their emotions by understanding that they contain important information about their needs, just as those who tend to be labile and feel victimized by their emotions can learn to ask themselves what their emotions are telling them about what they need right now.

This is the skill of emotional self-regulation, and you can walk the client through the process in the session: "Sue, you seem to be getting upset. See if you can take a couple of deep breaths. Okay, see if you can tell what else you may be feeling. Can you tell Tim what you're feeling or needing from him right now?" Give them the homework assignment of practicing this during the week.

Learning emotional self-responsibility is particularly important for those whose primary emotion is anger. Some people are so vulnerable that when they're hurt they attack, and it's common for one partner, like Sara, to feel hurt and show anger, and for the other, like Ann, to feel hurt and withdraw. Those prone to anger need help to see their anger not as a problem but as a signal of other emotions that are being stirred.

Help them learn to slow down their process by encouraging them to take several deep breaths and ask themselves what else may be happening: "I'm feeling angry or irritable; what's going on—am I worried, tired, frustrated, sad, something else?" Encourage them to then act responsibly—write down what they're worried about, talk to their partner about it, figure out a plan to deal with it, take a nap, get out their frustration by some form of exercise—rather than discharging on others or abusively on themselves.

With practice individuals can learn to recognize their own emotional patterns—"I get irritable, which usually means I'm stressed and need to go read a book or watch television to unwind." "I feel have the urge to cut on myself, which means that I'm annoyed about something and I need to figure it out." "I get angry at my partner, which tells me that my feelings are hurt." By recognizing the pattern and the information they can then take responsibility and help others better understand what makes them tick, as well as change the emotional climate between them.

The Ability to Be Aware of Who Has the Problem

If I feel or see a problem, it's mine. This is taking responsibility for oneself and sidesteps the "I feel bad but as soon as I can get you to change, I'll feel better." Sara's problem was her daughter not following through on chores and Ann's perceived undermining of her requests. Ann's problem was her disagreement with Sara's approach and the fact she was feeling dismissed. Clearly the problems overlap and feed into each other, but the starting point for discussion is helping the couple define who owns which problem. The next step for Sara and Ann might be to map out areas of agreement—yes, Sara agrees that Ann should have an equal role in parenting—and help them come up with standards they can agree on, as well as identifying areas of disagreement—no, Ann can't agree with Sara's tougher stance—and then see if Sara wants to help Ann with her problem, or help Ann say what she wants to do next.

Highlighting who's got the problem is the starting point for negotiation for the couple, part of clearing the clutter, not the endpoint. As we'll see in the next chapter, you may need to dig deeper to uncover the structural elements that hold the problem in place—to understand why Ann and Sara are so emotionally attached to their positions. Helping the couple see who has the problem is, however, the primary tool for breaking the overresponsible, underresponsible, dominant–submissive dynamic of the drama triangle and couple relationships. It offers the victim the opportunity to step out of the unempowered role and helps keep the rescuer from feeling burned out, overstressed, or resentful for having to do it all. Furthermore, it helps untangle the emotional enmeshment.

This clarification of responsibility does not mean that there should be an egocentric quality to intimate relationships—I take care of me and you take care of you. Actually, it is the opposite. Once the boundaries are clear, it is possible for each to be more compassionate toward the other. If Sara is having a hard time with her daughter, Ann is free to support her in a way that is helpful to Sara rather than blaming herself, feeling guilty, and feeling responsible for making Sara feel better.

You can help couples learn to adopt this perspective by encouraging them to practice these skills in other, less emotionally entangled relationships. Suggest they try and determine who has the problem when dealing with a work supervisor or an upset friend. Apply it to children. When Mary begins to melt down in Wal-Mart because she wants candy, help her dad see that it is not about candy and it is not about him. Rather it is Mary's upset, frustration, or tiredness; it is her emotional problem, and he doesn't need to fix it by buying her candy or feel resentful because she is having a hard time. Instead he needs to remain calm and clear, acknowledging her frustration but not giving in to her demands until she is able to calm herself down. With these successes under their belt the couple can then begin to apply these skills to themselves.

Be Honest

Being aware of emotions and labeling, using emotions as information, and realizing who has the problem all lay the foundation not only for self-responsibility but for honesty and genuineness. By self-focusing and recognizing and labeling your emotions, by defining and taking responsibility for your problems, you are being transparent. What you show is who you are. Without such honesty relationships become distorted—you don't speak up because you are afraid, or you assume others should know how you feel. Rather than being clear and direct you resort to manipulation.

But such honesty requires a willingness to take risks—to examine your own sincerity, to look deeper into yourself in order to help others fully understand what is going on inside. Once again you can take the lead. Encourage risk taking in the session by asking clients to clarify fuzzy language, by commenting on nonverbal cues so they can be brought into the conversation, by asking the hard questions—"Are you saying you are feeling _____, that you are wanting _____, that you are really thinking _____?" Model risk taking and clarity yourself. Resist settling into your own personal comfort zone. Be curious and press on while maintaining the client's trust. Stay in the moment and closely track the session process so that the client learns to do the same.

COUPLE SKILLS

By focusing more on themselves and less on the other, taking responsibility for their own emotions and using them for problem solving, and by being honest couples are best able to communicate and create a foundation for intimacy. But couples also need ways of clearing up inevitable misunderstandings, of effectively problem solving, of bringing positive emotions and experiences into their relationship. Here are some of the aspects of couple communication that you want to help them focus upon:

Awareness of Process

This has been mentioned several times and is vital for couples—the ability to distinguish between content and process, and, more importantly, perhaps, becoming sensitive to when the process is deteriorating. You want to begin helping them with this from the first meetings. Point out the dysfunctional patterns and the escalation of emotions that you see in the room: "Hold on, let's stop for a minute. You both seem to be getting angry. John, I notice that the more times you say to Ruth that she was wrong, the more you, Ruth, get angry and bring up details about the affair, which in turns makes you more angry, John, and more critical of Ruth. Can you see how you are bouncing off each other and escalating the argument?"

This interrupting and pointing out of the patterns is something that you will need to do over and over so that the couple develops that "third ear," and can recognize for themselves when the content is no longer carrying the message but merely serving as fuel for rising emotions. Help them become more sensitive by stopping them and asking if they can tell that the conversation is going off course or that neither one is listening well. They need your help to realize that the problem in the room is the escalating emotion, not the other's seeming inability to understand, to recognize that they are getting angry, and to have ways of calming down and cooling off before they can effectively tackle the content of the problem. Over time their increased awareness of the process will enable them to self-correct.

Active Listening

Active listening—reflecting back what you believe the other is saying and feeling—can both help keep a conversation on track and be an effective means of reducing the emotional temperature when it begins to rise. It is a basic clinical skill, and you'll be modeling this for clients. But some clinicians believe that it's valuable to teach this more formally and structure the conversation to hone these skills. This is where the clinician asks the partners to make I-statements rather than "you" statements, explaining that "you" statements reflexively cause the other to feel blamed and defensive.

Harville Hendrix asks partners to say what they thought they heard the other say and how they think they felt, and get the green light that they are correct from the other partner before replying: "It sounds like you are saying that you want me to help the kids with their homework after dinner and that you feel irritated that I seem to leave it to you—is that correct?" John Gottman will try to slow the process down by asking the partners to take turns taking notes—literally writing down what they think the other is saying before replying. Michael Nichols suggests that listeners elaborate on what the other said to show they are really interested, rather than quickly summarizing in order to switch to what the listener wants to say.

While some couples feel that the more structured approach gives them something solid to hold on to, other couples dislike this because it feels artificial. Some couples miss the point. Rather than slowing down and listening, they wind up arguing with each other over who is or isn't following the rules. Assure those who complain that the process feels awkward and artificial that it will seem more natural as they become more adept at the skills. For those who miss the point, help them recognize the power struggle and see how it undermines what they are trying to accomplish. Follow the process as it unfolds and help them stay on track.

No Name-Calling, Defensiveness, or Dredging Up of the Past

Your goal is not to help couples to be unemotional, but rather to help them learn to keep the emotions in bounds. Rather than "fighting dirty" they need to, as Gottman puts it, "fight clean." To do that they need to know what is out of bounds. Name-calling clearly falls in the dirty category and invariably undermines the process. Defensiveness—firing back with counterattacks ("But at least *I* didn't ... ") or weak excuses ("But you *knew* I was so stressed out about ... ") to retaliate or save face—shuts down active listening. Dredging up of the past ("And what about that argument you started last Christmas ... ") and especially of old wounds ("At least *I* didn't have an affair!") drags the conversation off course and just provides more ammunition in an escalating emotional battle.

The couple learns to become sensitive to these tactics by your pointing them out ("Jake, you're sounding defensive again"; "Molly, we're not talking about the affair right now; instead, can you say how you are feeling about what Tom said?"), and putting a halt to the interaction if necessary so that everyone can cool down. By doing this in the session and helping them map out a plan for better managing this at home, you help them avoid adding new emotional injuries to old ones.

Willingness to Return and Repair

Every couple will miscommunicate from time to time; that's to be expected. What prevents the miscommunication from undermining the relationship is the couple's willingness to come back together (return) and discuss (and repair) both the miscommunication ("Sorry I got so angry ... ") and the problem ("Let's try again. What do you think we should do about the dog?") when both partners have cooled down.

It's always surprising how many couples don't do this. Usually they never saw this modeled in their own families of origin, or because their argument felt so emotionally devastating, they fear that bringing up the topic again will only set off another war. So they try to sweep the argument and problem under the rug, go through the motions of making up ("Are you okay?—I'm fine"), and both silently agree to "forget about it." Usually the problem comes up again (sometimes as part of another fight) and sets off another war, only further confirming their fears and the need to avoid the topic. If they manage to really lock it away and not go there, we are back to the house metaphor where the rooms get filled and closed off, leading to the weather and kids' soccer as the only safe topics of conversation.

The ability to circle back around and rediscuss a problem is essential to avoiding a land-mined relationship. You can help couples do this by your doing this in the session process—stop the action, help both partners calm down, and begin the conversation again with active listening skills. If they again get heated, stop them once again. In the early stages of treatment when they may be gun-shy about rediscussing issues at home, you can ask them to stop arguments if they become too emotional and bring them back in to the next session to discuss. Once they have the experience of seeing that the discussion doesn't inevitably turn into World War III, their fear will be reduced, their courage will go up, and they can begin to do this themselves at home.

The key here is helping the individuals to take responsibility for their own emotions. They need to be able to calm themselves down, and be able to wait until they are emotionally calm before taking up the conversation again. Invariably the partners will differ on how long this takes (5 minutes versus 4 hours), and how well they can tolerate the unresolved tension, but it's important that neither one pressure the other to return and resolve before he or she is ready.

If one of the partners gets anxious and tends to push to resolve the issue prematurely, help him or her work up a plan such as going out for a walk, setting a timer for 30 or 60 minutes, or explicitly scheduling an appointment to talk again (tomorrow night after the kids go to bed). And if the topic should become emotional once again, they need to agree to stop and cool off, bring the problem to therapy so the emotional triggers can be explored and defused, or to write out their responses via a note or e-mail stating their feelings and position as clearly and cleanly as possible.

The Ability to Problem Solve

Some couples have no difficulty circling back to problems but lack the problem-solving skills needed to resolve them. They may have difficulty breaking the problem down into manageable chunks, articulating what it is that they want, or translating changes into specific behaviors. They may not know how to compromise.

Your job is to lead them through this process. You want to help them stay present and focused on the bottom line. If the discussion is about "helping around the house," encourage them to clearly define how, when, and by whom. Move them toward compromise by suggesting various options—"How about you both try taking turns making dinner during the week by agreeing to trade-offs"—"If you do _____, I'd be willing to do _____." Make clear to them that you are not trying to solve the problem for them, but instead trying to show them how the problem-solving process works. Finally, encourage them to try out the new agreed-upon behaviors at home and help them fine-tune them as needed.

Obviously you want to point out to couples when they are engaging in a power struggle—trying to get their own way rather than solving the problem—but stay alert to the lack of power as well, for example, Ann's passively agreeing with Sara in order to stop the conversation and reduce the tension. Good problem solving and effective compromise only come when partners have equal footing. If they don't, you need to support the one-down partner. Encourage him to speak up; with your support help her say what she wants most—"Beth, it seems like you are going along with what Tom wants, but is this really what you want?" Once both sides are clear and on more equal footing, compromise becomes a more viable, honest, and ultimately successful option.

Provide Positive Feedback

As mentioned earlier, you're looking for positives in your initial assessment. But even couples who aren't in crisis often fail to provide enough of the positive feedback needed to offset the negative. Instead they may settle for emotional safety through inflexible routines and patterns or, if prone to anger and arguments, use the emotional venting and making-up process as an acceptable substitute for other forms of intimacy.[3]

If you are successful in reducing the level of anger and blame and changing the emotional climate in the session, and have modeled positive feedback toward them yourself, they may spontaneously begin to be more open and positive themselves. Generally, however, you'll want to increase the amount of positive interaction through homework assignments—ask each to do something romantic for the other during the week, plan a time each day to debrief their day for 30 minutes, call each other in the middle of the day just to see how they are doing, each making an effort to thank or compliment the other.[4] Help each of the partners to say the types of things he or she would like to hear. Often what one partner sees as a positive gesture (he thinks that giving his wife sexy

---

[3]This same pattern can be found between parents and children where the only real interaction occurs during arguments. The venting and the making up process that bring the parents and children closer are subtle yet powerful reinforcers that keep the pattern intact.

[4]Leonard Zunin (1982), a psychiatrist, in his book *Contact: The First Four Minutes* (New York: Ballantine), did research on initial impressions and advocated for couples to particularly pay attention to those emotional points of contact during the day—waking up together in the morning, coming back together in the evening—because they set the tone for the hours after. Because partners oftentimes drift in and out of the house with merely a grunt, suggesting to couples that they pay specific attention to how they enter and leave their lives together—a hug, a kiss, a smile as greetings and departing gestures—goes a long way toward creating a positive emotional climate.

lingerie is romantic) is totally off the mark (she would prefer a massage or candlelight dinner). In sessions look for times when compliments are offered but are not acknowledged or minimized by the other—"Don't make a big deal about it, it was nothing." Individuals who grew up in critical homes have a difficult time not only making positive comments, but accepting them as well. You can help them by gently (you don't want to re-create the criticism that they are sensitive to) pointing out their minimizing response and encouraging them to allow themselves to take the compliment in.

While couples may complain that, like the active listening responses, these suggestions feel awkward and artificial, underscore their importance and purpose and reassure couples that they will become more natural with time. Watch out for couples who use homework assignments as additional fuel for unresolved anger ("I complimented Joan 12 times last week and she only complimented me once!"). If this happens, point out the competition or the falling into a martyr role; help them identify the underlying emotions driving the behaviors and encourage the individuals to once again be responsible for themselves.

The combination of individual and couple skills lays a foundation for stopping destructive patterns, and moving partners toward self-responsibility and emotional honesty. These skills allow couples to solve problems rather than being derailed by their emotions, and provides them with the respect and appreciation they each need to maintain good feelings and promote intimacy. Developing these skills in couples not only provides a practical and neutral frame for the beginning stage of treatment, but more importantly allows them to become independent of you. Rather than all three of you falling into the pattern of playing out the "Fight of the Week" session after session, you are instead helping them learn how to sort out their own disagreements at home without mediator or referee at hand. This is what enables them to handle the twists and curves as they move up and down the developmental rollercoaster of the relationship.

Again, for some couples doing this will be enough. They are able to fix a nagging problem that has been undermining their relationship; they are able to pull it out of the negative ruts that are all too easy to fall into and with practice replace negative patterns with positive, more loving interactions. But other couples will need this and more. They will need to move aside the emotional boulders of the past that prevent them from moving forward. In the next chapter we return to Sara and Ann and look at these dynamics more closely.

Looking Within: Chapter 5 Exercises

1. How well are you able to recognize and label your own emotions? Are you able to be assertive? Can you use your emotions as information to tell you what you need and want? What emotions in yourself or others do you have difficulty with? How do they affect your work as a therapist?

2. How quickly are you able to tell when conversations in your personal life are becoming derailed? Are you able to fight clean? Can you return and repair? Are you generous with your positive statements? Are there certain emotions or topics that you are particularly sensitive to and that trigger an overreaction on your part?

3. How do you tend to respond when witnessing the arguing of others close to you in your personal life? Do you feel anxious or overwhelmed? Does your tolerance tend to be low and do you find yourself wanting to jump in to end the argument or fix the issue? How does this possibly interfere with your clinical work?

4. Reflecting on your own clinical style, what priority do you put on skill training? How much of the treatment do you feel should be focused on these areas? Are there other aspects of the relationship that you feel are more important?

Chapter 6

Drilling Down
Core Issues

Sara and Ann come in for the sixth session. There's been improvement. They were able to come up with a list of chores for Amy that they both could agree on. Ann felt more like an equal parent and Sara was happy that Ann was not undermining their plan. But now there's a tension in the room as they both sit down.

"How was your week?"

Silence. Sara finally speaks up: "Actually I thought we were doing better. I was beginning to feel that Ann and I were on the same page as parents." She looks over at Ann who is huddled in the corner of the couch and turned away. "And then we had a fight Sunday night."

"What about?"

Ann comes out of her corner. "Sara was giving Amy a hard time about how she was washing the dishes." Her voice is quiet but has a mean edge.

"Come on, Ann, you know she was doing a lousy job!" Sara is angry already. "Even you would agree that she was trying to just get it done so she could call her friend!"

"Yes, but it was the way you reacted—you were just so angry, so critical." Ann's sitting upright now, getting louder herself.

"I wasn't that angry and I hate it when she tries to cut corners like that. She knows better and it just pisses me off!"

"But you didn't even see that look on her face, did you?" Ann's voice is quieter, less angry. "She was just about crying."

"She was fine."

"You always ride her. She can't do anything right."

"She's my daughter. There are certain things I expect from her!"

"That's right, she's *your* daughter. Fine." Ann pulls back, huddling back in the corner.

They're back to where they were 3 weeks ago. Although they made some behavioral changes, they have fallen back into the same emotional patterns and have gotten stuck at exactly the same point: Sara gets angry, Ann pushes back for a while, but then collapses and withdraws. This is the core pattern that has been played out over and over. While it is again about Amy and parenting, it's easy to imagine that this same dynamic coming up in arguments about money, sex, or who does what around the house.

You have two options at this point. One would be to do what we did last time—support Ann in speaking up, help her to be assertive so they can better understand each other's positions and work out a solution. But the pull of this pattern is so strong and so central, it may be best to see what is emotionally holding it in place.

"Hold on a minute, please. Do you see what has just happened? Does this feel familiar?"

"It sure does," says Sara. "Once again Ann's taking Amy's side and undermining me." Ann shoots her a look but says nothing.

"What I'm noticing is not so much that you're disagreeing but more about how this argument plays out. It seems like you both get stuck, and it's not about Amy. It is something between you. Sara, you seem to get angry quickly, and Ann, you seem to do a good job of saying how you feel, but then you suddenly withdraw. I'm not sure why. Do you feel that Sara is pulling rank by saying Amy is her daughter? Do you feel like she's not going to listen anymore?"

"I just feel overpowered," says Ann. "Yes, I guess I feel that she's not going to listen to me."

"Sara, what's happening for you?"

"I get angry because I feel like it's me against Ann and Amy. Like I'm the bad person. Like I can't depend on Ann to stand by me. When Ann shuts down and pulls back, I feel like I'm back to being a single parent with no support." Sara's voice is softer, tired.

"I'm wondering if these feelings—Ann, of being overpowered, not being listened to, Sara, of feeling unsupported, that you can't depend on Ann to stand by you—are familiar to both of you, whether you've felt them before in other relationships?"

"I had the same problem in my former relationship," says Sara. "My partner and I didn't fight about Amy but we did about money. I felt we were never on the same page."

"I've always had a hard time with people who seem critical and angry," says Ann. "My mother was like that and now my boss. I spend a lot of my energy just trying to stay away from him."

They are both acknowledging links to the past and the replication of individual patterns. This is a good time to tie these pieces together so they can begin to see the interplay of their own dynamics rather than getting stuck on what the other seems to be doing to them.

"It seems like this is where you both get stuck. Ann, you're sensitive to Sara's anger and criticism. When Ann tries to speak up, it feels to you, Sara, like she is undermining you, which makes you feel angry. Sara's anger starts to overwhelm you, Ann, and once again you feel like no one listens. You pull back, which leaves you, Sara, feeling angry but also once again deserted, like you can't depend on anybody. It's a circle that you've both experienced before and that leaves you both feeling those same old feelings. I'm wondering if there's a way for you both to break out of the circle and feel differently."

Let's stop here with this interpretation and talk about the larger process that is unfolding. As mentioned in the last chapter, some couples are able to make substantial changes to their relationship just by improving their communication. In the beginning your focus is on helping them bring into the session topics that they can't yet safely approach at home. You help them shape the conversation so that it is different— more complete, more complex, more productive. As they learn individual and couple communication skills, they apply them tentatively at first, but over time they get better at separating process and content; you and they notice that they are more responsible for their emotions and self-confident in their behaviors. You intervene less and when you do it is usually in the form of reminders—a fine-tuning of what they already know.

But sometimes they will, like Sara and Ann, then get stuck. A problem that you thought was put to rest rises up again a couple of weeks later. Or a new problem emerges, but the dynamic is the same and the couple reaches the same emotional impasse. They reach their stuck point, the core pattern through which they can't seem to move. Even though they may intellectually know the skills to apply, the skills seem to go right out the window—Ann continues to collapse and give in to Sara's demands, Sara continues to get angry whenever Ann seems to do anything out of line with Sara's expectations. Emotions escalate; responses to seemingly simple or innocuous issues seem out of proportion.

The dynamics of the drama triangle, triggered by one particular topic or an off-the-cuff remark, are played out right there in the room. You try to slow the process down, try to help them define more clearly what they are thinking and feeling, but even if they do it seems to do little to change the emotional climate. Something below the surface is getting activated, fueling and distorting the situation. You need to uncover this layer.

ANATOMY OF THE CORE DYNAMIC

You can think of the couple's core pattern—the stuck point that gets played out over and over and leads to an impasse—as the basic unit of their dysfunction. Sara and Ann's pattern is common—the escalation of emotion until someone collapses and gives in. In other couples the ramping up leads to an explosion, abuse, or walking away. Less volatile couples may get too anxious at the first sign of conflict and mutually avoid it by changing the topic and cutting off the communication or shifting the focus to something else—a child, the dog, the weather. Whatever the pattern, old wounds are reactivated, familiar modes of coping come into play, and, as Sara and Ann confirmed, are replicated and reinforced over and over. Your job is to help the couple move beyond these points so they can change their roles, emotions, and perceptions of the relationship.

What makes these patterns so tenacious isn't just the repetition and reinforcement, but also the complementarity of each partner's response. As mentioned earlier, complementarity is one of the binding forces of relationships.[1] The introvert is attracted to the extrovert; the extrovert finds the introvert quiet and mysterious; the emotional one is attracted to the less emotional, more intellectual one. This counterpoint is positive and works well under low stress—the extrovert drags the introvert out into society, opening up his world; the angry one is calmed by the quiet affection of the other; the one who is emotionally overwhelmed appreciates the clear reasoning of the more cognitive partner. The differences fill deficits and lend support.

But problems arise when old wounds are triggered by developmental changes—the birth of, or leaving home of children—or by high stress. What was complementary and supportive is now polarizing and divisive. This is where we find Sara and Ann. The nurturing qualities

---

[1]The theory of complementarity in relationships was one of the foundational concepts of the early marriage and family therapists, especially Don Jackson and John Weakland. See, for example, Jackson, D. D. (1965). Family Rules: Marital Quid Pro Quo. *Archives of General Psychiatry, 12,* 589–594.

of Ann that were attractive to Sara at the start of the relationship are now in the same emotional camp as Ann's seeming inability to hold the line with Amy. Sara's organization and ability to take charge, qualities that Ann admired, have now taken on the hard edge of criticism and control. Even without exploring their pasts, we can wonder why it is so important for Sara, for example, to teach her daughter to follow rules and be responsible, while Ann feels it is important to be nurturing and teach trust. Each projects onto Amy her own sensitivities and polarized points of view, and as a result they wind up using her as a battleground for their own differences.

Their strong emotions are anchored to their own worldviews and core beliefs about others and relationships. Sara learned through earlier experiences that you can't trust others, that they will let you down, not back you up, that you have to go it alone. Her sensitivity to these issues signals the emotional wounds—the abandonment, betrayal, disappointment—that lie beneath. In response she learned to become highly independent and, in an effort to shield her daughter from the same pain, has made self-reliance and responsibility a framework for the daughter's development.

Under stress Sara goes on the offensive. Responsibility moves toward control, frustration and fear move toward criticism and anger, triggered by the old wound of abandonment—right now portrayed in the "undermining" by Ann. Her attempts to solve a problem in effect create it. Her invariable escalation drives Ann (and no doubt her daughter) away, re-creating the pain of abandonment and reinforcing her worldview that you always have to go it alone. A self-fulfilling prophesy is replicated over and over. She finds herself continually getting what she expects.

It's easy to see how Sara's coping style and worldview dovetail with Ann's. Ann, who is not angry and controlling, is hypersensitive to anger and control. She wants those she is close to listen to her and respect her but finds that they never do. Instead they always seem critical and dismissive. Where Sara has learned to attack and push, Ann has learned to back down and give up, each driving the coping style of the other. Just as Sara always winds up feeling abandoned and alone, Ann always winds up feeling overpowered and criticized.

Underneath it all both are feeling essentially the same. Ann feels minimized and dismissed by Sara's criticism and inability to listen just as Sara feels minimized and dismissed by Ann's taking Amy's side and not backing her up. Each wishes the other were finally the one to do it differently, to be the one to provide what they've wanted all along. They get angry and frustrated and depressed in their efforts to make it happen, and remain disappointed that it never does.

Some couples play these patterns out over and over until they reach some emotional bottom line, convince themselves that it will never change, and move on to other relationships, only to replay the dynamics yet again. Thomas, for example, came in for individual counseling after his fourth wife left him. As he described the history of his past relationships it was clear that he was always caught in the middle of a triangle and always wound up feeling jealous and left out. First it was with his own children, then with a new wife and her mother, then a third wife and her job, and finally with a fourth wife and her mentally ill daughter.

Each time the attention he received during the courtship and early months of the marriage made him feel optimistic, but then invariably, like Ann, he felt sidelined, unappreciated. He felt as he did when his father died and his mother was forced to care for six children as a single parent. Close to his father, he suddenly felt abandoned, alone, and alienated from his overwhelmed mother. Each marriage was an attempt to fill that emotional void, heal the childhood wound by finding someone who would give him the attention he was missing, but instead he succeeded only in replicating it.

What both Thomas and Sara and Ann need to do is move against their own grain—resist the temptation to leave, to control, to become passive—and move in the opposite direction, to stay and work things out, to let go of control and compromise, to speak up and be assertive. This breaks the dysfunctional core pattern, and by doing so allows new experiences and emotions to replace the old. They also each need to help their partners understand their needs and ask from them what they could not directly ask for as children from their parents. If they can do this, they are fixing the problem in the present while helping each other heal, rather than replicate, old hurts.

DRILLING DOWN

How do you uncover these core dynamics within a couple? You start with curiosity—Why have these two people come together? Why are they stuck at this point?—and observe and explore. You may have begun to detect these core issues through individual comments made when you were doing your assessment: A partner's mother, described as depressed and self-absorbed and having little to give, who left the children to fend for themselves; the alcoholic father whose moods floated up and down on his level of intoxication, and who taught the children to read him like an emotional seismometer; the always critical parent or ex-spouse that the partner gave up on ever pleasing and learned to avoid; the chaotic family that pushed the client to take refuge in the home life of a close friend, in the competitive arena of sports, or the numbing comfort of drugs and addiction. These one-line or longer recitations alert you not only to the potential replaying of coping patterns (self-reliance, hyper-vigilance, avoidance and withdrawal), but also to a sensitivity to and tolerance for these corresponding behaviors in the partner—depression, alcoholism, criticism, or a chaotic home life. The past becomes part and parcel of the present.

And if you didn't uncover these signs and signals in the assessment, you will undoubtedly uncover them now in the middle stages of treat-ment. As the couple becomes more trusting of you and the therapeutic process, they relax and bring up topics not mentioned before, or display strong emotions more openly. Often it is these emotional reactions and overly strong language that provide clues to unresolved past issues—"You always criticize me!" when it is clear that the partner does not; "I feel like you're trying to kill me!" when the partner gets angry or frustrated; "You always treat me like a 10-year-old!" when the partner is generally sensitive to the other's opinions. You find clues too in non-verbal behaviors—the partner who suddenly has a look of terror on his face, who physically cowers or collapses in a heap, or who blows up like a teenager. These signs tell you that old fears are being triggered. Old ways of coping that no longer fit the present situation are coming into play. Here, you suspect, are the childhood wounds that never healed, the childhood needs that were never fulfilled.

Once you hear these clues, and see the core pattern repeated over and over, you can begin to explore and see what holds it in place. The goal, of course, is to help them break the cycle, and the key to doing this is helping them separate the past from the present—cognitively, emo-tionally, behaviorally. Here are several ways you can do this:

Point Out What You Notice

Defining the reactions and emotions and making the client curious about them is often enough to begin the stepping-back process:

"Greg, I notice that unlike other issues that you disagree with Helen about, you seem particularly angry now and are having a hard time calming your-self down. I wonder what makes you especially sensitive to this one."

"Cheryl, I notice that when Tim starts to get angry, you physically curl up and seem to me to be trying to squeeze yourself into the corner of the couch almost like a scared little girl. I wonder how you are feeling."

"Hank, you just said that you feel as though Margaret is out to destroy you, and you have a frightened look on your face. Sometimes strong reactions like this are tied into some similar childhood experiences. I wonder if Margaret's reactions or your feelings remind you of something similar from your past."

"Tina, you mentioned a few weeks ago that your mom was always criticizing you and you learned to just tune her out as a way of coping with it. Anita seems to be trying to get you to understand how she feels, and just said that she feels that you are not listening to her. I wonder if you are feeling criticized right now by her, and tuning her out like you used to do with your mom."

What you're doing here is saying what you see and suggesting that there may be more going on that is fueling the individual's reactions. Sometimes simply making this connection cognitively allows the individual to slow and modify his or her behavior. Other times this may lead into a longer discussion of childhood experiences. The client will be able to talk about traumatic experiences and painful emotions. Expressing these feelings will make them less potent and help further reduce the firing of old reactions.

Occasionally you may have a client who makes no connection to the past—Hank, for example, says that no, Margaret's reactions don't remind him of anything from the past, or that he has few memories of his childhood. Such blocking of childhood memories or idealization of childhood is due to repression, usually of traumatic events. From a psychodynamic perspective you would gently push further to help the individual begin to uncover these memories; from a cognitive-behavioral perspective it's usually not necessary. Even if Hank doesn't make a connection, his partner, Margaret, generally has, and that in turn will help modify her reaction. Her recognizing that Hank is possibly responding to old wounds may enable her to take his reactions less personally and respond more empathically toward him. Coupling her awareness with specific behavioral changes that both of them can make will help break the cycle.

Have the Client Make Specific Reflective Childhood Statements

Harville Hendrix does this masterfully and it is one of the keys to his imago approach to couple therapy. Essentially you want to slow down the process and give the individual statements to complete: "When you criticize me about the children, it reminds me of _____, and I feel _____. What I needed back then and didn't receive was _____." These fill-in-the-blank statements can be emotionally powerful. They force clients to revive the past and identify the triggers for themselves and their partners. Once these past issues are separated from the present, you can then talk more effectively about ways of recognizing the triggers in the present and behaviorally changing the dysfunctional pattern.

Move into Deeper Experiential Techniques and Assignments

Depending on your style and orientation you may want to move into other experiential techniques that help drain old emotions and heal old wounds. Several options come to mind:

The Empty-Chair Technique

The empty-chair technique is one of the mainstays of Gestalt therapy. Once you and the client have made a connection between the present situation and the past, you can ask clients to imagine the parent, for example, sitting in the empty chair that you place across from them. You then ask them to talk to that parent in the present tense about how they felt as a child—"Dad, when you yell at me I feel _____." Essentially the person is saying what he or she never got to say in real life. The individual then switches chairs and takes the role of the parent— "What would your dad say," you ask, "if he heard you say this to him?" You can go back and forth, encouraging a deepening dialogue between them. If both roles seem to get stuck, with the dad staying critical, for example, and the child weakly complaining, you can intervene to shift the emotions.

For example, you may say to a client while she is in the dad role, "Dad, Sally sees you as angry all the time, but I guess that as a parent you are also worried about her. What is it you are most worried about?" to move toward the softer emotions. Or, "Sally only seems to see this one angry side of you. What is it that she doesn't understand about what makes you tick?" Or, "Sally sees you as angry all the time, but I suspect that as a parent you love her as well. Can you tell her how much you care about her?"

The client is forced to make something up, to wrestle with other perspectives and emotions. Clients report feeling differently as they shift between roles and get an emotional sense of what it may have felt like to be the parent. These two sides have often been incorporated within themselves as different aspects of their personalities and are now getting played out in your office. Through the exercise clients have the opportunity to separate the past and present, their current adult self from the parent and child subpersonalities within. They become less sensitive to the emotional triggers because their perceptions have changed.

Letter Writing

Like the empty-chair technique, letter writing is a way of getting past issues off one's chest and directing them where they need to go—to the person in the past, rather than the partner in the present. This is usually given as a homework assignment and can be written to a deceased parent, or to a living parent as he or she was perceived in the past. As with the empty-chair exercise, you want to encourage a dialogue. Generally it's most effective to have clients write three letters. The first is from clients to the parent (or grandparent, sibling, etc.) saying whatever they want to say that never was said about what bothered them the most, what they wished was different. The clients then write a letter back to themselves saying what they think the parent would write back if he or she actually received the letter (for example, "Mary, I'm sorry," or "Mary, you obviously have no respect for your parents and I refuse to talk about this!"). Finally, they write a third letter from the parent to themselves saying what ideally they wish the parents would say ("Mary, I am so sorry and realize now how much I hurt you through the years ... "). Clients can write as much as they like and are asked to bring the letters in to the next sessions, where you ask them to read the letters aloud.

Again, the process of writing the letters both stirs memories and feelings and provides an outlet. When they are read aloud, not only are old emotions drained, the partner has the opportunity to understand and empathize with the writer's pain.

Discussions with Parent about the Past

If parents are accessible to a client, conversations with them can be an optimal way of separating and repairing the past. Clients are often anxious about talking with their parents about their childhoods (which is why they have not done so before), and worry that what they might say will only make matters worse. To help desensitize them to these deeper conversations suggest that they simply start a dialogue the next time they see the parent or talk to him or her on the phone by asking a specific but relatively innocuous question about childhood ("Dad, what do you remember most about my childhood?" or "Mom, I was thinking about when you and Dad got divorced—that must have been hard for you.").

The goal is not to vent and tell the parents off but rather to change the process by opening doors into topics previously not discussed. It is an opportunity to share perspectives and perceptions and correct them—"How did you see me as a child?" "How did you feel after the divorce?" "Could tell how upset I was?" These questions help the client move away from the black/white perceptions of a child and replace with the complex and reality-based perceptions of an adult.

You can also invite the client to bring a parent in for a session. Because the parent will undoubtedly feel anxious, your first goal is help him or her relax. Define the purpose and context of the meeting: "As you probably know, Sue, her husband, and I have been working together on their relationship. I suggested to Sue that she invite you here just to talk about what you remember about her childhood that might help her better understand what is now happening in her marriage." Open the discussion and stay in charge of the process so everyone feels safe.

Make sure the discussion remains balanced, but steer it toward deeper, softer emotional levels. It's less about covering content than about changing process. The purpose is not to vent, or to put the parent on the hot seat. Think of it more as a consult by the parent, a sharing of his or her perspective, which you can process separately with the client later. End by thanking the parent for coming in, making sure he or she is feeling okay, and encouraging both parent and child to continue these types of discussions on their own if they both choose.

Guided Imagery

When Tim says he feels that his wife is treating him like a 10-year-old, or Cheryl feels neglected like she was when she was little, you can guide the client to imagine that scene in the past—Tim being scolded by his mother, for example, or Cheryl sitting in her room feeling lonely. Once they have the scene in their minds, have them begin to play it like a movie and describe to you what they see—"I'm sitting at the kitchen table and my mother keeps asking me if I have finished my homework." Provide suggestions that change the scene and make it more healing— for example, have Tim imagine telling his mother how he feels that she is nagging him rather than silently holding his emotions in, or showing her his homework rather than snapping back, or talking to his mother later and imagining her giving him a hug.

A powerful variation on this is to have the client imagine his or her inner child. Ask Cheryl, for example, to imagine herself feeling sad and lonely in her room, and imagine the adult her sitting down and asking in a gentle voice what it is that she, the little girl, needs and wants most. This is emotionally powerful and what she hears the little girl inside her say helps clarify basic unfulfilled needs—"I need someone to be proud of me"; "I need someone to tell me I'm lovable." These basic needs can then be connected to behavioral changes in the present.[2]

Sculpting

Okay, stand up. Grab someone there in the room with you. I'd like you to imagine you are a sculptor and you are going to make a sculpture of the relationship between you as a child and one of your parents. Do this without talking. Merely shape the other person in a position that seems to represent how you saw your parent most of the time—hunched in a corner and withdrawn, glaring at you from across the room, giving you a hug—and be sure to include facial expressions. Now put yourself into the sculpture, shaping yourself to represent how you felt in relation to your parent most of the time—reaching out and sad, hugging back but feeling stiff. Got it? Now do it again, making a sculpture of how you wish it could have been.

Because it is so stark and dramatic, doing this exercise with couples can be emotionally powerful for both partners. It forces them to crystallize their childhood relationships and gives you a way to reignite old emotions ("How does it feel," you ask the one in the parent pose, "to be standing so far away from your daughter? Do you ever wish you could get closer to her?"). After sculpting their parents' relationships, you can then ask the couple to each sculpt their current relationship, and compare and contrast them with that of the past. The image tends to linger and you can refer back to it when the past intrudes into the present ("John, as you're talking I'm seeing the image again of the frightened little boy crouching in the corner.").

What all of these experiential techniques have in common is their ability to clarify and help resolve past issues that are contaminating interactions in the present. Obviously some emotional blocks will be easier to move than others. For some clients, simply pointing out their

---

[2]Richard Schwartz has developed a therapeutic model that powerfully expands on this type of inner work with individuals. See Schwartz, R. C. (1994). *Internal Family Systems Therapy*. New York: Guilford Press.

strong reaction to a particular comment is enough to cause them to consciously shift their behavior, while with others you may need to try one
or even several of these tools to order to find one that is effective.

A trap you want to avoid is seeing the presence of old wounds as a
rationale to abandon couple therapy and replace it with individual therapy. This can seem like an alluring option for you as therapist and for
a couple. If you feel less skilled in couple therapy, or are uncomfortable
dealing with the inherent triangle, you can find yourself easily sidestep-
ping your anxiety by creating rationalizations for intensive individual
work.

Couples are tempted to look upon individual work as a way of
bypassing the middle-stage emotional angst of working through their
problems together. The one-on-one relationship with the therapist can
feel cozy, and the focus on the past can seem like a welcome distraction
from the complex and messy present. And for those partners still mired
in blame, having one partner seemingly more entrapped by the past can
leave the other feeling that yes, indeed, it's true what he or she believed
all along, that the other really is the one who is screwed up after all and
needs all the work. We're back to the one up-one one-down dynamic of
the drama triangle and the couple is unbalanced.

If this initial exploration does uncover deeper individual issues that
the client is eager to work on more intensively, this becomes a fork in the
road that you need to clarify with the couple: Does the individual want
to do individual therapy with someone else while continuing couple
therapy with you? Are they both agreeing to postpone (not stop) couple
therapy for now in order to focus on this individual work? Are they taking this path because they are feeling stuck or anxious about working
things through together?

If, for example, you are concerned that entering individual therapy
will only reinforce the one-down, person-with-the-problem position of
one of the partners, and aggravate rather than relieve their presenting
problems, voice your concern. Again, you're an advocate for their relationship, your focus is on their interactional process, and your job is to
help them think through the options and implications of any changes in
your therapeutic contract. Help them refrain from simply taking a path
of least resistance.

In most cases, this will not be an issue. You'll help them clear away
these impediments of the past and the couple can move forward. What
is important is that you next incorporate these insights into present
behaviors. Once Sara, for example, has greater emotional awareness of
the source of her control and sensitivity to feeling undermined, she will
still need help to move against her own grain, replace her old behaviors
with new ones. She will need to consciously resist taking control and

put a damper on her anger, just as Ann will need to consciously take the risk of holding her ground, rather than giving in, even when beginning to feel overwhelmed. Only by each one taking these steps will they finally and fully be able to break the hold of the past and the recurring dysfunctional pattern.

As with any new behaviors, their first attempts will be the most shaky. They will need a lot of support and positive feedback from you for taking the risk at all. It will be easy for them to fall back into old reactions, but each time the new behaviors will become easier. Over time, and with your support and reminders of what is past and present, the partners will be better able to stay more present focused and apply the skills they are developing.

HEALING COUPLE WOUNDS

While many emotional wounds can be tracked back to childhood, some may come from within the couple's relationship. Extramarital affairs are probably the most common source of injury, but there can be others— the hurt of feeling abandoned during pregnancy, injuries caused by the ways each partner coped during a stressful time involving a child's serious illness or parent's death, sometimes a simple but cutting remark that lingers and cannot be shaken. You uncover these wounds when one partner tells you about the affair, when a past incident is dredged up in the midst of a heated argument, or when they say they have an issue that always sits right below the surface that they both want to finally put to rest.

The question to yourself and the couple is why now—why is the past coming back into the present? Sometimes it's because the wound was swept under the rug but periodically gets triggered in the present. After the husband found out about his wife's affair, she told him she didn't know why it happened, and urged him to just move on, put it behind him. But it haunts him, especially when he is feeling neglected or when he sees his wife flirting at a party. Sometimes a partner holds on to the hurt as a weapon. When arguments get heated enough, the affair is pulled out in a last-ditch effort to stay on top—"At least I never _____!" Other times pain from the past has been unraveling slowly, and as the relationship and emotions become more open, or the partner feels more empowered through therapy and your support, these nagging old feelings are revealed—the wife really is angry that her husband wasn't more involved during her first pregnancy, or he has never forgiven her for not coming with him to his father's funeral.

The simple and obvious goal here is to get the conversation in the room, but as with other elements of the relationship, to not simply re-create the same familiar fight, the same familiar responses. Your job is to change the conversation, to make it more complete, to draw out the emotions that had not been expressed. The I-don't-know-why-it-happened response to the affair is no longer adequate. Time in the sessions need to be used to explore why it may have happened, to understand how it was a solution to another unidentified problem. The wife needs to express her anger about her feeling of abandonment during pregnancy, the couple needs to talk about how they each internally struggled, but never fully expressed how they felt when they were told that their child was autistic. What went unsaid needs to be said now.

What these discussions are really about is grief—the loss on one or both sides of the way the relationship and the partner were thought to be: Here was a woman whom I thought I could trust, and then I found out that she, like most of the women in my life, cannot be trusted; here was a relationship that we thought was strong enough to weather whatever life threw at us, only to find that it was more fragile than we thought, and that some of that foundation has eroded. You help them with these emotions by asking about them—"Did this feel like a loss to you?" "Were you sad?" "Did you feel angry?"—and then listening. You help them move away from blaming and arguing about what happened and toward these deeper emotions.

When the conversation seems one-sided—when the wife really doesn't want to sit there and hear again (especially when it was years ago) how hurt her husband felt by the affair—you offer support and acknowledge that it is difficult to hear, and help her understand that being willing to hear her partner and allowing him to grieve is part of the healing process. Show how what is happening in the room is part of the same problem and solution that initially brought them in—for example, the couple's tendency to sweep things under the rug, or to avoid taking the time to listen to each other.

As you do with childhood wounds, you want to connect the past to the present: Are there triggers in the present that the partners need to be aware of—flirting, not having sex for long periods of time, falling into silences and avoidance when problems loom on the horizon? Does the sudden stirring of old wounds—seemingly out-of-the-blue thinking about the past affair or sudden anger about past comments—offer a signal about an individual need or problem in the relationship that now needs to be addressed? Identifying these triggers, using memories as information help move the issue out of the psychological limbo it has been in, encourages the couple to stay active and focused in the present.

If, however, the topic is less about grief and more about power—a partner is using it to express anger in the only way he or she knows how, as a weapon in an argument, or as a way of stirring guilt in order to get what he or she wants—your job is to call it. It's dirty fighting, it's manipulation. Label it for what it is and get it off the table. Rather than talking about the affair, you say, let's talk about how you start to feel during the argument. Rather than stirring guilt by bringing up the past in order to get your partner to agree with what you want, see if you can be assertive and say directly what you want. Arguing isn't bad, but you want to help them fight clean, not dirty; say what you want in the present without leveraging it with the past.

And what if one of the partners can't seem to shake the hurt and anger? You need to wonder what's keeping it active. Often it is something from childhood, and the betrayal or abandonment in the relationship opened a similar, yet unexplored wound from an earlier time. "What else does this feeling remind you of?" you ask. "When else have you felt betrayed or abandoned? See what lies underneath."

Be careful again about reductionism, and turning a couple-defined wound in the relationship automatically into an individual childhood one. If you do, you're in danger of unbalancing the system. Transforming a legitimate couple issue into individual pathology—it's not about the hurt of the affair, it's about childhood abandonment—it mitigates the other's role in the creation of the problem. Start with what's presented, explore the issue within the relationship. If you then get stuck, go deeper, help repair the weak spot in the psychological flooring, and then bring it back to the present.

CHOOSE YOUR FORMAT

In light of all this discussion about the past and underlying issues, this is a good time to talk about the advantages and disadvantages of various session formats—that is, seeing the couple together versus doing couple therapy by working with individuals separately. We'll start with the poles—always couple and always individuals—and then move toward some combination.

Couple Only

Advantages

Working with the couple only when they are together in the room has the advantage of keeping absolutely everything out in the open. You can easily see the patterns as they unfold, and can stop or change them in the moment. You have an ideal forum for teaching skills as the couple plays out their interactions in front of you. You don't have to worry about mentally having to piece together two different sides of a story. Most of all, perhaps, this format reinforces to the couple that they are in this together, and that you're helping them understand each other and work together better as a unit.

Disadvantages

You always have a triangle. You need to be careful about balance in the room and you need to make sure you have a solid rapport with both. You need to be particularly alert to the effects of gender: Does the husband feel left out by the simple dynamics of having two women in the room with him? Is the wife in danger of feeling ganged up on by the two men? Think of these possibilities, look for the hesitations or tension, and address them. If you feel that there is some imbalance, some unspoken problem in your therapeutic relationship with one of the partners, bring it up in the session, or through a follow-up note—"John, you seemed quiet last week. I was wondering if you felt that I was taking Emily's side against you"—that they both can share.

Managing the process between the partners can be taxing, especially in the beginning when the couple may be in crisis. It can feel intimidating if you are clinically less experienced; plenty of supervisory coaching and support will be important. The fact that couple therapy feels less intimate than individual therapy might be disorienting until you grow more comfortable with it.

There is a danger that if you see only the couple some important issues could stay underground—Tom, for example, really does have some resentment over his wife's leaving their church but is afraid to bring it up because he doesn't know what stand you might take. You can offset this by making sure you raise the issue of issues—"Is there any lingering issue that we should be talking about? Anything that you feel is important but feel hesitant to bring up?" This lets them know that the therapeutic ground is wide. If they feel safe with you they eventually will.

Finally, due to the triangle, there is always the danger of the couple turning on the therapist. Police officers are familiar with this dynamic in domestic violence calls made by neighbors—as soon as the officer starts to intervene to break up the argument, the couple turns on the policeman, who they feel has no business being there. If a couple gangs up on you, the question to ask yourself is "Why?" Usually, just like with the police officers, it is about power, your use of your power. You're pushing too hard, applying too much pressure, perhaps because you are feeling overresponsible for the problem, and the couple unites against the common enemy of the moment, namely you. As with other bumps on the therapeutic road, the problem is found in the process. Hear them out, find out what is driving their reaction, fix the relationship, and clarify the expectations.

Individuals Only

Advantages

You can work with individuals and still focus on the couple relationship. Some clinicians split a session between each of the partners, some alternate weeks, some see each once a week. You can teach skills, coach on ways to step out of the dysfunctional patterns, and still explore triggers and uncover the past. You can give each individual your undivided attention, and it is easier to move between past and present. You don't have to worry about balancing out the process by the end of the session since each has your equal attention. For those trained in individual therapy or less skilled in working with couples, managing the process can seem easier; you feel like you have more control.

Disadvantages

If you're psychodynamically oriented, concerned more with tracking individual past dynamics and developing insight, this format may not seem to be much of a problem. But if you are following a behavioral, systems-oriented model, all that appears to be an advantage can be seen as a potential disadvantage. You're not able to observe the couple's interactions directly—you have to rely on detailed descriptions about what happens at home, piece stories together, or infer that your reactions and theirs may replicate what happens in the relationship. You can teach skills or suggest new behaviors to try, but you lack the opportunity to get immediate feedback and fine-tune your efforts.

As mentioned above, you need to remain clear about your model and clear with the couple around the clinical goals so that you don't wander toward individual therapy as a way of avoiding their or your own anxiety. A bigger danger, however, is that the couple's progress is artificial, propped up by an active, if unintentional, triangulation with you. Because the focus of the process is not directly on the interaction of the couple, but on the interaction of the couple through you, there is the danger that you become the stabilizing force for the couple. They don't argue as much because they individually know they can vent to you about the week's complaints; they feel better because you are serving as a surrogate ideal partner, offering support and quality time. You have become the stabilizing force, and though they seem to do better, little actually changes within the couple relationship.

It can be easy for you to collude with this process if you are not alert. The partners enjoy coming, and because they do, you enjoy seeing them. They each tell you that seeing you is making a difference, which together with the comfortable intimacy of the session, keeps you willing to keep it going. The work becomes long term, which you can rationalize as going deeper when in fact everyone is treading water.

The way to avoid this, of course, is to look for it, to track whether real changes in patterns, in behaviors, in the application of skills are taking place at home. Look whether the couple is taking real emotional risks and breaking new ground with each other, and talking with their partners about things they discuss with you. Be clear about the clinical goals, and make sure that everyone is working in the same direction.

Couple–Individual Combination

Advantages

The mixing of individual and couple sessions would seem to be the Goldilocks not too cold, not too hot, seemingly just-right option. Which side you lean toward will depend on your orientation (for example, psychodynamically oriented versus systems or communication oriented) and personal style. Using the model we are presenting the real clinical issue is knowing when and why to include individual sessions. Here are some clinical possibilities:

- *To build or repair rapport.* If you are having a hard time joining with one of the partners, if you are worried that he or she sees you as siding with the other partner, if you said something that was taken the wrong way perhaps, or created hurt feelings that weren't processed in the session, pull the individual aside to clarify and fix. Once you are back on solid ground, go back to the couple.
- *To uncover underlying issues.* Some clinicians meet with the individuals on a regular basis to see how each feels the treatment is going, and to see if there are any issues that are being stirred up but not brought up in couple sessions. If an issue has slipped under the radar ("We haven't talked about this much, but I'm more worried about Harry's depression than I've said"), talk about next steps for bringing it up in the next

couple session. This provides a way of moving aside clinical boulders that could cause the progress to stall or keep the process at a superficial level.

• *When an individual requests it.* Sometimes an individual will request a separate session to win you to his or her side or to relieve the tension of the couple interaction by having a deeper relationship with you. If this is the case, you are in danger of unbalancing the relationship, serving as a stabilizing leg of the triangle, or alienating the other partner. Listen to the individual's concerns, restate your focus on helping the couple's interactions and relationship, and then encourage him or her to raise any concerns in the couple session.

But sometimes a request for a separate session is about somewhat unrelated issues—Doris wants to talk to you about her aging mother and how to handle her when she gets explosive; Matt is struggling with his boss and wants some advice on handling it differently. This can be helpful in reducing stress that may be contributing to the relationship. The partner, however, should know what is being discussed so he or she doesn't get paranoid and assume the session involves some secret about the relationship. Similarly, these seeming side issues should not be a distraction from the couple work. If Doris's issues are more complex than you thought, for example, and need more than a couple of sessions of your time, consider referring her to see someone else about this, or talk with the couple about which issues they now see as priorities.

This raises the issue of deciding when individual therapy actually does trump couple work, and should indeed become the therapeutic priority. Two situations come to mind. The first is when an individual's struggle clearly makes couple work at the present time ineffective. This can include untreated major depression, obsessive–compulsive disorder (OCD), or an eating disorder, for example, as well as drug and alcohol addictions where the uncontrolled addiction undermines progress in couple therapy.

The other situation, closely related, is one where your recommendation of individual therapy is a way of setting priorities and encouraging personal responsibility. Again, addiction comes to mind, where an individual may minimize drug use or connect it to the relationship ("I only drink so much because my wife … "), but this can also apply to anger management, where by saying to the client "You need to get some help with your anger," you are underscoring that this really is a problem that the client needs to own and wrestle with, rather than diffusing the responsibility by blaming the partner.

In such situations it's generally best to ask that the individual begin treatment and get some traction, then you and the other clinician he is seeing can talk and make recommendations about when it would be best to begin couple work again. Sometimes couple or family therapy will be folded into the individual treatment. An outpatient substance abuse program, for example, may build in periodic family sessions, as part and parcel of the individual treatment. All these can be completed before tackling the couple's relationship issues more intensively.

Disadvantages

The only disadvantage to shifting between couple and individual sessions is that it can seem arbitrary and confusing for the couple. The easiest way to avoid this is to determine your preferences at the beginning and communicate them clearly to the couple ("We'll occasionally be meeting individually just as a type of check-in" or "You can feel free to ask me about an individual session if you ... "). You can set out the same parameters regarding family sessions ("If you ever want to bring in the children to nail down with them some of the parenting issues you've been talking about, feel free to say so.").

The theme that runs through this discussion of formats is clarity of clinical intention and communication. Sort through for yourself what clinically suits your own style and framework, and decide what you most want to help the couple accomplish and focus upon and what setting will be most productive. Communicate all this to the couple both at the beginning and when situations come up that require any change.

THE CORE OF THE WORK: A SUMMARY

This middle stage is where the bulk of the work is done. You will be moving through layers of problems and patterns beginning with clearing up the communication so that the conversations are more honest and specific, and then isolating and further exploring the core dynamics. Along the way some couples will improve and leave, relieved that the crisis and surface tension are reduced. Others will stay and, as they feel more safe and settled with you and each other, will drop their defensiveness and communicate more intimately. Again, what you want to avoid is the never-ending "fight of the week" rut, where you are essentially offering mediation or arbitration and where the couple has not been able to change its patterns or apply the skills of communication and problem solving. If this begins to happen, ask yourself, and them, why, and focus on the underlying problem.

There is, unfortunately, no recipe to lead you on a straight linear course. You will be plowing, prodding, and continually circling back to repeat themes, to point out recurring patterns, to pinpoint the triggers that stir the core dynamic. This is the nature of this stage of treatment. Helping the couple understand this prevents them from becoming discouraged and feeling that they are not moving fast enough. Some couples may do well for a couple of weeks, then suddenly regress when out-of-town company comes and stays a bit too long, or when job stress preoccupies one of the partners, leaving the other feeling abandoned or helpless, and the hurt stirs old wounds. Some couples appreciate having weekly homework assignments as a way of staying focused and maintaining momentum; others see the sessions themselves as a way of keeping them both accountable for applying what they are learning.

But if you are doing your job well, they reach a steady state of comfort. The crises and regressions are less frequent, and they are able to recover on their own more and more quickly. Your role in the session moves from teaching and guiding to commenting on the positives or underscoring variations on the theme. You may wish that they would spend more time together as a couple, or that the husband could feel more empowered overall, and you express your wish, but they nod and tend to brush it off. You bring up the question of reclarifying goals and little comes up. You sense they are not settling or avoiding their anxiety, but really are doing okay.

It's time to begin to terminate.

Looking Within: Chapter 6 Exercises

1. This is a good time to look more closely at your own clinical models and preferences. What do you set as a priority for treatment? What, in your mind, is the role of an individual's past in shaping current relationships? What is your preference and style for handling such issues in treatment?

2. What does your partner do that bothers you most? What in your past might have left you especially sensitive to that? Try one of the experiential exercises—empty chair, letter writing—as a way of defining and possibly settling some unfinished business from your own past.

3. A guided imagery exercise:

   Imagine yourself entering a theater. You walk into a lobby where there are a lot of people milling around. You walk through the lobby into the auditorium, where you take the best seat in the house. In front of you is a large stage with a curtain drawn across it.

You make yourself comfortable, and now the other members of the audience come in and take the seats around you. The house lights go dim and the stage lights go on. A play is about to start.

The curtain rises on the first act of the play. There we see your parents and the time is before you were born. Watch what happens, listen to what is said, see who else is there.

The curtain comes down. The curtain rises on the next act and we see you on the stage, and you are a young child. Again watch what happens, see who else is there, and listen to what is said.

The curtain comes down again. The curtain rises and we see you on stage, and now you are a teenager and are with one or both of your parents. They are talking to you about growing up—about relationships and sex, careers and education. Listen to what they say, listen to what you say back.

The curtain comes down. The curtain rises on the next act and we see you on stage and now you are a bit older. It is the time in your life when you are leaving home for the first time, literally moving out of the house—to go to college, to get an apartment with friends, to get married. On stage with you are one or both of your parents. Watch what happens, listen to what is said, see if you can tell how you are feeling at the moment.

The curtain comes down. The curtain rises on the next act and now you are a bit older and in a serious relationship—a boy- or girl-friend, a partner—and you are together on stage. Watch what happens, listens to what is said.

The curtain comes down. The curtain rises and the time is the present. You are on stage. Watch what happens.

The curtain comes down. The curtain rises again and the time is the future, 5 years from now. Watch what happens, listen to what is said, see who is there.

The play is over now and the curtain comes down, the stage lights go off and the house lights go on. The audience gets up and begins to leave the theater. You follow them out and you overhear them talking about the play. Listen to what they say about the play.

So what did you see? The question to ask yourself is: Out of the things you could have seen, why did you see what you did and what does it say about your life right now? What is the overall tone, what are the patterns that run through the scenes?

A quick framework for self-reflection:

The first scene of your parents is about early relationships—how did your parents get along? What were they doing? How is this a model for the early stages of your own relationships?

For the second scene, from your childhood, ask yourself: Out of all you could have imagined, why this scene—what does it say about your childhood, your life now? Were you happy, sad? Alone, with sibs, with parents? What were you doing?

The third scene is an expanded birds-and-bees talk about growing up: What did you hear? What did your parents say was important? Often these become the "shoulds" that drive our lives. What are yours?

The next scene involves leaving. How did you feel when you were packing up—excited, scared, depressed, smothered, guilty? Why? How is this feeling a possible emotional bottom line for you about leavings in general? How often do you decide to leave a relationship or job, even when you feel this way again?

An early relationship: What did you see? What was the tone? How was it like or unlike the first scene of your parents?

The present. Out of all that is going on in your life right now, what did you see? How is this similar to or different from the other scenes?

Five years in the future: What did you see? How is it similar to or different from what you consciously think about? How is it like or different from other scenes?

What did the audience say about your play—exciting, boring, glad you turned yourself around? How sensitive are you to what others say?

This isn't prophecy, only a different way of getting information about your life. Mull it over and see how it applies to your self and your work.

Chapter 7

Termination

Eventually it comes—the end of treatment. In this chapter, which concludes our look at overall structure—beginning, middle, and end—of treatment, we'll look at some of the common scenarios for termination, talk about handling the ones that go sour, and explore some of the countertransference issues that can underlie the process.

WHY STOP?

There are many reasons to terminate therapy. Termination may be initiated by the clients, or come as a joint decision, or you may initiate it yourself. Sometimes couples abruptly end therapy for logistical reasons—the wife is suddenly transferred in her job, and a couple needs to sell their house and move to Colorado in the next 2 weeks; Grandma has broken her hip and the husband is going to be staying with her for the next couple of months until she is stable again; their child has been in a serious accident and all their attention and resources are focused on him. Other times they simply drop out of sight—they cancel because the car breaks down, then the child gets sick, and they leave a message that they'll give you a call. They never do and seem to have faded away.

So you call and leave a message—you wish them the best of luck in Colorado and tell them you would be happy to pass on your impressions if they decide to go back into therapy and sign a release; you are sorry to hear about Grandma or their child and hope things work out okay, and say they should feel free to contact you if at some point they want to do therapy again or just need some support; you let them know that you haven't seen them for a few weeks say, they seem to have a lot going on and you seem to have lost touch, and encourage them to give you a call when they are ready to start again. This type of follow-up is human courtesy and support, but it often goes a long way toward leaving a couple with a good feeling about you and therapy in general.

And if you are wondering whether they are dropping away because the last session left them too shaken and shell-shocked, or discouraged, give them a call or write them a note, saying exactly that—"I wonder if you felt discouraged after our last session" or "I realize that our last session was emotionally difficult; I hope you are doing okay and would be happy to talk to you more about it; please give me a call." Maybe they will, maybe they won't, but at least you made a genuine attempt to reach out and reach some closure.

It's easy not to do this follow-up and just let them go. You tell yourself you are too busy and they are no doubt fine; your clinical training may tell you that you are being too invasive or overresponsible. Often beneath this reluctance are your own mixed feelings and anxiety—about letting go yourself, about admitting that you may have let them down somewhat, the fear that they will call back saying exactly that and you will feel the wound of rejection.

More often, however, terminations are clinically driven. Here are some of the common reasons, both sudden and planned, for ending:

Bad Fit

Hector and Teresa came for three sessions, then dropped out. You're surprised. You thought that they were motivated and committed, that everyone's expectations were clear, yet they faded away. The problem was with doing therapy itself. This may have been their first experience with it, and it turned out to be all too difficult—the focus on the details of process, the questions about events from the past, the stirring of emotions just felt too overwhelming or seemingly irrelevant. They had a heart-to-heart conversation late one night and decided they had had enough. They realized that they were committed to each other after all, had been getting along okay the past few weeks, and that they could use their copay for new shoes for the kids or some dinners out.

But sometimes the problem is about you. They had the impression that you would hear their problem, tell them what to do, and wrap it up quickly. Yes, you told them about your approach and tried to clarify expectations, but three sessions later they are feeling frustrated. Or, perhaps the husband is fine with you and your style, but the wife has a problem. There are sexual issues that she really wants to talk about (but hasn't brought up yet) and feels uncomfortable talking to you, as a man, about it. She would much rather have a female therapist.

Sometimes you have no control over these miscommunications—you ask the wife how she feels talking with a man and she seems to honestly say that she is comfortable; you explain why you might need several sessions to get a good idea of the problems, but a couple can't get their one- or two-session expectation out of their heads. But other times more of the responsibility is yours—though you thought you were clear in your expectations, you weren't; though you thought a couple was on board, you missed the signs of their restlessness or frustration; though you realized that the last session was emotional, you didn't leave enough time to debrief or didn't follow up. You don't need to castigate yourself for this, but instead see the sudden break as an opportunity for self-reflection.

The Crisis Is Over

As mentioned earlier, many clients are seeking—and much of outpatient therapy in general is often about—crisis reduction. Some couples are particularly crisis oriented and feel ready to stop once they return to their emotional baseline. Other couples don't have the energy for or see the value in going deeper—learning skills, exploring patterns. They talk about the presenting problem, see you as a mediator, reach some understanding, and feel they are done. Then there are still others who stay perpetually in motion, struggle with one crisis then another. The latest one—the turning off of electricity, problems with their child at school, a sick relative—takes center stage and pushes the relationship to the side.

While it can be helpful to map out with these couples the way their crisis thinking in itself can lead to problems (the underlying dynamics never get addressed), or show how developing skills and understanding patterns can actually make them more resilient, there is little value in seeming critical of their decision to stop or scaring them into continuing. Let them leave on a good note and walk, rather than run, away. Tell them they are welcome back whenever they feel the need. Your lack of pressure will help ensure that they do.

They Are Over a Developmental Hurdle

As we'll be exploring in later chapters and as we briefly discussed when talking about the relationship rollercoaster, couples often enter therapy because they are facing a developmental hurdle—the changes that come with the birth of a first or additional child, the loss of a parent, a serious emotional or physical illness, parenting difficulties with adolescents, or moving to a new town and feeling isolated and depressed. These stresses can push a couple to the limits of their skills (they know how to parent young children but can't shift to adolescents), uncover weaknesses in the relationship (the couple doesn't know how to partialize problems and discuss them together), or stir individual issues that have lain dormant (the husband has always struggled with low-level depression but slides deeper when his mother dies or he loses his job).

Your job is to help them overcome the hurdle—learn the new parenting skills, improve their communication skills, help the husband grieve his loss and get medication to relieve his depression. It's not an overhaul of a relationship as much as a psychological push up and over a hill on the road that is their life together as a couple. Once they are over it—the depression subsides, they set clear rules for the 14-year-old, they make friends and feel less isolated and irritable with each other—your work is done and they are ready to stop. When the next challenge comes up, they may be back.

They Have Become More Clear

Eric and Wendy came for therapy after it was uncovered that Eric was having an affair with a coworker. The couple had been married for almost 20 years and had separated for a few months about 6 years ago, but did not seek any counseling at that time and had continued to have difficulties since. They both agreed that they felt disconnected from each other. Wendy complained that Eric rarely talked to her, and though they interacted fairly well when they went out with other couples, they rarely went out as a couple alone. Eric, for his part, felt underappreciated for the hard work he did on his job, felt his wife showed little interest in his work, found himself going along with what Wendy wanted most of the time. In his mind he tied all this to the affair—he had found someone who showed interest in and admiration for him and understood the day-to-day grind. He said the affair was over, however, and was now committed to working out their disconnection.

And they tried to do that. The therapist encouraged them to plan time alone as a couple, rather than continuing their parallel lives. She encouraged Eric to speak up—about his work and about his desires—rather than defaulting into passivity. They made the changes, the therapist felt they were doing better. The conflicts that had been swept under the rug were now coming out, and both were doing a good job of listening and speaking up. But then they suddenly decided to stop therapy and were planning on divorce. What had happened?

What happened is that through the therapy process they became more clear. Many couples enter treatment with a high level of ambivalence. They are essentially sitting on the fence, unsure of their motivation, uncertain whether there has been too much water under the bridge, pessimistic whether either one of them can really change. Through therapy the issues and their emotions become more clear and often more glaring.

Eric, for example, felt more empowered through therapy, and paradoxically, because he was, he realized he could step away from the marriage, rather than drifting along frustrated as he had for many years. As Eric became more clear, so did Wendy. As he expressed his own needs and desires more openly, Wendy realized just what she did not want to do, and how much they had changed over the years. They weren't so much frightened by the emotions that came to the surface, but more realized, individually and together, that they simply didn't want to wrestle with them.

The case could be made, of course, for their pressing on. Now that they were able to acknowledge the elephant in the room with them, the next logical step would be to work together to push it out the front door. But some couples don't want to do that. As with those who focus on the crisis, you can map out options and help them place what is happening in a bigger context, but the decision is their own.

The other common variation on this scenario is one that is more one-sided. Wendy is willing to see the change process through, but Eric is ready to quit. Perhaps he was more ambivalent than you thought. Though he seemed committed, he was going through the motions; in the back of his mind he was hanging in there long enough to be certain that you were around to mop up and take care of Wendy emotionally after he left. Or perhaps while he said he had ended the affair, he really had not; the seemingly grinding, sluggish progress in the marriage was no match for the initial thrills of the new relationship. Again, you can try to put the actions in a different context, can talk about the affair as merely a solution to deeper individual problems, but it may not matter. While you are committed to the relationship and working to change the dynamics, you are shaping the process, not controlling the outcome. That is up to each of the individuals.

With the ending of the couple work, the focus may shift to individual or family therapy. Eric drops out, but Wendy continues to see you. Ann and Sara may have initially come in because they are struggling over the roles of stepparent and parent, but within a few sessions you all agree that bringing the daughter in and doing family therapy would actually get to the heart of the problems and relieve the stress a couple is feeling. Tom and Allyse initially seem to be scrabbling over money, but it becomes apparent that the underlying problem for both of them is Allyse's eating disorder and its control over all their lives.

As mentioned in the last chapter, such shifts in treatment can be effective but need to be based upon a sound clinical rationale, rather than a means of avoiding the anxiety of doing couple work. Discuss with the couple your perspective, make sure everyone understands and agrees with the shift, be clear about goals. If unclear yourself talk to your supervisor or a trusted colleague.

They Learned the Basic Skills and Have Cleared Away the Major Psychological Barriers

Alice has learned to recognize the signs of her growing anger, and rather than verbally pummeling her husband when he hits the front door, she is able to pull back, settle herself, and figure out what is going on. Serge has learned to speak up and tell his wife what he wants rather than retreating into video games and beers. Ken and Karen have learned how to successfully negotiate to balance their differing needs for individual versus couple time, and no longer take their differences so personally. Their agendas each week get shorter, the overall climate is tremendously improved, they are able to recover increasingly quickly and independently when communication and emotions go awry.

Basically they stop because they have accomplished their goals and developed a solid foundation. They have learned to manage and self-correct the process. Everyone has worked hard and it's paid off. Your work is done.

CLINICIAN-INITIATED TERMINATIONS

Sometimes, however, your work is done because you have inadvertently undermined the very process that you are ostensibly encouraging. These are the countertransference issues—your own personal reactions and triggers—that can move like an powerful undertow beneath the treatment process. By looking back on your pattern with cases, by obtaining regular feedback through clinical supervision, by staying aware of and honestly admitting your own strong emotional reactions, you can avoid many of these. Here are some of the most common sources:

You Feel Clinically Over Your Head

If you are new to the field or new to couple therapy, if your professional self-confidence is shaky and you lack supervisory support, it's easy to feel overwhelmed with the seemingly complex dynamics thrust upon you. One way of coping with all this is to essentially push the problems and the couple away. You can do this by overly normalizing or minimizing the severity of the problems or of a couple's distress ("It appears you both are under a lot of stress with the move here. I suspect that once things have settled down in a few weeks, things will be fine"), by shifting the focus to one more clinically comfortable for you ("I'm concerned about your depression, Mary, and from your history it sounds like you have been wounded in many ways; I'm wondering if our doing some individual work in these areas might be most helpful to you"), or by passively discouraging follow-through (not returning a couple's phone calls, finding it difficult to find a suitable appointment time, canceling appointments at the last minute, failing to pick up on problems in rapport even when you are openly aware of them).

Sorting all this out can be tricky. You may be correct and the couple may be simply overwhelmed by the stress of the move and quickly get back on track; Mary may very well do better clinically by focusing individually on her history and depression right now; your logistical problems may not be avoidance at all but real problems in scheduling or follow-through. It's a question of the source—is it your emotional reaction that is driving what unfolds or professional and well-thought-out clinical judgment? Honesty and supervision are the means for understanding what is really going on.

You Get Inducted into the System

Wilson and Lydia have been married for 10 years and have struggled for much of that time. Decision making is difficult. They snap and snarl at each other. They spend most of their time wrapped up in their separate individual lives. When they come to see you they are pessimistic and exhausted.

So you work with them to get their various issues on the table. You help them to problem solve and reach solutions and compromises. You encourage them to find positive ways of connecting and replace the snarling with open and honest communication. They try, do well for a couple of weeks, but then slide back to their old ways and routines. You too start to feel discouraged and tired. You try various options and approaches, but only halfheartedly believe they will be effective. You're beginning to feel frustrated and burned out. When they call to cancel you make little effort to call them back.

You essentially wind up feeling the way they do. You and they are getting stuck because you are working on several fronts at once, trying to pin down skills rather than dealing with the problem in the room, namely, the process of getting stuck itself. Instead of moving them to a deeper level—toward the core patterns and issues—you are staying on the surface, replicating what they have been doing for years. You've become inducted into their emotional system.

The notion of induction into the family system is a familiar and key concept of structural family therapy, and prevention, namely by anticipating and staying alert to such dangers as part of your initial formulation, is the best way to avoid it.[1] If, however, you do find yourself becoming caught in the couple's patterns and reactions and are losing your effectiveness as a change agent, you need to talk to your supervisor or a trusted colleague as a way of stepping back and regrouping. He or she can often see the parallel process unfolding more easily than you can, and can help break the process by responding to you in the way you need to respond to the couple.

You Encourage the Couple to Act Out Your Own Issues

Because the personal and professional so easily overlap when doing any type of therapy, overidentifying with a certain issue, stance, or client is always a danger. But as was mentioned in the first chapter, when doing couple therapy it's easy for these issues to be even more intense. The couple reminds you of your parents, or of your current relationship, or your relationship when you were younger. You find yourself pushing them to do what you wished your parents had done, or what you emotionally can't bring yourself to do now. Instead of tracking their concerns, you find yourself harping on issues that you are particularly sensitive to. You encourage them to fight battles that you, in your personal life, never finished fighting or are afraid to approach.

It's all countertransference, and this is where focusing on the neutral ground of process, rather than the more charged arena of outcomes, is valuable. As with other countertransference issues, outside supervision

---

[1] Salvador Minuchin, the developer of structural family therapy, has several books on his approach. For his latest thinking see Minuchin, S., et al. (2006). *Assessing Families and Couples: From Symptom to System.* Boston: Allyn & Bacon.

and support are important, as well as the self-supervision of looking for patterns in your own work. If a majority of your work is always reduced to the same one or two issues, if you find yourself reaching the same dead-end points in treatment, or if you are filled with an overly strong sense of "right," rather than clinical awareness of dynamics and options, it's time for you to step back and rethink about who's in treatment.

WRAPPING IT UP

If the process goes well and you and the couple are on the same page and moving toward termination, the question comes up of how to best wrap things up. The standard options are the drop-dead stop date or the more gradual fadeaway. The first is what it says. You and the couple decide on a set time to stop—three more sessions, a month, a week—and you stick to it. While traditional thinking about termination braces you to expect crises or regression, in couple therapy this is less likely to happen—the clients, unlike the individual who has relied on you for a major source of support, can lean on the other.

If there is a sliding back, don't assume you need to change plans, but rather that you need to explore what is happening. While you, for example, may feel that a couple is on a solid footing, they may suddenly realize how dependent on you they have become, or worry that you are permanently kicking them out. See where the anxiety is coming from, underscore how quickly they have been able to get back on track, reassure them that if they find themselves falling back into old ruts they can always come back. They will only know they are in good shape when they can get through those first mini-crises without you.

The fadeaway approach counters many of these concerns. You believe that they are doing better, they agree, and you suggest that they skip a week or two and see how it goes. If it goes well and they can weather the disruptions that come up, you can stretch out the intervals between sessions on a timetable that feels comfortable to them. Sometimes you may suggest moving to an as-needed basis, and find that no, they would rather schedule another appointment for next month, only to have them cancel a few days before. That's fine—they needed to know that the safety net was there if they needed it and the knowing allows them to put their skills into use.

The keys to managing terminations are the same as those you have been using from the beginning—be clear, be honest, be positive; track their reactions, encourage them to take risks.

LEFT BEHIND

This is a good time to talk about those situations where the couple therapy unravels and one of the partners pulls out, leaving the other behind. In the ideal psychological world in which one partner decided that the relationship was over or that he or she wanted a separation, a couple would take the time to understand why this was occurring. They would slowly unravel and disconnect and work through the grief process together, rather than suddenly chopping the relationship off.

But life is not ideal and more often than not, it doesn't work this way. As mentioned above, one partner may have started therapy with his or her mind already made up. Clients may secretly agree to come for a few sessions to "give therapy a try," to relieve their guilt, to make a final declaration in a safer environment. Such declarations can be dramatic and emotionally wrenching—a spouse of 20 years suddenly announces that he is gay and is moving out—or can be simply sad—that they know that they have been unhappy together for a long time and now the partner has reached a decision. He is ready to move on and sitting in sessions and rehashing what went wrong, he says, is just too painful. The talking is over.

So you are left with the left-behind partner. Sometimes these partners are angry—at the other for leaving, at you for failing to save the relationship—and because they see no point in continuing, decide to leave therapy as well. It's a good idea to still keep the door open. Make a phone call to check in in a couple of weeks, say that he or she is welcome to come back if there is the need, and do the same for the partner who is leaving as well. They may not call back, or may return weeks or months later ready to put together the pieces or get support in starting anew.

More often, however, the left-behind partners will want to continue, and you need to be available to them. If you don't practice individual therapy, believe that starting over with someone else is clinically best for them, or find that they cannot afford your services any longer, you need to provide transition to another therapist. Ethically you can't abandon a client who is in crisis and in need of services, and from a clinical perspective, to do so is only replicating what just happened to them. Be clear and honest, but make provisions for a transition if that is what is needed.

If you continue to see them your goal is helping them deal with normal grief that follows any loss. The same stages of shock and denial, anger, bargaining, depression, and resolution will all be there, but there are additional factors that make this loss unique. One is often the impact of children. The left-behind partners suddenly feel stuck with most, if not all, of the responsibility for the kids. Even if the other partner is visiting and paying child support, or had little involvement as a parent, those left behind are suddenly aware of the weight of providing day-to-day emotional support to the children. The other partner, in their mind, is moving toward what he or she wanted while the left-behind partners feel trapped with responsibilities that they did not choose, in a future that at the moment seems dim. The left-behind partners can easily overidentify with the children's pain, see the children, like themselves, as victims of a chaotic or frightening world.

Environmental changes can make these feelings all the stronger. Literally, there are holes about the house—the couch or desk has been taken out, the bed is suddenly only half filled and seems vastly lonely, a closet is empty. There's an empty seat at dinner, or the kids are eating KFC three nights a week because your client never really did any cooking. The car breaks down and your client doesn't know who to call. These are painful and constant reminders of what has changed, what has been lost, how life itself has been altered.

And finally, while the relationship may be legally or physically over, usually the emotional intensity is not. The other partner isn't dead and gone, but seen every Saturday when the kids are dropped off for visits. Your client bumps into her ex (with a new girlfriend) at the mall, notices how he has lost weight and seems happy. What were annoyances before now become the source of major battles and power struggles—the quiet husband who talked little now never returns phone calls; the partner prone to anger is now harassing her ex to get his tools out of the garage; the disorganized, impulsive partner who promises to take the kids every Saturday calls up Friday night to say that he has to go out of town for the weekend. Your client is terribly angry, massively depressed, or switches between the two within minutes.

How do you help? Here are some tasks for you to focus on to help your clients successfully get through this process:

Monitor Their Emotional State

Are they depressed? Are they losing weight, having sleep disturbances? Are they enraged a good deal of the time, emotionally numb, drinking or taking drugs to self medicate? Are they becoming workaholic or spending the weekend vegetating on the couch?

Their response will obviously depend on their own ego strength, coping style, and past experiences, and the particulars of their situation. If a couple had separated before or they had been talking about it on and off for years, their response may be very different than if the partner walked out suddenly with only 2 weeks' notice. But even when there is no surprise, loss is loss. Consider referring clients to their family doctor or to a psychiatrist for medication evaluation if you are concerned about depression, overwhelming anxiety, obsessive thinking, or anger. The medication can help them sleep, calm some of their obsessive thinking, make them less reactive, reduce self-medication with drugs or alcohol, and keep them productive so they don't jeopardize their job.

Educate Them about the Process

Being able to talk about the normal grief of the divorce process helps reduce the tunnel vision that clients usually have. Mapping out for them realistic time frames for moving through the process helps keep what seems like an endless wave of misery from overwhelming them. Let them know that they may feel numb and in shock for 2–3 weeks, may feel somewhat unstable emotionally for about 3 months, and will not really feel like they are back on their feet for about a year. It may be 2 years until they are really stable and feel like most of this is behind them.[2] Help them understand that though they may realize intellectually that the relationship never would have been able to make it, they still feel miserable because what they are feeling often has less to do with love and more to do with psychological attachment (this is particularly helpful for those who end abusive relationships and can't understand why they still feel depressed). It's normal grief, it's part of the human condition.

Clients may also benefit from legal advice. While it is helpful for you to be somewhat familiar with the overall divorce process in your state (grounds for divorce, separation agreements, time frames) to help counter the hearsay information that they may get from friends or colleagues, this is no substitute for their seeking sound legal guidance.

---

[2]Bibliotherapy can also be helpful at this time. Some books to recommend: Vaughn, D. (1990). *Uncoupling: Turning Points in Intimate Relationships*. New York: Vintage; Fisher, B. (2005). *Rebuilding: When Your Relationship Ends, 3rd Edition*. New York: Impact; McWilliams, P. (1993). *How to Survive the Loss of a Love*. New York: Prelude Press; Oberlin, L. (2005). *Surviving Separation and Divorce, 2nd Edition*. Avon, MA: Adams Media; Trafford, A. (1992). *Crazy Time: Surviving Divorce and Building a New Life*. New York: HarperCollins. You can also suggest that clients self-select reading material by simply going to Barnes & Noble, *Amazon.com*, etc., and browsing for something that seems interesting or relevant to them.

Many lawyers will schedule a no-cost initial appointment; legal aid is available in most locales for those in financial difficulty. Knowing the legal options can help clients feel more empowered and prevent them from making psychologically or economically costly mistakes out of normal but relatively temporary guilt, regret, or anger.

Allow Clients to Talk, Provide Support

Most of your sessions, especially soon after the separation, are consumed with the venting of emotions—blow-by-blows of the week's events, stresses and aggravations, fears and obsessions about the past and the future. They are processing what has happened, and their obsessions are ways of trying to make sense of it. Over time the obsessive thinking usually decreases (again, medication can help this from being too overwhelming) as gradually a story or theory is developed about what happened and why it happened as it did. Having someone who is nonjudgmental to talk to aloud about all this reduces overall anxiety and speeds up the healing process.

It's helpful for you to be clear about your own limits. Being reactive and feeling overwhelmed, clients in these early stages of loss may be tempted to call you several times a day or in rapid response to the latest upset. Decide in advance how you want to handle this clinically and be clear with the clients—it's okay to call and leave a message, to write you an e-mail, and that they should contact the answering or emergency service if they can't reach you. To help them better manage their crisis response, consider increasing individual sessions during the week or arrange for scheduled phone check-ins.

Encourage clients to create a base of outside emotional support. Many are reluctant to do this—they don't want to tell their family what has happened, they are embarrassed to tell their friends and colleagues about this change in their lives, and they don't know how to approach former mutual friends. Some of this represents their own denial about what is occurring, sometimes it reflects long-standing dynamics—struggles, for example, dealing with critical parents or having mostly superficial relationships and few close friends—and sometimes the natural social awkwardness of this new transitional state. Help them walk through their fears, role-play conversations and requests, encourage them to take acceptable social risks so they are less isolated.

Similarly, help clients develop healthy self-care. Help parents who are adjusting to being the sole parent, or feeling work pressures on top of the emotional ones, find daily ways of reducing their stress. Planned outings with friends and family, quiet time after the kids go to bed, journaling, meditation, simple bedtime rituals of warm baths and time with a good novel can help them recenter and reduce the sense that they always have to be doing for others.

Help Them Move Beyond Black-and-White Thinking

As clients wrestle with the process of making sense of their lives—"Was our marriage a hoax all along?" "Why didn't I realize how she was feeling sooner?"—it's easy for them to fall into black-and-white thinking. The early versions of their story often reflect this simplicity—he left because he was having a midlife crisis, because he always wanted sex; she left because all her friends were getting divorced, because she is just like her mother. It was my fault, his fault, her fault, but often not our fault. The danger of holding on to such a simple story is that it is distorted, and important elements are overlooked and left out. If this explanation solidifies into *the* explanation for the downfall of the relationship, the moral of the story that was the relationship, the psychological foundation upon which future relationships are built will be weak. Past mistakes are more likely to be repeated.

There is no *right* explanation for what has occurred, of course, and it is likely that the story of the relationship will change over time as the clients gain perspective and grow. But your job is to help the clients see the complexity as much as they are able, to challenge the quick one-line explanation "He's just like his father." As you do all along, you look for the holes, you turn up the edges of the story to help them see what might lie underneath.

You can do this by exploring history, especially if you have not had much opportunity to do this before. "What were your parents like?" "How did you hope your relationship would be different than theirs?" "How did you decide to act differently than them, and what price did you pay for acting in that way?" "How was your spouse like your father/mother?" "Is there a danger that in the attempt to avoid being like them you swung too far in the opposite direction?" "Could you imagine that your parents felt the same way about their relationship that you did sometimes?"

You can raise provocative questions about the relationship: "Why do you think your spouse decided to have an affair now, rather than 5 years ago?" "Do you think he ever felt jealous of the children?" "How much was sex an issue?" "If things had kept going the way they were and hadn't changed, what would you have done 5 years from now?" "What do you regret the most?" Because you have met with the couple, you can often fold in information from past joint sessions (of course, not breaking confidentiality by sharing information from individual sessions): "Do you remember when Dave said to you that he felt lonely at home?" "Do you remember when you were assertive in that early session and Sara got really angry?" Your goal is to shake up the thinking—to make the clients curious about why this and why now—not to find the culprit but to help them see how mutual patterns unfolded over time, how problems were poor solutions.

You need to be sensitive to the timing and pacing of all this. In the early stages of the separation process, clients just need to vent, get their bearings, cope with everyday situations—stirring up history and old emotions too quickly can make them feel even more overwhelmed or guilty. But as they get their sea legs and are more emotionally stable, as the black-and-white begins to move toward gray, take the lead in exploring the larger picture.

Coach Them on Managing the Children

Not only are the children dealing with their own sense of loss and often blaming the left-behind parent for what's happened, they are also feeling the psychological pull to fill the hole in the family. This is where the oldest child steps in as the junior parent and becomes overresponsible or, perhaps, like the absent parent, feels angry, aggressive, or entitled. The left-behind parent may be faced not only with setting up new structure and routines, but also with the challenge of melding roles—to be more of a disciplinarian, for example, than in the past because the other is not there to discipline, or to be more nurturing because the nurturing parent is no longer available.

You can help parents with these transitions by educating them about the children's normal reactions.[3] When Tommy throws a fit about bedtime, the kids are crazy after spending the weekend with Mom, or Maria digs in and refuses to eat her breakfast, it's good for the parent to know it's not about her, but a normal sign of the child's adjustment to change. You need to help the parent fill in the holes—step into the nurturer and disciplinarian roles, set a new structure, balance out care

---

[3]Again bibliotherapy can be helpful. Some books to consider: Wallerstein, J. (2003). *What about the Kids?: Raising Your Children before, during and after Divorce*. New York: Hyperion; Emery, R. (2006). *The Truth about Children and Divorce: Dealing with the Emotions So You and Your Children Can Thrive*. New York: Plume; Long, N. (2002). *Making Divorce Easier on Your Child: 50 Effective Ways to Help Children Adjust*. New York: McGraw-Hill. There are also many picture books for parents to read to their children—encourage parents to check them out.

for the children with self care. This can be new ground for some parents and you may need to give them detailed coaching and lots of support.

You need to be careful to not fall into a surrogate role yourself. If Denise, for example, is having a hard time with 14-year-old Brett, you'd do better to hold off seeing him when she asks if you could talk with him about his behavior—she may reflexively be trying to fill the void in the family with you. Her response may be more automatic if you are a male, but not necessarily. It's usually more about your seeming power and skills, and less about gender. Instead, with your support and suggestions, help Denise develop the skills to set limits with Brett or, alternatively, agree to meet with both of them with the focus on supporting them as she talks through the problems with him. Rather than rescuing her, help her feel empowered.

Coach Them through Rebound Relationships

There is the old adage "Sometimes the best way to get over someone is to get under someone else." Stereotypically, it's men who fall into this pattern, but women can do so as well. Once you are focused on someone else, there is the excitement of someone new and of being wanted; the natural rush of hormones and endorphins makes it hard not to feel better. The attraction of rebound relationships is often formed on a simple theory—"My husband never listened to me and Brad is so wonderful because he is a great listener"; "Alice was always critical and angry, and Lesley is so even tempered and good natured." Here is the breath of fresh air, the kind of relationship they were secretly wishing for those many years.

Powerful stuff. But the fact that the clients are continuing to show up in your office and not running away to get married in Mexico is a good sign that they need something from you in all this. Clarify what they are seeking—"Are you asking for my permission? Feedback?" Ask how you can help them most. You don't need to be the scolding parent, but you can be the reality check—"Phil, what you are saying about what is happening in this new relationship seems to me to be a variation of the problems you were having with Laura." Just what you tried to do in the couple counseling you want to do now, namely, advocate for the less empowered parts of themselves, help them think in different ways, and encourage them to make decisions that can consider all their needs, rather than just fill the immediate gaps.

So take the consultant role. Offer to have them bring the new person into counseling if they feel that would be helpful. Link what is happening in their new relationship and in your sessions to their initial goals—"I'm asking about this because you said when we started that you wanted to learn to be more assertive." Be careful not to encourage clients to vicariously act out your own needs or encourage dependency in their relationship with you that becomes an end in itself. By providing a safe forum and steady support you can help these clients heal and move on to the next chapters of their own lives.

This finishes up our exploration of the beginning, middle, and ending phases of couple therapy. Each phase has its own challenges and task, each phase flows on the dynamics and success of the last. In the next chapter we look more closely at the complex power issues of relationships—money, sex, children.

Looking Within: Chapter 7 Exercises

1. What are your own personal values regarding divorce and separation? Where do these values come from—parents, your own experience? How do they color your attitudes and work?

2. Think back about the play fantasy that you created in the last chapter and the scene about leaving home. What patterns do you see in your own life? How have you ended important relationships? What did you do well, or poorly, and what do you wish you had done differently? How do your own emotional bottom lines and these experiences affect your attitudes about clients who leave treatment prematurely, or leave relationships?

3. Are there patterns in your own endings with clients? Do you tend to go only so far and then stop? What triggers this? Have you encouraged clients to vicariously act out your own personal struggles, needs, desires?

Chapter 8

Of Money, Sex, and Children
Handling the Power Issues

Money, sex, kids—these are often the thorny issues of couple therapy: Who controls the finances, how sexually compatible are the partners, how well can they work together as parents? These topics may be the presenting problem, or weave in and out of other issues. As with other problems that couples face, there are hands-on skills and information that can make navigating these issues easier—how to set up a budget and stick to it, how to be sexually sensitive and satisfying, how to provide the right mix of nurturance and structure for children—and they may look to you to help them figure it all out.

But in common with all issues, there's also the process side balancing out the content—not only what our financial priorities are but how we talk about them; not only knowing what turns you on, but what I do and do we when I feel sexually vulnerable; not only what the rules are for the kids but what we do when we disagree about just what these rules should be. And finally there is the power element that these issues generate—not what we decide but who decides, what we do when we begin to resent the ways decisions have been made. These become the source of the stuck points; they bring out the core patterns and dynamics of the couple that you see unfolding in your office. As we saw with Sara and Ann, these are the issues that can easily become the battleground for other tensions in the relationship—rather than talking directly about how I feel pushed to the side and ignored, we fight over the kids and what they need.

In this chapter we explore the clinical aspects and approaches to each of these common and core issues. While the previous chapters have discussed more of the process of all couple work, in this chapter we look at the specific clinical challenges that each of these areas present.

MONEY

Edna and Sam are actually on the same page when it comes to money—"We don't have any." They are struggling to manage their bills, and it's all gotten worse since Sam lost his job.

"What drives me crazy," says Neena, "is that Kwan will go off and buy a new motorcycle without saying a word about it to me!"

Martin is the saver in the family. He hates debt and gets anxious whenever the saving account drops below the several months' salary that he likes to always have on hand. His wife, Melissa, on the other hand, freely uses credit cards and is not concerned about debt as long as they can pay their bills. She feels that Martin is a bit too obsessed about saving.

Alice has handled the money for all 18 years of the marriage; Josh essentially hands over his paycheck, leaving out a few dollars a week for gas and lunch. Periodically, it becomes the source of violent arguments with Josh screaming that he resents being treated like an 8-year-old.

The different faces of money. Sometimes money is the presenting problem; other times it weaves into the conversation when you ask about decision making or stressors. Before you can know how to help, you need to understand how the role of money, and the problems associated with it, fit within the framework of the couple's financial skills, ability to communicate, and their individual and joint means of handling emotions. Here are some questions to ask about money, along with the clinical issues behind them:

- *How well does the couple manage money? Are they in debt, being pursued by creditors, having utilities turned off, or always on the edge of a financial crisis?* Couples who are always short of money are also constantly stressed or in emotional crisis. If they do understand the basic skills—of budgeting, or banking—the question is what undermines their ability to be successful. If they lack the skills, what help do they need to acquire them?
- *Does the couple discuss money together? How do these conversations usually turn out?* Some couples are much less open about money than

they are in other areas of their relationship. While some may approach the topic calmly and rationally, others argue or simply avoid the topic because of the emotions it generates. If they have trouble communicating around this topic, why? Do problems in this area reflect larger problems with communication and/or communication skills in general? Is it a topic that is swept under the rug?

• *Do they share the same philosophy about money, for example, saving versus spending, or do they both manage money differently?* Couples often differ in their learned approaches to money and when anxious may attack each other or try and convert the other to their point of view. Often beneath the stance are core fears—of abandonment, of control or loss of it. Uncovering these fears can help dissipate emotions and make problem solving easier.

• *Does one or both of the partners act out with money—for example, go on periodic spending sprees, suddenly buying large items without consulting the other?* Money can often be a way of coping with individual or couple stress and depression, or be a means of expressing anger and resentment toward partners or others; money can be used as a weapon.

• *Does the issue of money come up periodically as an issue but then die down and never really get resolved?* Money issues can also be an indicator of other stressors—I worry, for example, more about the bills or my low salary when I have too many other things on my plate to deal with. Money becomes the "comfortable problem" for the couple—the battleground for other issues they can't approach.

• *Is one person in charge of money? Why? What happens if the other person disagrees with the way the first one handles the money? Do they each have money to spend on things of their own choosing?* Again, be curious. You want to separate out good thinking, old habits, and efficiency from power dynamics. Is one person more capable or comfortable managing it? Is it role or gender linked? Does this reflect a general lack of trust? Is it a means of controlling the other person or the relationship? Does it fuel the drama triangle with one person on top, one on the bottom, and the periodic resentment over the other's control or the other's lack of appreciation and help?

What these questions reflect is the complexity of money as an issue, the various ways it can function within the relationship, and the aspects of it that can be a source of struggle. What you will usually hear is the simple stating of the problem—"He spends too much money"; "We fight all the time"; "We are constantly in debt"—and then it is up to you to begin to tease it all apart. Let's talk about the common tasks and discuss how they shape money issues.

Supporting Money Skills

Obviously a couple's skills and knowledge will vary with the population you are serving. If, for example, you work in a public clinic serving
low-income couples, money skills are more likely to be a factor than,
say, they would be in a private practice. Like Edna and Sam, mentioned
above, your clients may lack a concrete understanding of how money
works and find themselves always at the edge economically. They may
have difficulty setting priorities, or not understand how to balance a
checkbook and consequently always find themselves bouncing checks.
They may be intellectually or emotionally overwhelmed—they receive
a letter from the disability office, and not being sure what it means or
being unable to read it, put it aside rather than responding. And if there
are underlying mental health issues such as addictions that are draining
away money, these only add to the crises they constantly face.

So you find out what they know. If they raise the issue of money ask:
Do they have a budget? Do they use a checking account, have a savings
account? Some couples will say yes even if they don't because they do
not want to appear incompetent; others may become suspicious by your
question and fear that you will report them to creditors. Put your questions in context—"I am asking because I know managing money can be
complicated. I'm wondering if you are struggling partly because you get
confused about how to handle it sometimes." Offer to walk through the
setting up of a budget or help them understand how checking works if
you and they are comfortable doing this. Don't be afraid to refer them
to other professionals who can supply the guidance they need.[1]

For those couples who are emotionally overwhelmed and intellectually unable to manage their own affairs over the long term, they may
need payor services where someone is legally appointed to manage their
money and pay their bills. Contact your local community mental health
center to learn about these options.

Managing the Communication

Couples may squabble over money in the same way they squabble over
almost everything else. They become defensive, lost in content, caught
in a tit-for-tat banter just like when they disagree about the kids, the
in-laws, or who didn't take the dog out. But the volatility is often higher;

---

[1] A good place to start is with local consumer credit counseling agencies. There are hun-
dreds of these nonprofit organizations across the country that help with budgeting and
debt management. You can find out about them and their locations by checking out the
website of the National Foundation for Credit Counseling (*www.nfcc.org*).

emotions flare up more quickly due to toxic mix of power, resentment, and stress. Within moments the discussion can disintegrate into a power struggle. Your task, as it is with other difficult topics, is to slow the process down in order to change the emotional climate and help the individuals articulate their worries and be assertive about their needs.

If Jada and Noah's conversation, for example, quickly moves from the unbalanced checkbook to angry accusations over who is contributing more to the household fund, you want to hold up your hand, stop the escalation, and ask questions and make comments about both the process and content. Some possibilities:

"You both are getting angry. Jada, what is it that you want Noah to most understand about how you feel?"

"Noah, you started talking about the checkbook, but are now shifting to the household fund—what happened?"

"Hold on a minute. Can you tell you both are getting defensive?"

"You both are talking about two separate problems—can we take one at a time?"

"Noah, it sounds like you feel that the current arrangement is unfair—how would you like it different?"

Statements like these help a couple to separate the issues, and slow and clarify the process.

Exploring Differences in Philosophy

The savers versus the spenders. The folks who never buy on credit and the ones who only do. The ones who pay their bills on time and the ones who are constantly in debt and have creditors always snapping at their heels. These opposites often find themselves together in a relationship; polarization flares.

Differences in philosophy sometimes reflect the influence of individual family cultures—ingrained notions of thrift and the necessity of staying within a budget versus little worry about money because there was always plenty. These childhood lessons may also include gender typing—the husband is always in charge of the money, for example, or the wife is always in charge of household and children's needs, while the husband is responsible for just about everything else—leading to expectations that may or may not match.

But while some of us swallow our parents' views on money whole, others of us walk out of childhood with fear and anxieties based on our own perceptions. Angela, for example, grew up in a financially comfortable household until she was 12 years old. In that year her father suddenly left her mother and offered nothing in the way of child support. The mother became severely depressed, the family struggled financially. When the mother was finally able to get back on her feet, she was forced to take a low-paying job as a hotel maid to support the children. Now Angela works as a well-paid office manager for a law firm and feels compelled to save most of her income. If her savings falls below $30,000 she becomes anxious and pressures her husband to curtail his own spending so she is able to make up the difference. Feeling that her reactions are irrational and unnecessary and that she is treating him like a child, he becomes resentful. The money issues become, for them, a repetitive source of conflict.

The problem, and ultimately the solution for this couple, lay in allaying the fears that her parents' divorce had created in Angela. At first glance, her concern was a simple one about money—she didn't want to ever wind up in the financial situation that her mother was forced to deal with. We could say, "So the fact that the divorce left your mother impoverished seems to make you anxious to have a cushion of savings?" and see how she responds. But it may be more complicated than that, and we may want to explore what the money represents as well—independence, possibly escape and freedom (she would not have to stay in a marriage for money), an antidote, in her mind perhaps, to inevitable despair.

If this is the case, then she is using money to fix possible problems in the relationship, and her efforts to prevent a problem—controlling the money and controlling her husband—were, in fact, in danger of creating it, by causing strife and pushing her husband away.

While for Angela the moral of the story of her parents' divorce was the importance of saving money in order to be ever prepared for disaster, for others the lessons of childhood are very different. Seventeen-year-old Ramon, for example, was a member of a small, yet active gang in his hometown. His father had struggled with poverty and alcoholism, his uncle had died of AIDS, and he had a good friend who had been killed in a drive-by shooting. He confidently said that he didn't expect to live past 25. He spent money freely, carelessly, living the life he imagined that his father never could. While Angela saw money as protection against the future, Ramon, in his mind, had no future to protect.

If, hypothetically, Angela and Ramon were to marry, we could imagine that it would not take long for major conflicts to develop, and for them to get polarized around money. While Angela might initially be attracted to the carefree lifestyle a Ramon might represent, just as Ramon might appreciate the stability that Angela, in contrast to his father, seemed to offer, these attractions would quickly wear off. Each one's behavior would ignite the other—the more Ramon spent, the more anxious Angela would become. The more controlling and conservative Angela became, the more Ramon would act out his resentment and worldview by spending.

But even in a less dramatic situation such polarization and power struggles can easily unfold. The struggle is fueled by underlying fears and resentments, and disarming the struggle means helping each understand the other's driving emotions. Angela's husband needs to understand her fear, just as she needs to understand his resentment. You may need to help Angela unravel and separate those old emotions of the past from the present. Together a couple may need to negotiate what is fiscally reasonable to save, rather than making purely emotional decisions. She may need help to identify the triggers for her money anxiety and learn to see her anxiety as information about underlying stressors or unmet needs within the relationship. Again, if we think of her control of money as a bad solution, we need to help her and her husband recognize the underlying problem and address it directly.

This last point is crucial. While identifying Angela's fears and creating a more adult perspective are important, the old childhood emotions will continue to lag behind and be triggered in the present. An argument with her husband over something as innocuous as laundry might ignite fantasies that he is unhappy and will leave. What needs to be mapped out are means of prevention (things her husband can do to help her feel more secure overall in the relationship) and emotional first aid (what he can do—honest communication, a hug, speedy reassurance—when Angela feels threatened and is tempted to return to her old ways of coping). These changes are what will, over time, create trust and dispel the remnants of Angela's past.

Putting Acting Out in Context

Shopping therapy, gambling, that sudden purchase of a new Harley—if money can symbolize security or freedom, it can also reflect anger or depression. One of the first dynamics to explore with partners who are overspending is the enactment of the drama triangle, where the rescuer or victim gets fed up, moves to the persecutor role, and goes on the spending spree. Again, what drives this is resentment and anger—for the rescuer that he is having to do it all and receiving little back, for the victim that he feels controlled and unempowered. Both feel that they deserve to do what they do—the rescuer has gone unappreciated for way too long, the victim has endured feeling controlled for far too long.

Sometimes the spending is less a burst of resentment and more a means maintaining the stability of roles. The partner, for example, who feels unempowered and controlled in other aspects of the relationship compensates, in her own mind, by spending the other's money, while he complains but tolerates it. Each feels like a victim of the other but their behaviors interlock. The one in control finds a reason for staying in control because the other is, in his mind, constantly demonstrating her irresponsibility, while she uses the control as a rationale for continuing to spend. Both stay within their emotional comfort zones and are able to avoid the conflict that real change might require.

Other times, however, these spending patterns are more indicative of individual rather than relationship distress. Shopping therapy or gambling addictions, for example, may represent an individual's long-standing way of coping with anxiety or depression, even preceding the relationship. The relationship may help abate some of these underlying drivers or, by adding stress, aggravate them.

You can sort this all out by careful exploration: Does the spending come up periodically, feel deserved, tied to feelings of being unappreciated or resentful? Does the behavior have an addictive quality—the inability to stop, the relentless drive that seems to be somewhat independent of everyday stress? Is there a history of addiction in other forms or prior to the relationship? Do the individuals tie their behavior to their internal state, such as feeling depressed or anxious, and head off to the mall or shop online, thinking that it will help them feel better? Because these can be sensitive issues and the individuals can easily hear your comments as criticism of their behavior even when there is none, talk gently. Put the questions in context—"I'm not criticizing your behavior, I'm wondering more about emotions that seem to upset you that may be triggering the behavior."

Obviously, however, you can have several issues making up the one. The person with a gambling addiction, for example, will need help dealing with the addiction itself, as well as any stresses in the relationship that make it worse. The person suffering from depression may need medication, but also need help to be more assertive and move out of the victim role in the relationship. You may need to refer them for outside treatment, such as a medication evaluation or individual therapy, while you focus upon the relationship dynamics.

Finally, you will often need to do some detective work to sort out how many or which of the issues presented here—lack of financial skills, poor communication, differences in philosophy, acting-out behaviors—

are folded into the larger problem of money. Again ask the leading questions: What do they know about handling money? Are they philosophically on the same page? Are problems driven by emotions and stress within the relationship and/or within the individual? Be prepared to tackle the problem from multiple perspectives—through education, communication and negotiation, by uncovering and allaying childhood fears, with referrals for medication or individual therapy. Help the couple understand that behavior regarding money is often the solution to a deeper problem, and help them understand the underlying dynamics. Be clear in your own mind and with them about who has and what is the problem. Help them see the issue in a new and more productive way.

THE COMPLEX WORLD OF SEX

Sexual problems share many of the same dynamics as those of money—issues of skill, problems with poor communication, differences in attitudes and expectations, behaviors as a means of expressing strong emotions, sensitivity to power imbalances—but all these concerns are heightened and made more complex. Sex taps into our core issues of vulnerability, of safety and trust, the most basic of our needs, as well as feelings of pleasure, desire, excitement, soothing. Just as money, psychologically, is never just money, sex is never just sex.

But while money is above ground, sex is often not. We heard our parents talking about money, saw in our family the consequences that came with it even if we didn't understand all the details. In our everyday lives we have fairly easy means of measuring and tracking it through account balances and budgets; funds can be moved, spent, or saved. It's out there in black and white. Sex, on the other hand, is all too often an underground world marked by subtlety and innuendoes. Most of us probably knew little about our parents' sex lives, and what we did hear from them was more likely to be a list of cautions and prohibitions than anything else. Like other aspects of our childhood, we somehow cobbled together a mix of messages and impressions about the role of sex in adult relationships and combined them with our own attitudes and expectations shaped by our early sexual experiences.

If these experiences were in some way traumatic, the residues of the trauma can color our response to physical sensations. Emotions can easily be stirred that leave us feeling confused, angry, or numb; we may become hyperalert and overly sensitive to the power of others. Because talking to our partners about what makes us feel vulnerable can in the moment make us feel vulnerable, many couples develop their own verbal shorthand and repertoire of nonverbal pokes or looks. Misinterpretation is easy; honest and open communication is difficult.

If our individual differences were not enough of a basis for potential conflict, you can add the influence of our biology, brain, and social-ization. Research tells us now that many men, for example, see sex as means of reducing individual stress and repairing a relationship, while many women instinctively feel the opposite—that they need to feel relaxed and the relationship needs to be repaired before sex can hap-pen.[2] We all know that antidepressants can effectively kill a partner's libido, that work stress can dampen sexual performance, that hormonal changes brought on by pregnancy or aging can radically change one's attitudes and sexual needs. All these factors can change the landscape of a couple's sexual relationship and weave together to create the problems that a couple brings to you.

Your job is to help couples tease these various sources and stuck points apart. It starts with communication, your communication. For couples who do not bring in sex as the presenting problem, it valuable to bring it up as part of the assessment—matter-of-fact questions like "And how is your sex life? Are you both happy with it?" or "What does sex mean for each of you?" or "How do you make decisions between you, like about sex?" This opens the door to the topic, lets them know that you are comfortable talking about their concerns, and helps you begin to place the issue within the larger context of the relationship. They may say little at this point, but once they feel safe with you and the process, they may then bring up problems.

The Tale of Tina and Paul

Tina and Paul have been married 3 years and have an 18-month-old daughter. "I feel that Paul is pressuring me for sex all the time," says Tina, moments into the first session. "That's because we never have it," chimes in Paul with an angry edge to his voice. And this is the problem, according to him—that they have sex only a couple of times a month. On her side, Tina feels that that is all Paul wants—he doesn't talk to

---

[2]There is a wealth of information available on the impact of brain chemistry, physical dif-ferences, and socialization on gender and sexual behavior. See Canary, D., et al. (1997). *Sex and Gender Differences in Personal Relationships.* New York: Guilford Press; Schwartz, P., & Rutter, V. (1998). *The Gender of Sexuality: Exploring Sexual Possibilities.* Walnut Creek, CA: AltaMira Press; Blum, D. (1998). *Sex on the Brain: The Biological Differences between Men and Women.* New York: Penguin; Rhoads, S. (2005). *Taking Sex Differences Seriously.* San Francisco: Encounter Books.

her, he isn't affectionate, and what drives her crazy is that he seems to be always grabbing her behind or breasts, even in public, or making jabbing comments to her about what he is not getting. Tina feels hurt and abused; Paul feels angry, frustrated, and ignored.

Let's stop it right there. How do you start thinking about the problem? How do you begin to separate the various layers of emotion and behavior? Here are some questions to get us started:

What other problems do they see in the relationship? Is this the arena where other issues and tensions in the relationship are played out? Do the same dynamics spill over to other areas as well?

How do they interpret each other's behavior—does Tina see Paul's actions as being sexually awkward, for example, or does she interpret them as something more malicious—deliberately mean and hurtful, perhaps? And if so, why does she think so?

What are the interactional patterns? What actually happens when Paul "pressures" Tina for sex or touches her inappropriately? What does Tina do? What happens next?

How long has this problem been going on? Did they, for example, get along better before the daughter was born? How has the child changed their relationship or changed Tina's libido or overall energy?

Does Paul tend to express his anger in a passive–aggressive way? Rather than communicating his frustration or anger about sex or other issues, does he resort to doing what annoys Tina? Does this carry over to other areas of their relationship?

When they do have sex, what prompts it? Does Tina give in, does Paul approach Tina differently? Once they have sex is it satisfying for both of them? Are there problems with skills and techniques for either one?

Is the couple engaging in a power struggle—the more Tina resists, the more Paul pressures and visa versa, ultimately becoming a question of who is going to get his or her way?

What other ways do the couple have of connecting? Why is it that Paul is not affectionate or doesn't talk much? Is it part of his own upbringing, or something within the relationship that discourages such behavior? Is sex his only means of connecting? Can he, for example, be affectionate with his daughter?

Is there any history of trauma for either one, but especially Tina, that makes sex emotionally difficult? How does she handle the power of others?

Threaded through the questions are ways of approaching the problem from different perspectives and placing it in a larger context. Their purpose is to separate skills from emotions, identify the behavioral patterns that keep the problem alive as well as the holes that the individuals and the couple may need to move toward, and to uncover the underlying problems that make the presenting one a symptom or solution. You ask these questions to help you pick apart the problem and help a couple open up about the issue and begin to talk about it differently than they do at home. You're encouraging them to express what is unexpressed—emotions that are never fully conveyed, the more complete explanations for their thinking and behavior that your deeper questions are able to pry loose.

If, for example, Tina says that things were fine until their daughter was born, the conversation turns to this life change. Does she have less interest in sex because of hormonal changes and simple exhaustion, does Paul perhaps feel left out of their close mother–daughter twosome, have they lost the opportunity to have couple time? Have they talked at home about these changes and feelings, and if not, why not? Where do they get stuck in their own process, and how can they problem solve more successfully? What doesn't the other understand about what they each need most now and how can they each get it?

If Paul, on the other hand, feels that while their sexual frequency has declined since the birth of their child, there has always been tension in the relationship around sex, you explore these dynamics. How, for example, does he explain this tension to himself—that Tina is simply uptight about sex, that she really doesn't care about his needs or feelings? His theory tells you where he feels the solution lies. How does he view his own level of affection—is he concerned, is there something that Tina can do or should not do that would make it easier for him to be more affectionate, does he see a relationship between Tina's desire for affection and communication as a way of connecting and her interest in sex?

Does Tina agree that there has been this tension all along? If yes, what is her explanation? Perhaps Paul, for example, is too sexually forceful or aggressive, his techniques leave her unsatisfied, or he pushes for spontaneity while she is more comfortable with the familiar. They each need to share their perspectives, and you want to help them turn this into a dialogue. Help them identify and label their emotions, check and see if the other understands and agrees. Help them realize how the behavior of one shapes the behavior of the other.

And when the process gets stuck in the room, help them sort it out—"Paul, you are sounding angry; what hurt your feelings?" "Tina, you seem to just be nodding your head and going along with what Paul is saying, but I wonder how you feel, what you are thinking." Help them see how their interactions, the ways they each express or don't express their emotions and feelings for each other, may be played out in the sexual relationship.

Obviously, the exploration should not be reductionistic. There may not be one core problem but several. The couple really has not had much couple time since the baby was born and need to get emotionally reconnected. Paul does have a difficult time with affection outside the bedroom and needs clear encouragement and affection from Tina to help him make changes. Tina really doesn't enjoy sex with Paul because there is not enough foreplay and she is unsatisfied; she may need your help to explicitly say what she needs and Paul may need support to follow through.[3] Paul may express his anger and frustration through negative remarks and aggressive touching, and needs to understand from Tina how that only makes matters worse. He may need her feedback and your help to develop more direct and responsible ways of expressing his feelings. All of these may be worked on together, or taken one by one as individual goals based on what the couple themselves see as priorities.

Again you want balance and behavioral change. Tina's view of the problem needs to be heard and addressed just as Paul's is. Communication and understanding can help them separate and clarify the issues, but then the understanding needs to be translated into new action. Pacing and realistic timelines are important here. If the sexual problems really are a reflection of other problems in the relationship, these need to be addressed first. If Tina, for example, generally feels overpowered by Paul, helping her be more assertive in other areas first—working on a budget together and encouraging her to speak up—allows her to build her communication skills and increase her self-confidence before tackling the more sensitive sexual issue. Similarly, if Paul feels Tina is not just withholding about sex but about compliments, encouragement, and

---

[3]If couples are struggling with sexual techniques and skills, it is often helpful for them to go to their local Barnes & Noble or Borders and pick out a book together on sexual techniques. This allows both to get involved in learning new behaviors and you can use the text as a basis for further discussion or questions in the sessions. Educating yourself is also important and many of the skills of sexual therapy can be self-taught. Obviously, if you are too uncomfortable or are clinically unsure how to approach more serious sexual dysfunctions, don't hesitate to refer the couple out to someone else or get closer consultation yourself from a supervisor or skilled colleague. For professional texts that deal with sexual therapy see Kaplan, H. S. (1995). *Sexual Desire Disorders: Dysfunctional Regulation of Sexual Motivation*. New York: Routledge; Schnarch, D. M. (1991). *Constructing the Sexual Crucible: An Integration of Sexual and Marital Therapy*. New York: Norton.

appreciation, this can be worked on as a way of changing the overall patterns of interaction and reducing the drama triangle dynamics.

If there is a power struggle going on—it is less about the problem and more about who is going to get his or her way—you need to call it, stop it, and help the couple sort out what is driving it. There may be resentment about other issues in the relationship, not fully discussed or resolved, that make sex the last stand and line of personal defense. One of the partners may be overwhelmed by fear, but rather than expressing it becomes resistant instead, causing the other to respond in kind. Go back to basics—ask about caring, trust, and safety, problem solving, control, power, decision making. Watch the patterns in the room, see what triggers the emotional digging in of heels and communication roadblocks.

And if there is trauma—if Tina, for example does have a history of abuse that gets triggered by Paul's subtle or unsubtle comments or behavior—handle this as you would handle other emotional obstacles in the relationship. Help her separate past from present, track and identify the past memories and emotions, and bring these out in the open so they are less haunting and so Paul can understand better what triggers these reactions.[4] And if these past experiences are too powerful and generate posttraumatic stress symptoms, consider referring the partner out for some individual work so these can be resolved rather than replicated.

As mentioned at the onset, sexual problems share the same underlying issues as money problems do—questions of skill, communication, individual differences in attitudes and philosophy, issues of power and control—but in more subtle and usually more complex forms. You want to help the couple feel safe enough to begin to unravel these elements,

---

[4]One of the best exercises to help couples develop trust and open communication and reduce contamination by the past is the sensate focus exercise developed by Masters and Johnson in the 1970s. There are two versions of this exercise, a nonsexual and sexual one that are generally done sequentially.

Essentially the partners take turns being a giver and receiver of touch. The receiver is in charge and in control, and directs the other where and how to touch his or her body as they lie down, clothed or unclothed. The receiver gives feedback along the way—that feels good, that is too hard—and the giver needs to do what the receiver asks. When the couple is successful with the nonsexual form, they can try the sexual one, where genital touching is included.

The ability to follow the other's direction is absolutely essential. If you feel that the couple is not emotionally ready—that it will turn into a power struggle, that one person will shut down and not be aware or able to direct—clear away these roadblocks first in order to create a good experience and not simply a replication of dysfunctional patterns.

identify the problems under the presenting problems, correct distortions, encourage the taking of acceptable risks.

You also need to be more sensitive to the transference issues. Your own gender can become an impediment to open communication. A woman talking about her side of the issue in a room with two men may assume that you will not understand, that you will take his side, or she may simply feel embarrassed. Similarly, if one of the partners is sensitive to power, be careful about your own—watch your tone of voice, be careful you are not seeming pushy, and inadvertently replicating the problem. If you sense hesitation or worry that one of the partners is feeling overpowered, bring the issue out in the open. If the partner is uncomfortable consider seeing him or her separately to build safety and trust, or bring in a cotherapist to create balance.

Similarly, be aware of your own countertransference reactions. If you feel awkward because of your own lack of skill in this area, get some support from your supervisor or trusted colleague. If a couple reminds you of your parents, for example, and you find yourself pushing their sexual issues to a back burner or reframing them as something else more within your personal comfort zone in order to avoid your own anxiety, you are in danger of doing what the couple is probably already doing. And if a couple is struggling with sexual issues that you personally are struggling with, be careful that you do not vicariously try and fix your own problem through them. Again, be honest with yourself, be aware of your own triggers and of who has the problem. Get the support you need to take the lead or consider transferring the case to someone else.

THE CHALLENGE OF CHILDREN

While money and sex are directly within each partner's control, children are not. They actively bring their own personalities and problems into the mix, shaping the family and ultimately the couple's relationship. Instinctively, children learn how to get attention from each parent, pick up on parents' tensions and act them out, try to split parents in order to get their way.

As with money and sex, there is a set of skills that are important for the parents to master in order to be successful as parents—how to nurture, how to set limits and consequences, how to communicate clearly and honestly, how to work effectively together as a team and present a united front. But unlike money and sexual skills that once learned continue to work, those of parenting must be constantly revised and updated. Managing a 3-year-old is not the same as managing a 10-year-old or 17-year-old. Parents need to be able to change their approach to fit the changing needs of the child. Those who can't can feel frustrated and stuck, all of which can leak into the couple's relationship.

Again the past comes into play and shapes each partner's parenting style, often in black-and-white terms. Sam, for example, remembered his own father as being strict with him when he was a child, but while admitting it was not always easy, he respected his father and felt that his father's ways turned him into the responsible man that he has become. If, however, Sam left childhood only aware of the resentment and wounds inflicted by his father's criticism and control, it's easy to imagine that his pain could drive him to swing too far in the opposite direction—becoming lenient and laid back—in an effort to avoid injuring his children in the same way he felt he was.

As we saw earlier with Sara and Ann, such childhood fears and worries easily interlock with those of the partner, and instead of changing history wind up replicating it. Sara's criticism of her daughter, Amy, for example, reminded Ann of her own critical mother. Ann overidentified with Amy's emotions, overcompensated for Sara's harshness by being even more lenient with Amy, and felt like a kid herself, essentially giving up her parenting and partner role. Ann's way of coping, in turn, stirred Sara's own old fears of being unsupported and abandoned. They became polarized, emotionally stuck, and found their own histories repeating themselves.

As with money and sex, the tensions between the partners are easily played out in the arena of child rearing. Just as frustration and resentments can surface over bill payments or sexual demands, the same feelings can just as easily fuel arguments over bedtimes or children's chores. Because children are so able to contour themselves to the parents' needs, unmet needs within a couple's relationship—for affection, for attention—can be filled in the relationship with a child. Children's problems can distract a couple from their own, just as the children's achievements can be a vicarious outlet for the parent's own desires. The complexity of these dynamics requires that you separate a couple's relationship problems from those directly linked to their parenting, and support them as partners as well as parents.

As a way of unraveling these couple/parenting dynamics, let's look more closely at some of the common presentations related to children:

Parents Are Overwhelmed and Can't Manage

Sol and Greta don't know what to do about their 6-year-old son, Nathan. He never listens to what they say, quickly throws tantrums, can't seem to stay still for more than a few minutes. Greta tends to yell but eventually gives up, Sol tries to set firmer limits but then gets frustrated and spanks. The spankings work briefly, but then seem to "wear off." Both parents are feeling stymied by Nathan's behavior, and each believes that the other is doing the best he or she can. Other areas of their relationship are described as good, their communication seems open and honest, and overall they seem supportive of each other.

Where do you start? An assessment of Nathan seems a logical choice—determining, for example, whether he has attention deficit disorder—as a way of addressing their presenting concerns and separating child issues from those of the couple. If it turns out that Nathan, in fact, does, the next step might be to educate them to the problem, and help them modify their parenting skills. Sol and Greta, for example, may need specific coaching on setting up a consistent structure in the home, giving Nathan directions that don't overload him, establishing clear expectations and supports so that Nathan can successfully complete his schoolwork, and so that they as parents can keep from feeling frustrated.

It's likely that the partners will differ in their abilities to implement these steps. They may need not only differing amounts of support from you, but also increased support from each other. If Greta, for example, easily becomes frustrated when Nathan seems unable to focus on his homework and she copes by giving in and letting him skip it, Sol may need to be available and know specifically how to support Greta in the moment so that she doesn't back down. Similarly, if Sol is quickly aggravated when he sees that Nathan has still not finished cleaning his room, Greta may need to step in and help Sol calm down and apply the responses they agreed to use. If you can treat Greta and Sol the way they need to treat Nathan—with consistency, understanding, and support—they will be able to make the transition and integrate the new skills into their parenting.

Sometimes, however, learning and applying new skills doesn't necessarily put the problems to rest. Because of their needs children with chronic mental and physical conditions—severe autism or cerebral palsy, for example—often become the common focus of the parents. Should, the child begin to do better (taking a new medication, for example, and becoming more independent) or do worse and enter residential treatment, the couple can feel at a loss and be destabilized. A hole is suddenly created in their relationship. While ideally a couple would see this as an opportunity to fill some of the hole with more of their relationship, they may instead find that it has in fact withered. They know each other as parents but not as partners. Rather than facing this new challenge, they may be tempted to stay preoccupied with the child in a new way—endlessly talking about the treatment, visiting each and every weekend—or redirecting their focus to another child in the family.

You can help such couples with this transition by getting issues and emotions out in the open—normalizing their sense of loss, confusion, or anxiety as the child becomes less of a focus and helping them see the development of their relationship as a couple as a natural and healthy challenge and goal, rather than filling in the hole with more of the same. They will need your help to explore these other areas of their relationship and clear out the obstacles that get in the way of their own intimacy. Once again, you need to take the lead.

One Parent Can Manage, the Other Can't

This is a variation on the one above. Both parents agree about parenting, but one parent is feeling frustrated either because he or she has trouble with the children, or the more competent one feels frustrated at times because the other is not. Renee, for example, know that she needs to be more strict with the kids and get them to bed on time but just gets overwhelmed. She then calls in her husband, David, who raises his voice and tells the kids to get to bed now or, hearing the uproar, goes upstairs and simply takes over. This more or less works until David has to work the evening shift; then Renee panics and winds up calling David at work so he can yell through the phone at the kids to go to bed. This aggravates David, and when he comes home he scolds Renee for bothering him at work and not handling it herself.

Ideally, both parents need to be able to nurture and set limits, though their individual styles may differ. The patterns David and Renee have created, however, are powerful. The children have clearly learned to ignore Mom and listen only to Dad, and each time the pattern unfolds it is behaviorally reinforced. But emotionally reinforcing the pattern may be the partners' own individual fears. Renee, for example, may believe that the kids will hate her if she is strict, or that she will lose control if she were to really try and enforce limits, or that David might drift away and leave her if she didn't have this pattern pulling him into the family. For all his complaining David may also appreciate being needed by Renee and fear losing his role or his control if she were in fact more independent. The pattern is effective in keeping these fears at bay.

If Renee and David are serious in their desire to change these patterns, Renee will obviously need to learn to set the limits herself, and, like Greta did, she may need David's support initially in doing so. Both will need support to resist the urge to let him take over. Of course the kids are part of this dynamic, and it would be helpful to predict to the couple that the kids are likely to escalate at first in response to Renee's limit setting before eventually giving in. This needs to be mapped out behaviorally and specifically—discussing all the possible scenarios and pitfalls—so that Renee can be successful. And finally you need raise the issues that they do not—namely, other ways David can be needed by Renee, other ways to ensure that he won't leave or that the children won't hate her. They will need to find healthier, less problem-oriented ways of connecting as a couple.

For some couples the presenting problem represents only the tip of the iceberg. Does Renee, for example, feel incompetent in other ways and rely on David to hold her up? If so, why? There may be concrete reasons—that she has a medical problem or untreated major depression that makes it difficult for her to function. She may have always adopted a helpless role in relationships, with men like David playing the complementary part as a way of staying connected. Similarly, is David controlling in other areas of the relationship and Renee's difficulty being assertive with him mirrors what she struggles with the children? All this can be explored as part of assessing the problem.

Battles over Parenting

This is probably one of the most common presenting problem that couples bring to counseling. They disagree about how to parent the children; each sees what the other is doing as wrong. They may battle all the time and get nowhere. The kids learn to split the parents or squeeze between the cracks. They come to counseling wanting you to say who is right and get the other to change.

The issue, however, is not over who is right, but about the process between them. This is what we did with Sara and Ann. You wonder aloud what keeps them from getting on the same page. Have what used to be small differences grown huge due to polarization? What prevents them from talking this through on their own? Is this issue a battleground for other, unspoken issues in the relationship? What other ways do they have to express anger? What ways do they have to express caring and affection?

Once again you want to help a couple to put the problem in a larger context. You want to see how they communicate, what they do with emotions in other areas; you want to explore the fears and the possible replication of their childhoods that are driving their militant positions. Each feels they are stuck because the other is stubborn and myopic. You want to uncover the anxiety and fear that drive the stubbornness. You want to point out the power struggle when it surfaces, change the emotional climate in the room by asking about softer emotions, assess what skill deficits and emotional patterns block successful communication.

Ultimately, you don't want to arbitrate the problem but rather to help them understand what drives it. Be clear in your role (I'm not going to be the judge, but I will help you talk this out and make decisions together), guide them toward the holes, help them better understand each other's perspective, and help them move toward the middle in a way that addresses their concerns and encourages them to be more flexible in their parental roles. Educate them about the value of a united front and endorse the notion that they are both right, and that there is much that they can learn from each other. And if there are other problems that are lying under the rug, drag them out so that everything isn't dumped into the problem of parenting.

Children as Surrogates

Daisy is angry that Henry seems to favor their son Brad, ignoring her and the other two children. She spends a majority of her time parenting them, and rarely do they spend time together as a couple.

Kevin is never at home, always out helping his friends work on their houses or cars. Shirley, his wife, says little to Kevin about his behavior, but instead pushes the kids to voice their complaints openly to their dad.

In both these relationships the children have come to replace the partner in their lives. In structural family therapy terms, the parental hierarchy has collapsed. Sometimes this pattern arises from the extended absence of the partner. Military families and families where one partner's job requires constant travel come to mind. By default the left-at-home parent becomes essentially a single parent and, in the partner's absence, leans on the children for support.

Other times this comes about from a parent's identification with one of the children, who shares a similar temperament or problems. "Brad reminds me of me," says Henry. "I was overweight, I struggled with school too, had other kids pick on me, and so I want to help him get through it." Henry is trying to repair his own childhood by helping his child. Daisy, feeling that the other children are being left out, as she is, spends her parenting time with them. The couple breaks into separate camps and over the years grows apart more and more.

Finally, the structure may be driven more directly by childhood histories. Kevin, for example, spent his childhood in multiple foster homes, never really bonded with any of his foster parents, and essentially spent his childhood emotionally caring for himself and living on the streets with friends. He married Shirley when he was 19. Shirley had grown up in a chaotic family with two alcoholic parents and, as the oldest of the children, assumed the caretaker role for her siblings. The marriage of Kevin and Shirley essentially re-created each of their childhoods. Kevin continued to be detached from his family and get his emotional support, however limited, from friends, while Shirley continued in her caretaker role with the children and used them to voice her own anger and frustration. Both stayed within their emotional comfort zones and found support and purpose from others rather than each other.

Couples like these are often thrown into a relationship crisis when the children become more independent as teens. Like the parents of a child with a chronic illness, what has been missing in their relationship, namely the ability to lean on each other for their emotional needs, becomes apparent as the children leave home or pull away. An initial goal would be to simply open up the communication—helping Henry talk about his childhood and fears for Brad, helping Shirley voice her anger at Kevin's absence—to essentially help them better understand each other and desensitize them to communication itself and to each other's emotions in order to increase intimacy. Help them see how their history is being re-created; explore with them how they evolved into separate camps. Next encourage them to take acceptable behavioral risks—for example, going out on dates, doing what they initially did, but have long forgotten, when they first met.

Simply by being in the room together with you and talking about anything at all concerning themselves, they are, in fact, plowing new ground. As they take behavioral risks, you need to be careful that they move slowly—spending a week together alone in Florida will likely result in Kevin golfing by himself and Shirley shopping, or discovering that one of the kids really doesn't feel well and their canceling the trip. Closely track their individual comfort zones, encouraging them to take acceptable but not overwhelming risks. Get feedback on their reactions to behavioral change. Coach them on providing large amounts of positive feedback to ensure slow and steady progress and success.

Again, you need to be the detective and sort out what are couple problems and parenting child problems. You may be working on two fronts simultaneously—helping couples communicate their concerns, for example, while providing concrete parenting suggestions or evaluation of the child. Your being able to untangle and separate out the issues helps couples do the same and fosters a change in the emotional climate between them and within the home.

COMMON THREADS

In surveying the clinical territory that money, sex, and children covers we see that they each are concrete problems in their own right, and a gauge of the strengths and weaknesses of the relationship itself. As with all problems that couples present, you begin with a clear understanding of their concern, the meaning of the problem to each of them, their personal theory on the cause and possible solution. You then need to place the problem in the larger context of the relationship by wondering why a couple defines this as a problem rather than something else in the relationship, why now, and what patterns and process from the present and past hold the problem in place. Finally, you want to look at their individual and joint skills in understanding and managing the problem, as well as the poor communication, power imbalances, childhood wounds that prevent them from solving the problem on their own.

As we have been saying all along, problems such as these represent emotional and behavioral limits that the couple have reached. The fact that they are defining the problem and bringing it to you to help them solve says that they are at least at the edge of being ready to move beyond these limits. What you offer a couple is the opportunity to see their concerns in this light, as a challenge for growth and expanded intimacy rather than a sign of failure. With your clarity, optimism, and sensitivity to their natural hesitations you can help them not only see possible solutions to the problem, but embrace change itself. And that perhaps is your greatest goal.

This concludes the first section of the book, on the basic concepts, concerns, and goals of couple therapy. In the second section we explore the presenting problems and clinical challenges as couples moves through the stages of family life.

Looking Within: Chapter 8 Exercises

1. Consider your own relationship to money. What is your own philosophy? How would you rate your own skill in managing it? Do you treat money as a way of coping with stress or expressing emotions? How sensitive are you to others controlling your income or spending?

2. Think about your own sexual history—the ways your attitudes toward sex have changed over time, its role in your past and current

life? How have your parents' attitudes shaped your own? What does sex mean to you? What for you is the relationship between sex and intimacy, between sex and love? How comfortable do your feel with your own sexuality, your skill, your sensitivity? What about your personal sexual life would you like to change? How do these insights affect your therapeutic work?

3. When you look back on your own childhood what is it that you most want to re-create and avoid re-creating as a parent? If one or both of your parents were to tell the story of your childhood, how would it be different from your own? What are your own values regarding good parenting?

4. In considering your clinical work, what are emotional triggers for you in the areas of money, sex, or parenting? In what ways may you need to be careful not to overreact or overidentify with a client? What support can you get to help you with this?

5. When you look at your past and current relationships, what has been a source of power struggles? What are you most hypersensitive about? What can make you feel like a victim? How has that changed over time?

6. Write a short paragraph assessing your own clinical skills and strengths regarding couple work.

Chapter 9

The Challenges of the Early Years

Keith and Rachel have been married just 6 months and they are already showing signs of marital wear. The first few months were great, but lately they have been arguing, a lot—about laundry and chores around the house, about how to spend their time together on the weekends, about the frequent visits by Rachel's parents who live close by. They are weary of the fighting, feel like it doesn't go anywhere, and they are, in fact, feeling a bit scared by it all.

Sure, you're going to be doing all the things that we've talked about so far—helping them with communication and process, helping them to avoid the power struggles and be responsible for their own emotions and problems, helping them move aside the boulders of the past that get in the way of their solving problems and moving on. But being new to couplehood poses it own unique challenges. In this chapter and the ones that follow, we explore the emotional and behavioral terrain of the couple life cycle, look at the challenges that the various stages offer and the common presenting problems that you are likely to see, and discuss ways to navigate the interplay between the drama triangle and the developmental relationship rollercoaster.

BUILDING THE FOUNDATION

To use a well-known simile, the early years of a relationship—and the first year in particular—are like building a foundation of house. The strength of the foundation determines how well the relationship will be able to handle the weight of life's additional challenges. The key challenges can be dramatized by your trying the following exercise:[1]

Begin clapping your hands. Okay, stop when your hands are together. Here is the couple, committed, united as one forever and ever. It's great, but ... after some period of time—2 hours, 4 days, 3 months—one or both of the partners begin to feel a bit too confined, too close, a bit suffocated (keep your hands together but start wiggling them). Couples face two challenges at this point—figuring out "How do we get space between us and how far apart do we go?"

Some couples get the space by periodically exploding apart through anger (go ahead, make your hands explode apart). Some do it by talking it through—they just agree to some schedule or routines for being apart (clasp your hands again and then just separate them). Sometimes one partner tries to sneak off (wiggle one hand so that it slips out from the clasp)—going off to get milk for 6 hours, getting drunk on the weekend, forgetting to mention that the guys invited him to go fishing this Saturday. Openly and clearly, or not, a couple has to negotiate expectations about time apart and together.

Even if they somehow work out how to separate, there is still the question of how far apart to go. Are they going to be long distance lovers (move your hands far apart)—the husband works out of town 5 days a week—or short-distance lovers (move your hands just a few inches apart). Usually each of the partners has his or her own expectations about this, derived from childhood experiences. Finally the big question—*who* decides what kind of lovers will they be? Do you go far off until I call you back, or until you've had enough and wander back into the relationship? Do you stay close by because I hold you on a short leash, because you feel anxious if you move further away, because it is the compromise we agreed on? How is this decision made and by whom?

There is a psychological tension underneath this dynamic driven by gender and complementarity. As the partners come back together (start moving your hands toward each other), they ultimately reach a tension point: One partner gets within a certain distance and begins to get anxious, and as John Gottman's research has shown, most often this is the male—who fears that if he gets too close he will get sucked in by the other (have one hand grasp for the other). It is a fear of emotional invasion and intrusion and he instinctively starts to back up. For the other partner the tension comes when the first pulls back beyond his

---

[1]This demonstration is borrowed from psychologist and writer Sam Keen. It is a useful one to demonstrate to couples.

comfort zone. The fear is that if this person goes too far, he will drift away and not come back. This is the fear of abandonment, often felt by the female, and her instinct when that point is reached is to pull the other back in. You can see the predicament—there is this gray zone (place your hands a few inches apart) where one partner reaches the psychological line and instinctively begins to back up, which threatens the other, who in turn reaches out to pull him back in (have one hand move away and the other reach out and grasp it).

What this all translates into in the real world of relationships is the challenge for couples to create compatible routines, to clarify expectations about how much time will be spent together and apart, and to set appropriate boundaries between themselves and the outside world. They need to build enough positive feedback into the relationship so that each partner feels appreciated, understood, and safe, and so that communication can be open. Finally they need to have an effective process for expressing emotions, making decisions, and problem solving. This is what you want to explore with couples like Keith and Rachel, and this is part of your assessment.

You can also show them the drama triangle and ask how it fits them. How much are their arguments about laundry, for example, not only a reflection of different expectations about who does chores and how, but also an outcome of a power imbalance where Keith, for example, has taken on the rescuer role, is overresponsible, and works hard to "be good" and make Rachel happy, only to periodically become resentful and unappreciated and start fuming about socks on the floor.

Similarly, did Rachel initially appreciate Keith's being in charge, but then start to feel like the victim, controlled and discounted, causing her to periodically blow up or act out? While helping them sort through the content of their disagreements (for example, come up together with a plan for chores) and develop the communication tools to do so, help them also see the larger patterns already at work—the power imbalances, the roles that they naturally bring in from their childhood experience, and the way these roles complement each other yet limit their emotional range and assertiveness.

Help them individually move toward their emotional and behavioral holes and toward the adult, differentiated stance. Ask Keith, for example, to notice what drives his actions—the shoulds versus the wants, his worry that Rachel will not be happy or be mad at him. Have him experiment with giving up some of the tasks he automatically takes on, make him curious about how he may play out his "good kid" role in other areas of life. Similarly, help Rachel be more assertive with Keith and experiment with speaking up in the session and at home when she feels he is being too directive or overbearing rather than just going along. She needs to begin to use Keith as a consultant to help her make changes and be more independent, rather than relying on him to do things completely for her.

Explore with them their ways of connecting and showing caring. This is where new couples often struggle because their styles differ. As mentioned earlier there is often one partner who has learned to "do for" the other person: helping out around the house, buying gifts—behaviors that demonstrate consideration and caring. The other partner often has a "do to" style. He or she is demonstrative when it comes to affection— the hugs and kisses and sex—and is less inclined to do things for the other. Problems develop over the months or years when they both feel that they are doing their best to show the other how they feel but getting little appreciation in return.

The problem is that each is expecting the other to be like him or her, and copy his or her own style. The person who "does for" may be relatively indifferent to affection and keeps wishing the other would vacuum the house, bring flowers, cook a special dinner, or simply listen to complaints about the work day. Their partner, in the meantime, who isn't particularly impassioned about meatloaf, feels starved for affection. Both eventually feel like the other really doesn't care.

Bring up the topic, help them see how their styles are based on a learned difference rather than personal indifference. Encourage them each to stretch—to do more of what the other expects while also appreciating what the other does for them—and to be creative in developing their own rituals and forms of connecting as a couple. Stay alert to the power struggle—not what we do but who decides—and point it out if it begins to unfold.

THE ANATOMY OF ANGER

Anger and conflict can obviously be a concern in the relationship at any point, but for new couples who are making the transition between romantic dating life and the realistic committed relationship, conflicts can feel particularly threatening and are often what brings them into therapy. Rachel may remark, for example, that there was one occasion when Keith became furious over a minor incident when they were dating, but he explained it as stress, apologized, and they made up. But now such incidents are becoming more frequent. She feels that he has a hair-trigger temper and is constantly trying to read his moods to prevent explosions.

Typically, it's mostly the environment that has changed, not Keith himself. Keith probably had a problem with anger before, but it was less apparent because he was on his best behavior during the dating process and was able to use distance to reduce his stress. Now that they are settled into the relationship and together in everyday life, Keith can no longer pull away to cope. The stress of meeting the challenges of coupling and living together leads to more conflict.

The problem needs to be addressed on several levels. One obvious place to start is by looking more closely at the couple's dynamics—the playing out of drama triangle imbalances resulting in Keith moving into the persecutor role. As mentioned in Chapter 4 you want to help a couple develop a plan for managing conflict. In order to keep arguments from escalating into power struggles and emotional and/or physical violence, each partner needs to be aware of and take responsibility for stopping a deteriorating process. You want to work on communication so that Keith doesn't bottle up his resentments, Rachel can be assertive rather than victimized, and each learns what triggers the other is sensitive to. You want to help them identify stresses and take individual responsibility for reducing them (Keith, for example, finds a way to unwind after work rather than bringing his work frustrations home and dumping them on Rachel), as well as ways of jointly reducing overall tension levels (for example, consciously increasing positive feedback or planning Friday night date nights).

You also want to assess personal responsibility. If Keith, for example, constantly blames Rachel for his anger and feels he deserves to feel the way he does because of her actions, he is being an adolescent more than a responsible adult. This becomes your focus—helping him move beyond thinking that his anger is her fault.

What is often underneath this couple's dynamic is a playing out of their parents' marital relationships. Rachel's mother, for example, was an alcoholic and had an explosive temper. Rachel constantly felt that she was walking on eggshells around her. While she consciously thought that Keith, who doesn't drink, was more emotionally stable, she unconsciously had found someone who emotionally replicated her mother's role. She instinctively reverted back to her hyperalert, cautious ways, and her past experience created within her a high tolerance for such aggressive behavior. Keith, for his part, identified with his father, who was the aggressor in his family of origin. Like him, Keith rationalizes his behavior and has difficulty regulating his emotions. Each partner plays the counterpoint to the other's role.

You can help couples who are insightful and willing to explore the past separate out the past from the present and step back from the patterns they are reenacting. You also need to develop a behavioral plan with them that interrupts their autopilot behavior. Rachel, for example, may need to say aloud when she feels like she is walking on eggshells around Keith to alert him to the tension and allow her to be more proactive. Similarly, Keith may need to write down annoyances that come up during the week and talk about them in therapy, rather than biting his tongue and exploding. If they can sustain these behaviors, they will eventually replace the old patterns and each one's emotional reactions will change as well.

But Keith may also need individual therapy to help him manage his anger. Traditional anger management treatment focuses upon helping individuals recognize triggers (for example, making the list of annoyances and stresses over the course of a week) and monitoring their emotional reactions (checking in with themselves to note their emotional state frequently throughout the day) in order to catch them before they reach the point of no return and are unable to self regulate. It teaches them how to be assertive and proactive rather than reactive in response to their environmental stressors and problems (deciding how they want to organize their time rather than having to deal with whatever lands in their lap). These are all effective tools that address the anger directly. What this approach sometimes misses, however, is addressing the broader context and underlying dynamics that can make someone prone to anger to begin with.

Keith, for example, may lack emotional flexibility. All his emotional energy gets translated into anger, and he has difficulty identifying softer emotions such as sadness, worry, fear. His angry response triggers a consistent and matching response in Rachel of withdrawal or anxiety, making it difficult for either of them to break the pattern. What he needs help learning is how to identify these other emotions, to see his anger as a signal that some other emotion lies just beneath the surface that he needs to label and broadcast to Rachel.

You can help him in the session by slowing down the process, translating his vocabulary of anger into that of sadness or fear, and helping him identify these underlying dynamics: "Keith, you sound angry. See if you can tell what else you may be feeling ... sad, worried, afraid? Focus on your feelings and see what image comes up." The shift is from anger management to seeing anger as information about other, more subtle emotions.

Keith's anger may also reflect an overall state of hypervigilance. Where Rachel's hypervigilance causes her to be timid and cautious, others become aggressive. This is easy to see in children who are diagnosed with oppositional defiant disorder. They are always scanning their environment, are extremely reactive and overreactive, and see everything as a threat. They automatically say no to requests by their teacher and are ready to pounce on a classmate who approaches them too quickly. What drives the anger is anxiety, often generated by living in a chaotic and unsafe family environment. These children can never relax, have learned to be always ready to fight or flee as a means of protecting themselves. They are at risk for alcohol or drug abuse as teens and adults because they find this is the only way they can calm themselves down; essentially they are self medicating to reduce their anxiety.

Keith may be doing the same. You could explore with Keith his childhood family life and look for signs of chaos and trauma. You could help him realize how the coping styles of childhood no longer apply, encourage him to talk about his childhood experiences and reactions as a way of draining old wounds and emotions, and coach him on changing his self-talk so he acknowledges that he is no longer as vulnerable as an adult as he once was as a child, and sees Rachel's reactions as less of a threat. Doing this work with Rachel present can also help her redefine Keith's actions in her own mind and help her react more compassionately.

Finally, some who struggle with anger are actually struggling with unresolved grief. There is a well-known play, which later became a successful movie starring Alan Alda, entitled *Same Time, Next Year*, by Bernard Slater. The story is about George and Doris, who have an affair that consists of their spending a weekend together at the same time each year. It's a two-character play and the scenes track their meetings and the changes in themselves and their relationship at 5-year intervals. At the opening of one particularly dramatic scene we see that George is acting very differently. He unpacks a suitcase full of liquor; instead of his easygoing comical self, he is angry and irritable, complaining about his work, his life. Doris is taken aback and presses to find out what is wrong; she succeeds only in making him even more belligerent.

At the climax of the scene she asks about his children and he finally tells her that his oldest son had been killed a few months before in Vietnam. As she starts to cry and asks how he felt, George says, "That's just it—I felt nothing. I thought it was a delayed reaction, that I was staying strong for my wife, that I would feel it later, but I never did. All I felt was numb. And then all I felt all the time was this incredible anger." While still crying, Doris reaches out and hugs him. He initially resists her, then leans into her, and finally breaks down and sobs uncontrollably, for the first time since his son died.

And so it is with some clients—there is a direct correlation between an ungrieved loss and an increase in overall irritability or bursts of anger. Some will even make the connection themselves—"I realize that I've been different since my mother died"—and bring it up to you. As it did for George, the anger substitutes for the sadness and keeps it at bay. Whenever clients present with problems of anger, go ahead and ask about loss, about their response, about whether there is an increase in their irritability and anger since that time. If this is the case, explore it further and help them express these emotions—letter writing to the deceased person saying what they were not able to say, visits to the cemetery, simple discussion of their thoughts and feelings about the relationship and the death. Again, if the partner is present, their witnessing of this process can help change their own attitudes and behaviors, as well as define ways they can be a support.

Of course, you will usually find yourself working on anger from multiple perspectives at the same time—increasing emotional flexibility, helping a couple move out of the drama triangle and persecutor roles, reducing stress and triggers, exploring the past and loss. The overall goal is redefining the anger, uncovering the dynamics that drive it, uncoupling the patterns that maintain or exacerbate it. Be curious, be pragmatic, help the client and couple focus on understanding and recognizing the emotional process rather than getting lost in the content.

DRAWING THE LINE: HANDLING THE IN-LAWS

Denise and Roy come for counseling on the advice of their minister. They had been attending premarital classes through their church, where in a group setting they were learning about communication skills, conflict resolution, practicalities of budget making—all aimed at creating a more solid and realistic foundation for married life. But the couple is struggling over the role of parents, particularly Denise's mother, in the planning of their wedding and in their everyday lives.

In the first therapy session Roy is open about his impatience and irritation. He feels that Denise's mother, Wanda, is micromanaging the wedding, he is resentful that she frequently "drops over" unannounced to see Denise and discuss details, that she brings gifts that she thinks will "help brighten up their apartment." Roy is distant and stiff around her, feels that Wanda accepts but doesn't particularly like him. He has tried to talk with Denise about all this, but she easily gets defensive, saying that that is just the way her mother is, and that she is just excited about the wedding. Roy wants Denise to take a stronger stand and set boundaries with her mother. He is angry because she hasn't.

Defining the role of extended family is often a major challenge for young couples. Like Roy, one partner may feel invaded by in-laws; what is unfolding is different from the expectation he or she had at the start. Their family cultures may be different—one partner is close to his family while the other is distant. The amount of family contact that was tolerable during dating is now intolerable; what one sees as caring by parents, the other sees as control.

Psychologically, however, the challenge is about leaving home and separating from the family of origin. The young couple is struggling with how and how far to pull away, how to shift psychic energy from parents to partner, while at the same time the parents are having to downshift their primary parenting role to something less intense, more peerlike. Often there is a sense of loss for the parents, especially if they have been heavily child-centered in their own relationship and are anxious about the hole they see looming in their own marriage.

Some couples are on the same page and clear about this from the onset. Both are trying to break away from home. Unconsciously or consciously they see the relationship as a support for doing this, and they easily move states away from their families—to go to school, to start the career, or because housing is cheaper. Sometimes the partner welcomes the involvement of the in-laws. If Roy, for example, had come to see Denise's family as a substitute for the one he didn't have, the parents' involvement might have been openly welcomed. But often the reactions are more complex, mixing feelings of jealousy and loyalty as the partners jockey for power and recognition. You hear Roy saying things like "I'm marrying you, not your mother," and Denise saying how she feels caught in the middle, having to choose whom to please.

Just as they need to determine their own individual boundaries, couples have to decide where to set the boundaries between them as a couple and the outside world. How much and in what way will extended family and friends be incorporated into their lives? As with other decisions there is an opportunity for a power struggle over whose vision of the marriage will prevail, who ultimately decides—Roy, Denise, or both of them together. Much will depend upon their individual coping styles. If, for example, Denise's way of coping with the demands of others has always been to concede in order to avoid conflict, it's easy to see how she now feels caught in a bind, struggling to please two people who are important to her. New problems will challenge her to handle old problems in new ways.

So how do you help this couple? Obviously the starting point is helping them air their feelings and thoughts clearly, expanding the conversation beyond its stalemated limits. For example, you ask Roy what specifically is bothering him about Wanda's planning of the wedding—

that she is taking over without asking permission or that she is taking over at all? Is he worried that she will continue to interfere and control their relationship? Is he transferring any of his feelings about his own parents onto her? What does Denise's going along with her mother mean to him—that her mother is more important than he is, that she is afraid to be fully committed to him, that she is afraid to make decisions on her own?

Similarly, when Denise says she feels caught between her mother and Roy, ask her what "feeling caught" means to her. Is she afraid to be assertive with her mother? Does she feel that Roy needs to be more understanding—of her, of her mother? Is she afraid of Roy's disapproval or anger? Does she see him as another parent that she needs to please? Does she have ways of showing Roy that she cares about him and that he is important besides doing what he wants? How is her vision of married life and the involvement of parents different from his? Can she say what she ideally would like?

What's behind all these questions is a clarifying of each partner's needs, wants, and fears. As always it is less about the content—how much wedding planning Wanda should do—than more about the stuck points in the process. Let them, for example, talk until they start to argue or show signs of emotion; then talk to them one at a time to clarify ideas and detoxify emotions. Then ask if they think the partner understands, and have them talk together again. By focusing and changing the process, you help them change the content. You encourage Denise to better define what she wants, help Roy feel less threatened and be more supportive, help them learn to take a unified stand. Your job is to highlight the issues, facilitate the process, draw out the underlying feelings. You do not need to find a solution, but help them work through a solution together.

Situations like these can stir transference issues that you need to stay alert to. For example, you may notice that Denise seems to be cautious and accommodating with you as she is with her mother, rather than being open and honest. Or Roy, who was ambivalent about coming to begin with, sees therapy as even more intrusion into their relationship and seems defensive. You may need to spend more time on building rapport and reducing their fears.

You also may find it useful to bring the problem more directly into the room—to invite Wanda into a session with the couple. Start by helping Wanda feel comfortable with you by introducing yourself, finding out a little bit about her. Find out what she knows about the purpose of the session and what her own agenda might be. With your support Roy can talk directly with Wanda about how he feels about their relationship, Denise may be able to say to her mother that she feels caught in the middle, or you can help them take a united stand and kindly but assertively tell Wanda what role they would like to play in their wedding planning. Encourage them to talk about their softer emotions—worry, concern, hurt—rather than anger and annoyance.

Ask Wanda what she thinks, how she feels. Expand the conversation and the couple's perspective on Wanda by asking her, for example, to talk about what the wedding means to her, or how she feels as a mother now that her daughter is truly beginning a new life apart from her. Make sure that it ends on a good note, that everyone feels heard, that no one feels angry or hurt.

Regardless what approaches you choose, your goal is to help couples not only successfully communicate and negotiate this particular conflict, but gain tools and develop the trust that they can navigate this process again in the future.

HERE COME THE KIDS

The entrance of children into the relationship can exacerbate problems between the young couple and their own parents. While some couples welcome the enthusiastic advice giving and offers to babysit, especially during the weeks after the birth of the child, others feel threatened. They worry about their parents spoiling the children and undermining their fragile identity and skills as new parents. Again, boundary setting is in order, but this may pose a challenge for a couple.

The entrance of children not only tests the couple's boundaries with their parents, but obviously brings its own set of stresses and challenges. Some of these are physical—the nighttime feedings and sleep deprivation that plague a couple for the first several months, the decrease in the wife's interest in sex due to hormonal changes, which unfortunately, in the husband's mind, often comes on the heels of decreasing sexual activity during the final of months of the pregnancy. But the biggest challenges are psychological—the couple is a couple no longer, but instead becomes an awkward triangle.

The introduction of a child can bring the weaknesses of the relationship—poor communication, power imbalances, inability to solve problems or make decisions together—to the forefront, especially for those with an unplanned pregnancy or other existing stressors. The husband may worry about money, or the wife may secretly worry that she will follow in the footsteps of her own abusive mother. If the partners are unable to verbalize these fears and lean on each other for support, they are forced to internalize or act out these worries and frustrations. Studies have shown, for example, that domestic violence increases and postpartum depression is greater in mothers who feel unsupported by their partners, and it is important to ask about these issues as part of your assessment.[2] If you are working with couples with these risk factors, you need to think in terms of crisis prevention. Focus with them on problem partialization, skill building, responsible behavior, and open communication. Help them get issues on the table, and help them learn to support each other and reach solutions.

But even for those couples who seem relatively stable, excited, and prepared, the changes in the relationship that a child brings can catch the best of them off guard. Marie initiated therapy in the sixth month of the couple's pregnancy because she felt that her husband, Harold, was spending more and more time on his job, arriving home late at night, talking to her little. At first Harold explained that he was working over-time because he was worried about money, especially with Marie's plans to stay home from her job for the first 3 months after their son was born. But as the conversation continued, it was clear that he felt jealous of Marie's focus on the pregnancy and the baby, and admitted with some embarrassment, "I feel like he has already become more important to her than me." His work behavior, though rationally driven by financial worry, was also a way of using distance as a means of coping with his feelings of abandonment.

These were familiar emotions for Harold. His younger sister was born with cerebral palsy, and the attention she received, especially from his mother, left him feeling cast aside and less important. His father, perhaps at least partially because he too didn't know how to enter into the family dynamics, also was a workaholic, and distant from his children and wife. Marie's parents, in contrast, were actively engaged with the children. Marie says, "We kids were the focus of their world." In fact she could remember only few times that her parents went out on their own. This child-centered view of marriage and family is what she expected for Harold and herself, and she was understandably mystified and disturbed by his reaction.

Again the couple is struggling over whose vision, driven by childhood example and individual wounds, will be played out. An initial clinical goal would seem to be helping Harold express his fears and help-

---

[2]Summaries of research and numerous helpful articles on the impact of pregnancy on relationships can be found online. See, for example, the websites of the Family Violence Prevention Fund (*endabuse.org*) and the Pan American Health Organization (*www.paho. org*).

ing Marie better understand and be sensitive to them so that he feels a part of the family and connected as a parent—doing, in fact, what Harold's mother and father were not able to do. They want to avoid replicating Harold's family, with him being wedded to work, her to the children.

But while that's important, there's another, more subtle, aspect of their dynamic that should not be overlooked. The other challenge that they share, and don't quite see, is not only learning to be united and involved together as parents, but also being involved with each other as couple. They lacked role models for this type of intimacy. If they are to successfully continue their relationship once the children leave home, this is a connection they will need to make.

As Bowenian family theory points out, the triangle that children create is powerful in its ability to at best distract a couple from their relationship and problems and at worst pull them apart. Like all triangles this one can quickly create a dysfunctional stability in which a couple's conflicts and problems with intimacy are deflected to the children. The antidote is maintaining a structural hierarchy between the parents and children and breaking the triangle into functional dyads—keeping issues between the couple between the couple, helping the parents develop their individual relationships with each of the children, and working as a united front, rather than compensating for problems in one relationship by focusing on another.

Your challenge is to help couples do this—to see what lies ahead and encourage them to approach the conflicts between them directly and openly. They need to recognize when issues are not about children but about their own differences. They need to develop a united front toward the children, yet be able to privately and honestly hammer out their parenting differences.

What this means is that you want to help Harold be aware of the dangers of following in his father's footsteps. Help him to talk about his old childhood abandonment wounds so he can better realize when they are getting triggered, separate them from the present, and be less reactive. Help him identify what he needs Marie to do to help him (probably what he needed from his mom) when he feels lonely. Help him express his feelings while taking responsibility for them. Similarly, you help Marie look more closely at her own parents' relationship, and be curious about their relationship apart from the children. Help her to be sensitive to Harold's feelings, yet not feel that she has to choose between her husband and child.

Finally, you want to help them look together at their own relationship—to actively discuss their fears, values, and priorities as parents.

Help them find ways to increase their intimacy at home by planned couple time. In the session process deepen their communication by asking the hard questions, pushing them to clarify what they verbally or nonverbally only infer, and encouraging them to take emotional risks. This challenging yet supportive approach will help prevent new couples like Marie and Harold from going on autopilot. It will help them establish a strong foundation upon which they can handle the developmental challenges that lie ahead.

These are the goals of these first few years—to become a committed couple rather than just a couple who dates; to work out how the everyday process of their lives will work; to make decisions and solve problems in a way that truly solves them rather than just sweeping them under the rug. It can be a difficult time. Many couples crash emotionally because they think of marriage as legal dating and assume the romance and excitement will continue. Others are more realistic but reach the limits of their interpersonal skills, or find the patterns of their parents that they so wanted to avoid slowly creeping into their everyday lives. Still others are hammered by outside stressors—struggling to survive together as a family on a minimum wage job, trying to create a career, dealing with criticism or intrusion by parents and extended family, trying to sanely adjust to the birth of a child.

These struggles will appear as a variety of presenting problems—complaints about parents who visit too long or are too critical, or children who don't sleep and exhaust couples who are trying to hold down full-time jobs, or couples who never argued during courtship finding that all they do now is argue about petty things such as snoring, not returning phone calls, leaving the milk out on the counter. They need your help to develop the long-term skills: to give up the alluring or accommodating talk of dating and replace it with the honest yet sensitive talk of commitment, to learn how to substitute the former part-time needs of a girlfriend or boyfriend with the full-time needs of a partner—lifelong lessons that you can help them to learn.

Looking Within: Chapter 9 Exercises

1. If you are not married, take a few moments to reflect on how your own expectations copy or compensate for your parents' relationship. If you are married consider how your own relationships may be replicating your parents' struggles.

2. Think back to your own impressions of your parents' life before you were born. Think of photos, things your parents may have told you— what is the image you gathered about their early life? How has it become a template for your own early marriage?

3. What is most stressful for you in starting a committed relationship? What issues are you particularly sensitive to? Why would you get married, and if you are, why, looking back on it, did you at that time in your life?

4. What potential countertransference issues do you need to be aware of when working with young couples—problems that resonate too strongly with your own, personalities that remind you of your own past, age similarities or differences? What type of support do you need to manage this better?

5. Think about children as the start of triangles in your relationships. How have you managed other triangular relationships? What role do you believe children should have in the broader landscape of your family?

Chapter 10

Re-creating the Vision

Pizza and a video with the kids are a Friday night tradition for Ken and Andrea, just as is the Saturday night sex. Weekends are filled with soccer games, grocery shopping, and mowing the lawn, while weekday afternoons and evenings are crammed with soccer practices, dance lessons, and the ever-present homework. The young couple has developed their own routines and patterns, their own lines of communication—unspoken rules for what they talk about and what they don't, who initiates the conversations, how they manage and solve problems. They have consciously and unconsciously created a structure for their family and their relationship. Emotionally, Ken has his feet planted firmly in his career, and Andrea often takes up the slack with the kids. She now works part time so she can be home with the children after school. Most of her waking time, it seems, is tied up with them.

And it's okay. They are realistic enough to know that the excitement of that dating time naturally fades. While the busyness and the routines can seem deadening at times, while Ken will wake up in the middle of night worrying about work or Andrea will occasionally miss the fulfillment and camaraderie of her former, full-time job, things are turning out more or less as they expected. They have made the transition to parenthood, they are committed to putting the children first. They have no major complaints. They are following their 5-year vision. Psychologically and emotionally they feel they are on track.

A VISION DERAILED

While Ken and Andrea are satisfied that they are living out the vision they initially created, many other couples, especially those who come to you for therapy, are finding that their early vision has been derailed. Conflict, frustration, anger, disappointment with each other have begun to take their toll. Environmental stresses—poverty, struggles with employment, health problems—may have been unceasing. Their ongoing struggle has robbed them of the opportunity to establish a stable base on which to build and taxed their ability to cope. They move from crisis to crisis, reach out for help when overwhelmed, pull back and try to catch their breath when there seems to be a break.

Let's take a look at ways of helping couples like these. Here are three couples with different presenting problems. Read each summary and write down what might be your initial hypothesis, focus, and goals for this couple before moving onto the next. When you're done we will brainstorm possible questions and options and compare notes.

*   *   *

Rita and Ruben have been married 5 years. While their oldest child, 4-year-old Maria, seems to be doing well, their 3-year-old son, Tony, has been having behavioral problems, first at day care and now in preschool. The pediatrician has labeled him as having attention-deficit/hyperactivity disorder (ADHD). Because of Tony's age, he is unwilling to prescribe medication, is recommending that the parents manage it behaviorally, and has provided them with a handout of parenting guidelines to follow. Rita says that she has tried to follow them but feels that they don't work, and she admits that she usually winds up giving in to Tony's demands. Ruben, her husband, does a better job of setting limits with Tony, but his long work hours make him essentially unavailable except for weekends. Rita is worried about Tony and feels overwhelmed by his behavior and criticized by Ruben. They argue constantly, it seems, about how to best handle him.

*   *   *

Logan and Sally worked full time in the first several years of their marriage; Logan worked evenings as a chef, Sally ran a florist shop during the day. When their first child was born they decided to keep their jobs and, given their schedules, manage the child care between them. But while Logan seems to be a good father, Sally is frustrated by Logan's underemployment—he has moved from restaurant to restaurant, taking ever lower-paying positions or even part-time work. She also is upset about his now daily marijuana use.

*   *   *

Rashan and Tameca have been trying to get pregnant for almost 2 years. The specialists they have consulted have provided a mix of opinions—some have said they see no medical problems that should pose an obstacle, while others suggest some subtle factors may be at work. The couple themselves are frustrated and divided about how much and how long to pursue further medical intervention before calling it quits. They vacillate between arguments and distance.

*   *   *

There are obviously multiple starting points and perspectives that we could take on each of these cases. Let's look at options.

Rita and Ruben

Here we have layers of problems—the behavioral problems with Tony himself, Rita's struggle managing him, the couple's own understanding of and reactions to the diagnosis, their differing parenting styles, the impact of the problem upon their relationship. Following the model outlined earlier, we want to start by understanding the details of the presenting complaint, determine who has and what is the problem, and expand the focus to include both of them, not just one partner. Rita, for example, may not understand fully what ADHD means. She may not even agree with the diagnosis, or may feel guilty, believing that she is somehow the cause. She may see Ruben as unsupportive or too harsh with Tony, tied, perhaps, to her own childhood or Tony's complaints to her privately. Ruben sounds alike he's already overloaded by the demands of his job. Does he see this as one more problem laid in his lap? Perhaps he believes that Rita's struggles are clearly of her own making. We need to ask, listen, and hear both sides.

We may find that they need concrete help with parenting skills, particularly the skills that parenting a child with ADHD requires. Their daughter, Maria, is doing well by all reports, which says something about her temperament but also indicates something positive about her parents' abilities. Rita may believe that what works with Maria should work with Tony, or she may not understand the guidelines or the importance that the doctor gave them.

Asking how they handle behaviors and consequences with Maria may give us information about their styles and differences, as well as help them feel more positive overall about themselves as parents. Going over the handout, educating them about ADHD, and explaining how such children can be impulsive and benefit from structure all may be helpful. They may need to expand their repertoire of skills. They need to see that being united in their view of Tony's problem and in their response is important in managing him successfully.

And then there are their own couple skills in communication, problem solving, and support. Can they voice their concerns clearly and honestly or do one or both of them bite their tongues? What drives their arguments, how bad do they get? While they may struggle over Tony, can they be supportive of each other in other ways? Does Ruben need more appreciation for working so hard? Does Rita need appreciation for attempting to hold down the fort with the kids when he's gone? Does she need Ruben to better understand her frustration?

Is there a danger that Rita lets Tony get away with things because she has a difficult time with conflict in general or because her primary connection is with her children rather than Ruben? Is at least part of the reason the couple is struggling that they are acting out marital issues in the arena of childrearing? How have Tony's problems derailed their vision of family life? Is there a sense of loss that neither one can speak about?

Finally, there is the management of Tony himself—how can Ruben help Rita set the structure that Tony needs without taking over and being critical? What other emotional supports need to be in place so that the parents feel more unified as a couple?

We will need to watch the session process—see whether communication breaks down, and whether they are able to get back on track. We will need to ask these questions and see where they most want help. If your approach focuses primarily on communication, you may spend much of your time in a session, especially in the beginning, helping them discuss all this openly, cleanly, and clearly. The session becomes a safe forum for open discussion and problem solving of all these possible issues. If you are more psychodynamically oriented you may explore their pasts and lead them to see how their experiences have shaped their own behaviors and expectations of married and family life and have made them sensitive to these particular aspects of their interactions. If you have good skills in child or family therapy, you may invite them to bring Tony in for an assessment, or have them bring both children in to see the family dynamics in action.

All these are possibilities and may be effective. The keys will be linking your style and view of the problems with their own priorities and expectations. Ask what they expect and what they most need help with, laying out your thinking, and see whether they are on board. What don't you want to do? Disrupt the balance by taking sides; unconsciously step in for Ruben as the primary support for Rita; take over the treatment of Tony and leave Rita and Ruben sitting out in the waiting room.

Logan and Sally

When you read the summary what grabs your attention, what are you most curious about? The fact that their work schedules leave them with little time to be together? How they connect with each other? Why this lifestyle seems emotionally okay for them? How they learned to structure their relationship and time this way?

Are you wondering about Logan's marijuana use—whether he is psychologically dependent upon it, how it may affect his work or attitude? If marijuana is a bad solution, what might be Logan's problem? Who's got the problem? Is he concerned about his marijuana use or his work, or is it only Sally's problem right now? Clearly Sally is having a problem with Logan, but is he having a problem with her?

All these are questions to listen for and raise. Ask what brings them in. Listen to and clarify each one's view of problems. Watch the process in the room—does Logan, for example, get quickly defensive or tune Sally out? Can he be assertive? Is he engaged in the therapy process, does he see it as potentially helpful, or is he just "going along" to pacify Sally? Can Sally talk about her worries—about Logan's employment, about his drug use—rather than just voice her complaints?

Ask the hard questions that deepen the conversation. How has the couple's vision of the future changed? What did they expect and want when they first started out? If it has changed, why do they think so? Ask about their childhoods. Are they playing out scripts from childhood— the nagging, unsupportive wife, the passive, less responsible husband?

Can we help them move toward the holes, stop the dysfunctional patterns? If Logan tends to avoid conflict, can we encourage him to voice his annoyances and anger rather than retreating? Does he feel like a victim? Can we help him step out of that role and define more clearly his own needs and wants? If Sally is in danger of falling into a martyr enabling role, can we help her shift toward the adult role by defining her problems, stating what she would like, but not trying to reduce her own anxiety by pressuring Logan to change?

Can we help them connect as a couple in positive ways? Can they carve out couple time? Can they create a common vision? If we can help them change the process, move them toward new conversations right there in the session, we may be able to break their one-dimensional view of each other. If we can stop the power struggles and expand their emotional range right there in the session, the experience may carry over to home.

What are the pitfalls we want to avoid? We want to encourage

Logan to speak up without sounding like a nagging, critical parent. In supporting him we need to be careful that Sally doesn't feel like her own concerns and frustrations are minimized or that we are taking Logan's side against her. If we are concerned about possible drug addiction in Logan, we need to matter-of-factly, but clearly, approach it—to take the role of a consultant, and offer options for possible treatment without leaving the impression that he really is the problem after all, that Sally was right. We talk about Logan's possible addiction as a solution to other issues that are important, and offer to help sort out and solve these other issues.

Rashan and Tameca

Again, start with curiosity. It certainly is understandable that they are frustrated. It is common in situations like this for each to have different theories about the cause of the problem; they may secretly blame themselves or the other. It is also common for couples to polarize around it—one partner is resigned or ready to give up or consider other options, while the other is more obsessed, more driven to keep trying to find a solution. The "working at it" itself becomes a source of strain that is hard to talk about openly without seeming uncaring or disloyal. But what also comes to mind is loss—not only over the possibility of not having children, but also of the vision that they initially created together.

We can start there. Listen to their frustrations but also their sadness. Ask about theories, guilt or blame, worst- and best-case scenarios. How do they explain this problem in their lives—not only the reason for the difficulty, but what it means to them to have to face this problem at all? How has it changed their view of themselves as individuals, themselves as a couple, their view of the future? Have they individually or together had to deal with other losses in their lives?

What gets in the way of their being a support to each other? Can they communicate and make decisions together in other areas? What makes this different?

We raise these questions and see what unfolds in terms of new emotions, patterns of connection or disengagement, and the search for the core pattern that defines where they get stuck in the process. We want to know what they want most from us—help making a decision, reducing the tension? Help talking about possible options or visions for the future rather than just the stalemate of the present? Help with grieving and taking action in a new way?

What do we want to avoid? Bypassing the deep emotional issues by focusing only on the medical ones, as they have, or replicating the triangle by not keeping the relationships and focus balanced.

Compare your own ideas on these cases to the ones above. No doubt some of your ideas are similar; no doubt you may be drawn to certain dynamics rather than others, may pick one starting point over another. Again, there are many approaches to take that would be effective. Your goal is to be clear—about what the couple is seeking, clear about your thinking and what you can offer, clear in your ability to follow the process, present your concern and your questions, and expand their perspectives.

REALIGNING THE STRUCTURE

You can feel the tension in the room as Matt and Ellen enter the room. They sit at opposite ends of the couch, pulling away from each other, Ellen looking at you, Matt at the floor.

After introducing yourself you ask why they are here.

"So go ahead," says Matt, "tell him." His voice is quiet but you can hear an edge to it.

Ellen takes a deep breath. "Matt had an affair." While you see her eyes start to water, she too has an edge to her voice.

"It's over," says Matt, looking at you. "I ended it as soon as Ellen found out about it. It had only been going on for a few months."

"But why?" snaps Ellen. She is crying now. "Why? I thought we were happy."

"I don't know, I don't know. I was just stupid. Because I could, I don't know." Matt sounds angry and is clenching his fist. Then he relaxes and says quietly to no one, "I felt numb all the time."

While couples like Logan and Sally, Ruben and Rita often come to therapy in those early years to learn new skills or resolve a seemingly unresolvable problem, there comes a point in the relationship where the challenge is about redefining and realigning the foundation of the relationship itself. This is the notorious 7-year itch, that dangerous time when couples are susceptible to divorce.

While to the couple, Matt's affair seems to be the classic cause for their marital deterioration, it is not. It is merely a bad solution, a symptom of other problems within the structure of the relationship itself. They could have just as easily come in talking about a career change decision that they can't resolve, or increasing resentment over the other's seemingly overbearing control. Somehow they have disconnected—

while Ellen thinks they're happy, Matt is numb and neither one is able to really talk about it.

Theorists of adult development talk about normal patterns of stability (usually 6 to 8 years) followed by periods of transition (2 to 3 years) over the life cycle.[1] In the language of the drama triangle, the 7-year itch sometimes marks not just a another round of moves from rescuer to persecutor, or victim to persecutor, but an attempt to break out of roles and shift toward an adult position. In terms of the relationship rollercoaster metaphor, this represents the climb up the first long hill and ending of the initial psychological contract. This is the heart of the struggle for a couple—recognizing that the basis of the relationship, formed during courtship and those first years, no longer fits. They need to decide what now needs to take its place.

As we discussed in Chapter 2, people like Matt and Ellen each had particular needs that they most wanted to have filled at the time they came together. Whatever they were—stability, excitement, feeling important, being taken care of—the couple's roles and routines were built around getting those needs met. But now, 6, 7, or 8 years later, those needs are needs no longer—Matt and Ellen have given each other what they each needed, have filled up those emotional holes. They have, in fact, been successful in accomplishing what they set out to do psychologically. But the same roles and routines persist, and the gap between the internal life and external one grows. Matt begins to feels numb. The affair not only brings excitement, it lets him know that his needs have changed.

While usually it seems that one partner is leading the charge, and may be more at the edge of individual change, it is a mistake to assume that it is one-sided. The other partner will often acknowledge that yes, the basic fabric of the relationship has shifted in some way, that no, they are not themselves the same person they were at the start. They may not be able to articulate this well, or may feel guilty or disloyal to the relationship if they voice a need for change. They may be frightened by the process of change itself.

Partners often differ in their individual tolerance for change. Matt, for example, described himself as someone who is always willing to try new things. This risk taking was actually one of the things that Ellen

---

[1]There are several classics on adult development that are worthwhile to explore. See Sheehy, G. (2006). *Passages: Predictable Crises of Adult Life*. New York: Ballantine Books; Levinson, D. (1986). *The Seasons of a Man's Life*. New York: Ballantine Books; Erikson, E. (1980). *Identity and the Life Cycle*. New York: Norton; Demick, J., & Andreotti, C. (Eds.). (2003). *Handbook of Adult Development*. New York: Springer.

found attractive about him. She herself had a cautious personality and not surprisingly, had always counted upon the stability of the relationship. We may wonder if her need for stability may have blinded her to the changes that were in fact unfolding. This ability to accept and incorporate change into the relationship can be seen as the meta-challenge of the relationship. Not only does a couple need to revise and revamp the psychological contract that holds them together, they also need to approach the anxiety that change itself brings.

Finally, these changes in the relationship often coincide with or are fueled by other developmental issues. Matt, for example, may also be at that point in his career when he is questioning the trajectory he is on, and may be restless or depressed about his workplace. Ellen may be at that point in her biological cycle where she is acutely aware that the opportunity to have children is steadily decreasing. If Matt can't talk about his work, if Ellen and he can't agree on or even discuss the issue of whether to have children or not, the emotions become internalized and add fuel to the tension and distance between them.

One of the dangers here is that if all these issues, emotions, and needs seem too overwhelming, if they lack the skills or the courage to face them, couples can choose to sweep them all under the rug. Matt's affair becomes something that "just happened." He is sorry and guilty, vows to make it up to Ellen, and she is willing to forget about it as best she can as long as Matt goes back to his former more comfortable and familiar ways. Other couples, sensing the distance between them, decide to fill it with distractions. They throw themselves into their careers, or the couple decides to have another child as a way of jump-starting the flailing relationship. It works in that it gives them a common focus for a while, but the danger is that it backfires—the child becomes the emotional focus for one of the partners, while the other emotionally leans more on one of the other children or work, or the child initially brings them together but then they drift apart once again.

Other couples don't use children or careers to distract themselves, but money. They buy a boat, go on an expensive vacation, redecorate the house or move to a new one. Sensing the undertow that is pulling the relationship off course, they try as best they can to resist it. They come to you in debt or depressed because what they thought would turn things around didn't. Finally, you may see some couples who rather than fleeing report simply fighting more. They are getting on each other's nerves–she can't stand how much time he spends at work, he is fed up with her involvement with her extended family or the way she coddles the kids. Tension is leaking out all over. The power struggle and aggravation are signs that the structure is falling apart.

You, the clinician, need to be alert to these underlying dynamics, especially when seeing couples at that 6- to 9-year mark. You need to be careful that you don't become too complacent and agree too readily with Matt and Ellen that they need to get this behind them and move on. Sure, you want to help them talk about the guilt, anger, and hurt in order to mend the wound. But to leave it at that and encourage them to simply make room for some quality time in their busy lives is essentially colluding with them. Similarly, merely helping a couple shore up their parenting after a new child or discussing with them how they go about making decisions on big money issues misses the point that deeper dynamics are at work here that need to be addressed.

Of course, some couples won't like to hear this and are not ready to take this on. Ellen may be frightened by such talk, Matt may come to therapy simply as a peace offering to Ellen and want to simply move on. That's obviously their choice. Your job, however, is to provide the outside perspective, to make them curious—why this problem, why now, and what is it trying to wake up between them?

So how do you do this? You start, of course, by listening, by helping them get their story out. You help define and drain the emotions that came with the affair. But then you need to turn the corner. "Tell me more about that numb feeling," you say to Matt. "Do you understand what Matt is saying?" you ask Ellen. "Do you ever feel that way?" "Tell me what attracted you to each other back when you first met. Looking back on that time, what is it that you thought you needed most from each other?" "How have you each changed?" "What do you need most now in your life, in your relationship?" "If you could change one thing, what would it be?"

By asking these questions you are trying to put the affair in a bigger context, showing that it was a bad solution to something else. You are creating an emotional experience by changing, through your questions, the emotional climate in the room. After you have created the experience, but not before, you can provide the explanation that helps them put together the pieces of the puzzle that is their relationship. Draw for them the drama triangle and explain it using the words they just said to you. Talk about the relationship rollercoaster, explain how it is natural for relationships to change over time, that perhaps some of Matt's feelings reflect this common disconnect between his external behaviors and roles and how he feels inside. You are offering them a new cognitive framework that should make sense because it ties together what they have already told you.

So present your ideas and then wait and watch and see what they do next. Do they nod their heads and agree? Does Matt agree, but Ellen seems anxious and fearful? Focus on the problem in the room. Ask Matt what resonates about what you are saying. Ask Ellen how she is feeling or say that she looks worried and help her to talk about it. You are presenting a couple with a new problem to replace their old one—not only how to repair a wound, but how to rebuild their relationship. You want to demonstrate that you can provide the leadership to help them tackle this new problem. You want to help them feel safe so they can learn and can let you guide them. You want to make sure they are with you and looking in the same direction as you are before moving any further ahead.

What you do next will depend upon your style, their interests. Ellen may need to spend more time emotionally putting the affair, and the sense of loss that comes with it, to rest, just as Matt may need help making sense of what happened and better define what it is that he needs from Ellen. You may need to spend time talking with Ellen about her strong fear of change, or encourage Matt to talk about the pressure or resentment he feels on his job. You may want to explore their pasts to define any childhood wounds that may have helped create the affair, or fueled Ellen's need for stability. You'll be assessing and shoring up communication skills as you go along, and looking for weaknesses in the infrastructure.

But regardless of your style, your goals are essentially the same. You want to help a couple to redefine their relationship and bring it up to date psychologically. You want to help each define what they need and want now—more time together, less time, more independence, less control. They need to be able to say what they want the other to stop doing, but you also need to help them say what they want substituted instead. If Ellen, for example, says she wants Matt to stop being so closed and instead be more open, you want to help her describe exactly what she means by that, what it is she is really looking for. Then you need to see if Matt understands, if he is willing to try what she asks, if he needs some concrete support from her in order to be able to do it—"What can Ellen do to help you do what she is asking for?"

Individual change within a relationship is not one person pressuring the other to do something different, but both looking at the ways they contribute to the patterns and taking responsibility for breaking them. Help them track the patterns, see how the pattern is the problem, and encourage them to change it in the session. Look for triggers in the process that cause Matt, for example, to close down, explore then and there what happened, and say what Ellen did to trigger it. Give them homework that helps put new behaviors into action, changes old emotions, and lets them and you know exactly where they get stuck. This is basic couple repair, but what makes it invaluable is that issues are being honestly and clearly voiced.

Desensitize them to change by helping them take emotional and verbal risks in order to build intimacy through honesty. Look for the themes, the holes, the childhood wounds that they are trying to repair. Does Ellen need to learn to be more assertive in order to feel more empowered, like she never could when she was younger? Does Matt have to experiment with trust and letting go in order to step away from his childhood? Pose this as a challenge. Show them how their old ways of coping are triggering anger and resentment rooted in the past and keeping them from getting what they want in the present.

Don't be surprised or frightened if arguments seem to get worse for a short period of time. As mentioned earlier, this often is a sign that a couple is feeling more trusting toward you, more safe and relaxed and able to speak more openly. For couples at this stage, these arguments amount to clear the upstairs rooms and closets of emotional junk that had been sealed away over the years. The hurt feelings from that Christmas 3 years ago. The time you didn't want to come with me to see my mother in the hospital. The way you seemed uninterested when I had that struggle with my supervisor at work.

Let them get this out, but referee these conversations closely so they don't retraumatize each other. Move toward the softer emotions rather than getting lost in content or anger. Encourage them to use I-statements. Help them put the event in a larger context, and help them define the moral of the story—"It sounds like your feelings were hurt when Matt didn't come to the hospital. What is it that you want Matt to most understand about it? What is it that you would like him to do differently if something like that were to come up again?"

But while cleaning out the emotional junk of the past is part of the repair, the other part is connection. Getting things off your chest helps you feel less burdened, perhaps, but not reunited. Ask the couple to talk about their vision for the future. Again, counter the anger with softer emotions like hurt or worry, but help them see how these emotions are shared—how Matt too has mixed feelings about having children, or how Ellen, for all her need for stability, is like Matt, frustrated about her job. Assign them date nights as homework, and let them know that they may strain to talk about anything else but work for a while. Ask them to take the time to connect with each other after work, and to consciously show each other affection during the week. Be clear with them about what you are thinking—that you want to help them be more open and honest and able to lean on each other. Unless they build ways of doing that into their everyday lives, they will fall back into their patterns of drifting apart.

You will know you are finished with the process for now when they are more open, more emotionally flexible, when their communication skills are solid enough for honesty, good listening, and problem solving, when they are curious about what lies underneath annoyances and arguments. When they are aware that the surfacing of old battles about laundry is a signal of individual stress or couple disconnection, that thinking about the affair of the past means that something is missing in the present. In sessions they will have less to talk about, the tension will be gone, they will be able to pick up on shifts in the process in the room. In many ways, they will, on their own, be taking up your role.

What happens to those couples who bypass this process of updating the psychological contract? Statistically we know that a good number will divorce. Ellen decides that Matt is simply a man who can't be trusted, or Matt decides to leave Ellen for the other woman and it's over. They get remarried to someone else 2, 3, 4 years later and find themselves in an outwardly different but emotionally similar place 6 or 7 years down the road. The repetition scares them and they either divorce again or hold on just so they avoid the pain of divorce again. But unless they can find a way to update the contract and close the gap between their internal and external lives, the emotional struggle will likely continue.

Those who don't divorce may use distraction—Matt and Ellen will have the child, they will move to California, Ellen may take that promotion. The family becomes more child centered, perhaps, lives become more parallel. Their couple issues go underground until 7 years later when the children begin to leave home. Finally, they may simply battle—endless arguments over the children, each others' jobs, the lack of sex. The topics are merely means of putting resentments and needs into words. This may go on for years and the issues are never really solved because they are needed as outlets.

If these couples come into your office, look beyond the presenting issue. Help them realize that rather than thinking their relationship will be better once they solve these problems, it is by making their relationship better first that these problems will get solved.

Looking Within: Chapter 10 Exercises

1. If you are married, in a committed relationship, or have been in a long term relationship in the past, look back over those early years. Was your own vision derailed in some way, did you struggle with the 7 year itch in which the initial attraction and needs had changed?

How did these changes manifest themselves? How were you able to manage the transition?

2. Is there a pattern to the structure of your relationships? What roles do you find yourself taking on? How do they create personal problems for you? How do they successfully match your own personality?

3. When you look back at your parents' relationship, how do you feel they handled those early developmental challenges? What about their relationship has made you sensitive to particular issues in your own?

4. How difficult, in general, is change for you? What makes it more tolerable? More difficult? What support do you need to learn to manage change more easily? How does your own experience with change affect your work with clients?

Chapter 11

Battle and Loss
Managing the Teenage Years

Take a moment and think back to your teenage years. What kind of kid were you—a bit wild and rebellious? Fairly mild, one to follow the rules? How did you get along with your parents? What did it feel like to simply be at home? Was it a place of safety and security? Were there big arguments, little ones, none? With whom? Were your parents strict? Lax? Did they agree on the rules and consequences? Were they worried about you? Did you feel they understood you? Did their relationship with you change over those years? What is it that you wish they had done differently?

How could a therapist have been helpful to you at that time? Given you space to air your concerns, helped with peer relationships, sexuality, depression, anger? Brought your parents in to sort out problems or helped them understand you better and give you more of what you needed? What would the therapist have needed to do to win your confidence? What would have turned you off? What was the moral of the story of your adolescence?

Just as we walk out of our childhood with strong, black-and-white impressions of what those years were like, our impressions of our adolescent years are often powerful and lasting. These years are often difficult, and at times pivotal, ones in the life of the family and a couple. For the teen it is a time of separation from the parents, usually by bonding with a peer group or a boy- or girlfriend. It can be a time of experimentation—of sex, drugs, new roles, the breaking of routines. It can be a time of battles between parent and child—over clothes and curfews, friends, school performance. Lots of drama, doors slamming, and seemingly endless power struggles.

Some teens, of course, seem to bypass all this commotion. They are the good kids, often the only or the oldest, who may or may not date, and have one or two good friends, who plod ahead academically, are liked by their teachers. For some, their being good is a way of coping, of avoiding conflict. Rather than acting out they may internalize, or "act in," developing eating disorders, depression. Suicide attempt rates peak during this time. Those who have suffered trauma at an earlier age, have grown up in chaotic families, or have undiagnosed mental illnesses are at risk of drug abuse as a means of self medicating.

All these dangers activate parental fears. These fears are triggered not only by what parents see going on around them, but by what is going on within them. If their own teen years were tumultuous ones—early sex or pregnancy, bad boyfriends, gangs or drugs, trouble with the law, academic struggles—these memories can come back to haunt them. They see in their teen a younger version of themselves, and see the present as the last opportunity to correct or avoid mistakes, to turn things around for their child, for themselves.

As to those parents who seemed to sail through, who were good and high achieving, it's easy for them to expect the same of their own kids. When their son is cutting classes or smoking pot, their daughter is not eating for days at a time or cutting on herself, they are at a loss. They blame it on the friends they hang out with—the bad kids up on the corner, the skinny cheerleaders. Their frustration flows over into rants toward the child and battles between them.

And for those parents who look back and feel that they were too stifled as teens, too controlled by overbearing parents, too responsible and never carefree, they may be tempted to swing too far in the other direction, not setting enough structure and limits for their teen, minimizing potentially dangerous behaviors—and often triggering their spouse to counter their stance. The double messages become confusing for the teen, who instinctively tries to slip through the cracks.

If these fears make it difficult for couples to determine what parental path to follow, the limits of their own skills and old wounds can block the path altogether. Kurt and Louise, for example, were actively involved with their children when they were young. Kurt, who believed strongly in rules, took on the role of the disciplinarian with threats and physical punishment, while Louise, who tended to be anxious, tended to micromanage and hover about the children. While their styles and skills worked well enough when the children were young, they were not as effective as the children moved toward adolescence. Kurt's punitive style no longer intimidated the oldest children, and they now challenged him, just as they openly resented Louise's hovering and direction—either yelling at her to leave them alone or simply ignoring her. The frustrations the parents felt were taken out on each other—Kurt constantly nagging Louise to be more consistent and not let the kids get away with their attitude, Louise feeling that she was always walking on eggshells, waiting for Kurt to explode.

These couple dynamics were fueled by their own histories. Kurt's own father, a domineering patriarch, had died suddenly when Kurt was 12 years old, and looking back he always felt that he had never really grieved his father's death. Not only was he emotionally frozen by his own grief, but what he had left were only those early memories of his father's parenting, impressions no doubt distorted by the filter of his younger child's eyes. He had no role model for fathering to carry him forward beyond what he himself had received, and could only continue what he was doing or withdraw. Louise, for her part, was in many ways like Kurt's mother, anxious and child centered, and Kurt was similar to her own father—at times explosive and critical; the tension and the feeling of hypervigilance were something she had long been familiar with. She was in danger of re-creating her parents' relationship and handing her own wounds down to her children.

In order to successfully move through their children's adolescence, couples need to learn to be flexible in order to adjust to their seemingly ever-changing teen. They need to be able to support each other to prevent their fears from enveloping them and combine the strengths that each has to offer. Like Kurt and Louise they may need to separate past emotions from present ones in order to heal old wounds and be able to give to each other what they could not get as teens. If they cannot, they risk conflict or isolation. Or they may simply burn out—give up being parents and leave the youngest children to their own devices.

COUPLE OPTIONS

Much of how all this turns out will obviously depend upon the strength of the couple's own relationship. While weaknesses in their structure and skills as a couple may have created ever-widening fissures, in the earlier years the stress of adolescence can threaten to collapse the entire system. Those couples who distracted themselves and failed to renegotiate the psychological contract back during the 7-year itch now find these old, undiscussed issues rising to the surface. Before we discuss how to help support these couples, let's quickly look at some of the common ways the teenage years may impact a couple's relationship.

Polarization

This is probably the most common negative effect on a couple. They may have been polarized in their parenting styles all along but now the rift between them has grown even wider. The mother becomes even more punitive and angry, the father even more supportive and laid back, each overcompensating for the other. Their individual fears, childhood wounds, and the sense that time to shape their children is running out fuel the dynamics leading to entrenchment. If their communication skills are poor, it becomes even more difficult for them to break through this seeming impasse.

All this leaves the partners feeling isolated. The mother who is afraid that her daughter could become a teen mother like she did cannot share her underlying fears nor gain the support and perspective she needs if her partner seems not to care at all about the daughter's behavior or is critical of his wife's control, or if they fall into shouting matches in which neither is heard. Similarly, the father who has vivid memories of abuse by his own father but has not shared any of it with his spouse may seem distant and aloof to her. In his own mind he is protecting his family by stepping back, perhaps too far, in order to avoid unintentionally exploding and becoming just like his father. What his wife feels is disconnected and isolated, which drives her toward the children, leaving the father more isolated himself, and more at risk for explosion.

Parent in the Middle

If we imagine the polarized parents are standing at opposite sides of the ring, here we find the more punitive parent battling with the teens while the other parent tries to act as referee. The parent in the middle is usually understanding toward each side—"I understand why Harold is so upset and Phyllis needs to be more respectful, but he doesn't need to get into a shouting match with her. She winds up feeling that he doesn't care about her." He or she often uses shuttle diplomacy: "Phyllis, your father isn't angry, just upset—why don't you go and apologize to him?" "Harold, I think Phyllis is snappy because she is upset about that commotion with her boyfriend. Why don't you offer to drive her to the mall on Saturday?" All this is fraught with projection, the middle parent overidentifying with the child, perhaps replicating a role he or she played in his or her own family of origin while the punitive parent feels unsupported, undermined, and even more angry.

United as Victims

Some parents feel that they are the victims of the teen's outrageous behavior—Angie and her sleazy boyfriend sneaking out at night, Tom's unrelenting marijuana use and poor grades, Terry's rants and open disrespect are driving the couple crazy. Thank God for 6-year-old Timmy, who is the perfect child and the apple of their eye. The parents feel overwhelmed and console each other in their helpless efforts to turn things around. They may be lacking the skills to step up and be the parents. They may have initially based their attraction and built their marital relationship on an "us against the world" stance, and the escalating problems of the children ensure that they continue to cling to each other for support.

Widening Parallel Lives

The parallel lives of distance and isolation set early in the relationship or as a response to the challenge of the 7-year itch may grow wider as the children become teens. Frank has become the VP at his company and either works 14-hour days, or is traveling out of town 3 days a week. Megan, his wife, is left home to deal with the children on her own, and is a de facto single parent. She vacillates between getting angry and rigid with the children and burned out and lax. While Frank may criticize her from the sidelines, or even at times empathize with her struggle, he is essentially married not to Megan but to his work. His weak relationship with his own children and his little time at home leave no trace. While Megan tries to micromanage the kids, he comes home and automatically retreats to his computer in his home office. In the language of structural family therapy Frank is the classic disengaged father.

Alongside the risk of burnout is the danger that Megan will use one of her teens as a surrogate partner. This is always a possibility with an isolated single parent but becomes even more so as the children become older and more adult-like, and may feel their own pressure to fill the hole in the marital relationship. This, of course, only makes matters worse. The chosen child feels needed and more special, the parenting partner has someone to support her, the absent parent feels there is no way to break into their close relationship and uses that to rationalize staying involved in work. In the most dysfunctional form of this, the elevation of the teen to surrogate partner is complete, and the risk of sexual abuse becomes real.

UNITED WE STAND

What runs through each of these options is the couple's inability to form a united front and establish a parental hierarchy due to weaknesses in their own relationship. This is the focus of your treatment. Let's discuss the clinical goals for each of these options:

Polarization

Antonio and Carla have been married 16 years and have two daughters, ages 15 and 13. While the 15-year-old, Lanea, is a model student, quiet, and stays close to home, her 13-year-old sister, Toni, is the opposite. She was interested in boys at age 11, has snuck out of the house to see her 15-year-old boyfriend on several occasions, and is always irritable at home and easily enraged. Antonio, who grew up in a strict military family, has no tolerance for Toni's attitude, and he and Toni quickly battle, which usually ends with Toni shouting she hates her father and stumping off to her room. Carla, who went through a similar period of acting out in her own early teen years, feels that Antonio is overreacting, further driving Toni to her boyfriend for support, and making matters worse rather than better. Carla tries her best to have "girl chats" with Toni when she picks her up from school, but they seem to have had little effect. The parents battle, usually after Antonio has a blowout with Toni. They call you up for therapy.

You could, of course, suggest family therapy with both the parents and the girls to initially open a dialogue between the parents and the children, and then look more closely at the subsystems—the couple, the siblings, an individual assessment of Toni to understand her own perspective not only on her father, but also on her mother and perfect sister, and in order to rule out depression or other underlying emotional stressors that may be affecting her. But if the couple presents the problem in terms of their own conflict and frustration with each other and their inability to see eye to eye, that's your obvious starting point.

Couples who come in with this presentation often believe that you will solve their problems by deciding who is right. Avoid being the arbitrator and focus instead on the problem in the room—their conflict, their inability to communicate effectively or understand each other's point of view, their struggle to take a united stand. Help them understand that their daughter will invariably slip through the cracks if they are not on the same page. Build on their common desire to help their daughter, and underscore that they are united in their agreement that there is a problem between them.

The next step is to open the communication and change the emotional climate. Ask Antonio about his anger: Is he worried about his own strong reactions? Is he aware of what particularly triggers them? Is there anything that Carla can do to help him when he feels he is on the verge of exploding? Ask him to talk about his fears and worries and Toni—these underlie the anger and will help change the emotional climate. Ask Carla what she most worries about. If she is in fact less worried about Toni than Antonio is, why? In order for them to take a united stand each first needs to have his or her fears and worries, which drive the interactional patterns with Toni, to be acknowledged and allayed by the other rather than discounted or minimized. Individually and together they need to have ways of soothing each other when each one's anger and anxiety are triggered. You may want to explore their histories at this time to see whether old wounds are further fueling their reactions. You may find, for example, that Antonio's sensitivity to feeling dismissed by Toni and Carla is a re-creation of his own childhood, or that Carla's reactions to Antonio's anger are triggered by her own past experiences with emotional abuse.

In order to place these parenting issues within the larger context of the couple's relationship, you'll need to explore their relationship more deeply. Do they, for example, battle around other issues—money, in-laws, setting priorities on their time? Are they able to make decisions together in these areas? How well can they communicate, use each other for support, be affectionate, and provide positive feedback to each other? Is the power balanced between them or does Carla overall feel in a one-down position, which fuels her support of Toni? If Toni is their only source of contact, albeit negative, it will be hard to give it up as a problem unless there is something positive to replace it.

If you find that a couple relationship is fairly solid, you can help them explore the stuck points that they present around the parenting, or suggest they consider starting family therapy. If you find, however, that Toni is one of several unresolved problems, if you uncover dysfunctional patterns that are undermining their overall ability to work together, the discussion needs to shift toward their relationship. Offer your perspective, connect your concerns about their relationship structure and dynamics to their concern for their daughter—pointing out that working together is important to the balance of nurturance and structure that she needs to be successful—and see how they react.

If they are hesitant to focus more directly on themselves, they may be re-creating the problem in the room, namely, trying to retreat from looking at their relationship and preferring instead to make Toni the comfortable focus. Focus on the problem in the room. Explore further what makes them feel uncomfortable, or ways they may disagree about what you said, and find out what they most need from you. Reduce their anxiety by hearing them out; help them feel safe so they can begin to explore the stuck points in their relationship.

If, however, they agree with you that the problem is in fact between them, help them plot out what they can concretely do differently at home to change the patterns with Toni and within their relationship. When Antonio, for example, begins to get angry, can he agree to stop and figure out what he is worried about and talk to Carla about it? And when Carla sees that Antonio is getting frustrated, is there something specific that he would like her to do to help him recognize what is going on within him and help him stay in check? Can she, for example, give him a hug, suggest that he take a break, or give him some nonverbal sign that lets him be more aware of the irritation that seems to be building?

Can you help them expand their roles? Rather than only being the "easy" parent to Toni, can Carla begin to set some limits so that Antonio can step into a more nurturing role himself? And what about Lanea? Do they have any concerns about her? Is there anything she needs that they together as parents may be missing? Raise the question so they can begin to move away from their tunnel vision and see the larger picture of their relationship and family.

And if they are struggling over other problems—in-laws or budgets, sex or time together—obviously offer to use therapy as a forum for resolving these issues. Help them prioritize their goals. Point out to them when they are beginning to polarize, uncover the underlying emotions, help them move toward win–win options.

Parent in the Middle

Alex and Christina come together for an initial session to talk about their 15-year-old son, Mark, but the conversation quickly turns away from Mark to a focus on their relationship. Alex says that he is tired of the battles between Christina and Mark, and admits to being the go-between and would-be peacemaker. Christina, while understanding Alex's intentions to some degree, wishes that he would take a firm stand with Mark along with her. She feels that he minimizes the problems Mark seems to be having in school in his attempts to make peace.

Why does Alex feel like he needs to be the peacemaker, and where does he stand on the school issue? This may be a good place to start and it gives you an opportunity to see their communication skills in action. What you may notice, for example, is that Alex has a hard time being clear—he waffles and mumbles and seems to be looking for the answer you and Christina want to hear—a replication, perhaps, of his anxiety and lack of assertiveness in the home. Can Christina present her worry about Mark without getting angry, which invariably causes Alex to feel anxious, get defensive, or shut down? Slow down the conversation so you can track for yourself and them how this pattern unfolds. Do they see it and acknowledge it? Can you support Alex, voicing what he may be feeling or thinking so that Christina better understands his position and his own fears?

If Alex, however, is able to be assertive then and there and says that he simply disagrees with what Christina is doing, you wonder how their own theories of Mark's problems differ, and why, and wonder aloud why they can't effectively have this conversation at home. You don't need to have the answer, you only need to pose the question. Maybe they have tried but it quickly unravels and spins off into other topics, and they are never able to move toward the problem-solving stage. The other topics may be important: Alex's annoyance over Christina's lack of affection, perhaps, or Christina's resentment of Alex's close relationship with Mark, or the couple's old wounds—feelings of abandonment or deep hurt—that neither has been able to resolve. All these are important and need to be discussed, but in contrast to how they are addressed at home, they need to be addressed one at a time and separately from concerns about Mark.

Again you have options, and your own style and theory will dictate where you lead the couple—toward a larger exploration of their communication and problem-solving skills; toward the past, the history of their relationship, their own parental models, and learned ways of handling conflict. If you feel their expectations for Mark are unrealistic, or if you suspect that other individual issues may be affecting his school performance, voice your thoughts. Talk about normal teen development, suggest more productive ways they might intervene with the school.[1]

---

[1]For useful texts to help parents understand and manage their teens better consider Bradley, M. (2003). *Yes, Your Teen Is Crazy!: Loving Your Kid without Losing Your Mind.* New York: Harbor Press; Nichols, M. P. (2004). *Stop Arguing with Your Kids.* New York: Guilford Press; Walsh, D. (2004). *Why Do They Act That Way?: A Survival Guide to the Adolescent Brain for You and Your Teen.* San Francisco: Free Press; Pruitt, D. (2000). *Your Adolescent: Emotional, Behavioral, and Cognitive Development from Early Adolescence through the Teen Years.* New York: Collins Living; Steinberg, L. (1997). *You and Your Adolescent, Revised Edition.* New York: Collins Living.

You may wonder how Mark's problems serve not only as an expression of Mark's own internal struggles, but as a stabilizing dynamic in the larger family relationship. If Mark's problems vanished overnight, you ask, how would their own couple relationship change? Would Alex still find himself in the middle in some way? Would Christina still feel stuck in the role of the worrier and confronter of problems? Again your goals are to help them put this problem in a larger context, to bring out problems that may have been swept under the rug, to change the dynamics so that they can work more effectively as a parenting team and more supportively as a couple.

United as Victims

The difficulty in working with couples who adopt a "woe is us" stance and feel victimized by their own children is that they are usually hoping that you will sympathize with their plight. They will present a list of the troubles their children heap upon them and expect you to take over and fix the kids. This, needless to say, would be a clinical mistake. Essentially they are delegating their parenting to you while their own unempowered roles stay in place. The real challenge is helping them step up and be the parents while finding other ways to be a couple besides uniting as victims.

This is a several-step process. Toby and Karen were referred by their son Adam's truant officer. They immediately lamented how Adam refused to go to school, how there was nothing they could do to get him out of bed in the morning, how he wound up sitting around the house all day playing video games while they were at work. They quickly wanted to know when you could see him to start counseling. They thought they could get him to come in if they promised to take him to McDonald's for dinner after the session. Because their relationship is built upon collapsing together in the wake of outside pressures, your challenge is one of pacing. Pushing them too hard or too fast to take over would likely ignite the victim response and cause them to lapse into passivity and helplessness.[2]

---

[2]Cases like this are often more a community issue than a couple issue. If the court and community have required them to get their son to school you may be able to take a stronger stand—essentially you, together with the court, would be approaching and treating them the way they need to treat their son. You want to help them clear out the roadblocks so they can avoid the consequences and be successful. This may work in some instances, as the fear of the consequences might mobilize them to break out of their roles. But if the consequences are unclear, if they are ambivalent about schooling for their son, the outside pressure may only reinforce their stand. They might get angry and battle the

To build rapport you need to start where they are—acknowledge their frustration and struggle, find out how concerned they really are about their son's truancy, find out their own theory about his problem. The next step is a bit trickier—helping them see themselves as change agents rather than dumping this problem in your lap. You need to build on whatever motivation they have to fix the problem and help them eliminate the obstacles.

Again, talk their language. If they say they are afraid that their son will not finish school and wind up with a lousy job like they have, let them know that you want to help them with these worries. If they say that they are angry and frustrated that their son is getting his way but that they don't know what to do to stop it, agree that they are right, their son shouldn't be just doing what he wants and walking all over them, and you want to help them straighten him out. Link the problem to their energy and emotions. Get them to commit to giving it another try.

If they are willing to do this, the next steps are finding out exactly where they get stuck in the parenting process. If they try and get Adam out of bed, what exactly do they do, how does he respond, and what do they do next? If Adam gets angry when they try and remove the computer, how do they feel and what do they do? If at any point they seem ambivalent, if they seem to get passive in the process in the room and you are feeling that you are working harder than them, you need to stop and see what is going on: "You both are getting quiet—what are you thinking, feeling? Do you agree with what I am saying?" If you sense any resistance, gently inquire and draw it out so that you are sure that they are with you.

If Toby and Karen can be successful with their son and begin to break out of their victim roles, you need to build on this success and turn their attention to their own relationship as a couple—to ways of showing affection, appreciation, support. If you don't help them emotionally strengthen their own relationship, if you don't help them get their individual needs met through each other rather than through their dysfunctional relationships with their children, the progress they make with Adam will likely collapse and they will fall back into their old roles. Adam will try to slide and they will back off and let him skip school, or they will find themselves victimized by another one of their children.

You need to be sensitive to their anxiety when shifting the focus to their relationship. Explain to them why you are doing this, so they don't

system, or may "try" but be unsuccessful, and the son would eventually have to be pulled out of the home.

pull back—"Now that you are getting out of the woods with Adam, I'm wondering, Toby and Karen, how you are both doing as a couple. For a lot of couples like you, who have been struggling so long with the problems their kids have been having, it's easy to feel sometimes that their relationship has fallen to the sidelines, that they haven't had the time to stay connected with each other as partners." You want to help them move out of the drama triangle toward adult positions by helping them talk about themselves rather than only complaining about their kids. You want to encourage intimacy and clear up the problems that block it.

Float the questions to them and see how they react. Keep stating the thinking that is behind your questions. If one of them begins to speak up but the other holds back, focus on the process in the room—"Karen, it seems like you have some concerns, but Toby, you're getting quiet. What do you think about what Karen is talking about?" Make sure they are following your lead together. And if they don't follow through on what they agreed to do, you need to back up and find out what is going on, rather than pushing harder. They will only be able to move forward if they agree with your direction and feel safe enough to take acceptable behavioral risks.

Widening Parallel Lives

Let's return to Megan and Frank, whom we discussed earlier. Megan is battling and micromanaging the teens at home while Frank is caught up in the demands of his work, and stays disconnected from Megan and the children when he is not. Megan feels resentful and abandoned and fills the space with the children, just as Frank probably feels the same and fills his space with work. For all the distance, the fact that they feel the same—each feeling disconnected from the other—provides them with something that they share in common. This can be a good starting point for discussion.

As in the other scenarios, your role as the outsider to the relationship is to help them voice their initial complaints and then to draw out these shared emotions and help them verbalize what you see—that they have become caught in their own worlds, drifted apart, and seem to have lost the connection with each other. How have they gotten to this point? Again you are moving to the softer emotions underneath the angry ones—ask Frank how he feels at home, or Megan how she feels alone when Frank is out of town—in order to change the emotional climate.

Your goal is to change the communication by helping them move away from the language of blame and fault—of Megan not being strong enough, of Frank being a workaholic. Instead frame their behaviors as individual coping styles that over time have become more and more entrenched. You offer to help them break the patterns that leave them feeling lonely. You let them know that this will feel awkward at first because it is new ground. You guide them in the session toward more effective and open communication and underlying softer emotions so they can begin to experience a reconnection and once again lean on each other rather than on their children. And finally you circle back around to their presenting problem so that they can work together as parents to better manage the concerns they have about the children.

The theme that runs throughout these scenarios is clear—that the problem with the teens is both a problem and a solution for structural and skill weaknesses within the couple's relationship. Both the parenting issues and the couple's relationship that undermines the parenting process need to be addressed. The danger for you is that you inadvertently replicate the process—by unbalancing the system and taking one partner's side, by focusing only on the parenting skills and not exploring the underlying dynamics that set the stage for the problems to begin with, by allowing a couple to replay the dysfunctional patterns and feeling frustrated like them, or getting pushed into taking on the role of parent. If you feel you are vulnerable to any of these dangers, line up good supervision to help keep you on track.

EMPTY NEST AND THE STALE RELATIONSHIP

The stress of the teen years can push many couples to the limits of their relationship. Those who have a strong foundation and good skills, are lucky enough to have relatively good kids, and are able to maintain a common perspective can support each other as they weather the storm that adolescence may bring together. But for others whose relationships are already stressed, teen problems—drug addiction, deteriorating school performance, sexual acting out—can create wear and tear upon the couple that psychologically flattens them. They may divorce or separate, or give up and disconnect psychologically. One or both may have affairs or lapse into their own forms of addiction—shopping, alcohol, Internet pornography—as a means of individually coping. Others mentally agree to tough it out for the sake of the children, plowing on until the children are launched.

Unfortunately, these crises and stresses are often complicated by each partner's own developmental challenges. At 40 or 55 or somewhere in between there is suddenly the sense that time is limited and running out. The questions arise: "Do I want to keep doing what I am doing for the next 20 years? What happened to those dreams that I had when I was younger? What happened to the person I wanted to be? If I don't act now, when?" The 45-year-old midlevel manager who has worked hard to move up the company career ladder faces the fact that he has been passed over for promotion and is not going to be the vice president he always dreamed he could become. The 53-year-old mom who sidetracked her career to be home with the children now finds it hard to stay at home when the children are never home or rant against her when they are. The factory worker who has long been burned out and dulled by the endless repetition of the daily grind fantasizes all day about the delicatessen that he wish he could open near the downtown mall.

The midlife crisis hits. If a couple's relationship is strong, all these regrets and dreams can be openly discussed. Even if there is a natural period of introspection, of depression or anger, as losses are mentally reviewed and life so far tallied, the emotional and mental storm can generally be weathered with support by the partner. But if the support is not there, if there is isolation, these feelings can smolder.

Or they can be acted out, in the brief fling, the classic sports car, the plastic surgery, the exotic and expensive vacation—signals of what lies beneath the surface. Sometimes the behavior is driven less by depression and more by a feeling of entitlement—I deserve this after all these years. There is a desire for change, some change, any change. For many the changes represent a healthy breaking out of the drama triangle roles. The rescuer decides finally that there is too much to do and too little appreciation, and that others need to pull their weight. The victim realizes that he has more power than he thinks and no longer needs to lean on others. Persecutors finally understand that they are responsible for always driving those close to them away and that they are alone. Enough is enough.

All this can come to a head as the children leave one by one and the empty nest looms. For child-centered couples, those who saw themselves more as Mom and Pop than Marcia and Phil, a huge hole that they filled for all those years with the children now stands between them. Those couples who are more balanced or who had no children also find themselves facing their second or third 7-year itch, where the gap between what they do and who they are has grown even wider. They discover that their conversations have truly withered to the weather and the job; they sense that their obligations are over and there is nothing to hold them together as a couple. The relationship is stale. Having closed off all those rooms of the house over the years, they really are standing together in the doorway of the house that was the relationship with nothing to say.

Owen, a 43-year-old computer technician, initially came into individual therapy for depression. Although he had tried a number of medications, none of them had made a significant difference. He ran his own business and, aside from the occasional headaches of management, was satisfied with his work. Physically he was having problems—two knee surgeries and a shoulder problem had all but eliminated his ability to play racquetball, a game that he loved. He had few friends; his three children were drifting away. One had already graduated from college and, though she was living in the area, was busy with her own life. A son was already in college in another state, and his younger daughter was a senior in high school and would be leaving in the fall. The house was empty of children most nights of the week, and he found himself in his office surfing the Net while his wife, Donna, was upstairs watching television. He dreaded what the next 20 years might be like.

It wasn't that he and Donna had arguments. Quite the opposite—they had come through the teen years with their children relatively easily, and in fact, he said, they never argued, or, as he pointed out, really even talked. Donna had spent much of her at-home time attending to the children's needs—cooking, driving, helping with homework. Their sexual life was limited—between the side effects of his medication and Donna's postmenopausal decrease in libido, contact was infrequent or perfunctory. He felt unimportant, sidelined, lonely. He thought his wife saw his depression as his problem to fix. Asked if he thought Donna had the same concerns about their future years, he said he didn't know—remember, he said, they didn't talk.

The distance between Owen and Donna, like that described earlier between Megan and Frank, was symptomatic of the state of their relationship. As with the relationship shifts of the 7-year itch, some couples at this time cope with any gap they sense by filling it in with things. They buy the boat and tool around the bay for a few weekends until they get bored and give it up. Others fill the hole created by the departure of the children with grandchildren, with dogs and cats, with alcoholic brothers who need a place to live. Still others begin to argue over laundry or mothers-in-law.

This arguing isn't necessarily a bad thing. If it can be contained and actually lead to problem solving, it can be a sign of a healthy awakening within the relationship. The couple is trying to redefine and reenergize the relationship, taking steps toward redefining power imbalances, and renegotiating the relationship contract. It is healthier and more productive than distracting themselves or filling in the gaps with substitutes for children.

Owen and Donna were experiencing one such stale marriage and were at risk of moving toward parallel lives. Donna had already voiced the notion of going back to graduate school after she retired from her job, a process that could occupy her more than full time for 2 to 3 years. After that who knew what would happen? Owen had fantasies of separating, of having affairs, but also realized that they were just fantasies. Mostly he imagined himself spending his nights working more or pushing himself to get involved in community activities. But that wasn't what he really wanted. Maybe he just needed better medication, he wondered aloud.

In working with couples like Owen and Donna you have two primary goals. As with the others described above, the starting point is getting them on the same page, seeing who has and what is the problem. The fact that Owen had not openly and honestly expressed to Donna his concerns and frustrations was an obvious place to start. The other goal is helping them move toward the holes. In this case it was relatively simple—they simply needed to talk to each other, initially about anything except the kids and work. This would help them desensitize themselves to talking and help them develop a connection. They then needed to go out and do things together, rather than living parallel lives, in order to create a portfolio of shared experiences. This would strengthen their base and encourage them to create a vision for the future upon which they could build. Finally they needed to learn how to argue, how to confront each other and fight for what each of them wanted rather than continuing to sweep emotions under the rug or avoid conflict through distance.

Donna did come in to the next session, and the session goal was for Owen to express his concerns and feelings about their future and see if she had the same worries. It was essentially a choreographed monologue that was about him rather than an attack on her. Donna took it well, she did understand. While she was looking forward to retirement and graduate school, and saw it not as a way of maintaining distance from Owen but as an individual goal, she did have some of the same worries that they would spin off into separate worlds. Both agreed to begin couple therapy with the aim of opening up communication, of using it as a way of pushing them out of their well-worn patterns.

While both seemed able to listen without getting too defensive, they each got stuck in the preverbal phase. They had fallen into the pattern of simply not communicating on a regular basis—there were no meetings to touch base at the end of the day to catch each other up on

their world and vent, there were no intimate conversations over romantic dinners because they rarely went out alone as a couple. Instead they
had built around the kids and now replaced kid time with individual
time rather than time together as a couple.

Part of this was personality and family background (both had
been relatively quiet, good kids whose parents were reserved and child
centered), and with it a learned anxiety over confrontation. Owen and
Donna were sensitive to each other and worked hard to do things they
thought would make the other happy, but unfortunately it was not
always what the other wanted or needed. In typical rescuer fashion they
were often driven by shoulds. They suppressed anger, and essentially
had formed a protection pact between them—I won't get angry if you
don't—no doubt replicating their own parents. Rather than speaking up
they chose instead to keep silent.

As with many couples, this easygoingness and lack of confrontation
was actually one of the bases of their attraction to each other—here is
someone who makes me feel safe. But over time this psychological contract had run out; Owen was voicing the need for something more. He,
and now Donna, were admitting that the safety had now hardened into
boredom and distance. In order to bring some vitality, connection, and
genuine intimacy into the relationship, especially now that the children
could no longer fill that void, they would need to speak up, talk about
wants rather than shoulds, about real emotions rather than safe topics.
Rather than continuing to be careful and cautious they needed to build
real trust by being honest.

This is what they needed to do in the sessions and at home. As
the leader you need to map out the ground and alert them to the challenges, but allow them to move at their own pace. As with the parents-
as-victims couple, trying to move them too quickly toward anger and
confrontation will only raise their anxiety, cause them to see you as the
aggressor, and trigger them to revert back to shutting down and using
distance. It would be easy for them to emotionally join forces against
you and drop out.

The early sessions focused upon getting them used to talking—
monologues about their dreams, explorations into their histories, discussions of their visions of the future. The process was one of gentle risk
taking—encouraging Owen to say more about his job frustrations rather
than resorting to his classic one sentence description; helping Donna
say what she missed most now that the oldest daughter had an independent life—nudging them toward more open and honest communication
and revealing of emotions.

They also were encouraged in sessions to talk about what was hard about talking, what they were afraid of—criticism, disinterest—so they help each other understand what emotional obstacles got in their way. Homework assignments focused upon doing things as a couple—a dinner out, a fix-up project on the weekend—rather than continuing their parallel living. Their follow through and success in their small risks were carefully tracked each week to see that they were moving forward rather than running out of steam and falling back into old patterns.

In the process of helping disengaged couples close some of the distance between them it's inevitable that some conflicts will emerge. This happened to Owen and Donna. As the connection grew, they gradually felt more safe and trusting and could talk more openly about problems in the relationship. At a session the week after Thanksgiving, the clinician asked matter-of-factly how their holiday was. Donna quickly picked up on it and replied that it was fine except ... and then she stopped and looked down. "Except what?" the therapist asked gently. "Except that I was angry with Owen for seeming to make fun of my brother." Owen looked down and away, and Donna continued. Owen was teasing her brother about his business, and implying that he didn't have much business sense. Donna could tell her brother's feelings were hurt, but he politely deflected Owen's comments. But Donna was upset that Owen had acted that way.

"Do you know what Donna is talking about?" asked the therapist. "Sure, but ... " and he was about to apologize as a way of closing off the topic. "But," he said, "she always made a big deal about his business, while never ever saying anything positive about what I have built over the years." He was getting louder and now it was Donna's turn to look down.

While some couples would within minutes turn this opening into World War III—but you did this, and remember when I said that—this was all relatively mild. But it was new territory for both of them, and they were going against their own grain. The clinician's job was to keep the process going forward rather than allowing them to retreat and superficially patch things up in order to avoid their anxiety. And they did—again, no venting of 20 years of rage, but a productive clearing of the air that went beyond apologies. Owen was able to say that he needed more positive feedback from Donna about his work, about himself in general. She was able to say that she felt embarrassed at times about how he acted in groups, and he was able to understand why she felt that way and what she wanted him to do instead. Not bad. They had pushed their boundaries, and survived emotionally. The therapist pointed out the process and acknowledged their taking the risk. They left feeling closer.

Over the next couple of months, more issues came up and they became less cautious, more open. Not surprisingly, the positive side of their relationship opened up as well. They began to have intimate, more open conversations. Their sex life improved, which brought them closer still. Donna still talked about graduate school, but also talked about doing it part time so it wouldn't cut into their time together as much. And Owen's depression abated. He was less pessimistic about the future. The relationship was no longer cramped and stale.

One of the dangers for the clinician in working with stale relationships is being too quick to see these couples—compared to those in major crisis and battle mode—as the walking well, who need relatively little from therapy. You accept what Owen offers and do ongoing individual therapy with him for his depression. You encourage couples to have date nights but, like them, avoid the conflicts swept under the rug. To return to an analogy presented earlier, you find yourself merely helping them get the clutter off the surface of the floor.

Instead you want to make them curious about what lies underneath. You want to pull up the emotional floorboards and take a look with them at the underlying structure, see what places need to be fortified or replaced. By being aware of the underlying dynamics and developmental challenges, by helping couples not only settle problems but also wonder what the problems are trying to teach, you can also help them to move together toward a new vision of the relationship, a wider perspective, one more reflective of their lives now.

Looking Within: Chapter 11 Exercises

1. If you are a parent of a teenager, take a few moments to reflect on the impact of these teen years on you and your relationship. How are these times different from the earlier years? What are your emotional triggers? What worries you the most about your child's struggles? If you are not a parent of a teen, look back at your own teen years— what, from your own experience, might you be reactive to with any children of your own or with the teens you see in your work? How did your own parents handle your teen years?

2. Midlife crises: What role models do you have for middle age and change? What changes, if any, do you imagine making in the second half of your life? How do you envision the older you? Are there any regrets that you most fear having? What for you would be a life unful-

filled? How might your views and fears affect your work with couples dealing with these issues?

3. You can look at life as something you build or something you discover. The builders see the ages of 20 to 60 as the time for creating what will be the testimony that is their lives. The discoverers look at life as unraveling before them, a winding path through the woods that leads them and they follow. What is your own view of life? How do you react to those who take the opposite stance toward their lives?

Chapter 12

One Big Happy Family
Working with Stepfamilies

Lucy and Ben have been fighting over the kids. Actually it is *his* kids—12-year-old son, Jason, and 15-year-old daughter, Jessie—whom they are fighting about. The couple has been married 3 years, a second marriage for each of them, and together have a 2-year-old son, Tim, who is Lucy's first child. Jason and Jessie have alternated their weeks between their parents' homes since the divorce 8 years ago. The rift between Lucy and Ben centers on what chores each thinks Jason and Jessie should do around the house. Lucy feels they should do more—clean their rooms, pick up behind themselves better—and is worried that they are not learning the responsibilities of being part of a family.

Ben, from his side, feels Lucy is being a bit too much like a drill sergeant. She doesn't realize, he says, that even kids their age need some room to be kids. He especially worries that Lucy is at risk of alienating rather than befriending Jessie. He also admits with some coaxing that he's afraid if Lucy keeps up her demands, the children will feel uncomfortable in their home and not want to come, or complain to their mom, who demands little of the children at home, potentially disrupting the icy truce between Ben and his ex-wife.

In this chapter we discuss in detail the treatment of Lucy and Ben in couple therapy, as well as the common challenges facing couples with stepchildren.

THE SECOND (OR THIRD) TIME AROUND

Thirteen hundred new stepfamilies are forming every day.

Over 50% of U.S. families are remarried or recoupled.

Fifty percent of first marriages divorce; 75% of those individuals remarry.

Sixty-seven percent of second marriages and 74% of third marriages end in divorce.

The median length of a second marriage that ends in divorce is 7 years.

Fifty percent of the 60 million children under the age of 13 are currently living with one biological parent and that parent's current partner.[1]

As these statistics make clear, stepfamilies are a growing segment of our population, and as these statistics suggest subsequent relationships are fraught with not only the challenges faced by first-time couples, but additional ones brought about by the complications of children and past histories. Like Ben and Lucy, couples often seek therapy because of problems managing stepchildren, but beneath these problems are often lingering remnants of past marriages as well as childhood wounds. The variety of presentations show just how complex these relationships can be.

Rebound Replication of Problems

Justin had been married over 20 years and had two children. He and his wife had had a parallel relationship—she heavily involved with the children, and Justin focused on his job. As the children began to leave home, Justin found himself thinking of leaving his wife. And then he met Paula, a new employee at his job.

Paula had three children a few years older than Justin's, all out of the home. She had divorced many years ago, had had a series of relationships with different men over the years, and when she met Justin had just ended a volatile relationship of 6 months. She and Justin hit it off. Unlike her ex-husband, who was violent, and unlike her boyfriends, who were emotionally abusive and unreliable, Justin seemed solid and even tempered. They talked about their kids, and Justin enjoyed her interest

---

[1]This information is based on the 2000 U.S. Census. There are a number of websites available that provide additional interesting statistics on divorce and marriage trends. See *www.stepfamily.org* as a good starting point.

in him, found himself opening up in a way he couldn't with his wife. They had an affair. Within 3 months he left his home and marriage and moved in with Paula, and 3 months later they were married.

Six months later they come in for therapy. The problem, according to Justin, is that Paula is always preoccupied with her children. Even though they are technically on their own, Paula talks to them several times a day, they drop over for dinner several nights a week, and she lends them money that he now sees as joint funds. Paula counters that Justin is being overly sensitive and demanding, and she is angry at him for being jealous of her children.

The problems of Justin's first marriage, and probably Paula's, are being continued with new faces. Making the dynamics all the worse is the short time span from their previous relationships. Both were rebounding. The excitement of their relationship not only distracted them and aborted any sense of loss that they might have felt over the ending of their relationships, but the relationship seemed to be the perfect antidote to each one's past problems. Justin felt neglected in his marriage because his wife was so tied up with the children, and dating Paula he received all the attention that he craved. Paula saw as her problem the abusive behavior of her boyfriends and found in Justin the calm and stability that she hadn't found in other relationships.

Because of their rebound relationship and short courtship, they didn't have the opportunity to reflect upon their own role in their past relationships in a more complex and realistic way; instead they were left with an explanation that was too black-and-white and simple. They looked at the problems as ones of content—the tending to young children, physical abuse—rather than understanding the process. Justin felt his past problems were conquered because he didn't see Paula running home to tend to children, just as she didn't fear abuse. What was being reignited for each of them through the process was their particular sensitivities. Justin was once again feeling neglected because of Paula's relatively distant but still active involvement with her children, but he could have just as easily come in complaining that she was too preoccupied by her job. Similarly the jealousy, demands, and sense of control that Paula felt from Justin were old triggers that left her feeling betrayed and angry. While the situations were thought to be different, the emotional end products were the same.

Repairing such relationships means repairing the old wounds and changing the old patterns that are being continued. To be successful Justin and Paula need to learn to do now what they weren't able to do before—learn to be more supportive and less sensitive, and connect rather than create parallel lives. The danger, of course, is that they will merely replicate the old solution as well—cut off the relationship, blame each other—only to potentially start the pattern all over again in some variation.

Integrating into a New Family

Unlike Justin and Paula, who have no children living with them, Lucy does. Her marriage to Ben brought with it a ready-made family, and she is suffering from culture shock. Unlike couples who start out together and develop their own patterns, priorities, and rituals over time, new stepparents must adjust to what is already in place. They may get some sense of the family culture during the dating process as they spend time with the children, but details of everyday life and the potential annoyances they bring are usually missed. The family's historic popcorn and movie tradition of Friday nights may be fine for the first couple of months, but then it starts to feel old. The once-a-month room cleaning may be tolerated during the dating time but drives the stepparent crazy when she has to see the mess 7 days a week. To pressure for change is to pressure for a major disruption of long-standing patterns. Resistance by the rest of the family and the partner is common and to be expected.

Underneath the culture shock issues, however, is the larger challenge of fitting in and finding a role. Can Lucy step in and impose her own order on the house or does she risk Ben and his kids ganging up on her? Does Ben need to be the point man for his own kids, or can Lucy enforce the parental rules unilaterally? If she can't and is left to care only for their son, Tim, is there a danger of the family falling into two separate camps—she and Tim, Ben and his children? Does this structure in some way replicate the patterns of their previous marriages?

All this can get tricky quickly. There is a fine line between the parenting issues and couple issues, between what makes good sense and what is in reality a power issue. New stepfathers, for example, are particularly prone, it seems, to come into the home and to take up a disciplinarian role. The children often resent and resist it with a "You are not my father" response, and the mother either feels caught in the middle or feels like she has to pick sides.

Generally the best approach for the new stepparent is to avoid making drastic changes or imposing heavy discipline at the beginning. The focus instead needs to be on developing a relationship with the stepchildren. This gives the children time to sort out their own feelings of being torn between the new parent and the old and see discipline when imposed as coming from a base of caring rather than control. Once the stepparent is trusted, he or she can gradually take on more and more disciplinary responsibilities over a period of months. If the natural parent, like Ben, tends to feel overwhelmed, or was unempowered as a parent in the previous marriage, and is in danger of easily falling into that role again, it is still best for the new stepparent, like Lucy, to lend him her support rather than taking over. This not only avoids sabotaging the stepparent's ability to form a more balanced relationship with the children, but avoids the replaying of dysfunctional patterns of the previous marriage.

But negotiating all this requires good communication skills between a couple, a common vision of family life, a clear vision of the stepparent's role, and a unified approach to parenting. They need to be able to separate the past problems from those of the present. This is a tall order that makes it easy for new stepparenting couples to get stuck.

The Mix of Children

The carting to four soccer games rather than two; the sharing of rooms and the fights over space; the two girls close in age who are competitive with each other; the alternating visits by children that keep a couple from ever having parenting downtime. These additional stresses and strains can threaten to polarize a couple: "I'm sympathetic to your children, but I feel you give mine a hard time." "The boys are not getting along, but it's your son who usually starts the conflicts." "My daughter is 15 and old enough to babysit our toddler, but you don't trust her." Are the couple's issues being filtered through parental ones?: Is my husband really taking out his anger on my children rather than me, or am I sensitive to it because my ex-husband used to do the same thing? Does her son really instigate conflicts or am I overidentifying with my son, who feels helpless and overpowered? Does not trusting my daughter's capabilities really say that my partner doesn't seem to trust me?

Again the skill for couples is the ability to keep the relationships and the problems clear and separate. They need to be able to be honest about real issues between them as a couple—trust, power, issues that create anger or anxiety—while presenting a united front as parents and supporting the children in making the transition to a new family structure. A parallel process is in operation here. The parents need to treat themselves and the children the way the children need to treat each other—with emotional honesty, support, and good problem-solving skills. If they can't, the children are in danger of acting out at their level the couple's struggles.

Tension from the Exes

Some divorced couples seem to spend more time together battling each other in court than they ever spent together when married. This type of stress is not only a financial drain on the new relationship but an emotional one as well. Other parents may not openly battle with their exes but nevertheless still feel the stress. Ben, for example, seemed to be always looking over his shoulder, restricting what he could and could not do so as not to create an uproar. Such stress filters down to the children, who must learn to fit into two worlds. Some children do their best to walk the fine line between them, while others stake out a primary allegiance with the natural parent and pile more resentment and stress on the stepparent.

In the best of all possible worlds, the unresolved issues between the former partners would be settled enough to allow the exes to work effectively as parents. If they can't do this themselves, you could offer to help them. Offer to invite the former partner to come into a couple session (or even the children, if they are teenagers, for a combined family session) to help facilitate the visits of children or to develop similar rules and routines at both houses. A couple may initially resist because they fear a disaster, but you can help them talk about their fears, let them know that your job is keep the meeting from getting out of control and staying productive. You could also refer them for formal mediation—a good alternative to battling in court. If the ex is not willing to participate in these options, you can coach the parent and stepparent on ways to unemotionally set clear limits and to communicate assertively and sensitively so as not to feel victimized or inflame the situation further.

Less Couple Time

Forming a new relationship when you already have children is sort of like hopping on a train while it is moving. Unlike the first relationship, which usually allowed the couple to focus on themselves and their needs, the focus this time around is filled with additional distractions and demands. While lack of couple time is usually not a presenting concern, it is often lying right below the surface. Suggesting as homework that they schedule some couple time often goes a long way in not only reducing stress, but in reinforcing the notion that it's important to see themselves as a couple and not just as parents of a gaggle of kids.

You want to be alert to any resistance to following through on these assignments. Couples will say they were too busy, or couldn't get a babysitter, and sometimes this is true. But often the problem is more their own anxiety. They may have focused so long on the parenting role, may have been so child centered in their previous marriage, or have operated for so long a time as a single parent that the shift to a more intimate relationship is challenging. They will need your help to be honest about the problems, to open up communication and intimacy in the session process, and to take risks at home with homework assignments.

LUCY AND BEN

Let's return to the treatment of Lucy and Ben and see how the treatment unfolds. The intake form merely says that they are arguing over responsibilities Jason and Jessie should have when the children are in the home. What questions come to your mind? Here are some possibilities:

• *What keeps them from solving this problem themselves?* Are there communication skills that they need to develop in order to hear each other better, in order to prevent the conversations from going off course and becoming too emotional, hurtful, and unproductive? How sensitive are they, and how well are they able to regulate their communication process? What keeps them from understanding each other's concerns? Are they in agreement about the basic notion of children having responsibilities but getting stuck on how much and how often, or are they really not on the same page at all?

• *If this problem over children is a symptom of or solution for other problems in their relationship, what might those problems be?* Are they playing out the drama triangle, with each stuck in a role, with someone seen on top, the other feeling on the bottom? Is Ben allying himself with his children and needing them for emotional support? Is Lucy feeling isolated from this subgroup and feeling lonely and resentful? Are they able to connect as a couple rather than just seeing themselves as battling parents? What are the holes for each—that is, what do they have trouble doing or saying that they need to move toward in order to solve the problem?

• *Why this particular problem rather than another?* What makes them sensitive to these particular issues? Are there old wounds from the past being stirred up, old dysfunctional patterns being replicated?

What is behind these questions is curiosity about their ability to communicate, and possible emotional barriers from the past that block progress in the present. Above all we will be helping them change the patterns in the room, take risks so they can begin to move toward their own solution.

Opening Moves

After initial introductions and rapport building, Ben and Lucy were asked to describe the problem. Lucy was the first to speak up, and described her frustration. She and Ben didn't agree on what responsibilities to impose on the children. She felt the children did little to help out. Ben quickly jumped in, saying that Lucy was too demanding, that kids needed some space to be kids. They quickly started talking over each other and were getting angry.

Time to stop the process. Is this what happens at home? Yes, they agree. Can you tell that the conversation is going off course? "Yes, but— she's not listening ... he is exaggerating ... " They need to learn to be more sensitive to the process in the room rather than using content to drive process. They need to slow it down, listen, and recognize when they are feeling defensive. They need to take responsibility by either being quiet and not fueling the conversation with more content, or stopping it altogether if it is getting too emotionally volatile—basic but vital communication skills.

You could have them start the conversation again and coach them on the process—"Ben, say what you think Lucy is saying"; "Lucy, you're sounding angry and interrupting—see if you can just listen"; "Ben, you are quiet and seem to be shutting down—can you tell Lucy how you are feeling?" See if they move through the process more productively.

But you can also slow down the process while focusing on the content. You could ask Lucy to tell you what her concerns are—what's her worry if the children don't have responsibilities? What is her theory about why Ben doesn't support her point of view? Talk about the underside of her frustration and anger—the worry, the hurt. Or expand the conversation even further: How does she feel being a stepparent? What does she find most difficult? Does she ever feel left out when Ben's kids come over? What did she like most about Ben when they met? How does she like being the mom of a 2-year-old?

Is she calming down, has the mood shifted? Is Ben listening or still upset or ruminating?

Turn to Ben—"What do you think about what Lucy is saying? Have you heard this before?" Expand his conversation—"What is it that you feel she doesn't understand about your children or your concerns? Knowing your kids best, what kinds of responsibilities do you think they can best handle?" "It's tough being a stepparent—what role do you think Lucy should have with your kids? She said that she feels left out at times—can you tell?" "What is your relationship like with your ex-wife?" Again, ask the hard questions, move toward content they don't normally discuss, bring out underlying emotions.

If you wonder about the drama triangle being played out, check it out in a calm, quiet voice. "Lucy, it sounds like you wind up doing a lot around the house because the kids and Ben aren't helping—a bit like Cinderella perhaps. Is that how you feel? Is that part of your frustration and blowing up?" "Ben, you are complaining that Lucy seems to be too pushy and controlling about all this—I understand you feel it's not good for the kids, but do you yourself ever feel like Lucy is pushing you too? What do you do then?" If you sense that the drama triangle dynamics are being played out, explain the drama triangle model to them and ask them to tell you what seems to fit.

All these moves are about creating change—in the conversation, the emotional climate, the process, their perceptions of the problem. You don't want them to leave feeling the way they do at home. You want to demonstrate leadership and make them curious about what is underneath the argument. You want to help them recognize the process between them. You want to know about their expectations so you can help fulfill them or change them to ones that are more appropriate. Fortunately they are not asking you to be the judge, take sides, or decide who is right and wrong. Each is trying to get the other one to be more like them—Ben wants Lucy to be more laid back and easygoing; Lucy wants Ben to step up, support her point of view, be a bit tougher on the children. The danger is that they get polarized and push harder for the other to change, creating the power struggle.

Move on to the Larger Context

Find out how this problem fits into the larger dynamics of their relationship.

> *"I know you both are busy with the children—do you do things together as a couple?"*

> *"Tell me the story of how you met and how you decided to get married. How much time was there between your first divorces and your own marriage?"*

> *"I understand you are getting stuck solving this problem—are there other problems that you get stuck on? How do you go about trying to solve them? How do you both feel you are doing parenting Tim?"*

"If you do have a disagreement, can you circle back later and talk about it?"

"Ben, I noticed you got quiet before—what usually makes that happen? Lucy, do you understand how Ben is feeling when he does that? Lucy, when you start to get angry, what would you like Ben to do that would help you the most?"

"What has changed most over the last few years? If you could change anything else in your relationship besides resolving this problem with the children, what would it be?"

You are listening for the process—can they answer these questions and hear each other? If not, shift focus to the process—what just happened? "Lucy, you are getting angry—what did you hear that hurt your feelings?" "Ben, what are you feeling that is making you withdraw and get quiet?" You are listening for the content—is their relationship more than parenting? Are they able to reapproach miscommunications and problems? Are there moments of intimacy and tenderness? Can they show it right there in the room? Is there a danger that other issues are being dumped into this one? Can you help them see this? Was this a rebound relationship with remnants of former relationships alive in this one?

Explore History

This may come up spontaneously: As you describe the drama triangle, Lucy says that she identifies with the rescuer. She grew up in a chaotic alcoholic family where she was the oldest and became the surrogate mom. She was the good kid and learned to be overresponsible for others. When asked what impression of parenting, men, and women she thinks she left her childhood with, she replies that she saw her father as undependable and unreliable, saw her mother as volatile and neglectful. She felt that she has turned out "all right" because she learned to become self-reliant. She also admitted that she struggled in her first marriage with a husband who, though not an alcoholic, had a hard time keeping a job, forcing her, she felt, to be the primary breadwinner and caretaker.

When asked about his own childhood Ben described being the youngest of four boys. His parents were rigid and strict, critical and controlling, providing little nurturance, and showing little interest in him. He left childhood feeling angry, withdrawn, and depressed and saw his first wife as being controlling and wrapped up in the children.

It's easy to see how their childhood wounds remain activated and complement each other to form their core dynamic. Lucy is sensitive to any signs that Ben is not following through and being actively responsible as a parent, which causes her to push him to step up and be different from the other men she has known. Her history as well leads her to want Ben's children to learn, as she did, to be more self sufficient and prepared for a tough world. The pushing, however, triggers Ben's old feelings of being criticized and controlled. He vacillates between overidentifying with his children and asserting their need to get the freedom that he did not get as child, and withdrawing when he feels assaulted by Lucy. His withdrawal only triggers Lucy to push harder.

Underneath this pattern are their mutual feelings of anxiety. Lucy gets anxious at what seems to be chaos and disorder in the house and tries to reduce it by pushing or doing things herself—hence the rescuer. Ben feels anxious and like a victim (once again) of Lucy's demands and controls. They are at a stalemate because each is trying to change the other—Ben wants Lucy to be more laid back, she wants Ben to be more responsible—but they both sound dismissive, and this does nothing to reduce each one's anxiety. In fact, it only makes it worse. Lucy can't step down and back off until she knows that Ben can step up. Ben can't step up until he knows that Lucy can step back and be supportive, rather than critical of him. These old wounds help explain why this issue, rather than something else, is a problem for them. These reactivated wounds, together with problems in communication and little couple time to offset the discord, leave them feeling miserable.

Where does all this information leave us regarding treatment? Your clinical style and theoretical orientation will obviously shape your priorities. But in terms of goals and treatment course there are clearly several directions to take:

Help the Couple with Communication Skills

Make them more aware of process by pointing out when they are starting to go off course, by encouraging them to make I-statements, by listening and recognizing when they are getting defensive. In order to help break the dysfunctional patterns, encourage Lucy to see her anger or desire for control as a signal of underlying anxiety and to talk about that. Encourage Ben to take Lucy's comments as information about her needs rather than criticisms of him. Encourage them to increase their positive feedback to each other in order to offset the negative.

Help Them Heal Each Other's Wounds

Have them talk about their pasts so they can emotionally separate the past from the present and help each other better understand the source of their sensitivities. Help them to do with each other what they were not able to do as children with their parents—to ask each other for help, to separate their shoulds from wants, to be assertive. Both will need to take risks in order to stop the re-creation of the past. Lucy will need to take the leap of faith and rather than micromanaging Ben, trust that he will follow through on what he agrees to; rather than silently handling her emotions herself, she needs to try telling Ben what he can do to help when she feels overwhelmed. Similarly, rather than becoming resentful, Ben needs to let Lucy know when he needs more positive feedback; rather than automatically siding with his children, he needs to try and step up and support her.

Help Them Develop a Joint Plan as Parents

To keep Ben from siding with his kids, they need to come up with a plan they can agree on. This is something you can focus on within a session. To reduce their tendency to move to the extremes—Lucy to toughness, Ben to being laid back—help them negotiate the middle ground based upon solid parenting skills and the children's developmental needs. It would be important to include in this dialogue a discussion about their vision of Lucy's role as stepparent, and ways she may best bond with Ben's children.

How you approach and prioritize these goals will depend on your own style and the expectations of the couple. You might take several sessions to do an assessment and then recommend a treatment plan, or could be less structured and focus upon improving their communication, or help them develop a chore list and see where they get stuck. If they remain defensive and angry in the sessions together, you may need to separate them to explore the underlying dynamics and map out with them ways of making the joint sessions more productive. What you want is to not have them replicate over and over the dysfunctional patterns, the same content, but instead change the patterns and emotional climate, to expand the content to provide a new perspective on the problem. They need to feel that something is changing, even if they can't yet tell where it is going to take them.

Obviously, as in any couple work, you want to stay sensitive to the balance. If you are a male you want to make sure that Lucy doesn't feel you are taking Ben's side, just as if you are female you don't want to

her around the house like a puppy or sitting for hours watching daytime television.

When they came in as a couple, Ken agreed that Eve was right. For the first few months he enjoyed catching up on his sleep, continued seeing friends from the plant, and worked through the to-do list that Eve had had posted on the refrigerator for what seemed like decades. But now he was caught up on his sleep, found that he had less and less to talk to work friends about, and had completed his projects. He was restless and bored and appeared a bit depressed.

Eve was sympathetic about Ken's transition—they had, in fact, talked about it months before retirement—but aggravated, feeling that he was underfoot and disrupting her daytime routine. They had planned to travel to see their children, who lived several states away, but the children were all busy right now and had suggested they come in a few months. Ken had plans to rebuild an old car that had been in the garage for years but found that the parts were more difficult to locate and more expensive than he originally thought, and he was reluctant to spend the money. He and Eve weren't so much fighting as snapping at each other.

When asked about their relationship prior to retirement, it became clear that in recent years they had moved toward living more parallel lives. About the time the children were leaving home, Ken was promoted to plant manager and shifted his focus and energy toward the new job. Eve began working part time at a local jewelry store and had many of her relationship needs filled with the friends that she made there. They had moved from a child-centered relationship in the earlier years to a relatively stable but admittedly somewhat stale post-empty-nest relationship. Now the lack of communication and intimacy that they had been managing with distance and distraction were coming to the fore.

The challenge for Ken and Eve was that of building or rebuilding a more intimate relationship. Like the stale empty-nest couple, they needed to go back upstairs and begin cleaning out all those closed-up rooms—talk about issues swept under the rug, acknowledge any unspoken wounds—in order to open up communication. They had to take the risk of moving against the grain, changing their patterns, and finding ways of connecting on an everyday basis—something that they hadn't needed to do before because of the distractions of children and work.

That being said, they also needed to negotiate their needs for individual time. This was a challenge, particularly for Ken. Like many men who were work focused, used to being in charge, or both, Ken needed to find ways of feeling good about himself aside from his job title. Even though he was in many ways looking forward to retirement, emotionally he was undoubtedly dealing with a loss and grieving. He would have to develop a new self-image, one not coupled to his job. He might need to find new friends with whom he has more in common. He might need to be willing to take the risk of exploring and experimenting, volunteering at the elementary school, taking bassoon lessons—drawing upon old interests and dreams that may have been pushed to the side over the years.

All this may be foreign to him. But he has the life experience of making transitions in the past and he can draw on those memories and be encouraged to take action. He will need support from Eve, friends, and possibly the therapist as he steps forward. And Eve will need to learn how to bend—to be less rigid about treating their home as her turf, and find ways to connect with Ken in the course of a day.

Treatment in such cases often is a combination of couple therapy to help them strengthen their relationship and negotiate these waters and individual therapy to help each of them chart their new course. Just as these changes may open up old, unresolved issues for a couple, they may open even older issues for either or both about their pasts—resentments about being the good child, perhaps, or the stirring of other losses such as the death of parents. Ken may benefit from medication to jump-start his risk taking if it seems as though he is sliding into a deeper depression or is having trouble taking action.

DEPRESSION

While Ken's depression is likely to be situational and to improve as he finds ways to replace the sources of self-esteem that he felt he had lost, for many other older adults the depression threatens to become chronic. Sometimes it has been there all along, untreated and undiagnosed, and becomes worse as stresses increase. For others the stresses themselves precipitate a depressive response.

Kim, 68 years old, was referred by her family doctor. He had been treating her for a host of physical ailments—back pain, headaches, skin rashes, pain in her chest—and, concerned about underlying depression and anxiety, suggested that she see a therapist for an evaluation before prescribing antidepressant or antianxiety medication.

Kim came in with her husband, Logan, because, she said, her nerves were just bothering her too much and she felt she couldn't drive. Logan, a quiet man, 72 years old, still worked part time doing repairs for neighbors in the trailer court where they live. Neither had been in any type of therapy before. When asked what she knew about the doctor's referral, Kim went into a lengthy recitation of her medical problems and medications. She said that she had had problems with her nerves all her life, but they seemed to have gotten worse in the past couple of years.

The couple had two grown children, a son and daughter. The son was married, had two children, and made what felt to Kim and Logan like stiff and formal visits to his family—the children and his wife would sit silently on the couch while their son would update them on family and work news. The children interacted little with the grandparents in spite of Kim's efforts to engage them. The couple's adult daughter was single, in and out of work and relationships, and an alcoholic. She would get drunk and call Kim late at night, usually blasting her about some incident from her childhood. These calls rattled Kim, but she seemed unable to set limits on them.

Logan had been alcoholic and at times abusive for the first 20 years of their marriage and sober and respectful for the last 20. Kim herself had grown up with abusive and severely alcoholic parents. The couple also had had a teenage daughter who had been killed in an auto accident about 30 years earlier. While Logan said he no longer thought about his deceased daughter much, Kim said she thought about her every day. Logan was worried about money—Kim's medications were costing a good deal each month and they were struggling living on social security and what little he made through his odd jobs. He himself seemed depressed.

Finally, on top of all these stressors was the recent death of Kim's good friend of many years from cancer. She knew it was coming, said Kim. Her friend had been struggling for years, yet it felt like a shock. Her friend had been one of her main social supports, and, she said, "Logan and me have never been good at talking."

Kim and Logan, who already have limited internal and external resources, are struggling with a number of stressors that are weakening them further. Kim undoubtedly learned early in her life to internalize and somatize many of her problems. Her marriage to Logan in those first 20 years was, we can imagine, merely a continuation of her childhood, with its abuse and neglect. While the partners have been a physical support for each other, there has been little emotional intimacy. They both had few positive relationship role models, and Logan's sobriety was only that—a cessation of drinking but not a closing of the emotional gap. Now, as they grow older, they have, like many older couples, become more isolated, their depressions have become contagious, and financial stress has increased their anxiety. The death of Kim's friend has probably set off an emotional cascade of the other unresolved losses in her life, leaving her more alone and increasing her depression and physical problems.

As it is for many older clients, especially of their economic status, the concept of therapy was alien to them. Because their doctor had referred them, they associated the process with the medical system, and much of the initial focus was on helping them understand the therapy process and the ways it could and couldn't help (no, we wouldn't be giving her more medicine here; no, they weren't crazy) and, most of all, on helping them feel safe. The goal was to provide support and begin to open the system by asking questions and essentially letting them talk about whatever was on their minds. They tended to talk about the past—their children, their childhoods, times when they were healthier, more active—probably because their day-to-day life was, in their eyes, uneventful.

Behaviorally the goal was desensitizing them to talking to each other and helping them experience a positive connection between talk-ing about emotions and the reduction of anxiety. Services were closely coordinated with the family doctor—he did go ahead and prescribe anti-depressant medication for Kim and, after some urging, Logan agreed to see the family doctor for medication as well. This didn't solve their environmental problems, but it helped break the downward spiral they were in.

One of the real possibilities here is that the therapy would only be a support—a place for Kim, especially, to talk about her week, the therapist essentially filling the role of her deceased friend. Such a focus might help her hold steady emotionally, but she would essentially be treading water, and it raises the ethical issue of creating dependency, that is, offering a relationship but providing no real change. Sorting this out can be a tough call that as a clinician you need to be sensitive to—to determine if the relationship really is helpful over the longer haul, or whether you are merely setting the couple up for another loss when therapy ends.

Two clinical goals seemed to be appropriate at the onset. One was helping the couple reduce the isolation brought on by age and family circumstance. The other was to help Kim find ways of approaching and solving problems more directly rather than continuing to internalize and somatize. One potential social support system for them that was already somewhat in place was their church. They were irregular attend-ees, but Kim in particular enjoyed it. She even had thought about vol-unteering to do service work with some of the members, and with some encouragement she started doing so. While she initially continued to complain about physical problems that caused her to stay home, she found over time that often she felt physically better if she pushed herself to go in spite of how she felt.

As they continued to talk about the past in sessions, their conversations were gently steered, so as to not overwhelm them, toward unresolved wounds. In one session, for example, Logan sat quietly while Kim talked about one birthday when he was drunk and turned over the table with the birthday cake on it. As she cried, he suddenly burst into tears himself, expressing his shame and guilt, and the moment caught them by surprise—they felt emotionally overwhelmed and embarrassed. The therapist reduced their anxiety by gently helping them understand that releasing rather than holding on to such emotions was not harmful but healing.

That emotional experience opened the door to others. They began to talk openly about the loss of their daughter, a topic they had previously avoided, and decided during one session to visit together the cemetery where she was buried, something they had not done in many years. Logan continued to voice his worry about money, and with the therapist's help they were not only able to come up with a budget, but were able to apply for and receive food stamps. Finally, Kim was gently encouraged to begin to set limits and be assertive—to tell her grown daughter, for example, that she wouldn't talk to her on the phone if she seemed drunk, and write a note to her son telling him how she wished to be more connected to his wife and children. While understandably anxious about such actions at first, she found that her daughter did indeed stop calling when she was drunk, and her son encouraged his children to talk more openly to their grandparents during visits.

As they were seen only every few weeks because of distance, all this was slow going. But over a period of a year, they took small but steady steps to gain more control over themselves and their lives, and they were able to be more proactive rather than reactive to the events and people in their lives. As the intimacy between them gradually grew, they individually felt less lonely and, realizing their time together as a couple was growing ever more limited, were more appreciative of each other, changing the emotional atmosphere at home.

Kim was still plagued by multiple physical problems, and she would have "bad nerve days" from time to time. Through therapy she learned to do emotional first aid, such as taking a walk, writing down how she was feeling, or even meditating when she felt upset, rather than grabbing for another pill. She learned that she could in some small ways change her life by changing herself.

PROBLEMS WITH ADULT CHILDREN

As with Kim's worries about her alcoholic adult daughter, many older couples have similar concerns about their adult children. We all have

seen elderly couples at the mall shepherding their 30-something mentally disabled child about, parents who anguish about care for their adult
handicapped children once they are gone. Other parents have sons and
daughter who have suddenly divorced and are now living in their basement, or they find themselves suddenly stepping in as full-time caregiv-
ers of their grandchildren so these adult children can work and get back
on their feet. They come in with concerns about the grandchild's angry
behavior in the home, about the daughter's seeming neglect of her children, about their son's depression and inability to get a job.

Facing these family problems, it's easy for the older parents to step
back into their old parenting patterns from before. While this support
can be helpful for their adult children, there is often confusion and
conflict over roles. In some ways it is like the challenge the stepparent
faces. The adult children are sensitive to being treated like 10-year-olds
again. Various triggers—from moving back into the childhood bedroom
to having the parents tell them to button their coat—set off old childhood patterns of resentment. The older couple themselves feel ambivalent—they want to help but resent having to help. They may feel guilty
about their own parenting job of the past and see this as an opportunity
to make it right—as does the adult child. For couples who are disconnected or were child-centered before, the focus on the adult child or the
problems of the grandchildren become a familiar, and at times welcome,
distraction from their own relationship issues.

A combination of couple and family therapy is helpful in such
cases. The initial goals focus upon helping everyone draw lines around
who has and what are the problems. When Jill and Henry came in, for
example, they talked about their concern for their 28-year-old daughter,
Leah. Leah had recently divorced and, with her two young children, had
moved in with them. The couple worried that Leah was not taking care
of her children well. She had started dating again, and her parents were
worried that she might relive her "wild and crazy days" of adolescence.
They felt sorry for the children, but also resented providing child care
for many hours during the week. When they had tried to talk to Leah
about it, Leah, they said, became defensive and ranted about how they
were criticizing and not supporting her yet again, and even insinuated
that her divorce was tied to her upbringing and indirectly their fault.

The first few sessions gave the couple room to vent their concerns
and to explore their own relationship (it was relatively solid after they
received some therapy several years back), and the therapist coached
them on concrete ways of talking with Leah that might allow her to
hear them without getting angry and replicating the patterns of adolescence. The couple also needed help defining their own limits. They were

conflicted—they did have guilt about Leah's life, and they did want to do the right thing, while realizing that Leah was now an adult. They were able to map out what they were and were not willing to do, and it was decided that they would invite Leah into a session to discuss the situation with her.

Leah came in with her parents and the therapist spent some time connecting with her, seeing how she felt about coming in, and whether she understood the purpose of the meeting. The therapist's clinical goal was to help them all move to the adult roles, in the reality of the present, rather than replicating the parent–child patterns they were falling into at home. With that in mind, Leah was asked to talk about the struggles of her transition, her own worries about her children, and her own experience living at home once again. She remained calm and open, and the couple, hearing of Leah's own ambivalence and worries, were able to see her as more insightful and adult-like than they had seen her be at home. The discussion was then about the parents' agenda for the meeting—namely, clarifying their role and tasks, and Leah was asked if she had any items that she wanted to talk about. She did talk about feeling micromanaged by her parents and worried that her children would come to see her more as a sister than a parent.

The therapist moved the three of them toward an agreement about specific tasks that the parents could and were willing to do. They were all able to discuss how and when the couple could discipline the kids and what the couple's expectations were for the children's behavior in the home, as well as ways they could best approach Leah if they felt anxious or had a question without Leah feeling criticized or micromanaged. They all agreed to have twice weekly meetings at home to check in and fine-tune the agreement.

The parents then voiced their concerns about her dating, and with help from the therapist were able to stick to the language of worry and the present rather than getting aggravated or bringing up examples from adolescence. Leah was helped to listen rather than get defensive, and she was able to help the parents hear that she was aware of their concern and that she was aware of her parenting responsibilities, but she was also clear that she needed them to support her as parents of an adult and not take over as parents of an adolescent.

While this focus worked effectively with this family, with other families who may have significant unresolved wounds from the past or with therapists who are more psychodynamically oriented, the focus can be on helping them explore these past issues, separate out the past from the present, and heal these wounds. This may have been a potentially lengthier process but just as effective. Whether you encourage the family to change present behaviors and patterns knowing that their perceptions and emotions will eventually change as well, or whether you tackle the emotions of the past more directly in order to drain them of their power so that behaviors are more easily changed in the present, the end result of moving the system to a new, more developmentally appropriate way of managing family problems is the same.

Leah and her parents agreed to come in for a series of follow-up meetings in order to provide some accountability for their plan and fine-tune it after it was put in place. These sessions were helpful in keeping communication open and preventing both sides from falling back into old patterns. Finally Leah called several weeks later and asked for a referral for individual therapy—another sign of her strength and openness.[1]

But sometimes long-standing childhood wounds are not so easily put to rest between a couple and their adult children. Penny and Hal, both retired engineers, came in because they had, out of the blue, received a scathing e-mail from their 32-year-old daughter, Janet. Janet was single, living with a long-term boyfriend. She was the couple's only child, and she had a long history of eating disorders for which she had not received treatment. The e-mail the couple received from Janet was angry and explicit—saying they had been insensitive to her needs while she was growing up, that she always felt she was never good enough in their eyes, that they had embroiled her in their own marital struggles. She said that they needed to get therapy to straighten themselves out and that she never wanted to talk to them again.

Needless to say, the couple was in shock and hurt. While Janet had seemed a bit more aloof in the past year, they had seen it as a sign that she was becoming less dependent on them, more able to stand on her own feet. In their eyes their relationship with her was good overall. Janet had never expressed any of the anger that she was displaying in the e-mail. They felt that they as parents had made sacrifices—helping

---

[1]There are a number of popular books that focus on the parent–adult child relationship and the healing of past wounds from both the parent and adult child's perspectives; some titles to check out: Lieber, P., et al. (2000). *Stop Treating Me Like a Child: Opening the Door to Healthy Relationships between Parents and Adult Children*. New York: Carol; Adams, J. (2004). *When Our Grown Kids Disappoint Us: Letting Go of Their Problems, Loving Them Anyway, and Getting On with Our Lives*. New York: Free Press; Campbell, R., & Chapman, G. (1999). *Parenting Your Adult Child: How You Can Help Them Achieve Their Full Potential*. Chicago: Northfield; Friel, J. (1990). *Adult Children: The Secret of Dysfunctional Families*. Deerfield Beach, FL: Health Communications; Farmer, S. (1990). *Adult Children of Abusive Parents: A Healing Program for Those Who Have Been Physically, Sexually, or Emotionally Abused*. New York: Ballantine Books; Isay, J. (2008). *Walking on Eggshells: Navigating the Delicate Relationship between Adult Children and Parents*. New York: Flying Dolphin Press.

her move several times, restarting her at a couple of colleges when she struggled after high school, offering refuge and support when she had broken up with past boyfriends and was depressed. Yes, they as a couple had had marital struggles, particularly during Janet's teen years. They admitted to coming close to separation, but finally had gotten into therapy when Janet went to college and were able to turn it around. They worried about Janet's eating disorder and had, with coaching from their therapist at the time, tried to talk with Janet about it, but to no avail. Like Joseph K. in Kafka's novel *The Trial*, they felt they were being punished for crimes they didn't know about, for events long past.

As strange as this all seemed to Penny and Hal, the pattern they were describing is itself not that extraordinary. Once they are physically and emotionally more independent and settled—with careers, with spouses and children—and leaning less on parents, many adult children in their early thirties develop the emotional strength and perspective to look back on their families of origin and their past with new eyes. Their own marriage or relationships with their children let them compare and contrast what is unfolding now from what unfolded before. This is a time when those who had abusive histories often begin to show signs of posttraumatic stress, suddenly having panic attacks, flashbacks, or disturbing nightmares over events long ago sealed over but not resolved.

The personality characteristics of those with eating disorders—the "good-kid" dynamics, the struggle with individuation, the suppression of anger, perfectionism, and feelings of never being good enough—all make Janet susceptible to this type of explosion. It is easy to imagine that now that she is maturing, and may even be in treatment herself, long-held anger about her childhood is exploding to the surface. It may also be overwhelming, and seem to her as if her only recourse is to cut off ties.

Where does this leave Hal and Penny? First, it would be helpful for them to understand this perspective on eating disorders and development, and try, even though it is painful for them, to see their daughter's action as a positive step by her toward individuation and healing. Secondly, it would be valuable for them to not retaliate, draw back, snap back in anger, or break off contact themselves. Instead, it is often helpful for the parents to write a letter together or each individually essentially apologizing for any hurt that they have caused in the past, and offer any perspective they might share that may be helpful to their daughter without sounding defensive—for example, "We were aware of your pain during those years and knew you were being drawn in. At the time we were overwhelmed ourselves and didn't know how to help you. We are truly sorry for any pain that we caused."

The advantage of writing, aside from the obvious fact that their daughter said she doesn't want to talk to them and would probably hang up the phone if they tried to call, is that it gives them a chance to be deliberate in the letter—to say more fully what their intentions are, to have the therapist or a friend read it to see that it doesn't sound defensive or angry. And the daughter can have the same opportunity: though she may receive the letter and immediately throw it out, she may also hold on to it and read it when she is ready; she can absorb what her parents are saying, without the reactions that might be triggered by facial expressions or voice tone.

Oftentimes the adult children will circle back around after they have worked through their own issues, have gone beyond their anger, and been able to achieve a more balanced perspective.[2] Part of the process for such children is grief—mourning the loss of a childhood they wished they had had—and like other grief this can take some time to work through, several years sometimes. If the parents react by cutting off ties, it can be more difficult for the adult child, who may still feel the need to save face, to reach out. Instead it's useful for parents to keep the communication door open—to periodically send two-sentence e-mails simply saying that they hope their daughter is doing okay, or by sending the birthday or Christmas card. The adult child needs to set the pace, but the parents need to show that they are willing to reconnect when the child is ready. In the absence of any communication by the parents the daughter will fill in the blank with her own interpretation.

Finally, there is the issue of therapy for Hal and Penny themselves that their daughter is advocating. They may feel that to begin therapy, and to let their daughter know that they have, will send a message to her that they are taking her concerns and suggestions seriously, and that this may help the daughter know that they care and reduce her anger. And they may be correct, but to do it only for that reason is like those couples who are ordered into counseling by the court—they are complying only to appease others and only going through the motions. Help them be clear about their goals and expectations. What you want to avoid is their beginning the therapy process with the magical thinking that their doing so will automatically turn their child around and create once again the big happy family. If they want to work on their relationship, they need to be motivated to do it for themselves.

---

[2]Natalie Goldberg, the well-known writer and writing teacher, offers an intimate look at the process of cutoff and reconciliation with her father, who sexually molested her. See her memoir *The Great Failure: A Bartender, a Monk, and My Unlikely Path to Truth* (2004). San Francisco: Harper.

Some couples are more than willing to do this. The adult child's recommendation, albeit an angry one, is a wake-up call to the parents to look at their past. Often deciding to write a clarifying and apologetic letter forces them to look hard and long at past behaviors that may have been swept under the rug. Couple therapy can be useful in helping them put their own past issues to rest.

RELATIONSHIP REPAIR

Masters and Johnson, the pioneering researchers into human sexuality, did their research in their sexual behavior laboratory with volunteers of all ages. One of the oldest couples they worked with were in their eighties. When asked what prompted them to volunteer, the couple said they realized that they probably had only a few years left together and wanted to do all they could to make their relationship the best it could be.

While it's easy for many older couples to fall into a "Why bother" attitude and believe that they are too old to make any changes in the relationship, some, like Masters and Johnson's volunteers, see this as the last opportunity to improve the time they have left. Sometimes it is prompted by a health crisis—a heart attack scare, a broken hip, a diagnosis of Alzheimer's—that makes a couple suddenly aware of the fragility of their lives and relationship. Other times, as for Hal and Penny, the prompt comes from some event within the extended family. Still others, like Ken and Eve described earlier, it is the increased proximity of their lives—in physical space and time—that increases the friction between them. They decide it's time to finally get some issues out of the way.

Lewis and Evelyn came for therapy "to help them communicate better." Lewis had had several falls in the last 4 months that had left him confined him to a wheelchair. He had always been energetic and taken the lead in the relationship, and now in addition to coping day to day with his own physical limitations, he was struggling emotionally with his sudden physical dependence upon Evelyn. His doctor, feeling that Lewis was understandably depressed and anxious, had placed him on antidepressant medication. While this helped reduce some of his irritability, the couple was arguing a good deal. Lewis was critical of Evelyn and Evelyn felt tired and unappreciated, and found herself increasingly snapping back. They realized that the patterns they were falling into were hurting them.

The challenge for this couple was that of adjusting to the changes in their lifestyle and relationship. The initial clinical goal was to help them talk more openly and deeply about the changes they were facing, rather than funneling these emotions into irritability and arguments. Their communication skills needed to be improved—to help them listen better, take responsibility for anger, and recognize the symptoms of stress and find concrete ways to reduce them (for example, Evelyn finding ways of getting relief, Lewis targeting his physical therapy toward helping him be more independent). But they were motivated and willing to take risks in the session and follow through with homework assignments.[3]

What they also needed to develop as a couple were new ways of being physically and emotionally intimate. They had had an active and satisfying sexual life before Lewis's medical problems, and had shared a common interest in outdoors activities. Now the negative aspects of their relationship seemed to be quickly overriding any positives, and the therapist voiced this observation. The couple agreed. Right away in the session they began to talk about solutions. They decided that they needed to make time for cuddling in bed; they decided they could give each other sexual and nonsexual massages. And they took up reading aloud to each other, something that they used to do when they were in college and dating. These moments became special to them, a way of sharing interests and creating positive couple time.

While there are specific challenges of old age that you need to be sensitive to and different presenting problems that you need to be alert to, the basics of your clinical approach should remain intact. What you may need to be careful about are the countertransference issues of this stage, especially with couples that remind you too closely of your own parents or grandparents. You may find yourself overidentifying with one or both of the partners or, driven by your own anxiety, minimizing problems, feeling impatient, or shuffling them toward medication or individual therapy. If you suspect this may be going on, as always talk to your supervisor or trusted colleague.

This completes our exploration of the challenges facing couples over the developmental cycle of the relationship. By knowing the landscape

---

[3]It's important for the therapist not to set expectations too low and assume that changes due to age need to be limited. The research on brain plasticity in the past decade has shown how even in older couples changes can be made not only behaviorally but neurologically. For more information on this research see Doidge, N. (2007). *The Brain That Changes Itself.* New York: Penguin; Schwartz, J., & Begley, S. (2003). *The Mind and the Brain: Neuroplasticity and the Power of Mental Force.* New York: HarperCollins; Whalley, L. (2003). *The Aging Brain.* New York: Columbia University Press; Cohen, G. (2005). *The Mature Mind.* New York: Basic Books.

that lies before them, you can feel free to be the guide and lead. You can help couples see the changes they face not as hurdles but opportunities for learning and growth.

Looking Within: Chapter 13 Exercises

1. Countertransference: Working with older couples is difficult for some therapists, especially younger ones. They feel like they are talking to their parents or grandparents, which makes them feel awkward or cautious. How do you respond to older couples? What topics might be difficult for you to talk about, what problems awkward to work with? What assumptions might you inadvertently make?

2. How do you envision your own elderly years? What is your greatest fear? What opportunities do you see for growth? What role models do you have for aging?

3. When you look back over a couple's entire life cycle, what stages do you feel most interested in or capable of working with? Why? What stages or problems are most challenging? Why? What support do you need to increase your range and feel more competent?

Chapter 14

One Helping Two, Two Helping One
Working with Individuals in Relationships

It's a Monday morning and you get a call from someone named Stacy who is requesting an appointment as soon as possible. She and her husband, David, she explains on the phone, have been arguing a lot lately, but it all came to head over the weekend when things really exploded. Both "said things they shouldn't have," and David punched a hole in a wall before taking off in the car. He returned several hours later, but for the rest of the weekend they simply avoided each other. Stacy has asked David to come with her to couple therapy, but he absolutely refuses, saying that he doesn't believe in talking about their problems with strangers. Even though he is unwilling to participate, she wants to come in to see what she can do to make the marriage better.

Situations where only one partner is willing to seek treatment to improve a troubled relationship are not unusual. In the first half of this chapter we explore ways of helping clients like Stacy become the change agent for the relationship. In the second half we discuss how two can help one, namely, how a couple can support the partner who may have a chronic mental illness.

MAKING TRANSITIONS

There are clients, of course, who start out in individual therapy for individual issues and over time see a value in moving to couple therapy. Michael, for example, originally sought individual therapy for help with his ADHD, as well as a low-grade but long-standing depression. He had been placed on medication for both conditions through his family doctor, but when the problems began to interfere more with his efficiency at work, his doctor suggested therapy as an adjunct approach. The initial focus was helping Michael organize his workplace so there were fewer distractions. The therapist encouraged him to talk directly to his supervisor about his problems and needs, something that he was reluctant to do. He tended to "take what he got" and was inclined to take a reactive stance rather than advocate for himself. Through role plays and coaching the therapist helped Michael learn the skills of assertive communication. He took the risk and was amazed and pleased by the willingness of his supervisor to accommodate his needs.

But this reactivity and desire to avoid conflict was not limited to work relationships. It carried over to his family as well. He felt, for example, that his children needed to do more around the house to help, but his wife usually undermined his attempts by going ahead and doing whatever the children didn't get done. This upset Michael, but rather than confronting his wife about it, he was inclined to say nothing and internalize his feelings. As the therapy proceeded he was able to see the connection among his behaviors, fears, and his emotions, and his success with his supervisor encouraged him to think that change could happen at home as well. He became more clear about what he wanted to be different at home and, somewhat to his own surprise, became more aware of his underlying anger and resentment toward his wife. As he did he felt less depressed, more energized. He felt ready to use therapy to do some work directly with his wife.

This shift from an individual to a couple focus becomes a clinical crossroad in the therapy process. For therapists who don't do couple therapy, the next step is clear—refer Michael and his wife to a couple therapist. The clinical issue becomes one of facilitating the transition—helping Michael, for example, talk to his wife about his concerns and his desire to start couple therapy, much as was done in approaching the supervisor, and, if she agrees, helping them find a couple therapist. The other clinical question to be decided is whether to stop individual therapy if his wife is willing to start couple therapy, or to continue with it as a concurrent process.

The obvious danger with continuing both therapies is confusion. What you don't want is Michael feeling scattered and pulled in opposite directions by two therapists or, because the individual therapy is more known and comfortable, holding back emotionally in couple therapy, or biting his tongue and saving his complaints for the individual therapist. This only re-creates the problem by undermining his ability to be assertive. If Michael were to continue to see the individual therapist, the focus and goals would need to be clear—that the work, for example, would center only on his organizing skills, for example.

All this would need to be discussed not only with Michael, but with the couple therapist as well. The two therapists may have very different approaches, for example, and might agree after discussion that the danger of confusion is too high. Given his ADHD Michael himself may feel that he could get too distracted working on two fronts, and choose to hold off on the individual therapy. If that is the case, then a plan for termination needs to be developed—having two or three individual sessions to summarize gains—or a brief handoff session planned with the new couple therapist where the individual therapist and Michael summarize the individual work for the couple therapist.

The other clinical option is to move from individual therapy to couple therapy with the same therapist. If you are comfortable doing the couple work, the obvious advantage of this is that you already know Michael and have some understanding of how his dynamics fit into the couple dynamics. The obvious challenge is that of balancing the system. Michael's wife is certainly going to feel at a disadvantage entering into treatment knowing that you and Michael have a long-standing relationship. She will assume you have been hearing all kinds of ugly stories about her and quite rightfully will feel that you are biased in your view. Michael, even if he agrees with the approach, may himself feel a bit deserted, betrayed, or anxious. The therapist is no longer on his side.

To make this work at all you need to spend time talking with Michael about his possible reactions to the change and show that you are sensitive to his emotions as the dynamics change. Obviously, you also need to get to know his wife and her views. You need to say at the start that you understand how she is probably thinking and feeling— that this feels awkward to her, as if you will take Michael's side or you will both gang up on her. You need to help her feel safe. Let her know that you want to take the time to get to know her, understand her view of the relationship, and map out with her her own goals for the couple therapy. If she is at all reluctant to do this, or feels at all that both of them may not be a good fit for you, let her know that you would be happy to refer them to another couple therapist. You are advocating now for the couple, rather than just the individual and need to help them find a format that will help ensure their success. You may find that your openness and flexibility will help quell the new client's concerns.

This building of rapport and understanding need not take long— two to three individual sessions is common. While you could also focus on these goals of rapport building and clarification in the opening sessions with the couple by focusing only on her with Michael as a silent witness, rapport building is usually easier if you see her alone. Again, you want to avoiding drifting toward individual therapy with her, and rather help her feel safe, open with you, and reassured that you can advocate for her needs as well as Michael's.

If Michael feel intimidated about the notion of approaching his wife at home about couple therapy, you may want to consider the option of having him invite her to one of his sessions. This is similar to other situations mentioned earlier where children or other family members are brought in to discuss a specific issue. The goal is simply to provide Michael support in talking with his wife about his concerns—for Michael to say to his wife what has been bothering him, to talk about his desire for couple therapy, and for you to facilitate the process so that both feel heard. If they can reach an agreement about couple therapy, you can then raise the question of whether continuing together with you or seeing someone new would be best.

Regardless of how you choose to help clients make the transition between individual and couple therapy, it is important that the clinical goals are clear and that you and the client take the time to sort through the emotions that come with transitions. Be aware of and honest with yourself about your own possible countertransference issues—be sure that you are not, for example, pushing Michael toward couple therapy because you feel burned out or clinically stuck in your individual therapy with him, or categorically dismissing couple therapy because you don't want to disrupt your individual work.

WORKING WITH STACY

Suppose you agree to see Stacy for her first appointment without David. What do you do next? One clinical option would be to try and get David to come in. There are two ways to do this. One is to reach out to David directly—to give him a call and invite him to come in for a session. This gives him a chance to hear your voice, to associate the therapy process with a person rather than just a principle. And if he raises objections—"I don't believe in counseling, it's a waste of time"; "It's her problem, not mine"—acknowledge his feelings and offer a counterperspective: "I understand what you are saying, and maybe it will not turn out to be helpful to you. Would you be willing, though, to come in one time and see what it is like? Even though it may be Stacy's problem, your point of view would be helpful in understanding the problems."

Often just listening even briefly to the other partner's perspective without the counterargument that he usually gets at home is enough to convince him to give it a try. If a phone call seems too invasive or awkward for you, you could send a note in the mail. This type of outreach is similar to what you might do to engage a reluctant family member to participate in family therapy.

The other route is to coach Stacy on how to talk to David about therapy: to talk in I-statements, to talk about her feelings and worries rather than criticizing him for his behavior—"I have a problem and I need your help"—to acknowledge that he doesn't believe in the process but ask if he would be willing to come in one time to see what it is like. This can be role-played and you can map out with Stacy where this conversation could go off course for either of them—that he might quickly say no and she would get angry, that he might get angry and she would have a difficult time not getting angry in return. She too can write him a note or send him an e-mail.

What is important is that she remain calm and keep the conversation short, making it an invitation rather than a springboard for another argument. It is also important to say that the other person only needs to commit to coming in once. Committing to weeks or months of therapy seems overwhelming to those who are reluctant and they quickly back off. Once he's there it's your job to persuade him to stay.

If Stacy seems reluctant to have you reach out to David or to invite him in, you need to wonder why. She may have a well-earned pessimism that David would change his mind—but if she believes in the couple therapy process, you can probably encourage her to make the attempt. She may be afraid to have the conversation because of David's reaction—the role play and coaching should help alleviate those fears. She may be ambivalent about couple therapy itself, and if so you need to raise the question and explore why. Perhaps she has been in individual counseling before and feels comfortable with this process, or she imagines that a joint session with you will only lead to another argument there in the room and both of them will walk out even more upset and unresolved. If this is her fear you will need to educate her to the process and assure her of your leadership role—that your job is to keep things from getting out of hand and not simply replicate what they can do on their own at home for free.

Her ambivalence may also be based less on her worry about the couple process than on her preference for that of individual therapy. She likes the intimacy of it, and rather than seeing it as an opportunity for her to make individual changes, she envisions using the therapist as a support for her. This can be seductive for both of you. If you are more comfortable doing individual rather than couple therapy, you could find yourself colluding with her. You both shift to individual therapy, and she uses you as a support to deal with a difficult relationship. You both stay within your comfort zone, little progress is made in the relationship, and the couple focus becomes lost.

Finally she seem ambivalent because she may feel that she needs to be comfortable with you first. The issue is one of trust. Before having David involved she needs to feel that you understand her side and can support her. This too is understandable; if she is comfortable with you, and less ambivalent, she will be able to make a stronger case to David for coming in. See her for a session or two to ease her mind, but help her understand your concern about imbalance.

The antidote to her ambivalence is clarity. Your job is to explore the client's fears, raise the questions, reassure and educate. Explain how you work, how you think about the process, and what your concerns are. By being clear about where you stand, you can help her to do the same.

STACY AS CHANGE AGENT

For all of your or Stacy's best efforts David may still refuse to come in. What do you do? One obvious option is to redefine the focus. Rather than focusing on the couple, offer Stacy the option of individual therapy to help her better understand her own psychological workings. Raise her curiosity about why this problem, this type of relationship. Help her develop greater insight into herself so that she is less reactive.

The other option is to see Stacy with the focus on helping her become the change agent for the relationship. Murray Bowen was a master of this and he helped individual clients to step out of the triangles that kept families dysfunctionally stable. The principle behind this is that of systems theory—if one changes the steps in the dance, the other has to follow suit. If Stacy can become more aware of the patterns that make up her relationship with David and deliberately change them, David will have to change as well.

What makes this approach different from seeing a couple together is that you cannot work on coordinating changes from both sides. The process is generally slower and more unpredictable. It's likely that David, for example, following the drama triangle model, will probably increase his behaviors or shift roles as Stacy begins to move toward the adult position. Your job will be to help Stacy anticipate this and support her so that she isn't drawn back into old roles and patterns.

Here are some of the goals and tasks to work on with Stacy:

Stop the Dysfunctional Patterns

Stacy came in because of escalating arguments. Start there. Map out with her the patterns of their arguments—the process—and help her learn to find ways to derail the escalation. If Stacy, for example, says she is particularly triggered to escalate when David brings up the past, calls her names, or storms out of the room, help her realize the dance they are engaged in and choreograph with her a different process. This will involve all the techniques mentioned earlier—remaining nonemotional, realizing that David's anger is his problem and indication of underlying pain rather than hers, using active listening to help David calm down, and having a specific behavioral plan if and when she herself begins to feel angry, such as deep breathing or even sitting in her car until she feels more settled.

Once Stacy begins to understand that she does not need to go on autopilot, can stop blaming David for the outcomes of arguments, and realizes that she can reshape the process between them, she will feel empowered. Role playing or even practicing similar behaviors with her children can help her feel confident of her ability to change.

Teach Her Communication Skills

This involves both talking more clearly with David about problems and concerns and increasing the positive feedback within the relationship. The first is the way of tackling the content of their issues. If, for example, they always fight about money or sex, explore her own position, help her sort out how much the issue is a power struggle, and coach her on talking to David about what she wants in an assertive, noncombative manner. This will involve using I-statements, talking about her own emotions, and clearly stating her intentions and worries, as well as her ability to anticipate David's thinking and weave it into her conversation. It may be helpful for her to write down what she wants to say and have her read it to you to get your feedback. She can then pick a good time to talk to David (like a Saturday morning when each of them is not stressed by the day's ordeal) or to even write him a note or e-mail and follow up with a conversation.

The second part of good communication, increasing positives, is often a harder sell. Why should she extend herself if he is not? Stacy may say. Again, your response is that she is the one who has volunteered to take the lead, that she will need to treat David the way she would like him to treat her in order to change the emotional climate of the relationship and move away from the tension and anger that they are feeling.

She needs to be prepared for less than immediate results. Let her know that her efforts to show David appreciation are likely to go unnoticed or minimally acknowledged at first. Stacy need not turn into a martyr, but she may need to take the lead for a few weeks until David begins to respond in kind. Your job is to give her support while she does this and assure her that her efforts can pay off.

Help Her to Deepen the Conversations

Stacy will need to take the lead in increasing the depth of the conversations between them as a way of changing the emotional climate and gaining a new perspective on David. Start by encouraging her to take the risk of being more open herself—brief monologues, for example, about what she has been learning in therapy, or talking to him about her dreams of the future—and inviting him to do the same. Again her expectations need to be kept low—the goal, you help her see, is not to get David to change, but to change the relationship process between them.

Explore the Past

She needs to explore both her past and his past. Understanding her past can help Stacy see her own triggers—the way David's criticism, for example, replicates that of her father, making her feel small and discounted—and help her separate the past from the present. Ask her about David's background. He may have come from an abusive or neglectful background, for example, and you can help Stacy understand that his understandable fear of control by others is what prompts what she sees as his stubbornness.

You want to help her see David from a different, less malevolent perspective; you want to give her a new lens through which to see his behavior. What you don't want to do is slip into both you and Stacy spending lots of time doing armchair analysis of David in order to determine why he has so many problems as a way of reducing her and your anxiety about moving forward. You don't want Stacy to use this perspective as fuel for arguments and power—"And my therapist says that people like you aren't capable of caring about anyone!" The aim is to create empathy. You want to help her see that David is coping the best he knows how (as is she), that behaviors that may upset her are his bad solutions to other problems, and that much of what she doesn't like is more about him and his past than her and the present. Stacy is most likely to hear this best when some of the negativity at home is already decreasing, when she feels more empowered and less angry, and has a more balanced view of herself.

Help Her Stay the Course

Stacy will need your encouragement and help to stay in the adult role and apply the skills you are helping her learn. David is likely at first to continue in his set ways, may get more angry, more controlling, more dependent for a short period of time out of his anxiety over her change and his effort to keep the patterns and roles as they have been. She will need your support to weather these times of escalation or discouragement, to set appropriate boundaries and protect herself from possible abuse. Help her understand that she is learning life skills, skills that can be applied to all of her relationships. She needs to hear from you that regardless of what David does or is able to do, she is learning to take risks, to be assertive, to ask for what she needs while taking responsibility for her own emotions and problems.

The therapy sessions themselves are valuable for this kind of tracking and accountability. Map out with Stacy clear goals for the week. Knowing that she is coming back to report to you about her progress helps her stay mindful and proactive in carrying out her goals. If she struggles to carry assignments out, find out where things break down—were the steps too big, were the emotions too overwhelming, does she need to better understand the purpose behind her taking the risk? Assure her that she need not worry about doing things right, but more about her doing them differently.

Working with individual clients in this way can be effective. At some point when David himself sees the beneficial effects of the therapy on Stacy, he may choose on his own to come in with her. If he does you're back to balancing the system—spending time with him to help him feel safe and understood—or, if they prefer, referring the couple to someone else. Even if David never comes in, Stacy may be able to facilitate enough change so that the relationship is feeling better for both of them.

On the other hand, things may continue to fall apart. Despite Stacy's concerted efforts, David may be recalcitrant in his behavioral patterns. He may have deeper issues of his own—untreated bipolar illness, for example, or alcoholism, or a personality disorder—that quickly override any changes Stacy may make. Or Stacy herself may not be able to go beyond thinking in terms of the quick fix and wanting changes within weeks if not days, or the initial emotional crisis may subside and after three sessions she may drop out. This is all beyond your control.

All you can do is be clear, be sensitive to what might unfold, be willing to offer your services. Beyond that it is the couple's journey. Stacy ultimately needs to set her own bottom line.

But what you can control are the dangers. Keep in mind that you are working as a team to help her change her relationship, rather than falling into thinking that you and she are conspiring to change David. If you ally too closely with her, rather than the relationship, and you spend your time talking about what outrageous things David did this past week, you're promoting the problems rather than helping change them. Stacy continues on because of your support, but nothing changes in the relationship, or worse yet, you encourage her toward divorce. To counteract this you need to keep your focus on the larger picture of the couple's patterns and skills rather than drifting toward Stacy's side of the story.

Again, these pulls can be powerful. The intimacy of individual therapy can replace for her the intimacy she should create with David. Just as you want to help Stacy take a leadership role, you need to do the same in her relationship with you. If you feel that she is drifting away from the couple and toward individual therapy and the triangle, it is up to you to raise the issue and clarify the goals. If she says she doesn't have the motivation and resolve to work on the relationship, that can be explored. But if you can set the pace and hold the course, it's likely that Stacy will as well.

TWO HELPING ONE

Let's turn now to another area where individual and couple therapy may overlap, those situations where one partner has an underlying mental illness. We cover three possible scenarios: where a couple is in therapy together, and the mental illness of one of the partners is acknowledged and woven into couple treatment; where an individual is in therapy for his or her illness and couple sessions are woven into the individual therapy; and finally, where a couple is in couple therapy and there is a probable underlying mental illness in one of the partners but it is not acknowledged by the affected client.

Couple Therapy and an Acknowledged Mental Illness

April has had a long history of anorexia but with much individual treatment and support has been stable for several years. She recently married Max, who had been married once before. He knew that April had an eating disorder, but dismissed it as simply "part of her past," and was still reeling himself from an awful divorce when they first met. He actually suggested they seek couple therapy to just "make sure our communication is solid."

The therapy proceeded well, with a focus on communication skills, an exploration of Max's first marriage—the mistakes made, the lessons learned, the triggers that could reignite past emotions and patterns—and an honest look at their expectations and priorities. All was moving along well until April's father had a severe stroke, which sent her into an emotional tailspin. She started restricting her diet, and quickly lost weight. Max, not fully understanding what was happening, did what many family members instinctively do—pressured April to eat, tried to supervise her meals—which only succeeded in making things worse.

April's relapse is understandable given her stress. To move back toward recovery she would probably need to restart individual therapy, have her family doctor medically track her and evaluate her for medication to reduce her anxiety and depression, and perhaps work with a nutritionist to provide a structured meal plan and support. While these individual aspects of her treatment are important, the couple dynamics need not be overlooked. But in addition to these individual dynamics are there are dynamics within the relationship that can be addressed in the couple therapy as well. Like April, there are many relationships in which one of the partners has a history of mental disorder—depression, drug addiction, anxiety or even psychosis—that gets worse with sufficient provocation. One issue becomes finding ways of helping the one partner best help the other who is struggling.

One obvious place to start is with education. You could spend a session outlining for Max the dynamics of eating disorders and direct him to books or websites. This will help take the mystery and confusion out of April's behaviors, help him understand that it is not about food but about handling emotions. But a perspective that may be even more valuable is the one that April can provide, not only educating Max about her experience, but letting him know what and what not to do to help her.

This is where the couple therapy intersects with the individual illness. Under the stress and shame of her disorder, April may be reluctant to speak up on her own about her needs. Sessions can provide a forum for these discussions. With your encouragement it would be valuable for her to let Max know that his micromanaging of her food, for all his good intentions, only makes her feel more anxious, not less, and increases her disordered eating.

Instead of encouraging her to eat, she might ask him to check in with her and ask at mealtime how she is feeling, give her a hug if she reports having a difficult day, or offer to eat meals with her, rather than her eating alone, but to not comment on what she is eating. She can tell him what triggers her negative thoughts and behaviors, and be firm in asking that he not leave the big bag of M&M's out on top of the refrigerator. By speaking up in this way April is not only taking charge of her illness but, rather than silently taking what she gets, actively shaping the support she needs. More important, perhaps, she is also practicing assertive communication—an important skill that will benefit her throughout the relationship.

The other valuable focus of this process is helping Max take care of himself. With your and April's coaching, he needs to understand what he can control and what he cannot. He needs to accept the reality that April's illness and recovery require his support but that they are at their base her journey. If Max does not do this, if he falls into an overresponsible mind-set, he is at risk not only of feeling like a martyr and burning out, but also of shifting to a persecutor role and becoming angry and blowing up or acting out.

Helping him see this is your responsibility. Empathize with his feelings of anxiety and helplessness, help him see how the desire to control or change April has more to do with managing his own anxiety than with her problem. Discuss with him ways he can take care of himself on a daily basis. Couple therapy can help open and keep open the lines of communication between them. But if he is still struggling with his own stress, consider recommending individual therapy for him, and/or a medication evaluation.

While relapses and flare-ups of chronic conditions like April's can derail a relationship, there are other situations where couples face a mental illness more suddenly. Warren, a 53-year-old accountant, fell quite rapidly into a major depression with periods of psychosis after the death of his mother. After a hospitalization and stabilization on medication his symptoms improved but he was still unable to work. All these changes were taking a toll on his 30-year marriage. His psychiatrist referred the couple for therapy.

Warren and his wife, Gale, came in together. Warren, his speech slow and halting due to the heavy medication he was on, tried to recount the history of his illness, with Gale nervously interjecting details. When the conversation turned toward the impact of the illness on their relationship, it was clear that both partners were devastated. Warren felt that he was letting the family down, was a burden rather than a provider. He felt helpless and ashamed. Gale, with tears in her eyes, spoke about having to watch Warren suffer and about she herself feeling helpless at times. They worried about the future.

As with Max, it's helpful to focus with Gale on her knowledge of Warren's illness, on clear ways that Warren feels she can be a support, and upon her own self care. But often in cases like this where the partners feel suddenly sideswiped by an illness, there is a strong, but often unspoken sense of loss—of Warren's vitality, for example, of the couple's financial security, the everyday fabric of their relationship. This is where you can be helpful—encouraging them to talk about and express their grief and sadness; providing a safe forum and guidance to solve their new problems together, to help them reshape their changing roles. You may, for example, help them develop a 6-month budget, or suggest that they talk with the doctor about prescribing less expensive medications. You may need to facilitate a discussion between them about ways Gale, depending on the course of Warren's treatment, could take more responsibility for the family income, and help them anticipate the problems that such changes might create.

Obviously, the stress of all this change can bring to the surface any weaknesses already in the relationship. If Warren and Gale have had poor communication skills, or Gale is easily prone to anger, these can all become worse and affect progress. Your job will be to strengthen the relationship in these areas through skill building and support, to help the couple partialize problems so as to feel less overwhelmed, to help them see the challenges as challenges rather than additional sources of hopelessness.

Finally, it is important in all these cases to maintain the balance of power within the relationship. There is always the danger of infantilizing the person with the illness—for Gale to take charge of everything and treat Warren like at child, or Max to begin to view April as incapacitated and unable to carry out her responsibilities. You can provide an important perspective in these situations, helping a couple explore and define what is realistic and reasonable in light of the changes and stresses. Gale and Warren may need to reshape their roles for a period of time, but you can also encourage them to continue to define for Warren a clear sense of his individual value and purpose.

Couple Therapy as an Adjunct to Individual Therapy

Carl sought individual therapy to help him cope with the stress of a new job. He had a long history of bipolar illness and had had a "bad episode" over the past year and a half that put him in the hospital and left him unemployed. He was now stable but was worried that the job stress would trigger a relapse.

The individual therapy focused on helping him manage his work stress by clarifying expectations with his supervisor, being assertive in obtaining the training that he needed, and finding ways of destressing over the course of the day. When asked about his marital relationship he talked about the ways his wife, Jean, had been so supportive and patient with him. When asked whether there were any areas of conflict, he mentioned their "differing philosophies regarding money"—he the saver, Jean more the spendthrift. While his wife's spending habits bothered him, he tended, especially after all she had done for him, not to press the issue. He was invited to have his wife come in with him to discuss this or just to touch base as a couple anytime he wished.[1]

Jean came in with Carl the next session. When asked what she felt about Carl's new job, his struggle the past year, and her own worries, she replied that she felt like she was always walking on eggshells. She was ever alert to Carl falling into another episode, and said she was glad that Carl was coming and getting the individual support he needed from someone besides herself. The rest of session then focused on Carl's financial concerns. Jean was understanding and receptive, and the couple quite readily agreed to sit down and work out a budget together. At the end of the session Jean said that she was glad she had come and thought it might be helpful to come together with Carl every couple of months just to touch base and make sure that things were continuing to go well in their relationship.

Using couple sessions as an adjunct to individual therapy can be helpful in several ways. Unlike Max and Gale, Jean was very familiar with the landscape of Carl's illness and had learned over the years how and when to provide the support Carl needed. Knowing that Carl had a good relationship with a therapist helped her feel she was not the sole support, and this in turn reduced her day-to-day stress and worry. She was able to relax more, lean into the relationship, and relate to Carl as an equal partner.

Knowing that she could return regularly further reduced her stress. She now had a forum for sharing her perspective and, in her mind, ensuring that the therapist had an accurate view of Carl and the relationship. Finally, the couple sessions allowed the therapist to ask the hard questions—about guilt and anxiety and anger, about problems that may have gone unvoiced for fear of upsetting one or the other. By

---

[1]In some public clinics it is the norm that several therapists work with one family or couple—one for the teenage daughter, individual therapists for each member of the couple, plus one couple therapist, another family therapist. My own bias here is that while the therapists learn to accept this system, it also can lend itself to confusion or splitting by the family or couple, and a danger of creating similar fragmented dynamics among the therapists.

having a means of airing important issues and emotions the couple was able to solve problems and increase their intimacy rather than remaining guarded and distant.

And this is what Jean's bimonthly visits were able to accomplish. It was less couple therapy in the traditional sense than a checking in to make sure things were really okay, to problem solve issues that were lingering, to talk openly about fears or fine-tune everyday routines so that both of them were able to relax and enjoy each other. Having a safe place to talk things out helped Carl to stay on track.

Couple Therapy Where an Individual Problem Is Not Acknowledged

Meg and Aaron came in because of escalating arguments. Aaron admitted that he was under a lot of financial stress due to a slowdown in his business, but he felt that Meg was cold and distant, and gave him little affection and even less sex. Meg, sounding angry and defensive, said she realized that Aaron was worried about money but had a hard time being close to him because he would drink, a lot, in the evenings and get "nasty" and critical of her, leading to the arguments, and her withdrawal.

Meg felt that if Aaron could just stop drinking, he wouldn't be so irritable and the atmosphere in the home would improve. Hearing this Aaron quickly got angry. Yes, he admitted, he did have something to drink every night, but he had always done so, and never really got that drunk. He didn't have a problem with drinking, his problem was that Meg was so unaffectionate. If she acted differently, his mood would change.

Situations like these can be among the most awkward ones to work with. While the relationship problems are certainly easy to see, the dynamics are being shaped at least in part by one or both of the partners' unacknowledged mental health or addiction issues. This early in the process it's important that you not take sides and align with one partner against the other. This only unbalances the system, the one feels ganged up on by two, and will likely refuse to come back. On the other hand in situations where a mental health problem is evident, and especially where it gets in the way of making any progress, you can't ignore what is happening and pretend it is not there. How it unfolds will depend upon your style, the seriousness of the problem, and the way the mental health issues are presented.

It's easy to see that this particular couple was at a standoff. Both were blaming the other for their reactions and problems, treating the therapy session as though it were a courtroom. Meg was hoping you would agree with her that Aaron is in fact the cause of the problems, just as he was lobbying for you to see his drinking as minimal and the issue as her coldness.

The couple's problem lay in the space between them, in the power struggle and pattern. Both were angry and defensive, communication was poor, each was having trouble taking responsibility for his and her individual emotions. This is where the initial therapy needed to focus—to move them out of the courtroom mentality, to change the emotional climate, help them see that they were in a power struggle. They each needed to move to the adult position, state their own needs more clearly and compassionately, and make efforts to break the dysfunctional patterns.

But the drinking was a concern. If Aaron was truly addicted, it would have a more powerful pull on him than anything Meg or the therapist could do and would sabotage the process. But, again, pacing and balance are important. If you spent too much time asking Aaron about his drinking and less on Meg's affection, Meg could easily hear that she was right and, given the emotional climate in the home, throw it up at Aaron all week long. Aaron would dismiss the therapy and therapist the same way he dismissed Meg's angry concerns.

What do you do in such situations? One starting point is your own assessment of the degree of risk. If Meg, for example, had started by describing not Aaron's drinking but instead a suicide attempt during the week, you would obviously take a strong stand. You might say that you are not trying to ally with Meg, but as a professional who is trying to be objective, you are terribly concerned that Aaron is clearly suffering and needs help. You would then talk firmly but gently with him privately, perhaps, or with Meg about his obvious need right now for more support. You would lead Meg to move away from her anger and to talk about her fear and worry. You would press Aaron to agree to go to the hospital for an evaluation. If he became angry and stormed out of the office, you would arrange for a temporary detention order so Aaron could be taken by authorities to a hospital. This is being responsible and ethical.

If, as described with Aaron's drinking, there is no homicidal or suicidal risk, no obvious need for immediate hospitalization, then the initial goal is to build rapport and assess further. You may see Aaron individually and ask, out of the heat of the moment with Meg, what he thinks about his drinking—does he ever get worried that he is too dependent? You can ask about family history and whether there are any examples of generational foreshadowing that he may be concerned about (for example, his grandfather died of alcoholism). Is he willing, for example, to try and not drink for a few weeks and see how he feels and see if that makes a difference in their relationship? Is he willing to see someone who is an addictions specialist to get a second, more objective opinion, or attend an AA meeting just to see what they are like? If drinking is a solution, what is the problem—does he have trouble handling stress, for example, or get depressed at times?

The purpose of this conversation is to see what his concerns are apart from the power struggle and the need to save face, to uncover if there is a family history that may dispose him toward greater risk, and to see what concerns he may have (his wife's nagging, his concern about following in family footsteps) that could motivate him to take action. Coupled with this you can provide education. Express your concerns that he may be using alcohol for self-medication, that other symptoms he may be concerned about—sleeping poorly, low energy, irritability—may be a result of the alcohol itself. If you listen to his concerns and resist being critical and controlling (the way he sees Meg), and if you can uncover a concern that may motivate him, you may be able to encourage him to take action on the problem.

If, however, you truly are convinced there is a major problem—if he admits to drinking a quart of bourbon each night but feels that it is fine—you are then clinically and ethically required to step in and take a stronger stand. Confront his denial head on. To do less is to collude with him and to undermine the therapy. Do this individually rather than in the presence of Meg. Be gentle, but firm. Talk about the concerns rather than the labels. Assure him it's not about taking sides, but rather concern about his emotional and physical health.

Finally, there are those cases that fall even more into the gray zone. Derek and Cynthia, for example, began couple therapy over problems with stepchildren. Both had been married before, and their respective children rotated in and out on a complicated visitation schedule; one weekend a month all the children were together. The children were having trouble getting along and this was rippling up to the parents, who were feeling pulled and stressed. The initial focus was helping them agree to create structure in the home, to plan ways for them to spend time with their own natural children while also reaching out and connecting with their stepchildren. This worked well, and after some expected testing by the children, they were all able to settle down and get along better.

But Derek continued to be upset by what he termed "Cynthia's OCD"—her anxiety about things getting out of place in the house, her tendency to seemingly always be after the children to pick up after themselves, to put things away, to clean up their rooms. Cynthia admitted that yes, this was something that really bothered her—she felt "nervous" when the house seemed to be in disarray, and her instinctive response to get everyone to stay on top of it. Derek felt it was continuing to create unnecessary tension in the house and that Cynthia just needed to "let go."

When asked, Cynthia said that she had always been like this, that her mother was much the same. At her job she felt her need for order was easier to manage, since she had her own office, but admitted that it had caused conflict when she tried to impose her standards on some of her supervisees. Like Derek and the children, her staff probably wished, she guessed, that she would just learn to relax. She agreed that maybe this was something she would like to change.

In cases like this you can focus upon the symptoms that the client herself sees spilling over to other relationships and situations. The motivation can come from her. Match your urgency with hers. Since this is something that she would "maybe" like to change, "maybe" she would consider getting an evaluation for medication to see if it would help. Similarly, if she said that while the issues at home do not concern her a great deal, but she is greatly concerned about the impact on her job, you may more adamantly urge her to talk to her doctor about medication options.

Again, these situations require that you move between the needs of a couple and those of the individual, that you be guided by individual concerns and motivation while remaining aware of the impact on a couple.[2] You want to remain balanced, unbiased, objective. You want to be sensitive and compassionate, yet lead. If you feel unclear, torn, or confused by the multiple demands, don't be hesitant to get what you need to give, namely support and feedback for yourself from others you trust.

---

[2]Psychoeducational materials can be a helpful adjunct to therapy for both the struggling client and couple. For depression see Golant, M., & Golant, S. (1998). *What to Do When Someone You Love Is Depressed: A Practical, Compassionate, and Helpful Guide.* New York: Owl Books; for bipolar illness, Torrey, E., & Knable, M. (2005). *Surviving Manic Depression: A Manual on Bipolar Disorder for Patients, Families, and Providers.* New York: Basic Books; for obsessive–compulsive disorder, Landsman, K., et al. (2005). *Loving Someone with OCD: Help for You and Your Family.* Oakland, CA: New Harbinger; for ADHD, Barkley, R., et al. (2007). *ADHD in Adults: What the Science Says.* New York: Guilford Press; for borderline personality, Mason, P. (1998). *Stop Walking on Eggshells.* Oakland, CA: New Harbinger.

Looking Within: Chapter 14 Exercises

1. How comfortable do you feel moving between individual and couple work, between couple and family work? What are your criteria for deciding whether to transfer an individual or couple to another therapist?

2. What mental illnesses are particularly difficult for you to work with? Why? Is it a matter of knowledge and skill, or something about the nature of the illness itself that triggers a reaction within you, or both? What do you need to learn or to do in order to feel more confident in working with clients who have these illnesses?

3. How do you respond—behaviorally, emotionally—to people who to you seem to be in denial about a problem or behavior they may have? Think not only about clients, but people in your personal life. When you look back at your own past, were there times when you realize now you were in denial about some aspect of yourself or your life? Looking back on it now, why do you think you were not able to acknowledge what was occurring?

4. If you work in a setting that uses multiple therapists for one family or couple, think about the advantages and disadvantages for you and the family. Ideally, how would you like it to be? Is there something you could do to facilitate changes if that is what you feel would be most clinically effective?

Chapter 15

Life in the Details
The Nuts and Bolts of Couple Therapy

As you have hopefully realized by now, couple therapy poses its own unique challenges and requires its own particular set of skills. In this closing chapter we look at a collection of small, yet important, items that you may be curious about and that can help you be successful and stay sane while doing couple therapy. Some of these suggestions can be applied to doing therapy in general, others are specific to couple work. As you have been doing all along, see how these ideas match up against your own.

SUPERVISION

One of the reasons couples come to you is because you are able to see—the blind spots, the bigger picture that is usually impossible for them to see themselves. The same is true for you —there are probably blind spots in your own perspective. Good supervisors can offer you that larger and different view that allows you to stay clear headed and challenged. They can also offer support and offset some of the loneliness that comes with the work.

In the mastery of any art or skill there are said to be four stages in the learning process: "Know what you don't know"; "Don't know what you know"; "Don't know what you don't know"; and "Know what you know." While this seems on the surface to be some type of word salad, actually it aptly describes how most of us learn—you as a therapist, and

257

the couple as masters of their own relationship. By understanding the different stages you can better see where you are and what lies ahead.

In the first stage, "Know what you don't know," you are the beginner, and, as one, what you are often most aware of is your ignorance, that is, what you don't know. You feel anxious. You watch colleagues doing couple therapy and have a hard time fully understanding what they are doing, and you are amazed at how easily things seem to unfold for them. You meet with a couple and feel certain that they can see right through you, that they are thinking to themselves that you really don't know what you are doing. You are often more aware of what is going on inside you than you are about what is going on in the room. Like the couples you see, it's easy for you to feel overwhelmed by the content of what they are talking about and have trouble tracking the process. Your tendency may be to give lectures about family life, about motivation, about whatever you learned at the last workshop you went to or about something a colleague mentioned in a staff meeting, to ask the same 20 questions to everyone. You work very hard and may struggle with burnout.

In the second stage, "Don't know what you know," you gain some experience and feel more steady. You are able to sort and shift out what is important from all a couple is saying. Your progress notes, that before used to fill volumes because of all the content you were constantly writing down, have become concise. Because you are less anxious, you are able to see the patterns, to take the lead rather than just take dictation. But session outcomes seem irregular—sometimes sessions go well, but the next time they fall apart. You find an approach that works effectively with one couple, but it falls flat when you try and apply to the next one. And you're not sure why the outcomes are different—a good night's sleep, your lucky dress? You have learned a great deal, but as in the middle stages of therapy, you are still in the process of conceptualizing and integrating what you do.

The third stage, "Don't know what you don't know," you finally have your sea legs and feel good about what you are doing. The danger of this stage is that you become overconfident—your success can leave you feeling swell-headed and cavalier. Where earlier you may have tended to blame yourself for the outcomes of cases, at this stage the danger is that you blame the couple—they are too resistant, they are not ready or willing to work. You become impatient and may come across as pushy or push away couples who you feel are not committed to the process. You have trouble seeing your own blind spots and acknowledging your clinical weaknesses.

When you reach the fourth stage, "Know what you know," your perspective has become more realistic and balanced. You're not the super-hero who can do it all—you know and accept your clinical strengths and weaknesses. What you interpreted earlier as a couple's resistance you now realize is more complicated than that. You have softened your stance, yet are able to use your power and skill appropriately. Your experience has given you not only a sense of mastery but on good days even a sense of wisdom.

Good supervisors can be valuable throughout this process, and really good ones, like good parents and partners, can match their approach and focus to your changing needs. In the first stage, you can lean on the supervisor for information. He or she can teach you and support you, just as you can do the same with a couple. Your supervisor can help you begin to look for process and patterns so that you don't, like a couple, get lost in content. She can help you break down what seems overwhelming into smaller, more focused and manageable pieces.

In the second stage, good supervisors can help you recognize what you know by giving you that steady feedback—this is what you are good at, this worked well, and why. They can help you conceptualize and integrate what may seem like a mishmash of skills or techniques into a more unified yet flexible approach. As your anxiety goes down, you can lean into the relationship and use the supervisor as a good role model.

The role of the good supervisor in the third stage is to help you stay balanced and, in some cases, in check. His job is to challenge you and keep you from becoming too cocky, to help you see that one size does not fit all, that what may seem like couple resistance is really a solution to a host of underlying dynamics, some of which may be generated by you. He can keep you moving forward rather than getting stuck in your own power.

Finally in the fourth stage, the good supervisor can help you apply your wisdom, accept your strengths and weaknesses. She can be someone with whom to problem-solve those stuck situations, and can encourage you to keep growing rather than lapsing into boredom or going on autopilot like the stale couple.[1]

To best supervise you in couple therapy, you obviously want a supervisor who knows couple work. If you have a clinical supervisor who is a good clinician with individuals but weak in couple work, not only will he or she not be able to offer the needed training and insight that

[1]For more information on this developmental approach to learning and clinical supervision see Taibbi, R. (1995). *Clinical Supervision: A Four-Stage Model of Growth and Discovery.* Milwaukee, WI: Families International Press, available from the author; Campbell. J. (2005). *Essentials of Clinical Supervision.* New York: Wiley.

comes from experience, but there is a danger that you will be encouraged to think only in terms of individual rather than couple dynamics. Similarly, if you have a supervisor who cannot be flexible and adapt to your changing clinical needs, you will either feel stuck or outgrow him or her. The good supervisor will ask you your opinion about your relationship and the supervisory process. If he or she does not, you need to be open and honest with your supervisor about your supervisory needs; you need to take the risk of letting him or her know what is helpful, what is not, and what you feel you need most.

If such supervision is not available at your workplace, you may need to seek it from someone outside the setting. Ask friends and colleagues for suggestions about good couple practitioners and supervisors in your area.

GROUP SUPERVISION

Group supervision can be an excellent way to learn and, if you are paying for it, is less expensive than individual supervision. The supervisory group gives you an opportunity to hear about a variety of approaches and styles, as well as a variety of cases—all of which can help expand your own creativity.

Resist, however, merely joining a supervisory group because it saves you money or is convenient. Make sure that at least a couple of the group members have more experience and skills than you do. If you are new to doing therapy or couple work, the "Know what you don't know" stage, you may find the group intimidating and overwhelming, leaving you feeling even more incompetent or anxious. It's better to get the support that you need from individual supervision and either use the group to supplement this supervision or wait until you feel less anxious and inexperienced before joining.

SELF-SUPERVISION

Maybe "self-reflection" is a better term. If you look back over your cases for the last 6 months or a year, what patterns do you see? What types of couples and problems were you most successful with and did you feel good about; which were more of a struggle or ended with mixed results? What does this say about skills that you may need to develop, points where your own countertransference issues have been stirred? How is your work now different from the way it was a year ago?

This type of self-analysis and reflection upon your work is valuable in that it helps you cultivate a reflective mind. Rather than judging yourself through the tunnel vision of those dramatic or problematic clients, you are able to step back and see the bigger picture of your work and practice. It helps you be proactive and plan a course of action for the next 6 months or year, rather than invariably falling into the same therapeutic holes. Take your analysis and reflections to your supervisor. Get his or her own perspective, and come up with a plan for change—perhaps more training, or more tracking of problem cases. Decide what you need to become more flexible and feel more competent.

TRAINING

Few of us leave graduate school with sufficient training in couple therapy. Further training is usually essential. Some of this will come through good supervision. But you may want to consider a training group or workshop to focus on specific skills or to supplement supervision. If you are new to the field, it's usually best to seek an approach that mirrors and supports your own. For example, if your overall therapeutic orientation is psychodynamic, find a training group (or supervisor for that matter) who shares that orientation and thinks the way you do. If you are more cognitive-behaviorally oriented, find someone similar who can speak that language. If you are just beginning to develop your own approach, one that is different from your own will be more difficult to integrate and may leave you feeling more overwhelmed and confused.

But once you feel more solid in your approach and style, different is better. Once you are at Stage 3, for example, it's a good time to stretch out and learn something different or fine-tune the skills you already have. By then you have a solid base on which to build and you will be more successful in translating and integrating a new model into your own. This is also a good time to consider extended training programs—a yearlong training program in imago or emotionally focused therapy or object relations approaches, for example. These can refresh and revitalize you, help you see what you don't know, and help you be more flexible as a couple therapist.

PERSONAL THERAPY

Because therapy is not like plumbing or computer repair, because the personal and professional so easily overlap, therapy for yourself is often a good thing to consider. Oftentimes we get stuck when working with certain types of clients or problems not because of lack of skills, but because of our own countertransference reactions. If you realize that you consistently have a hard time with angry or unfaithful husbands, with volatile or critical women, and you get passive or impatient or annoyed and find yourself shutting down, giving lectures, or not returning their phone calls, it's time to separate out what is an issue of skill and what is you. Start by talking with your supervisor as a way of helping you step back and assess the pattern. Decide whether therapy might be what you need to put the issue to rest.

You may obviously want to consider individual therapy, but think about couple therapy for you and your partner as well. This is especially important if you have any suspicion that you may be vicariously doing your own couple therapy through your clients—that is, inadvertently pushing them to make changes or tackle problems that you and your partner are yourselves afraid to make or acknowledge. Take care of your own issues so you can better help your couples with theirs.

COTHERAPY

Like family, in contrast to individual, therapy, couple therapy lends itself to use of a cotherapist. It is an attractive arrangement. Not only do you not have to shoulder the therapeutic load all by yourself, but working together as a team, you provide a couple with a healthy role model.

The common obstacles to cotherapy are logistics and cost: Does the person you want to work with have the time when you need it? Are you going to charge for two therapists and is the couple willing to pay for it? But in addition to these practical issues there are deeper clinical ones that you need to consider. What is the primary purpose of having a cotherapist—is it to support you or to maximize in a specific way the therapeutic impact on the couple? Is there any danger that one of the partners will feel more intimidated by having the additional person in the room? Is there good rapport between you and your colleague to keep you feeling relaxed rather than more tense? Do you think alike clinically or is there a danger that you might be tripping over each other and confusing the couple? Is someone going to take the lead and the other play the support?

All this needs to be carefully thought out and choreographed so that you can work effectively together and be the good role models for the couple that you would like to be. To decide to do cotherapy because your colleague is free and interested in couple work, or because you feel it "would be good for a couple" is too vague and is likely to lead to a breakdown in the process. This doesn't mean that sessions have to be scripted; couples can learn by seeing and hearing you work out cricks in the process as it unfolds, but the focus should ultimately be on them, not on you.

There are other occasions when you may bring in someone less as a cotherapist and more as a consultant. This is generally a one-time appearance and the purpose would be to either give you feedback after the session about your own work (for example, your supervisor providing live supervision for a particular session with a couple's permission), or to help "unstick" a couple or the process and provide them and you with feedback. If, for example, a couple seemed deadlocked on a particular issue—parenting their child with ADHD, managing symptoms through medication—you might have one of your colleagues sit in when they discuss the issue. He or she may be able, as an outsider to the system or as an expert in the field, to weigh in and make recommendations, or help break the stalemate by simply restating and underscoring things you may already have told the couple that they had trouble hearing. Having the extra therapeutic weight of the consultant may be enough to get everyone off the fence and heading in a new direction.

EVERYDAY STRATEGIES FOR SELF-CARE

Doing therapy is hard work and over time can take a toll. You need to stay alert and active, to be thinking and observing and balancing. Here are some suggestions to consider to help you manage the everyday stress:

Be in Charge of Your Caseload, Your Schedule, the Time

In some workplaces cases are automatically assigned to you and appointments are scheduled by someone else. On a Tuesday night you wind up with four volatile couples in court-ordered therapy after three afternoon appointments with hyperactive kids. This can be a recipe for burnout and ineffectiveness; you get exhausted, the cases start to blur, you go on autopilot. If this is the case for you, talk to your supervisor. So as not to sound as though you are merely complaining, try to talk in the language of her concerns and perspectives, namely clinical effectiveness and quality. You need, you say, a greater variety of cases and a more diversified schedule in order to stay focused and best do your job.

If you do schedule your own appointments, be conscious of the mix of cases over the course of the day. Yes, you may have couples gravitating toward those evening hours because that is the only time they can come in, but build around your own energy and style as well. Routinization will dull you. It's usually easier to be creative when you are engaging different parts of your brain and personality. Try and schedule more difficult sessions when you are most active and alert. Build in breaks and lunch. Take a breather between sessions (literally, take some deep breaths to help you relax, shake off the last session, get centered), move around.

End your sessions on time. Some therapists, especially new couple therapists, find this difficult. They don't want to cut anyone off, or leave the sessions unbalanced. Usually the problem is that they have trouble at first knowing the emotional terrain, anticipating where questions may lead, knowing how much time to leave for certain topics. While some of this is a matter of gaining experience, the underlying focus is that of developing your sensitivity to the session process, rather than once again getting caught up in the content. Video- or audiotaping or live supervision can be particularly helpful for doing this by allowing you to observe patterns and nonverbal behaviors.

You need to stay aware of the time (have clocks that you and the couple can see), and some clinicians like to give the couple a 10-minute warning. You can use some of this time to summarize the session and to give homework for the coming week. If you sense that a couple is feeling frustrated by the time limit, say what you think the clients may be thinking—"I know we just started talking about your mother and this is an emotional topic for you. I don't want to get too much into it today because I'm afraid it may just stir things up for you that we won't have time to fully discuss. Let's start with that next session." Clients appreciate this sensitivity and leadership.

They also appreciate knowing time limits from the onset. If a couple needs to fill out paperwork at the first session and you don't want to have that time cutting into your actual session, ask that they come a few minutes early to do the paperwork, and then let them know how long sessions will normally be. Be sensitive, be respectful of your and the couple's time, and have clear boundaries. If you don't they will be confused, and you will feel resentful and harried.

Similarly, be proactive in the handling of phone calls and messages. Decide in advance how and when you will respond to them. Some therapists leave a message on their voice mail saying that they may not be able to return calls until the end of the day. Others will call back between appointments but will say at the start that they only have 5 minutes to talk. Some allow or prefer e-mail messaging. Again be clear from the start.

Usually crisis calls or frequent calls reflect a clinical issue. In his book *The 7 Habits of Highly Effective People*, Stephen Covey divides work time into four quadrants:

Important/Urgent	Important/Not Urgent
Not Important/Urgent	Not Important/Not Urgent

This is helpful in looking at your own work time. A major portion of your work—therapy sessions, supervision, even paperwork—should be important but not urgent, the essential tasks of your job but without the crisis. Some tasks may be urgent but not important—your supervisor, for example, tells you that she needs to have all the Social Security numbers of your clients by 11:00. If you find that you are spending a good deal of your time doing these types of tasks, you need to talk to those above you about delegating some of them out to appropriate support staff.

"Important and urgent" is where crisis calls fall. While this may happen sometimes, if it happens too often with a particular couple, you need to ask yourself why. Do they need more support from you (more sessions in a week), more support from others apart from you (a friend or relative, for example)? Are there emotional triggers that need to be identified? Do you need to work more directly on helping the client develop ways of self-regulating his or her emotions? Is a client more comfortable talking on the phone than in person? Bring these concerns up in the next session so that some plan of action can be created to address them.

If you find that crises or too many phone calls are characteristic of not one or two of your clients but many, again ask yourself why. Are you having trouble with particular skills, such as setting boundaries? Are you inadvertently making your clients dependent upon you? Look at the patterns and discuss this with your supervisor or colleague.

These types of crisis calls should not be confused with client check-ins. Some clients find that calling in and leaving a message helps them be accountable—"I'm just leaving this message to let you know that I did the assignment, that I'm having a good day." Most therapists do not have a hard time with this; it does not demand more of their time, and is clinically valuable until the clients develop the skills to be more independent.

Finally there is the last quadrant—not important and not urgent. This is where you put your feet up on the desk and muse and reflect. Not only does it help you unwind, it can be a time for brainstorming, for thinking creative thoughts, for generating brilliant ideas without a deadline or agenda. While this may be the smallest portion of your work time, it is valuable.

Again the theme here is being proactive, deliberate, and clinically appropriate and clear. If you are constantly reacting to what comes at you, you will quickly feel burned out.

Relax

Easier said than done, of course. Beginning therapists, and beginning couple therapists, who are anxious and self-conscious about how they are doing, are apt to be hyperalert in sessions, feeling that they have to maintain eye contact at all times. Not only does this wear you out from the pumping of adrenaline, but it actually makes you less creative. A good part of doing good therapy is staying relaxed enough so that you remain open to the nonrational part of your brain—the images, fantasies, associations—that are stirred as you hear clients talk. This type of information—"While you were talking I just had an image of ... " "The word that keeps going through my mind is ... " "I'm remembering that scene you described a couple of sessions ago where you ... "—can provide valuable insights for you and the clients.

With experience and increased skill it obviously becomes easier to cultivate this state of mind. But you can foster the process by practicing relaxation with individual clients whom you know well, and in personal relationships with friends and family. Rather than hanging on to every word all the time, like a lawyer might, listen for the gist of the conversation, track the emotions and nonverbal responses, and pay attention to your own reactions and imagination. Be aware of your breathing. Allow yourself to look away. Try and stay in the moment and trust that you will be able to handle whatever might come up.

Create a Comfortable Workspace

Face it, a sizable part of your life is lived in your office. Create a space that is comfortable and reflects you. Get the good chair (one with rollers that allows you to move toward or away from clients as you need to), put the pictures on the wall that you want, have a desk that suits your needs.

Make it comfortable for the couple as well. Most couple offices are set up like living rooms, which helps couples relax and engage more easily. Have a choice of seating—the couch is fine—but having an additional chair for one person to sit in allows a couple to make eye contact and talk more directly to each other, or provides them with some distance if they are angry. An empty chair can be used to represent someone who is missing (a deceased parent, a child who has left home), a subtle but psychologically powerful technique. Sit in other colleagues' offices to see how you feel them—this may help you see things from the couple's perspective and give you clues about what you like.

Dress for Success

New therapists often wonder about this and usually wind up following the model of their coworkers. Dress for your own personality and comfort but also be aware of the impression you make on your clients. Generally dressing up—the suit, the dark dress—increases power and authority, while dressing down reduces it, and sometimes you want to be deliberate in your attire. If you know, for example, that a couple is unfamiliar with therapy and may be intimidated by the process, you may want to dress more casually to help them relax. Similarly, if you are meeting someone who you know is anxious and worried that the therapist may not understand or be skilled enough to help him, dressing up may help ease his mind. While you don't want to be artificial or manipulative— what will matter over the longer haul is your overall demeanor of respect and genuineness—be sensitive to these initial impressions.

Create Balance in Your Life

You have probably know people whose see their work as their life. While in some professions such a stance doesn't negatively affect the work, it can when your work is providing therapy. You risk needing your clients more than they need you; you may hold on too tight to outcomes and their journey may become yours.

Rather than putting all your needs in the work basket, diversify. Create balance by having strong, supportive relationships in your personal life. Stay physically active for your own health and to offset the sluggishness that can come from staying put all day. Engage in mentally stimulating activities—music, writing, woodworking, knitting. These can stimulate your other areas of your brain and even give you wonderful metaphors to offer to your clients. Do your best to practice what you preach—take acceptable risks so that you can continue to grow, remain curious about yourself and the world, and understand your stressors and triggers so you can step back from them when necessary. See life as the process it is rather than thinking only in terms of outcomes and content.

Again, self-reflection is invaluable. Once or twice a year, take some time to reflect on the broader landscape of your life over the past months—have you been happy, are your relationships satisfying and supportive, are you accomplishing your dreams, are you continuing to dream? What needs to change, what do you want to accomplish, what problems need to be put to rest, what experiences do you want to have that you are not having? Are you using your full potential in your work and in your life? Are you energized and creative, living out the values and sense of purpose that you always wanted to have?

You may not have immediate answers to any or all of these questions, but they are important to ask nonetheless. By asking, you open the door to the possibility of discovering the answers; by discovering the answers, you open the door to the life that you were meant to live.

Looking Within: Chapter 15 Exercises

1. We've come full circle and are back to purpose and visions. What is it that you most want to accomplish by doing couple therapy, by being a therapist, by living your life?

2. Evaluate your supervision. What about it is helpful, what do you need more or less of, what skills do you want your supervisor to help you develop?

3. If you have not done it recently, take time to do some self reflection: How are your work and life going now in contrast to what you imagined 5 years ago? Is there enough balance? If you could change one thing in your life, what would it be? Are there dreams of your past that have withered or been forgotten, but that you need to revitalize? Are there parts of yourself that have been neglected that you now want to give more attention to?

Epilogue

I once heard a comic say that deciding whether to get married or not was like choosing between being lonely for the rest of your life or being constantly irritated. While this is perhaps an exaggeration, it does seem that most of us are willing to take the irritation over the loneliness.

Seeing couples in therapy reminds us of this choice. It also reminds us of both the fragility of relationships and their strength; of the capacity for feelings of anger, even hate, within each of us to exist alongside those of caring and love; of the need to give to another while giving to ourselves, to speak up while being willing to listen. Balancing all of these and making sense of our relationships and lives can be a challenge, yet we try our best because our relationship with someone we care about allows us to feel cared for. It is this feeling that is perhaps our strongest defense against the isolation of the world. By helping us maintain our connection to humanity we, in turn, maintain our connection to ourselves.

Our challenge as clinicians sitting on the other side of the room is a similar mix of opposites. We need to listen and connect, yet lead. We need to note and decipher the smallest grains of interaction, yet be able to step back and see the wide expanse that makes up the relationship itself. We need to be realistic about what may or may not change, yet remain eternally optimistic about the process of change itself. On a good day the work allows us to make a difference; through the process we, like our clients, have the opportunity to become more of who we are—something to be grateful for indeed.

Thank you for taking the time to complete this journey with me. It is my hope that these words and ideas have encouraged you to begin to take the risk of discovering what your clients, your work, and your life may teach you. May you be well and enjoy what you do.

Index